POLITICAL PARTICIPATION AND INSTITUTIONAL INNOVATION
A Case Study of Zhejiang

WSPC-ZJUP Series on China's Regional Development

Print ISSN: 2661-3883
Online ISSN: 2661-3891

Series Editor
SHI Jinchuan *(School of Economics, Zhejiang University, China)*

Advisory Board Members
GU Yikang *(China Academy for Rural Development, Zhejiang University, China)*
MAO Dan *(School of Public Affairs, Zhejiang University, China)*
LU Lijun *(Zhejiang Institute of Administration, China)*
CHEN Lixu *(Zhejiang Institute of Administration, China)*
CHEN Shengyong *(School of Public Administration, Zhejiang Gongshang University, China)*

Since China's reform and opening-up in 1978, the world's most populous country has enjoyed rapid economic development. This book series sheds new light on China's phenomenal success by examining its regional development and disparity. The series starts from first few volumes focusing on Zhejiang province, one of the country's forerunners in economic, social and political transformation. These volumes analyse Zhejiang's local governance innovation, regional economic development, and social and cultural changes over the past few decades.

Published:

Vol. 5   *Political Participation and Institutional Innovation: A Case Study of Zhejiang*
by CHEN Shengyong, ZHONG Dongsheng, WU Xingzhi and ZHANG Bingxuan

Vol. 4   *The Belt and Road Initiative and the World's Largest Small Commodity Market: Yiwu Business Circle*
by LU Lijun *et al.*

Vol. 3   *Change of China's Rural Community: A Case Study of Zhejiang's Jianshanxia Village*
by MAO Dan

Vol. 2   *Rural Reform and Development: A Case Study of China's Zhejiang Province*
edited by GU Yikang and SHAO Feng

More information on this series can also be found at
https://www.worldscientific.com/series/wszjscrd

WSPC-ZJUP Series on China's Regional Development – Vol. 5

POLITICAL PARTICIPATION AND INSTITUTIONAL INNOVATION
A Case Study of Zhejiang

CHEN Shengyong
Zhejiang Gongshang University, China

ZHONG Dongsheng
Zhejiang Sci-Tech University, China

WU Xingzhi
Zhejiang Institute of Administration, China

ZHANG Bingxuan
Zhejiang Gongshang University, China

ZHEJIANG UNIVERSITY PRESS
浙江大学出版社

World Scientific

NEW JERSEY · LONDON · SINGAPORE · BEIJING · SHANGHAI · HONG KONG · TAIPEI · CHENNAI · TOKYO

Published by

World Scientific Publishing Co. Pte. Ltd.
5 Toh Tuck Link, Singapore 596224
USA office: 27 Warren Street, Suite 401-402, Hackensack, NJ 07601
UK office: 57 Shelton Street, Covent Garden, London WC2H 9HE

and

Zhejiang University Press
No. 148, Tianmushan Road
Xixi Campus of Zhejiang University
Hangzhou 310028, China

Library of Congress Cataloging-in-Publication Data
Names: Chen, Shengyong, author.
Title: Political participation and institutional innovation : a case study of Zhejiang /
   Shengyong Chen (Zhejiang Gongshang University, China), Dongsheng Zhong
   (Zhejiang Sci-Tech University, China), Xingzhi Wu (Zhejiang Institute of Administration, China)
   and Bingxuan Zhang (Zhejiang Gongshang University, China)
Description: Singapore ; Hackensack, NJ : World Seintific, 2020. | Series: WSPC-ZJUP series on
   China's regional development; Vol. 5 | Includes bibliographical references and index.
Identifiers: LCCN 2019047662 | ISBN 9789813279544 (hardcover)
Subjects: LCSH: Political participation--China--Zhejiang Sheng. | Public administration--China--
   Zhejiang Sheng--Citizen participation. | Zhejiang Sheng (China)--Politics and government.
Classification: LCC JS7365.Z443 A73 2020 | DDC 323/.0420951242--dc23
LC record available at https://lccn.loc.gov/2019047662

British Library Cataloguing-in-Publication Data
A catalogue record for this book is available from the British Library.

This edition is jointly published by World Scientific Publishing Co. Pte. Ltd. and Zhejiang University Press. This edition is distributed outside the Chinese mainland by World Scientific Publishing Co. Pte. Ltd.

Copyright © 2020 by World Scientific Publishing Co. Pte. Ltd. and Zhejiang University Press.

All rights reserved. This book, or parts thereof, may not be reproduced in any form or by any means, electronic or mechanical, including photocopying, recording or any information storage and retrieval system now known or to be invented, without written permission from the publisher.

For photocopying of material in this volume, please pay a copying fee through the Copyright Clearance Center, Inc., 222 Rosewood Drive, Danvers, MA 01923, USA. In this case permission to photocopy is not required from the publisher.

For any available supplementary material, please visit
https://www.worldscientific.com/worldscibooks/10.1142/11251#t=suppl

Desk Editors: Anthony Alexander/Lixi Dong

Typeset by Stallion Press
Email: enquiries@stallionpress.com

About the Authors

Chen Shengyong graduated from Hangzhou University (now renamed Zhejiang University). He first served as Professor at Zhejiang Academy of Social Sciences. He joined the Department of Political Science of Zhejiang University in 1998 as Director of the Local Governance Research Center and later served as Director of the Institute of Comparative Politics and Public Affairs, Director of Department of Political Science and Public Affairs, Head of the doctoral program of Zhejiang University, and Doctoral Tutor of political theory. Since 2009, he has acted as Director of the School of Public Administration at Zhejiang Gongshang University.

Zhong Dongsheng obtained his PhD in Politics from Zhejiang University and is Associate Professor of Law School at Zhejiang Sci-Tech University. His research interests include theory of political development and public administration.

Wu Xingzhi obtained his PhD in Politics from Zhejiang University. He is Professor of Department of Public Administration at Zhejiang Institute of Administration. His research interests include theory of political science, public administration, and local democratic governance.

Zhang Bingxuan obtained his PhD in Politics from Zhejiang University. He is Associate Professor of School of Public Administration at Zhejiang Gongshang University. His research interests include public administration theory, local government reform, and social governance.

Contents

About the Authors v

Chapter 1 Introduction

1.1 Topic selection and its significance 3
    1.1.1 Research background 3
    1.1.2 Theoretic value and practical meaning of the research 17
1.2 Several related concepts and theories 23
    1.2.1 On democracy 23
    1.2.2 Citizens and subjects 26
    1.2.3 Political participation in three modes of democracy 30
1.3 Research ideas and methods 38
    1.3.1 Research ideas 38
    1.3.2 Research methods 40
1.4 The basic structure of the book 43

Chapter 2 From Election to Governance: New Development of Grassroots Democracy in Zhejiang Province

2.1 The development of local democracy in China since the reform and opening-up 55
2.2 The development course of democracy at the grassroots level in Zhejiang 61

- 2.3 Innovation practice of democratic governance at the grassroots level in Zhejiang in recent years 68
  - 2.3.1 Innovation on democratic governance at the grassroots level in rural areas 71
  - 2.3.2 Innovation of democratic governance in urban communities 80
  - 2.3.3 Development of industry and social organizations 88
  - 2.3.4 Television governance, Internet and new forms of citizen participation 91
- 2.4 System changes and formation of the local democratic governance mechanism 99
  - 2.4.1 The objective demand of social development is a necessary condition for system change 100
  - 2.4.2 The realistic difficulties of local governance provide an opportunity for system innovation 103
  - 2.4.3 Innovation motive force and system supply of local governments are the guarantee of the system change 107
- 2.5 Value and significance of democratic governance innovation at the grassroots level in Zhejiang 111
  - 2.5.1 Innovation of democratic governance at the grassroots level is an important motive force to promote local development and social stability 112
  - 2.5.2 Innovation of democratic governance at the grassroots level is the practice of people's democratic idea in contemporary China 116
  - 2.5.3 Development of democracy at the grassroots level in China "one step ahead" 119

Chapter 3 Democratic Consultation: Deliberative Democracy and Local Public Policy

- 3.1 Wenling's democratic consultation: Deliberative democracy in local governance 128
  - 3.1.1 Background introduction 128

	3.1.2	The main form and its evolution process of Wenling's democratic consultation.. 130
	3.1.3	Democratic meaning of democratic consultation..................... 138
3.2	Participative budge consultation: Exploration of practice of deliberative democracy in Wenling.. 146	
	3.2.1	Democratic consultation of Zeguo Town pre-selection project for urban construction in 2006 150
	3.2.2	Democratic consultation of financial budget of Xinhe Town in 2006 157
3.3	Significance assessment: Deliberative democracy and local public policy formulation.. 168	
	3.3.1	Technical requirements for democratic consultation 169
	3.3.2	How does the deliberative democracy affect the formulation of public policy?... 174

Chapter 4 Hearing: Interest Expression and Interest Integration Mechanism

4.1	The system of hearing: Concept and theory 189	
	4.1.1	Hearing, citizen participation and procedural democracy......... 189
	4.1.2	China's development background and characteristics of the hearing system 190
	4.1.3	Government process theory: An analytical perspective 192
4.2	Three case studies of the hearing 197	
	4.2.1	Legislative hearing case 198
	4.2.2	Administrative hearing case 208
	4.2.3	Judicial hearing case... 215
4.3	Functional analysis of the hearing system 223	
	4.3.1	From the level of political system 224
	4.3.2	From the level of government process 225
	4.3.3	From the level of public policy 226
4.4	Institutional defects in the participation of political citizens 228	
	4.4.1	Defects and system "deviation" of the hearing system 228
	4.4.2	The negative effects of defects in the hearing system............... 232

4.5 Discussion and summary 234
    4.5.1 Hearing participation and the participation ability of contemporary Chinese citizens 235
    4.5.2 Improve local governance or officials make a show? 236
    4.5.3 The transformation of the target of the political participation in the hearing 239
    4.5.4 Improvement of government process theory and political participation in the hearing 244

Chapter 5 "Our Round Table Meeting": TV Political Consultation and Public Consultation

5.1 The rise of TV political consultation and "Our Round Table Meeting" 254
    5.1.1 Development course from "TV political consultation" to public consultation 255
    5.1.2 The establishment of "Our Round Table Meeting" and the characteristics of public participation 257
5.2 The composition and generation of the participants 261
    5.2.1 Composition of the participants 261
    5.2.2 The generation of the participants 264
5.3 The emergence and distribution of topics for consultation 268
    5.3.1 Topic setting 268
    5.3.2 Distribution and change of the topics 272
5.4 The operational process of "Our Round Table Meeting" 277
    5.4.1 Government guidance 277
    5.4.2 Host 279
    5.4.3 Citizen participation 280
    5.4.4 Constraint mechanism 286
5.5 The performance of "Our Round Table Meeting" TV political consultation 289
    5.5.1 Cultivation of public rationality and democratic consciousness 289

	5.5.2	The shaping of the public domain 290
	5.5.3	Expansion of civic participation 291
5.6	Discussion and conclusion 294
	5.6.1	Local and global democracy 295
	5.6.2	Government role of public consultation: Excessive or inferior 296
	5.6.3	Similar entertaining nature of public consultation 298
	5.6.4	Public consultation and local public policy 299

Chapter 6 Citizen Participation Platform on Internet

6.1	Citizen participation and democracy in the era of Internet 305
6.2	Internet political participation: Forms and fields of participation 309
	6.2.1 Forms of Internet political participation 309
	6.2.2 Analysis of Internet political participation factors 313
	6.2.3 Technological empowerment and system restraint: Logic of citizen participation in the era of the Internet 316
6.3	Technological empowerment: Examples of Internet participation platform and citizen participation 319
	6.3.1 Governments using Internet platforms to promote public negotiation and collect public opinions to provide service for people 320
	6.3.2 People's congress deputies, CPPCC members Internet participation platform 331
	6.3.3 Party and government information collection platform and mobilized participation 340
6.4	Information technology, government supervision and restrictive participation 344
	6.4.1 Technical constraints of Internet political participation 345
	6.4.2 Construction of Internet participation mechanism and strengthening of government supervision 347
	6.4.3 Diversion mechanism: Public service and social supervision 352

6.5 Discussion and conclusion 355
    6.5.1 Asymmetry of technological empowerment and constraint 355
    6.5.2 Insertion and absorption 357
    6.5.3 Internet citizen participation not equal to democracy 358
    6.5.4 Government and citizens in the era of the Internet 360

Chapter 7 Zhejiang Experience in Promoting Orderly Public Political Participation and Its Value

7.1 Characteristics of Zhejiang's experience in institutional innovation 367
    7.1.1 Providing concrete and practical approaches for public participation in local governance 368
    7.1.2 Innovative public participation system has clear objectives and roles 370
    7.1.3 Innovative public participation system reflects the values of democracy and the advanced participation technology 373
    7.1.4 Institutional innovation is the supplement and improvement for the national political system 375

7.2 Why did institutional innovation occur in Zhejiang? 379
    7.2.1 Local party committees and governments respond positively to the growing demand for participation in the transitional society 380
    7.2.2 A large number of local officials made active moves, bold exploration and practical innovation 384
    7.2.3 The cooperation between the government and citizens promotes institutional innovation in an orderly manner 386

7.3 What does Zhejiang's experience tell us? 389
    7.3.1 Citizens totally have the capability of taking care of their own affairs 390
    7.3.2 Democracy relies on the tangible participation system and channel 395

7.3.3 Safeguarding the public rights needs multi-level, functionally complementary participation system supply 398
 7.3.4 Enhancing public's orderly political participation is the basic way to promote social stability and construct a harmonious society 400

Chapter 8 Summary and Discussion

8.1 Characters of citizens and cultivation of participation-type citizens 407
8.2 Unbalance between political power and governing power in democracy and its solution 415
8.3 Political participation, institutional innovation and political stability 419

Bibliography 431

Postscript 443

Chapter

Introduction

1.1 Topic selection and its significance

1.1.1 Research background

China is the People's Republic. Popular Sovereignty is the fundamental property of the People's Republic. The principle of the republic is that the world is of the public, which means that the state power is in the hands of the common people, and the governance of the state is for the common cause of all citizens. The Constitution of the People's Republic of China (PRC) stipulates that all power of the PRC belongs to the people, which fundamentally determines that China must be a democratic country: People actively participate in politics and manage the public affairs of the country through institutionalized ways and means. This means to administer state affairs in accordance with the law, to manage economic and cultural undertakings, to manage social affairs and to exercise the right to be the master of the country. This kind of people's political form is a new type of modern democracy, namely people's democracy.

China is also a socialist country. Insisting on the leadership of the Communist Party of China (CPC) is an essential attribute of socialism with Chinese characteristics. This determines that in a socialist society, people's democracy must be unified with the leadership of the CPC and the rule of law. This unity is mainly reflected in two aspects: First, the Communist Party leads the people to run the country; second, it governs the country according to the law and governs for the people. The report of the 16th National Congress of the CPC points out: The ruling of the Communist Party is to lead and support the people to be the masters of the country, to mobilize and organize the people to manage state and social affairs in accordance with the law, to manage economic and cultural undertakings, and to safeguard and realize the fundamental interests of the people.

The question is, given China's national conditions and institutional background, how do the people govern themselves? By what means and in what way can they participate in the political life and exercise the political rights granted by the constitution? China is a large country with a large population and a vast territory. Even from the point of view of technology, it is impossible to promote the direct democracy of the Athenian city-states, in which the people directly participate in the national political life and manage public affairs at the national level, but instead, in China, the people elect their representatives to govern the country through representative democracy. At the same time, China is a country with thousands of years of authoritarian political tradition. The tradition of political culture and the power structure of autocratic monarchy have cultivated the submissive servile personality of the people and cast out the subject culture which seriously lacks in autonomy, consciousness of right and consciousness of democracy of traditional China. Therefore, although since the Opium War and after more than 100 years of development, especially after 40 years of reform and opening-up, China has completed the transition from an agricultural society to an industrial one, the democratic consciousness of the people is still relatively weak and the skills of democracy are not sufficient. The general public have always been paranoid and apathetic towards politics, and the people's initiative and participation with regard to politics has generally been low. Democracy, so to speak, in today's China, especially during the election in most remote and economically less-developed rural areas, to a large extent, is not the autonomy or self-consciousness of ordinary citizens, but the push of the ruling party, the government or the intellectual elite. The lack of consciousness of civil rights, democracy consciousness and political participation determines China's contemporary democracy is the democracy under the leadership of the CPC, namely socialist democracy.

Based on the above two considerations, after the founding of the PRC, the CPC established a complete political system to ensure that the people exercise their own power, participate in national politics and manage public affairs. According to the research of scholars, this system includes four aspects: (1) public opinion representative system, namely the system of people's congresses: It has achieved a wide range of civic political participation through the direct or indirect election of the people's congress deputies at all levels, as well as through the work of the people's representatives; (2) the system of political consultation, namely the multi-party cooperation and political consultation system under the leadership of the CPC. This is achieved through the participation of democratic parties, people's organizations and non-party personage; (3) social supervision system, including party and discipline supervision at all levels, supervision by the people's congress, administrative supervision, people's supervision and public opinion supervision, etc. Through direct participation by citizens, as well as indirect political participation, such as by letters, visits and whistle-blowing, citizens can supervise the power of the state; (4) public opinion system, that is, the public's opinions and appeals are input

Political Participation and Institutional Innovation:
A Case Study of Zhejiang

into the political system through the system of complaint letters, visits, leadership research and interviews with journalists and other channels.

These institutional arrangements, which guarantee citizens' political rights as the masters in form, are the main achievements of the development of democratic politics in China since the founding of the PRC. However, we must note that the system of civic participation established since the founding of the PRC, while ensuring that the people exercise the rights as the masters, is still imperfect and has some institutional deficiencies. According to the research of scholars, they are mainly reflected in the following two aspects.

First, from the dimension of the political system, the current political participation system has low degree of institutionalization and poor compatibility. In addition to the higher degree of institutionalization of participating channels, such as the National People's Congress (NPC) and the Chinese People's Political Consultative Conference (CPPCC), many more convenient channels of participation show low institutionalization of participation. Social supervision, public opinion and other aspects of the system are often based on work experiences and habits, with considerable contingency and randomness. In addition, the operable supporting measures are not strong, so that some participation systems are mostly confined to vague principles and are difficult to be implemented. This can easily lead to the unruliness of citizen participation. When it is difficult for people to use a channel of participation in the long term and in an effective way, it will inevitably lead to a decline in the trust in the whole political participation system and the apathy of political participation.

Second, from the aspect of structural function, the current political participation system is not highly differentiated and independent. Not every participation system is created solely for the needs of civic participation. In these systems, citizens are not the only actors, or even

Chapter 1 Introduction

the main actors. The existing participation system, while undertaking some functions of political participation, is often dominated by the party and government organs, and becomes a tool for political administration and social regulation by the ruling party and the government. For example, the NPC and the CPPCC, on the one hand, should undertake the functions of public opinion expression and encourage extensive participation in politics by all sectors of society. On the other hand, they should convey the ruling party and the government's policy decisions, and carry out extensive social mobilization functions to implement these decisions. In most cases, the latter is more attended to.

It must be pointed out that the civil political participation system established in the early days of the PRC has been adapted to the needs of the people in the planned economy to participate in political life. But with the reform and opening-up, industrialization, marketization and urbanization have been comprehensively promoted. Chinese society has changed from a traditional agricultural society to a modern society, and the social structure and social stratum have undergone fundamental changes. At the same time, with the deepening of the reform and opening-up, the ruling party and the government have been pushing forward market-oriented reform and institution-building, promoting the rule of law and democratic politics, reconstructing the model of state-to-society relations and giving citizens a range of economic, social and political rights. In the market economy, citizens have the opportunity to develop freely, and their own rights consciousness is awakening, and democratic consciousness is rising. Since the founding of the PRC, the institutional arrangements for the political participation of the citizens have been inadequate to meet the requirements of the times and social development.

First of all, with the century transformation of the Chinese society from a traditional agricultural society to an industrial society, and the consequent structural differentiation and reorganization of Chinese society, a batch of new social classes emerged, which has directly led to the diversification of the main body of social interests, thus forming a new social pattern of coexistence of multiple interests.

The differentiation and recombination of China's social structure are mainly reflected in two aspects. One is the differentiation and reorganization of the social structure. With the restructuring, closing down and bankruptcy of state-owned and collective-owned enterprises, the pattern of organizing and dominating the country by public enterprises in the planned economic era has been broken, and economic organizations such as private enterprises, joint-stock enterprises, and foreign-funded enterprises and township enterprises have developed rapidly. In the southeastern coastal area, the private economy with individual, private enterprises and stock enterprises as the main force has developed and emerged as the main economic organization in this area. Second, in line with the century-oriented transformation and structural differentiation of the Chinese society, the contemporary Chinese social strata have also undergone fission and reorganization, forming diversified interest groups. The five classes of the planned economy era, namely cadres, workers, farmers, intellectuals and class dissident stratum, have undergone fundamental differentiation and reorganization in the process of marketization and have a series of new careers, forming a batch of new social classes, such as managers, private entrepreneurs, individual businessmen, the urban unemployed and the semi-unemployed.

In the multi-social interest pattern formed by the social structure differentiation and the social stratum reorganization, how does the interest appeal of each social stratum express itself? In what channel is it expressed? How to integrate multiple interests into government's decision-making process? As mentioned above, the existing benefit expression mechanism and system arrangement, which are the products of the planned economy era, have been inadequate to adapt to the needs of society and the era, with the economic system reform and the differentiation of social structure. Facing the social reality of industrialization, marketization and urbanization, especially the reality of diversified social interests, how to set up a mechanism of interest representation, interest expression mechanism, interest coordination mechanism and interest integration mechanism to adapt to the pluralistic society and let different interest subjects play fair, free and equal games on the platform of the same legal system has become an important issue for the ruling party and the government to explore and solve.

Second, it is the rising awareness of civil rights and the rising consciousness of democracy. Since 1978, the ruling party and the government have emancipated the mind, kept pace with the times, and comprehensively pushed forward the reform and opening-up. While reforming and abolishing the old system that hampered the development of productive forces and social progress, the ruling party and the government actively promote the system construction of the state. At the same time, the new pattern of state and social relations has been designed and constructed: From the beginning of the reform and opening-up, the household contract responsibility system was started in the countryside, the people's communes were abolished, and the township government and the villagers' self-government system were fully implemented; then, the urban economic system reform was fully implemented, government functions were separated from enterprise management, the state-owned enterprise restructuring was implemented, the government quit completely from the microeconomic fields, and the transformation from planned economy system to market economic system was promoted. Since the 1990s, the ruling party has begun to promote the transformation of the all-inclusive government governance model, implement the transformation of government functions and the reform of the administrative system, and promote the rule of law and the construction of democratic politics. After entering the 21st century, the ruling party, in promoting the construction of democracy and the rule of law, has changed the ruling methods, improved the ruling ability while promoting the rule of law government, responsible government and service-oriented government construction. In this process, the ruling party and the government by the constitution and the law have gradually given each citizen their basic rights, gradually promoted the construction of grassroots democracy and the rule of law, implemented democratic elections, democratic management and democratic decision-making and democratic supervision in rural areas for villagers' autonomy, and have further promoted community autonomy and citizen education in the city. From the beginning of the reform and opening-up to free labor rights and production management rights (i.e. free land right, business right), after 40 years of efforts and struggle, Chinese citizens today have human rights such as personal rights, property rights, social rights, cultural rights and political rights.

For the contemporary Chinese, the era of the reform and opening-up is an era of "going to power", and it is an era of rising power and awareness of rights. In the past 40 years since the reform and opening-up, especially in the last 10 years, people have enjoyed freedom and development rights in the market economy, and gradually gained individual independence and autonomy. The consciousness of the rights of citizens has begun to sprout and develop. Some scholars have summarized this consciousness into three levels: The first is the individual's understanding of the interests and freedom that he or she should have. The second is the awareness of the individual's active recognition and maintenance of his or her rights as well as the consciousness of social individuals to make new claims on society and government according to the developments and changes of society. In practice, the consciousness of civil rights is reflected in case of infringement of power by citizens, and it will resist the power and the right to maintain it through legal means such as administrative reconsideration or administrative litigation. It is also reflected that citizens actively participate in the decision-making of the state and the government through direct or indirect democratic processes, and legally fight for their rights to establish freedom and rights in the way

Chapter 1 Introduction

of legislation. In other words, rights consciousness and democratic consciousness are actually interdependent and integrated, and the awakening of rights consciousness must be accompanied by the upsurge of democratic consciousness.

Third, the popularization of the Internet and the mobile Internet has created a new space and new world for mankind. The rise of Internet politics, the Internet portal BBS, blogs, microblogs, WeChat and other social media platforms have provided unprecedented space and stage for the political participation of Chinese citizens in modern times. Over the past decade or so, Chinese citizens have shown active and enthusiastic political participation on the Internet. Political participation in Internet politics, such as microblog political consultation, Internet corruption prevention and WeChat rights protection, has had a broad and profound impact on China's politics and society today.

China's Internet politics and citizen participation can be seen in its general form and characteristics, from typical cases of three forms of netizen political participation through microblog political consultation, Internet anti-corruption and WeChat rights protection.

For microblog political consultation, the most typical case is the case of netizen consultation after the railway bullet train crash in Wenzhou in 2011. On July 23, 2011, within the Ningbo–Wenzhou railway line of Zhejiang Province, the D301 train from Beijing to Fuzhou and the D3115 train from Hangzhou to Fuzhou were involved in a train rear-ended accident, with six carriages derailed, 40 people killed and 172 injured. Previously, such incidents were handled by the Ministry of Railways in conjunction with the public security department. This time, thanks to the popularity of smartphones and mobile Internet, tens of millions of netizens have tried their best to use microblogs to spread the truth about accidents on the Internet, investigate the cause of the accident and investigate the accident liability. From the cause of the accident, the on-site crisis management, the compensation standard of the victims, to the post-accountability of the Ministry of Railways, the government has been placed under strong supervision.

With regard to Internet anti-corruption campaigns, a classic case concerning a Chongqing official is "the case of Lei Zhengfu" in 2012. In November 2012, there was an Internet real-name report of suspected corruption case on Lei Zhengfu, a Chongqing Beibei District party official. A short article about this case was published on the Internet, attached with an indecent screenshot of a man and a woman. Because of the wide and rapid spread of the case through the Internet, the Chongqing Municipal Party Committee, which was forced to respond to it in a few days, relieved Lei Zhengfu from the post of secretary of the Beibei District Party Committee and investigated the case. Finally, Chongqing's No. 1 Intermediate People's Court sentenced Lei Zhengfu to 13 years in prison for bribery. In the period, local netizens resorted to human flesh search and other means to report officials with famous watches, mansions, mistresses and so on, to expose scandals, to expose privacy, to attract public attention, attracting attention of the netizens and public opinion on the concerned parties and forcing their superiors to quickly investigate and deal with them. A large number of officials have been punished for corruption, bribery or extravagance of private life.

With regard to WeChat rights protection, the May 2016 Lei Yang incident is a typical case. The case originally titled "Why did the man with a Master's degree from Renmin University of China who just became a father die in an hour?" was posted and spread through WeChat. The report drew attention to the mysterious death of the young man from Renmin University of China. Over the next few days, many netizens wrote about the cause of Lei's death, questioning the truth of the logic chain, calling on the police to make public the law enforcement process and calling for a third-party investigation. As a result, WeChat questioning succeeded in prompting the authorities to step in and lead the investigation by the Beijing Procuratorate.

Chapter 1 Introduction

Typical cases of microblog political consultation, Internet anti-corruption and WeChat rights protection show us the unique function and powerful influence of the Internet and citizens' political participation in the era of mobile Internet popularization. Due to the increasing catalytic effect of the network, incidents of some people protecting their rights or fighting against corruption occur on the Internet or continue to heat up with the attention of Internet users. The rapid change from individual events to public events has created powerful public opinion and public opinion pressure. We-media, like microblogs, blogs and WeChat, as a tool of online political participation, have combined the effects of individual participation and group participation, and have shown unparalleled influence on the Internet political field.

In today's China, despite the growing sophistication of the government's regulation over the Internet, rules are becoming more and more restrictive. However, due to the progress of mobile Internet and information technology, and the popularization of microblogs, WeChat, blogs and other we-media, the online political participation of Chinese citizens has already formed the potential of "peerless power", which is unstoppable as the tide of the Qianjiang River. Any ordinary person can use smartphones to express his/her interests and demands on the Internet anytime and anywhere, maintain basic rights, and pursue freedom, equality, fairness and justice; any ordinary Chinese will be able to supervise the governance of the ruling party and the government through the Internet and exercise the right of democracy to varying degrees; ordinary citizens can use the network to supervise the law enforcement department and crimes in judicial organs at all levels, and pursue judicial justice; expose official corruption, fight corruption, and pursue clear politics through the Internet. Internet citizens' political participation has become the norm. The network political participation profoundly affects China's present politics and society, and may continue to change and reshape the future of political and social structure in China.

Political Participation and Institutional Innovation:
A Case Study of Zhejiang

Finally, from the development of China's modernization process, due to the relative hysteresis of the political system reform, the centralized government management system formed in the era of planned economy is increasingly showing its inherent disadvantages in the market-oriented environment. Lord Acton, the British historian, once said that all power tended to corrupt and absolute power would lead to corruption absolutely. The government now controls most of the country's wealth and resources, such as land, taxes and mines. Major decisions are often made by the party and the government. The lack of necessary supervision and restriction of public power can easily lead to power rent-seeking and the breeding of government corruption. Moreover, the spread of power corruption is bound to form a violation of the legitimate rights and interests of citizens, and even civil liberties. Therefore, promoting the reform of the political system and the construction of modern state system, further enhancing democracy, promoting citizens' political participation, providing citizens with ways to influence, supervise and restrict state power, letting the people form the necessary supervision and restriction from their own government power, namely public power, preventing the infringement and coercion of civil liberties by public power, guaranteeing the freedom and rights of every citizen are the proper ways in which the ruling party and the government can promote the reform of the political system and the construction of democratic politics.

Rent-seeking corruption has been the most widespread and harmful phenomenon of power corruption since the reform and opening-up. The reason for rent-seeking corruption is that the government has too many resources. However, power is too centralized and lacks necessary supervision and restriction, which provides a lot of institutional rent and rent-seeking space for officials at all levels. In the economically developed southeastern coastal areas, the rent-seeking corruption of local government officials is often a direct violation of the interests of the public. Therefore, the public's discontent is aroused, which leads to antagonism and even confrontation between the officials and the

Chapter 1 Introduction

people. The series of mass incidents that have taken place over the past two decades are examples. Therefore, the question arises: how to enable citizens to participate in the governance of local public affairs through institutional channels and realize the benign interaction between government and citizens? In what ways can citizens supervise and restrict the power of the government? How to prevent the compulsory infringement of civil liberties and rights by government power? How to prevent and eliminate rent-seeking corruption and curb the spread of corrupted public power, so as to promote officials at all levels to strictly control and regulate the power in their hands, and make the operation of government power truly go along the track of "government of the people, by the people and for the people"? The solution to these problems depends on the deepening of the reform of the political and economic systems, on the development of modern national system construction and system innovation.

To enhance democratic political construction and local governance, we need to constantly promote citizens' orderly political participation, to realize the aspiration of the people to be the masters of the country, to enhance the positive interaction between the state and society, the government and citizens, and to gradually complete the process of democratization in the country. Over the past 10 years, the ruling party and the government have been exploring the practice of promoting democracy at the grassroots level, starting from regional and local reforms and experiments, actively promoting institutional construction and institutional innovation, and encouraging citizens to actively participate in local governance, cultivating and training citizens' consciousness of democratic rule of law, and shaping the spirit of citizenship and participatory personality. Taking Zhejiang as an example, these institutional innovations mainly include the following four aspects.

First, rural democracy and local governance, mainly including democratic consultation, citizens' council, residents or villagers' council and democratic financial committee.

Political Participation and Institutional Innovation:
A Case Study of Zhejiang

Second, the hearing of the city, mainly including legislative hearing, administrative hearing and judicial hearing, and residents' forum.

Third, the TV political consultation, the people's proposal solicitation system and democratic participation system for the major project, including various forms of TV political consultation programs, the people's daily proposal collection and public participation system of people's livelihood and major municipal construction projects.

Fourth, the network participation platform in the Internet age, including the government website BBS, network political consultation platform, "town hall", network performance platform of the NPC deputies, online contact room of representatives, online contact room of CPPCC members, as well as various participating platforms, such as microblogs, WeChat and APP, provided by government departments at all levels.

The party committees and governments at all levels in Zhejiang Province have introduced a series of institutional innovations to promote citizens' orderly political participation, and further improved the existing political participation system, opened up some political space for citizens to participate in public affairs and exercise their political rights as the masters of the country, setting up channels and means for participating in politics and expressing interest demands. They have conducted beneficial exploration and trials for the participation in local governance for citizens, and then to cultivate the participative citizen character, bridging the gap between the government and the power. This is the latest achievement of democracy construction and development in China.

From the practical dimension of local democracy, how are the performances of some institutional innovations introduced in recent years in Zhejiang Province in promoting orderly political participation and local governance? To what extent do these regional and local institutional innovations satisfy the desire of the people to be the masters of the country? What functions do they have in the process of realizing the expression, coordination and integration of social pluralistic interests and promoting the construction of a harmonious society? What role can it play? What problems exist in the system innovation itself and how to correct and improve it, so as to promote comprehensive and sustainable system innovation and system construction? And so on, a series of questions deserve our deep thinking and research.

From the perspective of political theory, there is a historical tension between sovereignty and democracy. Theoretically, the sovereignty belongs to the people's government, and it does not necessarily reflect and safeguard the interests of the people in the course of the operation of power. Therefore, the modern democratic politics always has faced tensions while trying to bridge the gap between people's sovereignty and power, and between democracy, freedom and equality. This book focuses on the question of what institutional arrangements can bridge the gap between regime and governance in the context of China's reality and make contemporary Chinese citizens not only have the power to be the masters of the country in theory, but also have the right to participate in the political life and manage the public affairs of the country equally in the real world. The above question is not only a major theoretical issue in contemporary Chinese political science, but also a major practical subject for development of socialist democracy in China. This book will serve as a preliminary discussion and answer to the major theoretical issues of political science through the study of Zhejiang's experience of promoting citizens' orderly political participation and system innovation.

1.1.2 Theoretic value and practical meaning of the research

Since 1911, when the Revolution of 1911 overthrew the autocratic monarchy and established a republic, developing democratic politics and building a modern state system of sovereignty among the people has been a century-old dream of the modern Chinese people and the

Political Participation and Institutional Innovation:
A Case Study of Zhejiang

goal for building a modern country. Because of the political and cultural tradition, the level of economic development, the social structure and the characteristics of national character and other historical and practical factor constraints, one of the biggest challenges facing the ruling party and the government in the process of building a democratic institutional system is how to get out of the predicament of democratic development, namely how to coordinate the people's participation and the internal tension of the state power. In other words, how to define the power relationship between government and market, state and citizens, state and society through institutional arrangement of the constitutional system? How to put the power of government into the orbit of the constitution and the law to regulate and supervise the operation of government power by law? How to establish a democratic participation system platform through system design, so that the people and the government can achieve benign interaction? We will actively create conditions to encourage citizens' orderly political participation, and promote the improvement of civil intelligence and the development of civil society. Ensuring every citizen enjoys and exercises the right to be the master, overcoming and dissolving the paradox of democratic politics itself so that the people not only have nominal power, but also in fact enjoy the benefits brought on by this power, preventing the power of the people to become a tool for harming the people, etc., are major issues that need to be seriously discussed and properly solved in the process of political democratization and modern state system construction in contemporary China.

Over the past 40 years of the reform and opening-up, in the process of building democracy at the grassroots level, party committees and governments at all levels in Zhejiang Province have actively explored and promoted institutional innovation, constantly expanded citizens' orderly political participation channels, cultivated participating-type citizens actively and encouraged citizens to participate in local public affairs. The practice of the democratic political development in Zhejiang Province provides us with empirical support to think and solve the

Chapter 1 Introduction

related problems in the process of China's democratic political development and system construction.

In Zhejiang Province, a series of institutional innovations is introduced, mainly embodied in four aspects: First, it has expanded the channels of citizen participation and promoted local governance; second, it has promoted the interest expression and the integration of interests of social pluralistic interest groups; third, it has enhanced political and governmental legitimacy; fourth, it has promoted the citizens' spirit of education and helped the cultivation of the participatory citizens. These functions have promoted the healthy development of grassroots democracy and enhanced the communication and interaction between citizens and the government. At the same time, it has bridged the gap between government and power, and made a beneficial exploration to overcome the paradox of democracy to some extent. In other words, a series of institutional innovations, such as democratic consultation, hearings, people's construction solicitation system, television political consultation, Internet political consultation and official and citizen dialogue on government websites, has been produced by the local party committee and the government and ordinary people in the practice of continuous interaction over many years with a strong vitality and embodying the Chinese characteristics of democracy.

We believe the fact that a series of institutional innovations of civic participation in public affairs that occurred in Zhejiang Province has deep social, economic and cultural roots. Zhejiang is one of the earliest and most developed provinces engaged in the market economy since China's reform and opening-up. From the economic, social and cultural to the overall political development, the local party committee and the government's institutional innovation has been leading the country. A remarkable feature of Zhejiang's economic development is that the start-up and market development of private enterprises is one step ahead of the vast majority of the country. And the growth of private enterprises and the expansion of the market are very rapid, with new

Political Participation and Institutional Innovation:
A Case Study of Zhejiang

economic activities' main subject and a new way of economic operation complementing each other, mutually reinforcing, and becoming the main driving force of regional economic development. Due to the unbalanced development of regional economy, the initial stage of economic development in Zhejiang Province is not a unified model. There are significant regional differences in institutional changes and economic development in different regions. These have formed a new social pattern of diversified interests and a Zhejiang model of co-existence and co-prosperity of various modes of economic development.

At the same time, Zhejiang is one of the provinces in the forefront of the construction of the government with regard to law, responsibility and public service. Since the reform and opening-up, the governments at all levels in Zhejiang Province have been committed to the modernization of the national governance system and governance capability, to actively promote institutional reform, to strengthen the government's own construction, to promote the government's administration in accordance with the law, to reform the model of all-powerful government governance, to transform government functions, to serve the market, to serve enterprises, and to serve for the people's well-being so as to create a favorable market environment and social environment for the development of market economy and private enterprises. From the perspective of development philosophy and development strategy, from acquiescence and non-interference to the "Wenzhou model", "Taizhou phenomenon" and private economic development in the initial reform to comprehensively promoting urbanization and private economic development in the province by the late 1990s, and launching the "eight–eight strategy", "rule of law Zhejiang", "peaceful Zhejiang" and the construction of the cultural province, promoting the development of education, science, technology, health, sports and the formation of the poverty alleviation strategy of "getting rid of poverty" after entering the new century, for complying with the changes of domestic and international development

Chapter 1 Introduction

environment, Zhejiang provincial party committee and government have formed a good pattern of economic growth, social development and government innovation, promoted the rapid development of local economy and the orderly transformation of society, and laid a solid social and economic foundation for promoting citizens' orderly political participation and the construction of grassroots democratic politics.

Viewing from the perspective of government administration and governance, the governments at all levels in Zhejiang Province, in response to the requirements of the era of industrialization, marketization and urbanization, constantly explore and innovate management modes, transform government functions and optimize the regional system environment to explore and adjust the management system and governance mode according to local conditions. By making government affairs public from Jinhua City to the whole province, from the "efficiency revolution" which was first carried out in Wenzhou to the provincial organ efficiency construction, and Hangzhou's assessment of "satisfaction and dissatisfaction" over the government, green GDP assessment in Huzhou and other places, "democratic consultation" of Wenling, etc., the governments at all levels are dedicated to the development of private enterprises and private venture capital's "soft environment". It can be said that the party committees and governments at all levels in Zhejiang Province have been promoting democracy and the rule of law for many years, promoting the reform of the government's own construction and administrative management system and promoting the transformation of governments at all levels from the all-inclusive government to the rule of law, responsible government and public service government, which has created a unique institutional advantage for Zhejiang's economic society to advance step by step. It is the creativity of the people, the vitality of the market mechanism and the development of government reform and institutional innovation that has created the Zhejiang model of social and economic development and the Zhejiang experience of grassroots democracy.

Political Participation and Institutional Innovation:
A Case Study of Zhejiang

In essence, the successful experience of the Zhejiang model and the pioneering effect of Zhejiang's social and economic development in China constitute the main basis for our choice of Zhejiang as the case. We hope that through this research, we will investigate and discuss the practice of local democracy construction and development in the private economically developed province since the reform and opening-up, summarize and upgrade the experience of system innovation introduced in Zhejiang Province in recent years. In view of the difficulties and new problems existing in the development of grassroots democratic political construction, some forward-looking and constructive policy suggestions are put forward. We believe that from the perspective of theory and practice, the series of institutional innovations to promote citizens' orderly political participation, like the experience of grassroots democratic political construction in Zhejiang Province, including democratic consultation, hearing, people's proposal solicitation system, television consultation, official and citizen dialogue platform via Internet, can provide useful reference and inspiration for the construction and development of grassroots democratic politics in China.

1.2 Several related concepts and theories

1.2.1 On democracy

Democracy is a controversial topic in political science. From the genetic dimension, democracy originated during the age of Athens in ancient Greece. Democracy refers to the rule of the people, referring to a state of political life of citizens. In the city of Athens, on the one hand, every citizen directly participated in the public relations practice of the city, elected the leader of the city, made public policy, and was the real ruler of the city. On the other hand, citizens were ruled and administered: they accepted the rule and administration of the city-state. Therefore, democracy in Athens is also a kind of institutional arrangement about political power. It is a form of government that is different from a monarchy and aristocracy. This form of government is called direct democracy or ancient democracy. For a variety of historical reasons, this form of democratic government existed only for a little more

Political Participation and Institutional Innovation: A Case Study of Zhejiang

than 200 years, and it was squeezed by both internal and external forces and disappeared in the space-time tunnel of ancient civilization.

In the history of democracy, there are paradoxes in the early democratic politics. In ancient Greece, the people were both the rulers and the ruled. Through the long Middle Ages to the present, the paradox of democracy is that: There exists great tension between the nominal attribution of power and the actual exercise of power. Modern politics is democratic politics. In theory, democratic politics is the politics of all power belonging to the people, and the sovereignty of the democratic state is in the hands of the people. In reality, however, at the national level, it is not possible for the people of the collective concept to directly exercise their power to govern the country. In most of today's supposedly democratic countries, including Western countries, the state sovereignty appears to belong to the people, but the power to govern the state, that is, the exercise of public power, has always been held by a few of the elite, and the people actually are subject to the power of the elite. It can be said that the relationship between the nominal power and the actual exercise of power, or equality and subordination, sovereignty and control, is a lasting tension embedded in democracy.

Around the paradox of democracy, democratic theorists and thinkers in modern times have been constantly exploring and thinking, trying to find some ways to bridge the gap between the nominal power and the actual exercise of power. Western modern political thinkers try to bridge this paradox from the natural state. Hobbes pushed the theory of mechanistic individualism to the extreme, making equality subject to the subordinate. Locke emphasized that the power exercised by the government is the delegated power of the people, thereby avoiding subordination and emphasizing equality. Rousseau used the concept of public will to limit democracy to a narrow group, so it could not become a modern workable model of democracy. Tocqueville tried to separate social democracy from political democracy, arguing that democracy could only be established in civil society and not in the political field. Satori distinguished between the nominal power and the exercise of power, trying to bridge the gap between democratic theory and democratic practice, public opinion and exercise of power.

The paradox of democracy exists in the realm of theory as well as in political practice. Since modern times, politicians and people have been exploring and trying to solve the problems caused by the paradox in the practice of democratic political development. From the perspective of the development of modern democracy, this paradox is mainly reflected in the fact that even in the democratic countries that claim to be popularly sovereign, it is often a few bureaucrats and members of the elite who rule the vast majority of the people. The establishment of representative democracy seemed to address the technical difficulties that direct democracy could not implement in expanded regions with large populations. However, the substitution of direct democracy at the national level for indirect democracy has not only failed to resolve, but in fact strengthened the paradox of democracy. Thus, there is the status of "semi-sovereign people" and meritocracy. During the second half of the 20th century, democratic countries promoted the reform of administrative decentralization and reconstructed the relationship between the central government and the local government. Through the continuous decentralization of local governments, they strengthened the local autonomy, provided right to local governments and power to people, tried to alleviate the paradox of democracy through the reconstruction of local governance structures. Participatory democracy emphasizes that citizens actively participate in local public affairs, and deliberative democratic theorists emphasize the use of public consultation channels to make up for the shortage of civic participation. Polycentric governance theorists emphasize to enhance the role of citizens and non-governmental organizations (NGOs) in social governance, and so on. These are all explorations and attempts to ease the tension of the regime and sovereignty and break the paradox of democracy.

Political Participation and Institutional Innovation:
A Case Study of Zhejiang

In China, democracy, as a political system and a form of governance, is undoubtedly a Western import. In modern times, advanced intellectuals and statesmen have been seeking the prosperity of the country and the democratization of politics. In theory, Kang Youwei, Yan Fu and others have detected the paradox between this equality and subordination, regime and sovereignty, in democracy. They advocated the establishment of a modern democratic system, and promoted the transition from traditional Chinese political culture to democratic political culture. In the political practice, the Wuxu Reform (or the Hundred Days' Reform) started the establishment of China's modern political system. Sun Yat-sen treated the modern democratic system as a national system goal and put it into practice in the Republic of China. Since the founding of the PRC, in order to guarantee equality, freedom and democracy for the people, the ruling party has established the system of people's congresses and local autonomy at the national level to ensure that the people exercise their rights as the masters of the country. Since the reform and opening-up, the ruling party and the government have promoted the construction of democratic politics at the grassroots level in rural areas, and explored the institutional innovation of local governance and grassroots democracy, such as villager autonomy, democratic consultation, people's proposal solicitation system, hearings, television political consultation and Internet political participation platforms, encouraging ordinary people to participate in local public affairs. In short, since modern times, Chinese people's pursuit of democracy has been manifested in two aspects: The first is to establish the modern democratic political system, including the representative system at the national level and the local autonomy system; the second is to explore the balance between democracy and authority, resolve the tension between equality and subordination, regime and sovereignty, and resolve the paradox of democracy while pursuing and building democracy.

1.2.2 Citizens and subjects

Who is a citizen? The definition of citizenship must be discussed in the context of public domain and democratic politics in order to

Chapter 1 Introduction

be meaningful. In Athens city democracy of ancient Greek, citizens referred to those who participate in the civic assembly, directly or indirectly, participate in the public affairs of the city-state, participate in the election of the decision-making people of the city, and be elected as part of the governing body of the city-state. Therefore, the citizens of Athens did not include women, children, and excluded slaves and gentiles. Here, citizens were the union of the ruler and the ruled. On the one hand, every citizen was the true ruler of the city-state; on the other hand, citizens were ruled and managed by the city-state. From the perspective of political science, citizenship is a kind of qualification and right, referring to individuals who participate in public affairs and thus have autonomy in the political country. For the so-called autonomy, the general statement is the matter of their own decision, the common decision of public affairs. Autonomy means the independence and perfection of personality, which is freedom from the bondage and enslavement of foreign powers. Citizens, therefore, are often associated with freedom, and citizenship means getting rid of the alien slavery force, the pursuit of independent and perfect personality, reflecting the value and moral concern of the people as a man and becoming a man. Citizenship also means personal autonomy in the private sphere, and personal affairs are exempt from interference or coercion by state power.

Citizens are the product of democratic politics and constitute the main subject of democratic politics. In democratic politics, individuals, as citizens, can participate directly or indirectly in public affairs. Democratic society recognizes, respects and maintains human autonomy. "Members of the community can, in general, participate directly or indirectly in decisions that affect the entire membership". It is also a minimalist expression of democracy. In a democracy, public affairs are a "matter of the people". Every citizen has the right to participate in the political life of the country, to administer the public affairs, and to make his own judgment and choice in the public interest.

Political Participation and Institutional Innovation: A Case Study of Zhejiang

Therefore, the individual as a citizen is the union of the ruler and the ruled. On the one hand, he must be the object of national governance and management, while on the other hand, state power and laws are operated by individuals with the participation of citizens.

A community of citizens, united by citizens, are called "the people". The people are not abstract concepts; they are superimposed by individuals or citizens of the community. In a democracy, the people, as a community of citizens, are the foundation and precondition of a political country. Democratic politics is the politics of people's sovereignty. Sovereignty is the basic property of democracy among the people. The people enjoy the supreme power in the political relations and the corresponding political countries. All the power of the state belongs to the people, and the people are the source, basis and end-result of the power of the political state.

The citizen corresponds to the subject. Subjects are the product of autocratic politics. In despotic politics, the individual exists only as the object of political rule and the enslavement of the political process. As the subject, the individual is passive to the public affairs. The individual exists purely as an object of economic exploitation and political oppression. Public affairs in an authoritarian state tend to be in the form of personal affairs, and are monopolized by the ruler, only by the affairs of a particular individual, the sovereign. Here, the individual is excluded from the public affairs of his own. Tyrants monopolize public affairs on the one hand and invade the private sphere on the other hand, and intervene and coerce pure personal affairs, imprison the whole of society in the state apparatus, and to the pervasive political rule of non-political life. In such totalitarian politics, state power is ubiquitous, and the boundaries between the public and private sectors are no longer there. It can be said that the lack of personal autonomy in the private sphere is the inevitable result of the lack of autonomy in the public domain.

Chapter 1 Introduction

In traditional Chinese society, there was only the family, the clan and the individual consciousness and no citizens or rights consciousness. At the level of the political country, Confucianism in the Han dynasty advocated the "principle of feudal moral conduct" (namely monarch is the guide of his subjects, father is the guide of his child, and husband is the guide of his wife), which is the natural and unchangeable order of people. Therefore, China's political ideology only had consciousness of subject and loyalty to the monarch, lacking a modern sense of citizenship and nation-state. In modern times, the concept of citizenship and nation-state began to be introduced from the West. Liang Qichao advocated the "theory of new people" and believed the key to China's political modernization lies in the cultivation of modern citizenship. Sun Yat-sen advocated civil rights and endeavoured to protect civil rights in the form of a constitution by initiating a revolution to overthrow the autocratic rule of the Qing dynasty and establish the Republic of China. After the founding of the PRC, especially the reform and opening-up, the ruling party and the government reformulated and promulgated the constitution in 1982. It stipulated the rights and obligations of citizens and guaranteed the citizens their rights. On the establishment of the state system, the people's representative system was established as the state's organ of power. The reality, however, is that, while the state has established laws and institutions guaranteeing civil rights, due to China's political tradition, the authoritarian and the subject consciousness is deeply rooted, and the formation of citizenship is not an overnight thing. This determines that the people of contemporary China will not be able to transform their roles from the subjects of the imperial dynasty to the citizens of the modern sense in a short period of time.

How to transform the role from the subjects to the citizens, and how to make the masses develop the consciousness of citizenship, the consciousness of rights and the rule of law, and cultivate the citizens in the modern sense? In addition to the promotion and dissemination of new ideas and new thinking, the state has continuously promoted the democracy and rule of law education for the people. More importantly, it should be the direct participation of the people in the democratic political system in public affairs. Participation in the process of local autonomy is only the process of getting people involved in public affairs and public decision-making. As a result, the people can truly enjoy the benefits of being the masters of their own affairs, understand democracy in the process, learn about democracy, learn to participate in the process, gradually master the skills of democracy and participation, and gradually complete the transformation of the role from subjects to citizens, cultivating a true sense of the new people. In this sense, the grassroots democratic political construction promoted since the reform and opening-up, as well as the practice of the system innovation carried out by local governments at all levels to promote the ownership of the citizens, is also a political experiment to cultivate citizens.

1.2.3 Political participation in three modes of democracy

Since the 1950s, there has been a general emphasis on citizens' participation in public decision-making and public affairs. This can be seen as an experiment in the democratic politics of countries, namely an attempt to mitigate the intrinsic paradoxes of democracy by expanding civic participation and cultivating participatory citizens.

Political democratization is often expressed and measured by the political participation of the masses, and political participation becomes one of the important fields of contemporary political science. In general, the research on political participation follows two routes: One is empirical research and the other is normative research. There is a consistency and tension of varying degrees between these researches. In order to better grasp and understand different types of political participations, they must be investigated in different democratic paradigms, so as to grasp their connotation and care. Otherwise, the exact connotation of political participation and the relationship between different types cannot be understood correctly. Let's discuss the political participation of the three most influential democratic paradigms today: responsive democracy, participatory democracy and deliberative democracy.

(1) *Three concepts of political participation*

  The political participation subjects in the three democratic forms are the common people. What these forms have in common is an emphasis on legal participation in the system. The differences are: (1) In the responsive democratic paradigm, political participation is a responsive participation that tries to influence decisions or decision-makers. Norman H. Nie and Sidney Verba believe that political participation refers to the legitimate activities of the civilian population, more or less, which influence the choice of government personnel and/or their actions for a direct purpose. This definition is macroscopic, and it is mainly based on empirical research at the national level. The representatives are Samuel Huntington, Norman H. Nie and Sidney Verba. (2) In the participatory democracy paradigm, political participation is defined as the formulation of direct participation in decision-making. Gould believes that such political participation is characterized by direct and immediate involvement of individuals in the decision-making process; Barber suggests that participatory democracy is a civic autonomy, not an autonomous government. Of course, participatory democracy theorists advocate political participation, but they have no intention of abolishing the representative system. It is to advocate for areas outside the traditional representative system, especially in small areas such as communities or workplaces, to expand opportunities for direct participation, such as solving community problems. (3) The model of deliberative democracy in political participation is a political discussion; as Chambers claims, participation in public consultation is not to directly make a decision, but to form opinions and points of view for the decision-making process. This discussion is intended to promote understanding of each other's views and perspectives through deliberation, so as to form opinions, even if no collective decisions are reached. The participation in the consultative democratic paradigm is mainly limited to a small scope. In short, in the responsive democratic paradigm, political participation refers to the behavior of trying to influence the government staff and their decision-making; in the participatory democratic paradigm, political participation is the formulation of citizens' direct participation in decision-making; in the consultative democratic paradigm, political participation refers to discussion, consultation or deliberation, which is the process of public consultation.

(2) *The results of three different kinds of political participation*

The three democratic theories differ not only in the concept of participation, but also in the outcome of political participation: (1) The responsive democratic paradigm focuses on systematically responding to the demands of citizens to achieve equal protection on an individual level. (2) The participatory democracy paradigm takes individual "self-development" as the primary criterion. As for self-development, Pateman believes that participatory democratic paradigm includes maximization of input (participation), not only policy output, but also the development of individual social and political capabilities. Of course, theorists have different definitions of self-development, but what they have in common is that they develop people's potential through political participation. (3) Deliberative democracy pays most attention to the legitimacy of the democratic system itself. The theory of deliberative democracy holds that legitimacy does not come from the predetermined will of individual formed by citizens, but from the process of formation of will itself, that is, deliberation.

(3) *The motivation of political participation*

Although scholars have their own views on the motivation of political participation, Jan Teorell argues that there is no fundamental difference between the three democratic paradigms, and he identifies factors that influence political participation as resources, incentives and actions. According to Coleman, the resources include physical capital (including income, personal wealth, telephone and Internet), human capital (including skills, ability, education and knowledge) and social capital (including social structure and human behavior in this structure). The number of opportunities for access to these resources, the increase or decrease of the likelihood of citizens resorting to political participation, and the use of different forms of political participation are also the different emphasis of different democratic paradigms on political participation, which is to try to influence decisions or decision-makers, direct decisions or political discussion.

In terms of the incentives to participate, Jan Teorell cites the general motivation and choice of motivation in Olsen's collective action theory. General incentives mainly aim at the common interests of all members of the group, while the choice incentives aim at individual member's interests within the group. As for how to mobilize people to participate in the collective business, Olsen believes that the choice incentives within the large group can mobilize the members to devote themselves to the collective affairs, while the general incentives are enough for the small group.

Why are citizens still reluctant to engage in public affairs when resources and incentives are available? First of all, in the nature of the relationship between motivation and resources, the two are not always dependent on each other, that is, the individuals with resources do not always have the incentive to devote themselves to the collective affairs. Second, resources shape incentives, that is, when incentives are merely coordination mechanisms, resources may indirectly influence participation. The participation behavior itself may be directed toward the resources of the investment material, person or social capital, and the existing participation experience also affects the will of future political participation. To this end, it is necessary to grasp the motivation of political participation from the reciprocal relationship among resources, incentives and actions.

(4) *Deliberative democracy theory*

Deliberative (or consultative) democracy theory is a democratic theory that emerged in Western political science in the late 20th century.

Political Participation and Institutional Innovation: A Case Study of Zhejiang

Political scientists define it from different perspectives. David Miller, Carolyn Hendriks and others interpret deliberative democracy as a democratic decision-making system or a rational form of decision-making. In this system, every citizen can participate equally in the formulation process of public policy, freely express opinions, listen to and consider different viewpoints and make decisions that are collectively binding in rational discussion and negotiation. Jorge M. Valadez and others argue that deliberative democracy is a form of democratic governance. Citizens with equality and freedom, in public interest, have reached consensus in dialogue and discussion and made decisions through public consultation (public deliberation). Public consultation is the process in which members of the political community participate in public discussion and critically examine public policies that are collectively binding.

According to Elster's definition, the so-called "deliberative democracy" means that all citizens or their representatives affected by the policy should be able to participate in collective decisions. And this collective decision is made by participants with a rational and selfless attitude through discussion and negotiation. Political scientists A. Gutmann and D. Thompson argue that deliberative democracy refers to such a form of democratic politics. That is, through extensive public discussion, all parties communicate with each other in public forum, to enable the parties to understand each other's positions and views, and to seek and achieve acceptable solutions on the premise of pursuing public interests. Based on this, deliberative democratic theory emphasizes that citizens are the participants of democratic institutions and their participation in public affairs should be promoted actively. This political participation of the citizens should not be limited to voting, or petition, or lobbyism, or to social movements. The public policy should be discussed openly in the context of the participants' full control of information, equality of opportunity and fair decision-making, whereby participants propose feasible solutions or suggestions.

Chapter 1 Introduction

The rise of deliberative democracy is a response to the many problems facing Western society. In particular, the deep and persistent moral conflicts underlying the multi-cultural society and the inequality of cognitive resources among ethnic cultural groups make it difficult for most people to participate effectively in public decision-making. Deliberative democracy reemphasizes citizens' responsibility for the public interest and emphasizes the qualitative improvement of public opinion. Through continuous public consultation, all parties can understand each other's positions and broaden their minds. On the basis of communication and understanding, the pure expediency is promoted to the appeal of public welfare, so as to make up for the system defect of electoral democracy and "majority decision". The theory of deliberative democracy is the result of the deep reflection on the essence of democracy by contemporary political scientists based on the flaws exposed by representative democracy in modern politics. It is a revision of contemporary political science to liberal democracy or electoral democracy that overemphasizes freedom and ignores equality. It is the new development of democratic theory in the contemporary era.

Deliberative democracy is both a democratic theory and a democratic practice. In this book, we mainly use it as an exploration for cultivating modern citizens and improving social governance to alleviate the paradox of democracy, or as a theoretical analysis tool. In the application of deliberative democratic theory to analyze citizens' political participation in contemporary China, the Chinese social environment needs to be investigated. At this point, scholars mainly have the following views in two aspects.

First, it is necessary to recognize that China is not fully equipped with the social environment and social structure required by the deliberative democratic theory. Professor Yu Keping believes that deliberative democracy is based on the political foundation of Western representative democracy and majority democracy. It is the perfection

Political Participation and Institutional Innovation: A Case Study of Zhejiang

and transcendence of Western representative democracy, majority democracy and remote democracy. If we deviate from this premise and look at deliberative democracy, we may deviate from the truth of history. In other words, deliberative democracy is not an isolated theory or practice: it is deeply rooted in Western tradition and reality. In a sense, China doesn't actually have the social environment for deliberative democracy. Some scholars believe that the dilemma of deliberative democracy in China comes from China's current multiple structures: (1) The rules of liberalism are missing in many aspects of China today. (2) The expression of republicanism is similar to that of a traditional Chinese family and cultural traditions, but there is an essential difference in logic. If republicanism expects the expression and maintenance of a common interest, then the expression and specification of liberalism is the most efficient premise. In the absence of such a liberal mechanism of expression, the theoretical nature of republicanism would be a reasonable cloak for autocracy and dictatorship. The discussion of the deficiency of liberalism and republicanism should be based on the development of political practice, so it has its rationality and legitimacy.

Second, the relationship between public consultation and the development of grassroots democracy in China. Since the 1980s, especially in the coastal areas such as Zhejiang, where the private economy is developed, with the promotion of grassroots democracy from democratic election to democratic governance, many new forms of deliberative democracy have developed in urban communities and rural societies, including advisory meetings, public hearings, democratic talks and consultations. Party committees and governments at all levels have initiated and encouraged the development of these systems, mainly for the following reasons: (1) Public consultation helps maintain the stability of local order. It is an effective way to solve the social interest differentiation and social tension problems caused by marketization,

Chapter 1 Introduction

and it is the way to realize the coordinated development of the economy and society. (2) The ruling party and the government are also trying to develop new ways of governance, by integrating administrative orders and democratic consultation mechanisms, and promoting cooperation between the government and the people to focus on local governance. (3) Deliberative democracy does not treat free election as the only sign of democracy.

1.3 Research ideas and methods

1.3.1 Research ideas

How to construct the system platform of political participation, promote citizens' orderly political participation, enhance citizens' participation in local governance, and realize the ideal of people as the masters of their own affairs? How to ensure the rights of the people for the benefits of the people and bridge the gap between power and governance? These questions are the basic issues focused on in this research. The research of this subject aims to provide a preliminary solution to the above problems on the basis of the empirical study of Zhejiang's institutional innovation, and expect academic and political circles to make further theoretical discussions on this issue while promoting the practice of local democratic political construction.

This subject is carried out synchronously with the research on this problem by domestic scholars. Being different

Chapter 1 Introduction

from the general description and general research on civil political participation made by some domestic scholars, from the historical background of the process of political democratization in contemporary China, this research attempts to study the different definitions of political participation through different democratic paradigms, and the research methods of structure-functionalism and empirical cases, to form a more accurate theoretical definition and scientific research method. Our research is based on an in-depth investigation of the cases of the expansion of civic participation system innovation across the Zhejiang Province. From the combination of theoretical thinking and case analysis, this research interprets and answers the question of how to resolve the democratic paradox in the contemporary Chinese context.

It must be pointed out that promoting political reform, developing democracy and enhancing citizens' political participation are unavoidable in the development of contemporary Chinese democratic politics. With the accelerating transformation of China's economic and social structure, the urgency of this issue is becoming more and more prominent. The key to the success of the transformation from the traditional country to the modern state is the speed and effectiveness of the construction of a modern national system. Due to the differences in political and cultural traditions, social economic structure and national character, the modern state system has different manifestations in different countries. In the process of constructing the modern state system, how to break through the traditional power structure, promote citizens' political participation, and realize the balance between people being the masters and government's power? It is well known that China's democratic political construction and the system innovation process of citizens' political participation are faced with many problems, such as the lack of civil intelligence, the lack of awareness of civic participation, the lack of enthusiasm for participation, and the lack of supply of a legal environment and supporting system. These problems greatly restrict and influence the effectiveness of system innovation. We believe that the solution to this problem requires the guidance of democratic theory on the one hand, and on the other hand, it needs to make a comprehensive summary and research on the practice of institutional innovation. Through the summary of practical experience and the reflection of theory, it supports the political practice. Therefore, we believe that the universality of democratic theory must be examined by localized experience. The research and summary of the local experience of democratic political development will certainly help to promote the combination of universality democratic theory and local experience. This is a valuable exploration in theory and practice in order to resolve the paradox of democracy in China by constructing a democratic governance paradigm suited to China's national conditions.

Based on this approach, we use structure-functionalism and empirical case studies in the study of the Zhejiang experience of promoting citizens' political participation and institutional innovation. According to the different meanings of political participation in different democratic paradigms, the characteristics, the mechanism, the structural function and the performance of the system innovation are reviewed over the hearing, the people's proposal solicitation system, the rural democratic consultation, the television political consultation, the Internet citizen participation platform and so on. It will conduct an in-depth analysis of the negative effects of factors hindering institutional innovation and their causes, put forward the objective principles of improving and perfecting citizens' orderly political participation, as well as the countermeasures and suggestions to promote institutional innovation and expand and perfect the citizen participation system.

1.3.2 Research methods

This book is mainly based on a social investigation and empirical analysis of relevant cases in Zhejiang Province in recent years.

Case study is one of the basic methods for the empirical investigation of events and phenomena in real-life situations. It

Chapter 1 Introduction

emphasizes the collection and processing of relevant data directly through the objects studied, and then the empirical description and analysis of the political phenomena, thus revealing the laws behind the political phenomena. With respect to data collected for the case, there are mainly data from literature and interviews; with respect to the case selection, there are mainly single case studies and multiple case studies. Case study method is used in the study of each chapter of this book. In regards to data collection, literature analysis and field investigation are considered. This includes a combination of case interviews with government officials and ordinary citizens, with a focus on multi-case studies.

In the process of case analysis, we try to use the relevant theories of modern political science as the analytical tools, and draw on and absorb other methods of political science research, which include the research methods of structural functionalism, the institutional research methods of new political economy and the research methods of political process. The study of the hearing system in this book absorbed the structural-functionalist approach of political science. This method focuses on the function of political system performance and the structure of executive function, emphasizes the analysis of the interrelationships between structure and function in each particular system, and attempts to reveal the law of political system operation by analyzing political structure and political function so as to provide an analytical framework for analyzing the political system. This book studies the hearing system, draws on the research paradigm in the famous works like Almond's *Politics in Developing Regions* and *Comparative Politics: Systems, Processes and Policies* and tries to use the structure of a political system—systems, processes and policies, as well as the functions of a political system—"transformation" (expression of interest, agglomeration of interests, political exchange, rulemaking, enforcement of rules, adjudication of rules), "maintenance" and "adaptation" and other research methods. Case study on the system of solicitation of people's suggestions, on the dialogue between the officials and the people over the Internet public

Political Participation and Institutional Innovation:
A Case Study of Zhejiang

forum attempts to reveal the role of two institutional innovations in the process of promoting local democracy and local autonomy and maintaining the political system.

The political process is often regarded as a research method that is different from the analysis of political systems. It regards political life as a continuous process, opposes the political system as the core content of political analysis, and advocates the political process as the core content of political analysis. This dynamic political research method provides an effective analytical tool for describing and interpreting changing political phenomena. An analysis of the hearing process in this book applies the government process to study the interest expression, interest integration, information feedback and function that affects public decision-making in the process of government and points out some problems of the hearing system, examining how the hearing system should be improved and enhanced from the theory of government process.

1.4 The basic structure of the book

Focusing on how to promote institutional innovation, promote citizens' orderly political participation and participation in local public affairs, and achieve the ideal of citizens being the masters of the country, this book selects a series of specific institutional innovations from theoretical and empirical dimensions. The book starts with a background introduction to the development of democratic politics at the grassroots level in Zhejiang Province, and examines the system innovation and its performance of democratic consultation, rural democracy, city hearing, people's proposal soliciting system, television political consultation, official and citizen dialogue through government website, public forum and so on that have promoted citizens' orderly political participation since the reform and opening-up in Zhejiang and other places. At the same time, we will look at the cases of mass activism and other non-institutional political participation in some areas of Zhejiang Province. We believe

Political Participation and Institutional Innovation:
A Case Study of Zhejiang

that the investigation and research on the two aspects will contribute to the understanding of the topic and the deepening of relevant research.

On the basis of analyzing and expounding the research background, the theoretical value and practical significance of the topic, this first chapter, "Introduction", focuses on a series of theoretical problems related to the promotion of citizens' orderly political participation and system innovation. The central question is how can citizens become the masters of their own country, in such a "popular sovereignty" socialist country like China. In what way do we participate in politics and manage public affairs? How can we effectively bridge the gap between sovereignty and power under the existing system and ensure that the power of the people is truly in the interests of the people? It should be said that the system of citizens' political participation established after the founding of the PRC still has institutional defects and deficiencies in safeguarding the people's right to be the masters of the country. With the differentiation of social benefits and social structure restructuring brought on by the reform and opening-up, these institutional defects and deficiencies are increasingly highlighted, pressing the ruling party and the government to promote political reform and institutional innovation, and provide necessary institutional supply for citizens to participate in local governance. Under the background of this era, in Zhejiang, one of the most developed and marketized regions in China's private economy, party committees and local governments at all levels actively promote institutional innovation and provide a new set of systems for citizens to participate in local governance, such as democratic consultation, rural democracy, city hearing, people's proposal soliciting system, television political consultation and Internet citizen participation platform, which has effectively promoted citizens' orderly political participation and improved the quality of local governance. Since the reform and opening-up, Zhejiang has developed a first-mover advantage in the process of industrialization, marketization and urbanization, especially the practice of "first step" in the construction of grassroots democratic politics, which has made Zhejiang experience research that have unique theoretical value to promote citizens' orderly political participation and system innovation.

In Chapter 2, "From Election to Governance: New Development of Grassroots Democracy in Zhejiang Province", through the review and investigation of the latest development of grassroots democratic politics in Zhejiang Province, we show the social and political background that Zhejiang has been promoting among its citizens for orderly political participation and institutional innovation since the reform and opening-up. As one of the most modern regions in China, Zhejiang's industrialization, marketization and development of private economy have attracted worldwide attention. With the rapid development of the private economy, the grassroots democracy and the rule of law have been advancing. The grassroots democratic practices in Wenling City, Yuhang District of Hangzhou City, Yuhuan County, Ningbo City and Wuyi County are also impressive. The experience of the democratic political construction in Zhejiang Province shows that there is no doubt about the importance of democratic election in the process of rural democracy construction. However, the villagers' election is only the beginning of grassroots democracy. Just having a democratic electoral system does not guarantee a healthy development of democracy at the grassroots level, nor does it guarantee that the grassroots society will inevitably lead to good governance.

Chapter 3 is titled "Democratic Consultation: Deliberative Democracy and Local Public Policy". In the construction of grassroots democratic politics in Zhejiang Province, the democratic consultation in Wenling City is represented by the grassroots practitioners who actively explore and seek the way of local governance on the basis of democratic elections and continue to promote the practice and innovation of grassroots democratic decision-making, democratic management and democratic supervision. The practice of democracy in Wenling and other places is a good answer to the following pressing problem in the process of rural democratic development: After the democratic election is fully promoted, how do we optimize governance in the countryside and promote good governance? It can be said that Wenling's democratic consultation has become a case that has a certain influence on the world, representing China's grassroots democratic political construction and local governance innovation model. In the process of analyzing the Wenling case, we try to analyze and dissect the institutional changes of Wenling's democratic consultation. The connotation of the democratic development of the grassroots villages and towns in Zhejiang Province reveals the mechanism and problems of the rural democratic governance innovation and emphasizes the path of further perfecting and deepening the rural democratic governance.

Chapter 4 is "Hearing: Interest Expression and Interest Integration Mechanism". The hearing system is not only a way for the expression of citizens' interests and the integration of interests, but also an effective way for citizens to participate in the management of local public affairs. In this chapter, the author makes a case study and analysis of the hearing system from the perspective of structure-functionalism by applying the government process theory, based on the definition of participation by responsive democratic paradigm. The mechanism of the hearing system is the result of the mutual promotion of the expression of interests and integration of China's social structure differentiation and restructuring, the diversification of interests, and the internal needs of local public governance. From the analysis of several cases of legislative hearing, administrative hearing and judicial hearing, we can see the role of hearing system in the process of interest expression and interest integration. From the three aspects of the hearing system, process and policy, the political participation of the hearing can be found to maintain the political system, including enhancing political legitimacy, maintaining political stability and accelerating the process of political democratization. The public transparency of the hearing process promotes the expression of the interests of citizens and the integration of interests. At the same time, the hearing also has the policy-influencing function of information feedback and social supervision. The current

Chapter 1 Introduction

hearing system still has some problems with the participants, hearing procedure and the cost of hearing. The improvement and perfection of the hearing system are needed with transformation from the decision consulting-type hearing of the opinions to the game-type hearing, from individual participated hearing to groups participated hearing, from government leading hearing to social diversity leading hearing, from power-dependent hearing to power restrictive supervisory hearing. To improve the political participation of the hearing, at the level of the participants, we need to improve the representativeness of the hearing representatives and establish a neutral moderator system; at the level of laws and regulations and procedures, we need to expand the scope of hearing, strengthen the hearing legislation, enhance the public hearing system, improve and perfect the supervision of the hearing and the inquiry system; and at the system level, we need to improve the hearing to influence decisions and reduce the cost of the hearing.

Chapter 5, "'Our Round Table Meeting': TV Political Consultation and Public Consultation", is a case study of the TV political consultation platform launched by the Hangzhou Municipal Government and the Hangzhou TV Station. The TV political consultation is a form of civic participation that has arisen since the beginning of new century. In the process of urban governance, Hangzhou Municipal Party Committee and Municipal Government implemented the new policy of "open decision" and "promoting people's livelihood with democracy"; as a result, "Our Round Table Meeting" came into being. As a public consultation platform involving multiple parties of government, media and society, to view from the composition of the participants, the way the participants were produced, the setting of the negotiation issues and the distribution of issues, "Our Round Table Meeting" features the diversity of participants, the uniqueness of communication channels and public consultation, and the diversity and universality of the negotiation issues. Through the investigation and analysis of the operation process of "Our Round Table Meeting" and the performance effect of TV, it is not hard to find that "Our Round Table Meeting" focuses on issues related to public interests and social group interests in the process of urban governance. It explores the solution of urban governance and people's livelihood in the discussion and consultation among government officials, people from all walks of life and ordinary citizens. It is a practice to promote urban governance through democratic consultation, and to some extent, it embodies the spirit of deliberative democracy. Of course, the form of such television questioning has its unavoidable limits in the application to the local governance, and the most prominent is the recreational tendency of public consultation.

Chapter 6 "Citizen Participation Platform on the Internet" is a study of Internet political participation and local governance based on several cases of Zhejiang's Internet political participation platforms. In recent years, the rise of the Internet, the invention and promotion of the progress of information network technology and the we-media and the popularity of smartphones have provided the citizens with an unprecedentedly grand stage for political participation in contemporary China. Our research, starting from the social and political nature of Internet and information technology, puts Internet political participation in the framework of national governance to examine China's Internet political participation and tries to explore the influence of technology empowerment, institutional constraint and government regulation on citizen participation through the system innovation of netizen participation in Zhejiang Province in recent years, including the government affairs forum, network inquiry, online collection of public opinions and service for people's livelihood, and the case analysis of citizens' participation in local governance through WeChat and microblogs. We believe that governments at all levels are promoting the construction of online civic participation mechanism and also bringing about the continuous strengthening of government regulation of Internet citizen participation, thus achieving the restrictive participation characteristics of current Chinese Internet political participation.

In the Internet age, the progress of information and network technology has brought new opportunities for the promotion of

Chapter 1 Introduction

citizens' political participation, and provided participants with new tools and new means. Public forum on government websites is oriented by civic participation. These public consultations and the official dialogue of the network platform have promoted the construction of government efficiency, helped to realize the interests expression and integration, to promote citizens' political participation, to cultivate participative citizens, to strengthen the public decision-making and public power legitimacy, thus promoting the construction of democracy at the grassroots level and improving the quality of local governance. However, there is no denying that Internet and information technology also bring huge risks and governance crises to citizens and society. Therefore, it is not enough to see only the opportunities brought about by the Internet, we must carefully consider the potential risks of the Internet as well. This will require the establishment of a modern state system of freedom, democracy and human rights guarantees that the ruling party and the government promote. This needs to start from a Chinese democracy and the rule of law construction, comprehensively deepen reform, promote system innovation and system supply, establish a legal system environment, and construct a participative political culture.

Chapter 7, "Zhejiang Experience in Promoting the Public Orderly Political Participation and Its Value", starts with summing up Zhejiang's experience of promoting citizens' orderly political participation and institutional innovation, probes into the basic experience and characteristics of institutional innovation in Zhejiang Province in recent years, and analyzes several independent variables and dependent variables of institutional innovation in Zhejiang Province and then reveals the enlightenment of Zhejiang experience in promoting citizens' orderly political participation and institutional innovation to the promotion of grassroots democracy in China.

Chapter 8, "Summary and Discussion", is the last chapter of the book. From the dimension of political theory, it gives some theoretical

Political Participation and Institutional Innovation: A Case Study of Zhejiang

thoughts on promoting citizens' orderly political participation and system innovation. We try to discuss the political theory value and practical significance of promoting citizens' orderly political participation and system innovation from the perspectives of transformation of roles and the cultivation of participatory citizens, the imbalance and defection of the regime and governance in democracy, political participation, institutional innovation and political stability.

We believe that in the process of promoting citizens' orderly political participation, enhancing grassroots democracy and the construction of the rule of law, a series of system innovations have been launched in various places, and public consultation has been introduced in local governance to encourage public participation. The widening of the channels for citizens to participate in local public affairs, and the promotion of the interaction between government and citizens, the understanding of the situation, absorption of public opinions and respondence to social needs, cultivation of citizens' consciousness of rights and democratic rule of law in the practice of grassroots democratic governance, enhancing of democratic participation awareness and participation capacity by party committees and governments at all levels in Zhejiang since the reform and opening-up, have effectively promoted and improved the quality of local governance.

The experience of Zhejiang, first of all, is to expand the institutional innovation of citizens' orderly political participation and provide concrete ways for the public to participate in local governance. Ordinary people can participate in the process of public consultation, express their interests, and strive for and defend their rights through democratic consultation, hearings, television political consultation, people's proposal solicitation activities, government network political consultation and online official and citizen dialogue. Second, the innovative civic participation system has clear objectives and functions,

Chapter 1 Introduction

namely promoting citizens' orderly political participation, and providing a platform for ordinary people to participate in public consultation and express interest demands. Through public consultation and interest coordination and integration mechanism, all classes are input to the local interests in the process of public policymaking, and balance among multiple stakeholders is achieved in the game of stakeholders. Third, the innovative civic participation system embodies the value of democracy and the advanced participation technology. In the Internet age, information communication technology (ICT) enables dual empowerment of citizens and governments, creating an infrastructure for the adjustment of state and social relations. Through "Internet plus" social governance, citizens can take part in public services and social governance to improve the quality of government public services. Finally, expanding the system innovation of citizens' political participation mechanism is not an alternative to the existing system of people's congresses and political consultation, but to complement and improve the national political system.

The practice of promoting citizens' orderly political participation and institutional innovation in Zhejiang Province and actively guiding citizens' direct and orderly political participation through institutionalized channels and legal procedures has improved the local governance, safeguarded the legitimate rights and interests of citizens, and promoted the self-construction of the government. It is the successful attempt of citizens to participate in local governance and exercise the political rights as the masters. It must be pointed out that the process of democracy and the rule of law in contemporary China have only a limited history. Similarly to other parts of the country, Zhejiang Province is facing many problems and challenges both in theory and practice in promoting the system construction of grassroots democratic politics and enhancing citizens' orderly political participation. The prospect of democracy, on the one hand, requires citizens to continuously cultivate and train the spirit of modern

Political Participation and Institutional Innovation: A Case Study of Zhejiang

citizenship in the practice of democracy, to enhance the consciousness of political participation and participation enthusiasm, to learn the methods and skills involved in improving participation; on the other hand, from the perspective of the ruling party and the government, we should comprehensively deepen the reform of the political systems, promote the construction of the modern state system, open up political space, promote democracy and the rule of law, promote the citizen education movement, solve the problems of expanding channels and institutionalizing the participation of citizens in a timely manner, enhance citizens' orderly political participation, promote the institutionalization and normalization of political participation in all levels of society, popularize the idea of democracy and make the system of democracy take root in China.

Chapter 2

From Election to Governance: New Development of Grassroots Democracy in Zhejiang Province

Political Participation and Institutional Innovation:
A Case Study of Zhejiang

Enhancing citizens' orderly political participation and promoting grassroots democratic governance are important contents of contemporary China's democratic politics construction. After the reform and opening-up, with the rapid development of industrialization, marketization and urbanization, especially the establishment of the socialist market economic system, the ruling party and the government reconstruct the structure of the relationship between the government and the market, and redefine the model of the relationship between the state and the society through institutional reform and opening-up to the outside world. As Wooyeal Paik points out, "Rapid economic development has increased mass political participation in China ... Many electoral authoritarian regimes with a good record of economic development have experienced the growing participation of elite/middle-class citizens".[1] The gradual withdrawal of state power from some areas of the economy and society has led to some fundamental changes of the power operation pattern in the economic field and the interests pattern in the social field, providing a certain space for social autonomous governance and grassroots democracy development. After more than 30 years of practice, a system of grassroots democratic autonomy is gradually being established, in which Rural Villagers' Committees and Urban Residents' Committees are the main forms. Through democratic election, democratic decision-making, democratic management, democratic supervision and other various forms, the masses can participate in the process of local public affairs governance, so as to improve local governance, local economy development and harmonious progress of the society. Therefore, observation and study of grassroots democracy and citizen participation process is an important window for understanding the characteristics of contemporary China's democratic political development and grasping the internal logic of local governance.

---

[1] Paik, W. Economic development and mass political participation in contemporary China: Determinants of provincial petition (Xinfang) activism 1994–2002. *International Political Science Review/Revue internationale de science politique*, 2012, 33 (1): 99–120.

2.1 The development of local democracy in China since the reform and opening-up

Democratization has been a major theme throughout the centennial history of political development in China in the 20th century, and will certainly be the theme of China's modernization and social transformation in the 21st century. Dorien Zandbergen argues that citizens' participation has emerged as one of the buzzwords of contemporary discussions as an important regime of knowledge and action. Politicians, policymakers, NGOs and corporations all promote participation as a means of achieving citizens' democratic empowerment. The grassroots democracy system in contemporary China has been formed and developed in the practice of democracy politics construction since the reform and opening-up, which is also the logical starting point and realistic basis for the continued development and progress of democracy politics in the 21st century.

Political Participation and Institutional Innovation: A Case Study of Zhejiang

The core of democracy development at the grassroots level in contemporary China lies in the promotion of autonomy and participation, enabling people to fully exercise their democratic rights and realize the vision of the people to be the masters of their own affairs. Therefore, it is one of the main contents of the construction and development of democracy at the grassroots level in China to let citizens participate in the management of local public affairs extensively, and to standardize and institutionalize citizen participation. For many years, the ruling party and the government have been emphasizing the promotion of citizens' orderly participation, enhancing democracy at the grassroots level, demanding that citizens' orderly political participation be guaranteed through rich democratic forms, encouraging or acquiescing local party committee and government officials at all levels to carry out active explorations and pilot projects, to promote community autonomy from rural to urban and institutional innovation of democratic governance at the grassroots level.

The changes start from rural areas. After the reform and opening-up, the biggest change in rural society is the implementation of the household contract responsibility system in terms of economy and the promotion of villagers' autonomy in the whole country in terms of politics. With the implementation of the household contract responsibility system in rural areas, the people's commune system established in the planned economy era has collapsed. The major changes in the original rural economic system lead to the paralysis of the organizational system at the grassroots level and the vacuum of power in the rural society. Faced with this situation, farmers in some villages in Yishan County, Guangxi, spontaneously reformed the management system of the production brigade in 1980, directly elected the villagers' committee by holding a general meeting of all members of the community and voting by secret ballot. China's first villagers' committee was born in Yishan County, Guangxi. Subsequently, many regions throughout the country used this method to elect many organizations similar to villagers' committees.

Chapter 2　From Election to Governance: New Development of Grassroots Democracy in Zhejiang Province

Based on the difficulties of governance in rural areas after the disintegration of the people's commune, the ruling party began to attach importance to and affirm the exploration and innovation of social governance at the grassroots level in Guangxi and other places. The 1982 Constitution confirmed the villagers' committee as the mass autonomy organization of the rural society at the grassroots level in China. Peng Zhen, then Chairman of the Standing Committee of the National People's Congress, pointed out in his statement of the 1982 Constitution that, the inclusion of villagers' committee in the constitutional provisions was to strengthen the construction of mass autonomy organization at the grassroots level and to ensure that the masses were the masters of their own affairs in the social life at the grassroots level. Since then, pilot work to establish villagers' committees was carried out in various localities in accordance with the requirements of the constitution. In October 1983, the Central Committee of the Communist Party of China issued the Notice on Implementation of the Separation of Government and Society and the Establishment of a Township Government, calling for the establishment of villagers' committees according to the living conditions of villagers while reforming the rural management system of integration of government and society. In 1987, the Organization Law of Villagers' Committee (Trial), China's first law on the organization and operation of village committees was promulgated and implemented, in which the nature, status, duty, generation mode, institutional framework and working mode of the villagers' committee as well as the power and organization form of the villagers' meeting were all stipulated in an all-round way. According to the law, the director, deputy director and committee members of the villagers' committee were directly elected by the villagers, each term of office was 3 years, and villagers over the age of 18 had the right to vote and to be elected.

Since 1987, the whole nation carried out demonstration activities of villagers' autonomy and popularized election of villagers' committee widely. By the end of 1989, 14 provinces, autonomous regions and municipalities directly under the central government had started to elect cadres of the villagers' committee in accordance with the law on the basis of the pilot project. In February 1994, the Ministry of Civil Affairs

Political Participation and Institutional Innovation:
A Case Study of Zhejiang

issued the Guiding Outline for the Demonstration Activities of Rural Villagers' Autonomy in China (Trial), which made comprehensive and systematic provisions on the objectives, tasks, guidelines, specific measures, etc., of the demonstration activities, and clearly proposed the establishment of "four democratic systems" for the first time, namely democratic election, democratic decision-making, democratic management and democratic supervision. In 1997, the report of the 15th National Congress of the Communist Party of China formally proposed that the expansion of democracy at the grassroots level should be regarded as "the most extensive practice of socialist democracy", so that democracy at the grassroots level, including villagers' autonomy, would usher in a broader space for development. In 1998, the Organization Law of Villagers' Committee (Trial), adopted at the Fifth Session of the Ninth Standing Committee of the National People's Congress, stipulated the basic principles for the implementation of villagers' autonomy and the specific measures. The work focus has also shifted from the establishment of rules and regulations to providing protection of rights for the masses of villagers, which indicates that the system of villagers' autonomy in China has formally entered the development track of institutionalization and legalization.

In the city, community residents' autonomy, as the main form of grassroots democratic politics construction, has also undergone a long-term process of gradual development. In the early days of the founding of the People's Republic of China, the Military Management Council, the People's Government and the working groups sent by the People's Government to the grassroots level organized the residents to carry out various democratic reform activities, assisted the local people's government in public security management, patriotic health and production services and other daily neighbourhood work, and set up neighborhood committees of various forms. On December 31, 1954, the Standing Committee of the National People's Congress formulated the Regulations on the Organization of Urban Residents' Committee, which clearly stipulated that a "residents' committee is a residents' organization

Chapter 2　From Election to Governance: New Development of Grassroots Democracy in Zhejiang Province

of mass autonomy". Since then, the autonomous organizations of community residents' committees have developed rapidly in various cities throughout the country, and have become the organizations at the grassroots level for the ruling party and the government to manage and control urban residents. After the Third Plenary Session of the 11th Central Committee of the Communist Party of China in 1978, with the disintegration of the planned economy system, the role of urban residents' committee as the management and control tool of the ruling party as well as the community system began to transform.

After the reform and opening-up, urban residents' autonomy in China began to enter a new stage of legalization. The Constitution of the People's Republic of China, promulgated in 1982, established for the first time the principle of residents' autonomy and the system of urban residents' committee in the form of the fundamental law of the state. On December 26, 1989, the 11th Session of the Seventh Standing Committee of the National People's Congress adopted the Organization Law of the Urban Residents' Committee of the People's Republic of China, through which the nature, task, organization form and other related systems of urban residents' autonomy under the conditions of the reform and opening-up are fully regulated, and for the first time, "carrying out community service activities for the benefit of people" was clearly defined as a primary responsibility of the residents' committee. In order to carry out the Organization Law of the Urban Residents' Committee, since 1990, all provinces, autonomous regions and municipalities directly under the central government have taken into account the local reality and started to formulate corresponding measures to implement community autonomy in an all-round way. Since then, the concept of "community building" has gradually combined with the function of residents' autonomy. In 1999, the Ministry of Civil Affairs carried out pilot and experimental work on community construction in some districts of 26 cities, and actively explored the development model of community construction. In the same year, the Ministry of Civil Affairs formulated the Implementation Plan for the Construction of Experimental Area in National Communities, through which the general requirements, basic principles, work steps, work contents, organization and leadership of the community construction in the experimental area were clearly stipulated. It also proposed to reform the management system of urban democracy at the grassroots level, cultivate and establish the management system and operation mechanism of community construction adapted to the socialist market economy system, which has greatly promoted the smooth development of community construction in all experimental communities and laid a good foundation for the overall promotion of community construction throughout the country.

After entering the 21st century, the ruling party and the government have successively formulated the construction of a harmonious society, advocated innovation in social management, and improved the public service and management capacity of communities at the grassroots level. In November 2000, the General Office of the CPC Central Committee and the General Office of the State Council put forward the views of the Ministry of Civil Affairs on promoting urban community construction throughout the country, which comprehensively and systematically expounded the connotation, objectives, significance, guiding ideology and main contents of community construction. It also pointed out the direction for expanding urban democracy at the grassroots level and promoting urban reform and development. In March 2001, community construction was included in the outline of the 10th 5-Year Plan for National Economic and Social Development, which means that community building has become an integral part of the economic and social development of contemporary China and an important indicator of economic and social development in various places. The construction of urban communities across the country is being carried out from point to plane, from large- and medium-sized cities to small- and medium-sized cities, and from the developed areas in the east to the developing areas in the west, and obvious results have been achieved in improving the community democratic election, community service function and other aspects.

2.2 The development course of democracy at the grassroots level in Zhejiang

Zhejiang lies on the south wing of the Yangtze River Delta on the southeast coast of China, with East China Sea on the east and Shanghai and Jiangsu in the north. Zhejiang has a land area of 105,500 square kilometers, about 1.1% of China's total land area, and is one of the smaller provinces in China. Since the reform and opening-up, Zhejiang has been well known for its market-oriented reform and the developed private economy. It is one of the provinces boasting the most active economy and the highest degree of marketization in China, and its per capita disposable income has ranked first in China for years in a row. In 2016, the gross domestic product (GDP) of Zhejiang reached RMB 4.6485 trillion yuan, an increase of 7.5% over the previous year, and the per capita GDP was 83,538 yuan (12,577 US dollars at annual average exchange rate), an increase of 6.7% over the previous year.

Political Participation and Institutional Innovation: A Case Study of Zhejiang

At the end of 2016, Zhejiang had a permanent resident population of 55.9 million, of which 99% were Han people.

Since the reform and opening-up, under the background of promoting the construction of democratic politics at the grassroots level in China, the progress and achievements of democracy at the grassroots level and construction of the rule of law in Zhejiang have been highly studied and praised by domestic and foreign academic circles. The achievements of democracy at the grassroots level in Zhejiang are mainly reflected in the main forms of social autonomy, such as rural villagers' election, the construction of democratic and legal village, community election in the city and other aspects.

In rural areas, as early as 1982, Zhejiang began the pilot work of villagers' committee election. In October 1983, after the Central Committee of the Communist Party of China and the State Council issued the Notice on Implementation of the Separation of Government and Society and the Establishment of a Township Government, the work of villagers' committee election in Zhejiang was generally pushed forward throughout the province. In June 1988, in accordance with the relevant provisions of the Organization Law of Villagers' Committee (Trial) formulated by the Standing Committee of the National People's Congress, combining the practical experience of villagers' election in the province, Zhejiang formulated the Measures for the Implementation of the Organization Law of Villagers' Committee of the People's Republic of China (Trial) in Zhejiang, which provided more specific norms and guidance for the work of villagers' election in the whole province. In 1998, after the Standing Committee of the National People's Congress formulated the Organization Law of Villagers' Committee, Zhejiang, in the following year, issued the Election Methods of Villagers' Committee in Zhejiang Province, which made detailed and specific regulations on the smooth development of villagers' election work from many aspects. So far, direct election of villagers' committee on the basis of village autonomy has been realized in rural areas of Zhejiang, even in some

Chapter 2　From Election to Governance: New Development of Grassroots Democracy in Zhejiang Province

remote mountain areas of Lishui, Wenzhou and other cities, and election of director of the villagers' committee has carried out the "audition" system. In many areas of the province, there are many innovative forms of the villagers' election, such as campaign speech of the candidate, lobbying and canvassing activities during the election process, and the "public election" of township and deputy county leaders, etc. Similarly, in the construction of democratic politics in urban communities, the community (residents' committee) election in Zhejiang has made great progress. In 2003, Zhejiang Provincial Party Committee and Provincial Government issued the Guidelines for Urban Community Construction in Zhejiang Province (2003–2010) (Trial), which clearly stipulated that the exercise of the autonomy right by the community (residents' committee) in accordance with the law shall be guaranteed by means such as democratic election, so as to promote the development of community non-governmental organizations, realize self-management, self-education and self-service of the community residents.

In the process of promoting democracy at the grassroots level, the party committees and governments at all levels in Zhejiang have comprehensively promoted the institutional construction of villagers' autonomy organization, and have generally established the meeting system of the villages, the village representatives and the villagers' committee. Meanwhile, the methods and mechanisms of democratic management of village affairs have been innovated constantly. The village affairs management system, especially the democratic deliberative consultation, financial audit supervision and democratic evaluation of village cadres, etc., has also been established and perfected, which greatly improves the degree of systematization, standardization and routinization of village affairs management. The construction of a democratic and legal village is an innovation of Zhejiang in the process of democratic politics construction at the grassroots level. At the beginning of 1998, Ningbo first proposed to establish democratic and legal villages in the whole country, and after that the construction of democratic and legal villages was carried out

Political Participation and Institutional Innovation:
A Case Study of Zhejiang

in various parts of Zhejiang one after another. By 2016, all villages in the province had carried out activities to create democratic and legal villages, and the vast majority of these villages had met the creating criteria, with more than 200 villages named as "National Demonstrative Democratic and Legal Village" by the Ministry of Justice and other units. Democracy and the rule of law have become the main melody of the construction of new socialist countryside in Zhejiang. Since the previous villagers' committee election, democratic and participation consciousness of the villagers has gradually strengthened, and the enthusiasm for taking part in the general election has gradually increased. In 2015, general election of the 10th villagers' committee of Zhejiang was held with a participation rate of eligible voters in the province reaching over 95%.

Openness of village affairs and standardization construction of democratic management are important contents of democratic politics construction at the grassroots level in China. In recent years, party committees and governments at all levels in Zhejiang have actively promoted the openness of village affairs and democratic management, participation of villagers in decision-making, management and supervision of village affairs, so that the "power of the village operates in the sunshine". To this end, Zhejiang Province has successively issued several documents on strengthening the openness and democratic management of village affairs, such as Notice on Further Improving the Openness of Village Affairs and Democratic Management System by General Office of the CPC Zhejiang Provincial Committee. General Office of the People's Government of Zhejiang Province, Notice on the Standardization Construction of Openness of Village Affairs and Democratic Management and Demonstration Unit Creating Activity, organized and carried out creating activities of demonstration unit for openness of village affairs, standardization construction of democratic management, and actively carried out multi-level evaluation activities, such as "Demonstration County (City, District) for Openness of Village Affairs and Democratic Management in Zhejiang Province",

Chapter 2　From Election to Governance: New Development of Grassroots Democracy in Zhejiang Province

"Demonstration Township (Town, Street) for Openness of Village Affairs and Democratic Management in Zhejiang Province" and "Demonstration Village for Openness of Village Affairs and Democratic Management in Zhejiang Province". In June 2005, General Office of Zhejiang Provincial Party Committee and General Office of the Provincial Government issued the Notice on Improving Openness of Village Affairs and Democratic Management System, which put forward the specific target task of the openness of village affairs. One of the important target tasks was to make clear the overall requirements of the openness of village affairs, and to make sure that the contents, forms and procedures are all standardized and orderly.

While vigorously developing democracy at the grassroots level, urban community democracy construction in Zhejiang has also achieved remarkable results. As early as in October 1949, the first urban residents' committee of the People's Republic of China was founded in Shangcheng District of Hangzhou, Zhejiang. After the reform and opening-up, with the transformation of social economy and gradual disintegration of the unit system, the social functions previously assumed by the government and enterprises have been gradually transferred to the community, meanwhile, the continuous increase of urban population and improvement of living standard also put forward new requirements to enhance the community function. In 1982, on the basis of summing up the experience of urban residents' autonomy, for the first time, the Constitution of the People's Republic of China clearly defined the nature, tasks and functions of the residents' committee in the form of a basic law, and pointed out that the residents' committee was a mass autonomous organization at the grassroots level. Under this background, organization and construction of urban residents' committees in Zhejiang has been fully restored and developed, and a new exploration of community democratic autonomy has begun all over the province. In accordance with the unified arrangement of the Zhejiang Provincial Government, the main duties of an urban community includes handling public affairs and public welfare in its own areas, mediating civil disputes, helping to maintain

Political Participation and Institutional Innovation: A Case Study of Zhejiang

public order, and reflecting the opinions, demands and suggestions of the masses to the people's government. In December 1989, Standing Committee of the National People's Congress adopted the Organization Law of the Urban Residents' Committee of the People's Republic of China, after which Zhejiang comprehensively regulated the nature, status and tasks of the residents' committee, emphasized the important duty of community residents' committee, "carrying out community service activities that are convenient to the people and benefit the people". In 2012, Zhejiang issued the Notice on Issuance of the 12th 5-Year Plan for Urban and Rural Community Development in Zhejiang Province, which emphasized once again the need to improve the community residents' autonomy mechanism, to promote the practice of democratic decision-making in the main forms such as residents' meeting, deliberative consultation and democratic hearing, practice of democratic management with self-management, self-education and self-service as its main purposes, practice of democratic supervision based on openness of home affairs and democratic evaluation, and to promote institutionalization and standardization of community residents' autonomy.

The main practice forms of urban community democracy in Zhejiang include residents' day of discussion, joint community meeting, online forum, people's sentiment talk, community dialogue and so on. Its main purpose is to ensure the community residents' right to know, participation and supervision. Since the beginning of the 21st century, Zhejiang has carried out the construction of a "democratic and legal village" in rural areas, meanwhile the construction of a "democratic and legal community" has also been widely carried out in urban communities, and the star evaluation activity of "democratic and legal community" has also been carried out actively, among which the democratic election of the community, democratic system construction and so on are important scoring items. By improving the organization system, convening special conferences, formulating policies and measures, strengthening supervision and inspection, recognizing advanced examples and other forms, the democratic construction of

Chapter 2　From Election to Governance: New Development of Grassroots Democracy in Zhejiang Province

urban communities in Zhejiang has been deepened and effectively carried out. The community autonomy organizations in the whole province obtain considerable development. For example, in the process of promoting community construction, Ningbo has established and perfected a democratic and autonomous mechanism led by community party organization, established a system including assembly of community resident representative as the "decision-maker", community residents' committee as the "executive level", community consultation council as the "deliberative level" and community party organization as the "leadership level", founding a relatively complete community autonomy system of self-management, self-education, self-service and self-supervision of the community residents. Haishu District of the city also takes the lead in realizing the direct election of all communities in the city. At present, in most cities of the province, general election of the party organizations and community residents' committees has basically realized democratic recommendation, campaign speeches and secret ballot elections.

Relying on the rapid development of industrialization, marketization and urbanization in Zhejiang since the reform and opening-up, and the overall prosperity and progress of the economy and society of the whole province, through the continuous exploration and practice of Zhejiang people over the years, rural democracy and community democracy in urban areas in Zhejiang have shown a good trend of development: The democratic electoral system at the grassroots level has been continuously improved, with the quality of the election improved, and the scope of the election expanded; construction of standardized system for democratic management of villagers' autonomy organization has been deepened continuously, and systems such as meeting of village representatives, supervision group for openness of village affairs, democratic financial management group have been gradually improved. The democratic management and democratic supervision system at the grassroots level, oriented by promoting citizen participation, has been established and operated throughout the province.

2.3 Innovation practice of democratic governance at the grassroots level in Zhejiang in recent years

Since 1980s, the construction of democratic politics at the grassroots level in Zhejiang has been comprehensively promoted. With the rapid development of industrialization, marketization and urbanization, social transformation and the growing differentiation of social structure, the development model with democratic election at the grassroots level as the main form has also met a series of new problems and challenges. On the one hand, this challenge is derived from the unbalanced development of democracy at the grassroots level in China; on the other hand, it is closely related to the complexity and diversity of the social and economic environment in the period of social transformation, in particular, the development of democracy at the grassroots level in Zhejiang.

As one of the most developed provinces in China, Zhejiang faces the most important challenge for the

Chapter 2　From Election to Governance: New Development of Grassroots Democracy in Zhejiang Province

development of democratic politics at the grassroots level, which is how to deal with the relationship between democratic election and democratic governance, as well as the relationship between social economic development and construction of democratic politics at the grassroots level. The rapid development of private economy has greatly stimulated the democratic consciousness and political participation consciousness of the masses, and promoted the rapid development of democratic politics at the grassroots level. However, the rapid development of industrialization, marketization and urbanization, the division of social classes and the diversification of interest subjects, as well as the resulting fierce and superficial game between subjects of interest, also lead to the phenomenon of bribery and disorderly competition in democratic election at the grassroots level; moreover, the general tendency of local government officials in the process of building democratic politics at the grassroots level to emphasize election and neglect governance has directly led to the corruption and dictatorship of the village officials elected in some areas as well as governance disorder, which seriously affect the healthy development of democracy at the grassroots level and even the harmony and stability of rural society at the grassroots level.

In recent years, the problem of bribery in the process of rural democratic election at the grassroots level is becoming more and more serious in Zhejiang. During the implementation of villagers' autonomy and villagers' election, although party committees, people's congresses and governments at all levels have strengthened prevention and punishment of bribery, there are still a large number of bribery cases in democratic election at the grassroots level because of the difficulties in defining and obtaining evidence for election bribery activities and the drive of realistic interests. It is quite common for candidates to use money and material promises or transactions to "canvass the votes cast" during the election process. Many villagers also believe that it is natural for both sides to "voluntarily" trade the votes with money. And once the candidates practising bribery in an election take office, they will hope and often use various means to get much more returns than the investment during the election period. Therefore, the bribery during elections is bound to have an inherent relationship with corruption. At the same time, in some villages, the clans are closely linked and become a community of interests, therefore, during the election of villagers' committee, there will be a situation in which one or more clans compete for their own clan members. Another dilemma of democratic election at the grassroots level is that even some village officials who come to power through fair elections find it difficult to avoid dictatorship and corruption because of the lack of necessary supervision and restriction in the management of public affairs, which finally infringes on the legitimate rights and interests of the villagers. Therefore, although the official insurance of the Organization Law of Villagers' Committee in November 1998 has gradually put governance at grassroots level in China on a regular track of development, according to our observation, in the practice of governance at the grassroots level, since the effective mechanism for democratic decision-making, democratic governance and democratic oversight has not been formed, villagers' committees elected by the villagers themselves in some areas tend to move toward the trend of bureaucracy and fail to become the organizational spokesmen for the interests of farmers. At the same time, in the practice of democratic politics at the grassroots level in Zhejiang, the interlaced relationship between capital and power is often accompanied by violence and black gold politics. Some of the new rich in villages use money to control the democratic election process and management of village public affairs, resulting in more and more contradictions and conflicts in rural society, and even large-scale mass incidents in some areas.

It should be pointed out that election is not the whole of democracy. Democracy with elections alone is not democracy in its entirety, and relying on the election system alone cannot effectively guarantee the healthy development of democratic politics at the grassroots level. In face of various problems in politics at the grassroots level, party

Chapter 2　From Election to Governance: New Development of Grassroots Democracy in Zhejiang Province

committees and governments at all levels in Zhejiang are actively exploring new ways to promote democratic construction at the grassroots level while deepening and perfecting democratic elections. In recent years, in the practice of democratic politics construction in various parts of Zhejiang, the question of how to promote and perfect democracy at the grassroots level has been continuously explored, among which the core problem is how to improve democratic governance at the grassroots level after the full implementation of democratic elections. Combining the reality of local democratic politics development, a group of local officials and practitioners of democracy at the grassroots level made great efforts to promote system construction and system innovation on the basis of democratic election, and to explore new mechanism for democratic decision-making, democratic management and democratic supervision, through which a number of flexible and diverse governance models of democracy at the grassroots level have been gradually formed.

2.3.1 Innovation on democratic governance at the grassroots level in rural areas

In recent years, for the system innovation of democratic construction at the grassroots level in Zhejiang, the most representative examples include democratic talks in Wenling, Taizhou, "democratic system establishment" in Yuhang District of Hangzhou, democratic hearings at the village level in Taizhou, Ningbo and other places, and supervision of village affairs in Wuyi County, Jinhua.

(1) *Democratic talks in Wenling, Taizhou*

The democratic talk began in June 1999 in Songmen Town of Wenling, and its prototype was "Agricultural Rural Modernization Education Forum". Different from the previous form of "cadres preaching to the masses", which is used to educate villagers and propagate, the Agricultural Rural Modernization Education Forum is a kind of negotiation process in the form of two-way dialogue and communication between the cadres and the masses, aimed at finally solving problems. Since 2000, Wenling Municipal Party Committee has gradually introduced the democratic talk system into the decision-making process of major matters at the grassroots level. In the form of documents of the municipal party committee, scope of the topic, participants, basic procedure, implementation and supervision links of democratic talks are clearly stipulated, and frequency and performance of democratic talks are included in the evaluation of political achievements at the same time.

After years of continuous exploration, various forms of democratic consultation systems have been formed in Wenling. The scope of democratic consultation extends from the village level and town level to community, party and municipal departments, and content of the negotiation has also been deepened, from the personal interests of a family to the core issues of urban planning, environmental protection, and even the deliberation and supervision of public budgets. The "democratic talk" in Wenling encourages citizens to participate in the formulation of policies and management of public affairs, and encourages consultation and dialogue between officials and citizens, which is a creative reform and an important breakthrough in the practice and construction of democracy at the grassroots level in China. In recent years, the "democratic talk" has been popularized in Zhejiang. The concept of democratic consultation has increasingly merged into the activities of democratic decision-making and democratic management at the grassroots level in Zhejiang, and has become a new type of democratic governance.

The democratic talk in Wenling originated from the democratic governance at the grassroots level in rural areas, which has been promoted by the local government after obvious practical results, expanding gradually from democracy at grassroots in rural areas to urban democracy. At present, the democratic governance form of democratic talks has been widely carried out in governance at the grassroots level in rural and urban areas.

Chapter 2　From Election to Governance: New Development of Grassroots Democracy in Zhejiang Province

(2) *"Democratic system establishment" in Yuhang District of Hangzhou*

Democratic system construction in Yuhang District refers to the system construction of democracy at the grassroots level, and the main contents of this include the following aspects.

(1) Standardization and refinement of the opening system of village affairs. All villages should make sure of the following: The opening column of village affairs moves from the inside wall to the conspicuous place outside the wall; the opening column of village affairs is not less than 4 square meters; village affairs are open to the public each quarter, with reception expenses disclosed one by one, and the candidates for the supervision group of village affairs democratically elected. Meanwhile, with regard to the contents, the emphasis shifts from the previous financial affairs to village affairs and financial affairs simultaneously, with financial revenue and expenditure, cadres' remuneration, entertainment expense at the village level, homestead examination and approval and other major matters made known to the public fully. At present, remuneration of cadres in 262 villages in the district has been made known to the public fully, and entertainment expense at the village level is basically made known to the public. On this basis, Yuhang District also introduced the remuneration mechanism of masses' comment on village cadres, through the way of directly linking the remuneration of village cadres with public comment to strengthen the supervision power of villagers.

(2) Carry out the principle of "establishing the system according to law and governing the village by system" and follow the way of institutionalized development of village-level governance. On the basis of formulating the Rules for Village Affairs in Yuhang District, various systems such as the original village rules and regulations have been revised, improved and standardized in 262 villages in Yuhang District within the scope of the general rules. The Rules for Village Affairs

Political Participation and Institutional Innovation:
A Case Study of Zhejiang

officially have become the code of conduct that the village cadres and villagers abide by in Yuhang District. The villages universally implement a series of systematic and standardized systems with the Rules for Village Affairs as the core, which cover all aspects of the implementation and protection of villagers' right to vote, to know, to participate and to supervise, define the working responsibilities and principles of the village party organizations, villagers' committees and economic associations, as well as make specific provisions on basic work, financial management, decision-making, democratic supervision, organization and discussion, accountability investigation and other aspects.

(3) The village accounting agency system is fully implemented, and the supervision group of democratic financial management is democratically elected by the villagers to manage and supervise financial affairs on behalf of the villagers. The financial statement must be signed by the head of the group before it can be published on the opening column of village affairs.

(4) Carry out "democratic decision-making process" and standardize democratic decision-making system in order to realize the democratic participation right of the villagers. The "flow chart of democratic decision-making" is posted in the conference rooms of each villagers' committee, which is composed of six parts: "Proposal of the topic, acceptance, consultation by the two committees, discussion of conditions of the people, voting of the village representative and opening". The "flow chart of democratic decision-making" is the further improvement and standardization of democratic decision-making in Yuhang District on the basis of the village representative meeting system. Many villages also display the following contents in the opening column of village affairs, such as the proposed issue, time, place, person, content of the vote, the number of people supposed to attend the vote and the actual number, number of affirmative votes, negative votes and abstention votes as well as the voting result; make

Chapter 2   From Election to Governance: New Development of Grassroots Democracy in Zhejiang Province

clear labor division of villagers' committee members, annual work target and quarterly work arrangement, and list and explain the content, form and procedure of democratic decision-making.

(5) Talk on conditions of the people shall be held at least once a quarter, through which the village cadres report main work to be done at present and important matters in the village affairs to all villagers, as well as seek public opinions. The masses participating in the meeting may put inquiries or questions to the village cadres on relevant matters, and the village cadres must give serious answers or explanations to the questions raised by the masses.

(6) Fully implement the village representative meeting system. Two or more village representative meetings must be held per year in each village to conduct democratic decision-making on matters authorized by the villagers' meeting according to law. Village collective economic projects and other investments valued more than 30,000 yuan and one-off non-productive expenditure more than 3,000 yuan must be decided by the village representative meeting. The "six must visit" system is implemented, requiring the village cadres to visit party members, village representatives, team leaders, difficult households, large households of agricultural cultivation and breeding, as well as enterprise owners. The Implementation Measures for the Contract Work of the Village Collective Economic Investment Project is formulated, stipulating that for houses and public welfare facilities construction above 10,000 yuan at the village level, transfer or one-off purchase of fixed assets more than 3,000 yuan, as well as contracting, leasing and other matters of collective assets, public bidding shall be invited, and be supervised by the discipline inspection department of the town, county (sub-district).

(3) *Democratic hearings at the village level in Taizhou, Ningbo and other places*

Yuhuan County of Taizhou has carried out the system of "two discussions, three openings and one supervision" in rural areas earlier in the province (party members' council and village representatives' council, openness of party affairs, village affairs as well as government affairs, and democratic supervision group of village affairs). In order to further promote construction of democratic politics at the village level, Yuhuan County takes its geographical advantages in Taizhou, which is reputed as a "hometown of democratic talks", and combines the successful experience of democratic talks, actively practices the innovation of "democratic hearings at the village level" on the basis of "two discussions, three openings and one supervision" system, which includes the following: standardize the working procedure at the village level, formulating the village rules and regulations or regulations on villagers' autonomy with strong operability; implement democratic evaluation and supervision of village cadres and establish a democratic evaluation mechanism that integrates reporting work of the villagers' committee, individual reporting, democratic evaluation and percentage system assessment, and the evaluation result shall be combined with remuneration and promotion of village cadres; adopt the principle of "bidirectional hearing", which means ordinary party members and villagers shall listen to the work report by the village party branch and the villagers' committee, and the village cadres shall listen to the opinions and suggestions of ordinary party members and villagers, and so on.

In the process of organizational governance at the village level in Ningbo, Zhejiang, the villagers' rights to know, participate, manage and supervise have been guaranteed through channels such as openness of village affairs, democratic hearings and democratic talks, and good results have been achieved. In summary, the democratic hearing at the village level in Ningbo includes the following:

(1) Define the scope of the issues of the democratic hearing. For matters such as decision-making on major community matters, actual projects, major financial arrangements, major investments in share economy cooperatives, development of reserved land, land acquisition,

Chapter 2　From Election to Governance: New Development of Grassroots Democracy in Zhejiang Province

renovation of old villages and resettlement schemes for households in difficult circumstances, etc., before making decisions, a democratic hearing shall be organized to solicit the opinions of the masses widely. Meanwhile, major issues such as work plans, village economic income and expenditure plans, financing of engineering projects, tender and bid plans shall be included in the scope of hearing.

(2) Each village adopts different ways of convening according to the actual situation in order to strengthen the pertinence and effectiveness of the democratic hearing. For major village affairs involving construction and development at the village level and the interests of villagers, the village party branch and the villagers' committee shall request all the villagers to vote in public to decide whether to implement or not implement the plan according to the provisions of the "major village affairs referendum system".

(3) Strengthen system construction and strict hearing procedure to prevent inequality and dominant acts in the hearing negotiation process. Specifically, formulate the detailed hearing procedures according to the laws and regulations to ensure the regularity and legitimacy of the democratic hearing; establish archives, and record form for each major decision of the democratic hearings must be filled out and filed; realize openness and transparency of the democratic hearing. Some villages also distribute the *Sunshine Journal* monthly to the villagers free of charge, in which main work completed in the previous month and key work plan of the current month are recorded in detail; moreover, financial statement of income and expenditure in the village for the previous month is also published.

(4) *Supervision of village affairs in Wuyi County, Jinhua*

On June 18, 2004, an election for members of the "Village Affairs Supervisory Committee" was held in Houchen Village, Wuyi County, Jinhua City. Notably, 32 Party members and 17 village representatives gathered in the meeting room of the villagers' committee and elected the 3 members of the Village Affairs Supervisory Committee through 2 rounds of elections. After the 2 rounds of elections, Zhang Shenan, who received the most votes, was elected as director of the Village Affairs Supervisory Committee. In this way, the first Village Affairs Supervisory Committee was formally established in Houchen Village which served as a prelude to the new democratic policy of village affairs supervision in Wuyi County. On October 28, 2010, the Standing Committee of the National People's Congress made it clear that village affairs supervisory committee or supervisory institutions in other forms shall be established. This is a full affirmation of Wuyi's experience and highlights the fact that the democracy at the grassroots level which originated from Zhejiang is moving forward on the track of rule of law.

The main methods of village supervision in Wuyi are as follows: (1) The village affairs supervisory committee is elected by the village representatives, with four candidates generally recommended within the village representatives and three members of the village affairs supervisory committee are subsequently elected through direct margin election, with the person who gets the most votes becoming the director of the village affairs supervision committee. (2) Formulate the System of Village Affairs Supervision, through which the village affairs supervisory committee is entrusted with nine specific duties, such as examining and verifying the village affairs and the financial disclosure list. (3) Define the supervision procedures for the village affairs supervisory committee in the performance of its own duties, in which it is specially stipulated that if the villagers have doubts about village affairs, financial contents and implementation situation by the two committees of the village, the village affairs supervisory committee may, with the consent of more than one-third of the village representatives, propose in writing to the villagers' committee to hold a hearing. In addition, for the village cadres assessed by the masses with more than 50% votes of no confidence, the village affairs supervisory committee has the right to request the villagers' committee to initiate the removal procedure. (4) The village affairs supervisory

Chapter 2　From Election to Governance: New Development of Grassroots Democracy in Zhejiang Province

committee is entrusted by the villager representatives' meeting to carry out supervision work of village affairs independently, and shall be responsible for the village representatives' meeting. The village representatives have the right to request the removal of members of the village affairs supervisory committee, which shall be voted by all the representatives, and the majority approval shall take effect. (5) The exercise situation of functions and powers of the village affairs supervisory committee itself is also subject to the supervision of the village representatives. For example, the provision of System of Village Affairs Supervision in Houchen Village stipulates that, as long as more than one-third of the villagers, or the party branch, make a resolution, it can call for a vote through the village representatives' meeting to decide whether to replace or re-elect the members of the village affairs supervisory committee.

Through many years of practice and exploration, the supervision system of village affairs in Wuyi has gradually matured and improved. In 2012, on the basis of the "Houchen Village's experience", Wuyi extended openness of village affairs and democratic management to group affairs and home affairs, established the supervision system of home affairs and group affairs, implemented supervision of the group affairs and home affairs, and formed a second-level governance and supervision system of village affairs. Since 2013, Wuyi has also constructed convenience services at the village level and opened platforms for party affairs, village affairs and financial information. With this platform of convenience services, villagers can check the relevant information of the village at home by means of television on demand, which can realize constant supervision and make the village affairs and financial affairs fully transparent. This is undoubtedly another innovative and epochal practice of the supervisory committee system of Wuyi in modern information society, which provides a broader real space to promote the active participation of villagers in decision-making, management and supervision of village affairs.

Political Participation and Institutional Innovation:
A Case Study of Zhejiang

In addition, in recent years, there have been more examples of system innovation of rural democracy at the grassroots level in Zhejiang, such as construction of "integrity project" with "integrity index" as the core content in Zhenhai District of Ningbo City, and the "communication day for conditions of the people" held on a regular monthly basis in Changshan County of Quzhou City, which have been of much interest in social circles. It can be said that the continuous emergence of innovative examples of governance at the grassroots level throughout Zhejiang has greatly promoted the development and improvement of democratic politics at the grassroots level in Zhejiang, which has opened up diversified channels for citizens to participate in the practice of governance at the grassroots level and to effectively exercise their democratic power as the masters, as well as made a positive exploration with leading significance for the construction and development of democratic politics at the grassroots level in China. Moreover, these innovative practices also provide us with a typical case that can be used for analysis and reference in thinking and exploring the feasible path of democratic governance at the grassroots level in China.

2.3.2 Innovation of democratic governance in urban communities

The rapid development of social economy promotes the process of urbanization in China and challenges the urban governance in the new era. As a community of social life organized by people living in a certain area, the urban community is the foundation of urban social development. Under the condition of current social transformation and system transition, it is of great significance to promote community democratic autonomy for speeding up the process of urbanization in China, satisfying the multi-level and diversified needs of the citizens, as well as deepening the reform and promoting social stability.

In recent years, the construction of urban communities in Zhejiang has developed healthily. In 2015 alone, Zhejiang won seven national community development awards, including the "Three Society Model:

Chapter 2   From Election to Governance: New Development of Grassroots Democracy in Zhejiang Province

Community Needs Discovery and Community Public Welfare to Promote the Growth of Community Social Organizations" of the Bureau of Civil Affairs in Shangcheng District of Hangzhou, "Exploring the New Mode of Rural Community Construction of the Bureau of Civil Affairs" in Yuhang District of Hangzhou, "Promoting the Development of Rural Community Around Life, Production and Ecology" of Ruiyan Community, Chaiqiao Sub-district, Beilun District, Ningbo, and "Standardizing Management, Expanding Service and Promoting the Construction of Rural Community in a Solid Way" of Cixi Civil Affairs Bureau, and so on. In terms of community democracy construction, Zhejiang lays emphasis on the construction of community democratic politics, which is an important carrier to implement the scientific development concept, to build a harmonious society, to improve the life quality of urban residents as well as urban management level. With the core of strengthening the main role of residents in community governance, Zhejiang explores a new model of diversified democratic governance in urban communities, which promotes the sustained, coordinated and healthy development of urban economy and society.

(1) *Innovation exploration of democratic governance structure of the community*

Haishu District of Ningbo is the first municipal district in which direct elections are held in all urban communities. Differential election, primary election, election campaign and secret voting room have become part of residents' committee election in communities of Ningbo. In recent years, Ningbo has continuously strengthened democratic governance of the community and carried out democratic decision-making, democratic management and democratic supervision in community autonomy affairs. The whole community autonomy organization is divided into 3 parts: community members' meeting, community construction council and community residents' committee with a term of 3 years. The community members' meeting is the decision-making body of the community, which elects and dismisses the members of the community residents' committee according to law, discusses and decides the important affairs of the community, and supervises the work of the community residents' committee. The member representatives shall be elected by the community residents and resident units in accordance with the prescribed procedures. The community construction council is the deliberative organ of the community, which exercises the functions of the representatives' meeting during the intersessional period and regularly consults on the important affairs of the community. The community residents' committee is the executive organ of community affairs and the main organ of community autonomy which is responsible for the management of daily affairs of the community according to the requirements of self-management, self-education, self-service and self-supervision under the leadership of the community party organization.

With the rapid development of urbanization, the importance of community party building work is becoming more and more obvious. How to further deepen the community party building work has become an important subject for strengthening the construction of the party's grassroots organizations in the city. On the basis of summing up the previous working experience, Wucheng District of Jinhua explores the establishment of representatives' meeting of sub-district community party building member units and meeting of community party members' representatives, innovates the organizational form and working mechanism of the party at the grassroots level. The main practices are as follows: (1) Make clear the conditions and quota arrangement of the representatives and organize the selection work on the basis of mastering the basic situation of party organizations and party members of sub-district units in an all-round way. (2) The sub-district and the community shall hold representatives' meeting of sub-street community party building member units and meeting of community party members' representatives, respectively, on the basis of selecting a good representative. (3) Perfect the supporting systems such as double evaluation of party construction performance of party organizations in the area of jurisdiction and establish a job guarantee mechanism.

Chapter 2 From Election to Governance: New Development of Grassroots Democracy in Zhejiang Province

At present, Jinhua has fully implemented the system of representatives' meeting of sub-street community party building member units and meeting of community party members' representative, as well as participation of serving party members in community construction and management system.

(2) *Community forum and community hearing system*

In the process of democratic community construction in the city, the community network forum has been gradually favored by residents' committees and community residents. In this respect, the Dejia Community of Hangzhou is in the forefront. The Dejia Community Forum was not very popular at the beginning of its founding, and residents only discussed issues such as community greening, dog keeping and how owners and security guards get along with each other at the forum. But later, more and more people participated in the discussion, and many residents made valuable comments and suggestions in the Community Forum. The director of the community residents' committee and the secretary of the party committee got to know the questions put forward by the residents on the Internet every day, spoke directly with the residents online, discussed or answered all kinds of questions raised by the residents, and encouraged the residents to participate in the management of the community through the network and accept the supervision of the masses. Community workers also discuss community work with residents on the Internet, so that residents can participate in community management through the network, conduct rational discussion on how to strengthen community service functions, improve service quality of the property management company, and strengthen coordination of the relationship between community construction units and other issues. This new management mode of community negotiation provides a new idea for the management of urban community, reflects the open characteristic of community life, and provides a good foundation for democratic autonomy of the community, which provides a platform for community residents to conduct consultative governance of community public affairs.

Political Participation and Institutional Innovation:
A Case Study of Zhejiang

On the basis of community autonomy, large- and medium-sized cities such as Hangzhou, Ningbo and Wenzhou have also established community hearing systems and public participation mechanisms for major projects related to the people's livelihood, so as to solicit citizens' views on urban development and community construction as widely as possible. In recent years, Hangzhou, the provincial capital, has issued a number of guiding documents on the construction of community democracy, covering various aspects such as community service planning, community party building, community daily affairs management, and so on. It also has formed a relatively perfect policy system, and established a variety of democratic governance mechanisms, such as community democratic talk, affairs coordination, consultation meeting of community council, community affairs hearing, people satisfaction assessment and effectiveness council, and so on.

(3) *Urban governance of "promoting people's livelihood through democracy"*

The practice of "promoting people's livelihood through democracy" introduced by Hangzhou more than 10 years ago is mainly to improve the mechanism of citizen participation and public opinion expression through open decision-making by the government, which means opening to the public major decisions and construction plans concerning people's livelihood, listening to the opinions and suggestions of the citizens directly, and accepting the supervision and restriction of people in the whole city. Relevant mechanisms include direct participation of the people in important decision-making, public evaluation of government work, solicitation of people's suggestions, and so on.

First, establish a mechanism for direct participation and opinion expression of the public in major decision-making. It is a further innovative practice for Hangzhou Municipal Government to carry out "open decision" on the basis of previous democratic decisions. Decision-making model of the government's standing committee is as follows: fully solicit public opinions before executive meeting of

Chapter 2　From Election to Governance: New Development of Grassroots Democracy in Zhejiang Province

the government, "before the meeting", and then submit government decision-making matters to the standing committee of the municipal, district (county) government, invite people's congress deputies, CPPCC members and citizen representatives to attend the meeting and issue their opinions "during the meeting". Citizens can also participate in decision-making and discussion by posting messages on the Internet or live video on the Internet, and the municipal, district (county) relevant departments shall respond to the Internet users in a timely manner, within 24 hours "after the meeting". This open decision-making model is characterized by greater transparency, direct interaction between the government and the people, and an important complement to the decision-making system of the head system, which embodies the features such as moderate open topic, wide open field, direct open expression, open promotion of interaction, transparent open process and so on.

Second, establishing the mechanism of direct evaluation by the masses on the government work. In June 1999, Hangzhou initiated the "12345" mayor's public telephone hotline and gradually formed a public service platform with telephone, e-mail, SMS and other forms as the carrier to absorb public comment. In 2000, Hangzhou created a "satisfactory or unsatisfactory" mechanism for citizens to comment on the government work. Units below the standard line for public comment scores were publicly admonished, and those at the bottom of the standard line were the "dissatisfied units" and were criticized by the municipal party committee and the municipal government. In case of three consecutive years as unsatisfactory unit, the municipal party committee adjusted the leading group. In July 2002, Hangzhou started the "96666" efficiency supervision telephone hotline, through which the public complained about the service attitude and effectiveness of the party and government staff by telephone. The hotline "12345" mainly dealt with the government (ask for the government's help in case of any event) while "96666" was mainly for people. The acceptance scope of complaint call on service attitude and effectiveness of the party and government staff included seven aspects. If a complaint call by the masses was found to be true after investigation, it was necessary to seriously push the relevant departments and relevant staff and investigate the responsibility of the unit's leaders. In practice, the number of people for evaluation increased year by year; the number of units to be evaluated expanded year by year; and the evaluation index became refined and the evaluation level improved.

Third, establishing the solicitation system for people's suggestions. In 2000, Hangzhou Municipal Government formulated the Implementation Opinions of Solicitation and Reward for People's Suggestions in Hangzhou (Trial), formally carrying out regular activities of soliciting people's suggestions, the essence of which is crystallization of the wisdom of the broad masses of the people and gathering of the insights from social circles, unimpeded channels for citizens to participate in political affairs, as well as an effective form for the people to be the masters of their own country. There are three ways of solicitation: daily solicitation, special topic solicitation and media solicitation, among which daily solicitation is the most extensive, and generally reflects the views of the majority; special topic solicitation has strong pertinence and is most favorable to absorbing the wisdom of the people; media solicitation is most favorable to giving full play to the media's powerful publicity advantage, which makes solicitation activities the focus of the masses' attention, and the socialized level of soliciting people's suggestions can be raised rapidly. Questions as to how to renovate West Lake scenic spots, how to improve the small lanes at the back of the street in urban areas, whether the design of the art gallery is feasible or not, which of the top 10 projects of the provincial and municipal governments that do practical work for the people are most urgently needed to be included, and all these need to be widely solicited for the suggestions and opinions of Hangzhou citizens. At the same time, the "Good Suggestions of Internet Users" column is jointly organized by "Hangzhou Website Council Chamber" of Hangzhou Website and Suggestion Solicitation Office of the People's Government of Hangzhou, which is to collect and publish constructive suggestions

Chapter 2 From Election to Governance: New Development of Grassroots Democracy in Zhejiang Province

sent by Internet users for construction and development of Hangzhou. The suggestions will be delivered to the Suggestion Solicitation Office for summary. In the "Online Service" column jointly organized with "12345", the suggestions sent by the Internet users are directly delivered to relevant departments for acceptance. By December 31, 2015, the "Good Suggestions of Internet Users" column and "Online Service" column had received more than 2,000 suggestions. Many suggestions of the Internet users delivered by the "Hangzhou Website Council Chamber" column are approved and adopted by the department. The establishment of solicitation system for people's suggestions provides a good system platform to encourage the public to participate in local governance and to realize the seamless communication between the government and the public.

(4) *Practice of democratic consultation and governance of the community*

The development of community governance is closely related to the democratic quality and ability of the residents. In recent years, the poor mass has been the main group to participate drastically more in China, which brings great pressure to governance at the grassroots level. In the democratic governance of the community in various areas of Zhejiang, the emphasis is laid on the communication practice of guiding the residents from the stranger society to the acquaintance society by the way of consultation among residents, which not only provides a broad public space for cultivating modern civic culture and democratic consciousness, but also provides a humanistic basis for improving the quality of democratic governance in urban community. In Wangjiang Sub-district of Hangzhou, the local government has made great efforts to build a new platform for comprehensive governance in the community to promote autonomy through consultation, which carries out meaningful exploration on how to build a positive logical connection between modern resident life, democratic politics and government governance. "Neighbourly Post" is located in Jinjiang Dongyuan Community of Wangjiang Sub-district with a total area of about 2,000 square meters, which is a "public sitting room" for residents of Wangjiang Sub-district that integrates visits, experiences, services, exchanges, entertainment and mutual aid. As for space layout, the "Neighbourly Post" is composed of three blocks: Neighborhood Communication Experience Center, Online E-point of People's Conditions and Social Organization Coordination Center. Each block has its own function, but all the three blocks revolve around the main line of promoting community residents' participation in community affairs and effective consultation and interaction among community residents. Therefore, the three blocks form an organic whole and jointly play a role in due efficiency of comprehensive governance platform in the community. Among them, the Neighborhood Communication Experience Center plays the most important role in community governance. Through various sharing communication spaces in the community, it increases opportunities and places for the residents' activities, guides communication and contact of residents, forms a new neighborhood with a sense of belonging, security and humanity, as well as strengthens the sense of belonging and identity of the community. Meanwhile, by constructing diversified ways of neighborhood communication, residents can communicate with each other in the process of democratic participation, independent participation and free visit, making neighborhood communication one of the ways in which people communicate emotions, promote understanding and mutual assistance, and strengthen their ability to manage themselves. The community common affairs problems were solved by the residents themselves as much as possible, so as to achieve the goal of self-management, self-service and self-education.

2.3.3 Development of industry and social organizations

Since Tocqueville, most of the democratic theorists in modern times believe that a civil society that is composed of autonomous social organizations that are independent of the state and can exert effective influence on the public policy of the state is the necessary prerequisite for the establishment of democratic system and the development of

Chapter 2　From Election to Governance: New Development of Grassroots Democracy in Zhejiang Province

democratic politics. Organization is an important form of human social activities, and the pluralistic development trend of contemporary society, economy and culture has greatly promoted the emergence and development of various social organizations. It is necessary to point out that China's civil society is different from Western society in terms of connotation, the prerequisites and conditions for development. It is the product of resource conditions such as China's local economy, society, culture and so on.

What kind of organizational structure will the civil society of China use to complete the reorganization of the society in the process of transition from an agricultural civilization to an industrial civilization? It is a difficult problem that must be solved in the course of China's modernization. In Zhejiang, marketization and the development of private economy bring great challenges to the traditional relationship between the government and enterprises, which also has a profound impact on the governance structure of private enterprises and the relationship between enterprises. With the withdrawal of local government power from many fields, the society gets more and more autonomy space. Along with it, various kinds of autonomous community organizations have been created and developed step by step, among which the development of folk chamber of commerce and industry association has been the most noticeable phenomenon in Zhejiang in recent years.

The rise and development of the folk chamber of commerce and industry association is most typical in Wenzhou. Since the establishment of the first group of folk chamber of commerce—Joint Chamber of Commerce of Foreign-funded Enterprises in Wenzhou, Food Industry and Commerce Association, and Department Store Industry Association in 1988—folk chambers of commerce in Wenzhou have developed rapidly in a short period of more than a decade, and have gradually spread to Hangzhou and all parts of Zhejiang. Unlike most of the industry associations organized by the government through channels within the system in other regions, folk chamber of commerce

Political Participation and Institutional Innovation: A Case Study of Zhejiang

in Zhejiang is a non-profit, self-disciplined and service-oriented industry management organization that mostly formed through channels outside the system, and formed voluntarily by private entrepreneurs in various industries in the local industrial and commercial fields. The large number, perfect organization and sound operating mechanism are the main reasons why folk chamber of commerce in Zhejiang is of interest to and praised by outsiders. Especially in Wenzhou, the development, expansion and external expansion of the private economy cannot be separated from the support and promotion of folk chamber of commerce, and this kind of influence will infiltrate into more and more non-economic fields with the improvement of folk chamber of commerce organizations. As an intermediary organization, the status and role of folk chamber of commerce is irreplaceable, which can undertake something that the government can't do well or finds to be inconvenient, form a joint effort to solve the problems that individual private enterprises can't cope with, as well as play a special role in the development of private economy, such as endorsement, coordination, rights protection, integration, and so on. For example, in 2003, under the guidance of Wenzhou Cigarette Utensil Industry Association, Wenzhou lighters enterprises responded bravely to the EU anti-dumping suit, which is also the first legal self-defense war for Chinese private enterprises.

The folk chamber of commerce and industry association shall adopt the election system and tenure system. The directors shall be elected by the general assembly, and the president and vice president shall be elected by the council, and it is stipulated that the president of the chamber of commerce can only be re-elected for two terms, ranging from 3 to 5 years per term. Most of the leaders of the chambers of commerce and associations are private entrepreneurs, and their leaders are democratically elected by their members according to articles of association. At present, in Wenzhou, president candidates for a number of folk chambers of commerce and industry associations have started to implement a differential election. The private entrepreneurs are highly motivated to run for leadership positions in the chamber of commerce

Chapter 2　From Election to Governance: New Development of Grassroots Democracy in Zhejiang Province

and to vote in elections. In recent years, there have been calls for "audition" in some private chambers of commerce. Through the practice of democratic governance of local civil organizations, such as the folk chamber of commerce, the private entrepreneurs can directly participate in local autonomy and democratic governance of social organizations, and receive training in methods of democratic management and political participation, so as to gradually develop their sense of political participation, participation ability and democratic spirit.

2.3.4 Television governance, Internet and new forms of citizen participation

With the advent of modern information society, network democratic forms have also developed rapidly. Since the 1990s, the Internet political participation in the mainland of China has shown a rapid development trend, and political participation forms such as Internet forum of government affairs and Internet dialogue have been widely used. By June 2005, 78 colleges and universities in the mainland had established a total of 123 BBS sites. Moreover, public forums of government affairs on the government website also grow rapidly. In Zhejiang, from 2000 to 2005, there were such forums on the websites of provincial, municipal and county governments, for example, Interaction between the Government and the Public of Government Affairs Network of Zhejiang Provincial People's Government, Forum of Government Affairs of Hangzhou, China, Ask for People's Suggestions of Quzhou Online Affairs Hall and so on. Some cities and counties also set up government efficiency network and civil affairs network, for example, Efficiency Network of Tiantai, Civil Affairs Network of Taizhou, Efficiency Network of Linhai, Efficiency Network of Wenling, Efficiency Network of Huangyan Organ, Efficiency Network of Yuhuan, Efficiency Network of Sanmen, Efficiency Network of Jiaojiang and so on (see Table 2.1). This kind of public forum is the product of the practice of democratic politics at the local grassroots level, and the prominent feature of which is political nature, that is, the forum is for

**Political Participation and Institutional Innovation:
A Case Study of Zhejiang**

Table 2.1. Establishment time of forums/websites for government affairs.

Forum/Website	Forum of Government Affairs of Hangzhou, China	Efficiency Network of Tiantai	Civil Affairs Network of Taizhou	Efficiency Network of Linhai	Efficiency Network of Sanmen
Establishment time	2003-06-28	2004-04-20	2005-12-01	2005-01-21	2005-01-01

the expression of public opinion, interaction between the government and the public, consultation and dialogue, and efficiency construction.

On the Column of Interaction between the Government and the Public of Government Affairs Network of Zhejiang Provincial People's Government, there are eight columns: Governor's Mailbox, Department Mailbox, Local Mailbox, Government Affairs Microblog, Online Live Broadcast, Online Survey, Data Opening and Responding to Concerns, which are of typical representational significance; Government Affairs Website of Hangzhou Municipal People's Government also sets up eight columns: Party Secretary's Mailbox, Mayor's Mailbox, Efficiency Complaint Platform, Online Reception Room, Online Live Broadcast, Online Hearing, Opinions and Suggestions and Online Survey.

After 2010, with the maturity of 3G and 4G technologies and the application of smartphones, network governance which is more realtime and controllable has developed rapidly. The Dialogue Column of Ningbo, China website was founded in 2001, to build a platform for communication between the party, the government and the masses, which is a news interactive exchange platform with great influence in Zhejiang and even China. During the program time, the average daily page views kept at more than 600,000, and the highest number reached 3.3 million. Wenzhou Political Situation and Public Opinion Intermediate Station is a large-scale talk show jointly organized by the Wenzhou CPPCC Office and Urban Life Channel of Wenzhou

Chapter 2　From Election to Governance: New Development of Grassroots Democracy in Zhejiang Province

Radio and Television Media Group. From June 28, 2002 to 2017, more than 660 episodes had been broadcast on Sunday evenings at 9:00 p.m., aiming to let people directly participate in politics, promote democratic supervision, build bridges for communication and convey people's aspirations. Our Round Table Meeting was jointly hosted by the General Office of the CPC Hangzhou Municipal Committee, Hangzhou Municipal Government General Office and Hangzhou Wenguang Group, which aims to organize face-to-face communication among various circles on the urban development, social management, social construction and innovative services of Hangzhou. From October 2010 to October 2015, a total of 714 episodes covering 463 topics were produced and broadcast for 5 years, with some topics discussed continuously in the program for 2–3 issues, each of which lasted 40 minutes, and 4,980 people participated in the round table discussions. Shaoxing People's Conditions Online originated from the "Interaction between Government and the Public" Column of Shaoxing website set up in August 2011 and was renamed as the "Online Platform for Shaoxing People's Conditions" in July 2013, which aims to listen to people's aspirations, gathers the wisdom of the people and responds to people's concerns. It has brought together 88 municipal departments and public enterprises and institutions, mainly covering policy promotion, answering consultations, responding to requests, listening to the recommendations, aiming to realize real-time inquiries by the Internet users, real-time responses by the departments and real-time administration by the government.

The lasting influence of Internet governance is that it has many participants and face-to-face conversations, combines television media, Internet technology with public governance, as well as presents serious and intractable governance issues in the form of entertainment, which lets the ordinary people have a sense of personal experience. Meanwhile, the forms of network governance are flexible and diverse, and the leaders of the party and government departments are organized together with ordinary people in the form of television programs to hold

Political Participation and Institutional Innovation:
A Case Study of Zhejiang

a real face-to-face dialogue between the government and the people, which is more controllable than government forums, among which, the "Our Round Table Meeting" in Hangzhou and television governance in Wenzhou are the most representative.

(1) *"Our Round Table Meeting" in Hangzhou*

Hangzhou not only takes the lead in carrying out "open decision", but also actively explores various paths, one of which is to make use of the mass media in a variety of ways to ensure scientific and fair decision-making. "Our Round Table Meeting" is an interactive talk show on the comprehensive channel of Hangzhou TV Station, which adheres to the concept of democracy promoting people's livelihood and invites experts, officials, citizens and other social representatives from all social circles to sit around a "table" for dialogue, communication, exchanges, understanding and win–win on the topics of common concern in the city. The 30-minute program is broadcast every Monday to Friday. The basic mode of each episode is that the host and 4–5 guests from different backgrounds have a discussion in the studio. A variety of open interactive participation forms such as field interview, background information review, telephone hotline, network observers, information broadcasting, investigation and publication are used in the process to increase the information amount in the program and enhance the artistic sense of the program, which has a wide influence in Hangzhou area. The program is based on communication, focuses on people's livelihood and gathers the voices of all parties around the table.

In terms of program style, each episode of "Our Round Table Meeting" invites people from the party and government, colleges and universities, industry and enterprises, as well as the media to meet at the round table meeting, who discuss 1–2 topics five consecutive days per week, and talk deeply and thoroughly about the topic through discussing layer by layer. In terms of conversation topic, the program fully embodies openness and universality, which pays more attention to the combination of concern of the people and concern of the party and government,

Chapter 2　From Election to Governance: New Development of Grassroots Democracy in Zhejiang Province

the combination of urban residents' life and economic and social development, the combination of news event and social phenomenon analysis, as well as the combination of psycho-social analysis, emotional guidance and deep thinking and background concerned by experts and scholars in the hotspots of public opinion. Through open dialogue and rational communication, not only is consensus reached through communication and understanding, but also wisdom of the public is gathered in the best way to achieve harmonious management. In order to promote the active participation of government departments, "Our Round Table Meeting" column also set up the linkage mechanism of government participation: Each episode is regarded as the work responsibility of the department related to the topic, through the form of a letter sent by the General Office of Municipal Party Committee, and the relevant department is requested to attend. Through joint action of all circles and active association, the column group establishes a column linkage mechanism with citizens, expert support, party and government guidance, media communication, industry and enterprise participation, as well as an effective linkage with the relevant functional departments, districts, counties and cities, which provide a channel to reflect the work and respond to emergencies, and forms an effective mechanism for issuing, explaining and soliciting suggestions. Meanwhile, the column also establishes a mutual linkage mechanism with the policymaking department, which is for opinions solicitation, publishing and feedback in the process of policy research, issuance and implementation.

Since its launch in 2010, "Our Round Table Meeting" has no longer been about policy communication, but has had a practical effect. With the desire for a better life, more and more citizens of Hangzhou are gathering in the round table meeting to contribute wisdom to the construction of the city and life of the masses. In order to listen to more aspirations of the citizens, in the second half of 2014, the column launched the WeChat public platform "Micro-Round Table" to collect discussion topics through WeChat. In 2014, Zhang Hongming, Deputy Secretary of Hangzhou Municipal Party Committee and Mayor of

**Political Participation and Institutional Innovation:
A Case Study of Zhejiang**

Hangzhou at that time, joined "Our Round Table Meeting" three times to talk about topics such as "Five Water Co-governance", "Garbage Classification" and "Ten Things for People's Livelihood in 2015" face to face with experts, scholars, people's congress deputies, CPPCC members and enthusiastic citizens. In 2015 alone, more than 1,400 guests went into the studio and more than 100 government officials from more than 30 functional departments had sincere dialogues and communication with enthusiastic citizens around more than 60 topics, such as urban blockage, flood prevention, garbage classification, atmospheric haze control, pollution control of clean water, food safety, property management, smart city and health care reform. As an integral part of urban social management, "Our Round Table Meeting" also plays a role in promoting all aspects of urban governance. After broadcasting of the program *Ten Things for People's Livelihood in 2015—Mayor Listens to You*, many people who participated in the program received replies from the relevant functional departments, and suggestions of the participants were also reflected in the project of "Ten Aspects of People's Livelihood" launched by the government in 2015.

(2) Television governance in Wenzhou, Lishui and other places

In television governance, through the way of live broadcast on television, ordinary people question government officials face to face about social security, food safety, and issues related to people's livelihood, while relevant government leaders answer or explain at the scene. In the new era of information society, television governance is the exposure platform for the problems, the mouthpiece for the people's feelings and wishes, and the inspection field for the cadres' attitude and ability, which makes government officials realize that they are supervised by the masses and should be responsible for the masses. The widespread development of television governance in Zhejiang in recent years has made it an important way of accountability.

In March 2014, Wenzhou carried out the first television governance activity. The topic was about the "water control" problem, which

Chapter 2   From Election to Governance: New Development of Grassroots Democracy in Zhejiang Province

was closely related to the living environment of the masses. Led by relevant municipal departments ("top leaders" from Municipal Water Conservancy Bureau, Environmental Protection Bureau, Housing and Urban-Rural Development Bureau, Administrative Law Enforcement Bureau, Municipal Agricultural Affairs Office, etc.) and citizen representatives from all walks of life (including people's congress deputies, CPPCC members, media and public representatives), two teams were formed, and the deficiencies of water control in the city photographed by the reporter secretly were broadcast from time to time on the large-scale television screen with the progress of the program. The broad masses below the stage scored at the scene according to the performance of the relevant departments. Through statement of leaders of relevant departments, questions of citizens and people's congress deputies, discussion of experts, evaluation of the masses, guidance of leaders and other links, the focus laid on progress in "regulation of two rivers" — the garbage river and the black stinky river, progress in construction of sewage treatment facilities in urban and rural areas, supervision of industrial pollution sources and regulation of heavy pollution industries along the river, household garbage disposal and river cleaning, prevention and control of agricultural source pollutions such as livestock and poultry breeding, protection of Shanxi Reservoir and other water sources, construction of green landscape and walking paths along the river. Subsequently, Wenzhou carried out television governance many times, covering urban civilization, congestion problem, municipal key project construction and so on. The participating units involved almost all the functional departments of the municipal government, and the masses were extremely active in participating. Resolution of each case was supervised and implemented by the Performance Appraisal Office and relevant responsibility departments of Wenzhou, followed up and reported by major media, which had a very good social effect.

Since July 2013, Lishui has also carried out the "television governance" activity in the form of *Governance Process*, combining monthly and annual governance, conducting live broadcasts each month, tracking and supervising the progress of solving hot social problems, as well as the "annual examination" of "face-to-face governance" at the end of the year, which judges the performance of the county (city, district) and municipal departments. During the first television governance on July 29, around the theme of "Building a National Hygienic City", responsible persons from six departments, including the Municipal Hygienic Office of Lishui, Liandu District Government of Lishui, Lishui Municipal Bureau of Construction and so on, answered the questions raised by citizen representatives, some party representatives, people's congress deputies, CPPCC members, experts, media and audiences at the scene. Many people who took part in television governance at the scene said that it was a good platform and its significance was far from supervising and pushing forward some difficult social work, and more importantly, realizing a kind of "interaction between government and masses" that had been missing for a long time. The contents of *Governance Process* were mainly drawn from the quantitative assessment work of provincial party committee and provincial government, key work of municipal party committee and municipal government, as well as hot issues of people's livelihood of interest to society. Problems discussed through the monthly live broadcast of *Governance Process* will be followed up.

2.4 System changes and formation of the local democratic governance mechanism

How does system change of democratic governance in various regions of Zhejiang take place? Is it merely a deliberate innovation of local governments, or is there an objective necessity for its emergence? In this regard, we need to find the answer from the process of complicated system change of democratic governance in Zhejiang.

Since the reform and opening-up, with regard to Chinese political and social systems, compulsory system changes were implemented by the government through policies, laws and decrees. The development of Zhejiang's private economy and the evolution of democratic governance at the grassroots level have their own unique characteristics, that is, with the establishment of the market economy system, formation of social autonomous governance space and constant strengthening of social autonomy, the inductive system change from bottom to top, which is dominated by microeconomic behaviors such as farmers, workers and enterprises, has gradually become a type of system change that cannot be ignored. In the process of system change, the behavioral agent at the grassroots level has system demand first because of discovery of potential profit opportunities, and then generates demand and recognition for the new system from bottom to top, so as to influence and urge the decision-makers to make timely adjustment to the existing system arrangements.

2.4.1 The objective demand of social development is a necessary condition for system change

At present, China is in the period of social transformation, and the important problem of the transitional society is interest differentiation, which will endanger the stability of the society if not solved effectively and on time. Modernity produces stability, but modernization produces instability. When per capita output value of developing countries increased from 800 to 1,000 US dollars, an eventful period of interest differentiation and even interest conflicts began. In 2004, per capita GDP in China was just over 800 US dollars, and per capita GDP in Zhejiang reached 3,400 US dollars in 2005; Gini coefficient in China approached 0.47 in 2005, while that of urban and rural integration in Zhejiang in 2004 reached as high as 0.4738. The international community thinks that when the Gini coefficient exceeds 0.4, countries often start to face social tension. Therefore, China has entered the high incidence period of interest differentiation at the beginning of the 21st century. So it is necessary to construct the mechanism of interest expression as well as the mechanism for coordinating and resolving interest contradictions and conflicts, so that different groups can express their interests, and their demands can be better coordinated and resolved. In terms of expressing citizens' interests, Zhejiang has carried out a series of system innovations, such as democratic talk, hearing, public opinion solicitation, mayor's mailbox 12345, forum of government affairs, efficiency network, civil affairs network and other

Chapter 2　From Election to Governance: New Development of Grassroots Democracy in Zhejiang Province

forms of consultation systems. Negotiation can't exist without interest. The participants are not afraid to talk about their interests and demands; they try to balance different interests and reach mutual understanding and consensus on preferences and the credibility of actions, and they try to reconcile various interests and reach consensus on how to solve the problem through negotiation. In a sense, these system innovations show that in order to deal with the interest differentiation and maintain social stability, decisions made by the government must be combined with public opinions, and the decision right of some public affairs should be changed from the government to the citizens.

The unique pattern of economic development in Zhejiang since the reform and opening-up has not only been the password of creating economic miracles in Zhejiang, but also the most important external cause of local governance system changes in Zhejiang. Zhejiang has a land area of 105,500 square kilometers, about 1.1% of China's total land area, and is one of the smaller provinces in China. The contradiction between more people and less land as well as the scarcity of resources compels Zhejiang people to find other ways in reality. Before the reform and opening-up, going inland, going south, going north and even sailing cross the ocean was the only choice for Zhejiang people to seek a way out, which also made Zhejiang people tough, pragmatic and innovative. In the recent 40 years of the reform and opening-up, Zhejiang people have seized the opportunities to develop rapidly, making economic development in Zhejiang with private economy as the main body in the forefront of the country. The rapid development of private economy poses a challenge to the traditional government process and social structure. The prosperity of market economy makes a relatively independent social structure system come into being rapidly outside the traditional system. The grasp of market opportunity and the amount of economic capital have gradually become the decisive factor in social and economic activities. As a result of this change, the contractual relationship based on equal status is gradually replacing the traditional and rigid relationship of the identity system. The rapid

Political Participation and Institutional Innovation: A Case Study of Zhejiang

changes in the social economy require corresponding adjustments in the political structure of the society, constantly incorporating new social demands into their own words to form a suitable state of various behavioral agents for the established system arrangement and system structure.

In addition to the rapid development of private economy, deepening of the national political system reform is also an important cause of democratic system changes at the grassroots level. Since the 1990s, economic and social structure in Zhejiang has been constantly divided, forming a pluralistic interest group, and resulting in diversified interest expression and political participation. For example, in cities, the number of traditional industrial workers has dropped, while the number of workers in the tertiary industry has increased, so the new rich class and the new poor class have emerged. The new rich class includes technicians of private enterprises, senior Chinese managers of foreign-funded enterprises and owners of private enterprises, etc. The new poor class includes unemployed and laid-off workers, disabled persons and retired workers with low income. The differentiation of social interests in the transitional period has strengthened the internal driving force for citizens' political participation and greatly promoted the development of political participation. However, the original participation channels cannot meet citizens' needs for political participation, and the obvious lack of supply in the participation system in China is bound to lead to instability of the political order. After analyzing the modernization process in developing countries, Samuel Huntington points out that because of the low degree of institutionalization of the national political system, demands on governments are difficult or impossible to be expressed through legal channels and are difficult to be mitigated and converged within the political system. Therefore, the rapid increase in political participation will lead to political instability. The interest differentiation in the transitional society speeds up political participation system reform in China to provide more institutionalized channels for citizens' political participation, including the hearing system.

Chapter 2　From Election to Governance: New Development of Grassroots Democracy in Zhejiang Province

The existing participation channels can't meet the growing needs for political participation of Chinese social groups, and when their political participation and economic interests arising from this kind of consciousness can't be satisfied in the traditional system environment, there is a potential demand for new system arrangements, which leads to an unbalanced state of old system arrangements, and the generation of innovative system forms, such as hearing and political participation. In this process, the government and farmers will form a two-way interactive game relationship. Eventually, the new system arrangements may be implemented when the government actively caters to or guides such social needs under a comprehensive weight. The new system scheme is accepted by the villagers to obtain the common increased interests, so as to jointly promote formation of a new system.

2.4.2 The realistic difficulties of local governance provide an opportunity for system innovation

If the objective demand of social development provides the possibility for the change of democratic system at the grassroots level in Zhejiang, then the practical difficulties encountered in the social governance in various places provide an opportunity for the system change of democracy at the grassroots level in Zhejiang. Although the causes of practical difficulties in social governance are diverse, the core lies in the defects of the existing system arrangements. In other words, the old system arrangements are no longer adapted to the actual demands of social development in China.

In rural grassroots governance, the dilemma of village affairs governance is the most direct motive force of innovative systems, such as the village affairs supervision committee of Wuyi, democratic talk of Wenling and so on. The emergence of village affairs supervision committee in Wuyi is not accidental. The fundamental reason lies in that the contradiction between the villagers' committee and the villagers has existed for a long time in village governance, which has led to the villagers' distrust of the villagers' committee and greatly weakened

Political Participation and Institutional Innovation:
A Case Study of Zhejiang

its legitimacy, and caused unfavorable situations in the work of the villagers' committee, as the powers of the village cadres are generally out of control without supervision. As a result, the vicious circle of obstruction in advance and petition afterward by the villagers in terms of village affairs occurred. The direct cause of the village affairs supervision committee was the investigation on or removal of five top leaders of the "two committees" of the village under the jurisdiction of the Baiyang Sub-district in early 2004, and one of them got criminal penalties. This trust crisis of "village official" exposed the absence of a regular democratic supervision mechanism in village governance, which stimulated the urgent attention of the government and the masses for village affairs supervision. The emergence of the democratic talk is also the result of realistic pressure to some extent. The predecessor of the democratic talk is the "agricultural rural modernization education", which has been carried out for 12 years in the rural areas. The main goal of this kind of educational activity is preaching to the villagers, by relevant technicians or experts after the mobilization meeting that is convened by the government. Villagers often express deep boredom about this kind of one-way presentation, and relevant government departments are also deeply troubled by this. Meanwhile, villagers complain that it is difficult to find better ways to express their interests. Innovation of the democratic talk lies in changing the traditional one-way "cadre education" into a two-way "dialogue between cadres and villagers", which changes villagers from traditional "receipts" to active "actors". For the government, as the enthusiasm of the villagers better mobilizes, the educational effect improves and the tasks arranged by the superiors are satisfactorily completed, the image of an open pro-people government is set up. While for the villagers, the democratic talk has become an important way to realize their own interests and demands.

In urban grassroots democratic governance, due to the rapid development of urbanization and the complexity of community construction, actual challenges also exist, such as the dilemma of participation in community governance, how to supervise and restrict

Chapter 2 From Election to Governance: New Development of Grassroots Democracy in Zhejiang Province

community public power and so on. Especially, the increase of "villages in the city", a large number of migrant workers, blurring of urban and rural governance boundaries, the incessant contradiction of land requisition and removal, the phenomenon of a high level of petition and so on, have brought unprecedented pressure to urban grassroots governance. Therefore, in recent years, Zhejiang has always put the innovation of urban democratic governance in an important position in political practice, and explored a variety of innovative modes of community governance, such as community council, resident representatives' meeting, community forums and so on, which greatly expanded the public domain and cooperative governance space of urban community life. It's believed that the practice of the public domain is due to the joint participation of actors in the operation of political power, which can produce a common sense of solidarity with community life in public domain, realizing that the fate of the whole community depends on the minds, actions and decisions of everyone involved in it. In urban grassroots public domain, the joint participation of multiple governance subjects promotes various feasible system arrangements that can solve practical problems, which builds a platform for public interest expression, coordination, gaming and integration.

Since the beginning of the 21st century, progressive communication and information technologies have empowered ordinary citizens and governments to promote the continuous evolution of citizen participation ways, which has brought new pressure and opportunity to government governance. The government actively establishes network participation platforms to absorb the opinions of the masses and at the same time supervises and restrains citizen participation so as to ensure citizens' orderly participation and social stability. As Zheng Yongnian points out in his book *Technology Empowerment: The Internet, State and Society in China* (*2008*), the Internet empowers both the country and the society, and both of them benefit from the development of Internet, which creates a basic structure for the country and the society to move closer to each other. However, in specific governance situations, the social and political attributes of technology tend to show two totally different and highly interdependent characteristics: the characteristic of production and empowerment, and the characteristic of intrusiveness, bondedness and opacity. The former brings new development opportunities, which can promote the democratic process, improve efficiency of the government and promote social welfare in the specific environment, while the latter brings latent crisis and disaster to social governance. Although technology and technology platforms have a two-way empowerment function for users and administrators, technology empowerment can trigger turmoil in countries such as Egypt, while in China it can improve the quality of public services and social governance, so as to consolidate the ruling system. Why does Internet participation in different countries lead to different results? Of course, in essence, technology has injected new meaning and value into social order, whether it is to impact or consolidate the system. The question should not be whether the determinism of technology is right or wrong, but to what extent, under what conditions, a specific technology is more capable of shaping the society. The framework also complements and clarifies the question of human mobility: To what extent, how and under what conditions, specific groups of people can shape their social technology system? Actually, technical parameters have been introduced into the bureaucratic system to distinguish between good and bad, to draw the line between "acceptable" and "unacceptable", to form new identity and knowledge, to rationalize the behavior of subjects, to set up a new moral order for the society, to develop a system of knowledge and power order, as well as to reproduce the new public order through behavioral norms, compulsory mechanisms, identity and cultural mechanisms. China's Internet participation is not only political. The state continuously creates a legal platform for Internet political participation of the citizens, expands the system, includes citizen participation into the political process, and strengthens toughness of the system. More importantly, Chinese governments at all levels actively

Chapter 2　From Election to Governance: New Development of Grassroots Democracy in Zhejiang Province

induce citizens to participate in public services and social governance, rather than in the political domain. In this regard, China's Internet political participation is characterized by order and stability, which is produced by the dual forces of technology empowerment and system constraint.

2.4.3 Innovation motive force and system supply of local governments are the guarantee of the system change

Since the reform and opening-up, on the one hand, with the promotion of the reform measures whereby the central government devolves power to the local government and the continuous adjustment of the system environment, the local government has gained unprecedented power to deal with the public affairs within the jurisdiction independently; on the other hand, the rapid development of local economy also enables the local government to bear the cost of system innovation. As a result, local governments gradually have the subjective motive force and objective condition to promote system innovation, and their important position in national system innovation is increasingly prominent.

For local governments, what is the motive force for government innovation? Any system arrangement costs a certain amount of money, including the cost of system design, the expected cost of implementing the new arrangement and so on. Generally speaking, only when the expected income is greater than the expected cost can the behavior subjects push forward and finally realize the system change. However, any system arrangement involves a variety of subjects, meanwhile, the utility functions of different behavior subjects are different, who may have different evaluation criteria for the benefits of system arrangements. Therefore, as the system provider of democratic governance changes at the grassroots level, the comprehensive consideration of these different factors by local governments will determine the fate of the whole democratic governance system at the grassroots level. From the practice cases of democratic governance innovation at the grassroots level in

Political Participation and Institutional Innovation: A Case Study of Zhejiang

Zhejiang, it can be found that the system innovation motive force of local governments mainly comes from the following aspects:

(1) Conforming to the objective requirements for the development of citizens' democratic consciousness, easing tensions between the government and citizens, so as to optimize the government administrative environment. Through providing channels for public interest expression and participation in local public affairs, governments at the grassroots level expect to win political support from local residents.

(2) The need to pursue interests within the government organization. At present, each local government has gradually become an economic organization with relatively independent target of economic interests, and has the motive of pursuing the rapid growth of the local economy. Some local governments hope to prevent corruption, promote the healthy development of local economy and increase government revenue by means of democratic hearing, village affairs supervision and other system innovation forms.

(3) Government officials themselves can also obtain considerable political benefits from system arrangements and accumulate credits for further promotion. After nearly 40 years of reform and opening-up, on the basis of raw material competition, product market competition and talent competition in the past, new forms of competition—system innovation competition—have been added in the competition among local governments in China. From the actual situation, if some partial system innovation forms, implemented by some officials during their term of office, produce a good social effect and are affirmed by the higher government, their promoters will be praised or promoted.

The rise of hearing system in China's local governance, to a large extent, is due to the fact that the local government complies with the development trend of contemporary public domain governance movement and responds positively to citizens' needs of interest expression. Through

Chapter 2   From Election to Governance: New Development of Grassroots Democracy in Zhejiang Province

the construction of organic interaction and communication mechanism between the government and social pluralistic subjects, optimization of local governance system and governance structure is constantly promoted. Hearing emphasizes that the government and citizens can reach unified public decision-making goals through institutional means, but instead of making decisions alone, the government must listen to public opinions for decision-making. A hearing is not an order given by the government to the citizens, but the process of communicating and consulting with the citizens, turning government decision-makings into conscious participation by the citizens. A hearing is a game between various social interest groups against the same decision goal, which reflects the process of polycentric authorities influencing decision-making in the process of game, and is the unity of political ruling and political management.

Combined with actual development situations of local governance, local governments make full use of Internet and other modern information technologies in practical exploration, such as "Our Round Table Meeting" and the public forums of government affairs, which are vivid practices of system innovation by the local government. Compared with Internet political participation in many other countries, in innovation of local governance in Zhejiang, although the Internet political participation is also strictly restricted and regulated by the state, this kind of participation is not merely political. The state not only continuously creates a legal platform for Internet political participation of the citizens, but also expands the system, as well as includes citizen participation into the political process to strengthen toughness of the system. More importantly, Chinese governments at all levels actively encourage citizens to participate in public services and social governance, rather than in political domain. In this regard, China's Internet political participation is characterized by order and stability, which is produced by the dual forces of technology empowerment and system constraint.

It can be seen that, although the reform and opening-up of China is essentially a process of system change under the guidance of the

Political Participation and Institutional Innovation:
A Case Study of Zhejiang

central government, with the innovation of supply-oriented system as the main model, there are other important factors to promote the change of democratic governance system at the grassroots level in China, such as the improvement of the democratic consciousness of the society and masses and the increasing interest demands, as well as the innovation motive force of the local government. Especially in Zhejiang, where economic development is relatively rapid, such development not only brings about social progress, but also induces many contradictions and conflicts, and democratic consciousness of the citizens also increases with the frequent social flows and social exchanges, which have become sources of external pressure on the government to promote system innovation in the process of grassroots governance in Zhejiang. In the process of two-way responses and multiple games between the government and the masses, various innovation systems have been established and developed.

2.5 Value and significance of democratic governance innovation at the grassroots level in Zhejiang

In the past 40 years of the reform and opening-up, development of democracy at the grassroots level in China has been carried out in a hierarchical manner on the premise of maintaining social stability and economic development, following the principle of from point to surface, from bottom to top. In the transformation process of construction and governance of democratic politics, innovation system of local government has undoubtedly played an important role as a pathfinder because civic participation outside of the political domain does push individuals to be more politically active. Party committees and governments at all levels in Zhejiang vigorously promote the construction of democratic politics at the grassroots level and carry out creative practical exploration and system innovation in improving and perfecting democratic elections, democratic management, democratic supervision and democratic decision-making, through which a great deal of valuable practical experiences have been accumulated. Zhejiang is not only one step ahead of the whole country in market-oriented reform and development of private economic strength, a series of endogenous system innovations of democratic politics, such as democratic talks, also shows the potential for democratization development of grassroots politics in China. As one of the provinces with the most developed private economy in China, Zhejiang faces a number of particular and pioneering problems in the process of social development and system reform, which may also be the problems that other provinces may face in the future. Therefore, the practices and experiences of system innovation in the process of democratic governance at the grassroots level in Zhejiang are of great value and significance.

2.5.1 Innovation of democratic governance at the grassroots level is an important motive force to promote local development and social stability

Innovation is the soul of national progress, the inexhaustible motive force of national prosperity and the deepest national endowment of the Chinese nation. The report of the 18th National Congress of the Communist Party of China emphasizes that it is necessary to uphold the status of the people as the main body, give full play to the spirit of the people as the masters, and adhere to the basic policy of governing the country by law under the leadership of the Party, mobilize and organize the people to manage state and social affairs as well as economic and cultural undertakings in accordance with the law, actively participate in the socialist modernization construction, better safeguard the rights and interests of the people, and better ensure that the people are the masters of their own affairs. In recent years, the Party Central Committee and governments throughout the country persist in promoting democratic innovation through theoretical innovation based on practice, adhere to and improve the existing political system, constantly build a system that is complete, scientific, standard and runs

Chapter 2　From Election to Governance: New Development of Grassroots Democracy in Zhejiang Province

effectively combined with the reality, as well as continuously promote the modernization of the local governance system and management ability. Looking back on the endeavor of the Communist Party of China over the past 100 years, it is not difficult to find that the Party always sums up the successful experience of revolutionary construction and reform conscientiously, promotes the practical, theoretical and system innovations of the Party in a timely manner, constantly improves democracy within the Party and the people's democratic system, making all the undertakings of the Party and the country always advance in the correct direction.

In recent years, with further deepening of China's reform and opening-up, contradictions and conflicts between government and citizens, economy and society exist in many places, including Zhejiang, and some even evolve into serious group incidents. In order to strengthen the control of village (community) organizations at the grassroots level, or to ensure the smooth progress of some construction projects, some local governments often conducted election and daily governance of village (community) organizations. As a result, conflicts have not been alleviated by democratic construction such as election at the grassroots level; on the contrary, conflicts between the officials and the masses have intensified, inducing distrust and antagonism among the masses toward the government and leading to instability in governance at the grassroots level. Especially with the rapid development of social economy, in rural areas along the eastern coast in which the social economy is in a stage of rapid development, the deep-level contradictions caused by environmental pollution, farmland compensation, land requisition and removal, democratic rights and the relationship between cadres and masses are increasingly prominent. Due to various reasons, the channels for farmers to submit the problems and the ways to solve the problems are often not smooth enough, thus some contradictions and conflicts can't be solved effectively or in a timely manner, resulting in the phenomenon of large numbers of complaint letters and visits by the masses. For the petitioners, they invest a lot of material resources, financial resources and energy, which not only become a heavy burden, but also inevitably affect their normal production and life. According to the current reality, when the interests of farmers are infringed, because of the influence of cost, degree of trust, legal consciousness and other factors, few people will choose judicial approach to solve the problem, and farmers lack social organizations such as trade unions and trade associations to protect their legitimate rights and interests through systematic, organized expression of interests. In this case, it is easy to make some people ask for help from outside the system. In recent years, mass rights protection incidents have occurred from time to time in various areas. In some areas, cult organizations, gangland organizations and local evil forces have a growing tendency in social life, all of which are caused by the lack of a normal mechanism for people to express and realize their interests. Therefore, it is of great significance to promote democratic governance innovation at the grassroots level, as well as to explore the effective and cooperative co-governing mechanism among the pluralistic subjects to promote development and stability at the grassroots level.

As early as the beginning of the reform and opening-up, when other parts of the country still hesitated about pertaining to socialism or capitalism, public or private, Zhejiang Provincial Government provided necessary system space for the development of market economy through the innovative power operation mode of the government "ruling without action", which provided a solid system foundation for a series of profound transformations from the traditional planned economy system to the market economy system, from the small economic province based on agriculture to the large economic province based on industry, and from the closed type to the open type as soon as possible; and as the problem of "growing up first and worrying next" gradually became apparent in Zhejiang, governments at all levels in Zhejiang quickly and comprehensively initiated innovation models of democratic governance, such as democratic talks at the grassroots level, democratic hearings, supervision of village affairs and television governance, which

Chapter 2 From Election to Governance: New Development of Grassroots Democracy in Zhejiang Province

provided a good mechanism for harmonious and balanced development of local economy and society. The practice shows that in the practice of political reform at the grassroots level in Zhejiang, through system innovations focusing on democratic decision-making, democratic management and democratic supervision of local public affairs, governance at the grassroots level has been greatly improved. The implementation of democratic talks of Wenling and democratic hearings of Ningbo and Yuhuan has stimulated and improved the democratic participation consciousness of the masses, promoted expression and realization of masses' interests, reduced subjective randomness as well as unnecessary guesses and misunderstandings, and effectively avoided non-institutional participation forms, such as the traditional illegal petition, noisy complaining and traffic blocking.

Another important purpose of transformation of governance at the grassroots level in Zhejiang is to stimulate the enthusiasm of citizens to participate in public governance and to strengthen the legitimacy foundation of the authority organs of governance at the grassroots level. Through adjustment of the operating mechanism of governance power at the grassroots level, strengthening expression of citizens' interests in public affairs, and dredging the communication channels between the citizens and the government, resistance to government policy formulation and implementation reduced and work performance of grassroots governments improved greatly. Most citizens have been given a voice in the management of village affairs involving their own interests. Their needs and opinions can be reflected through democratic talks, democratic hearings, village affairs supervision committees and so on, and can be expressed through television governance, network forums and other forms, and embodied in public policy, which ensures transparency of public power operation in local governance, and is conducive to the maintenance of public interests and restricting the power of officials. These system innovations also contribute to the expansion and deepening of democratic decision-making, democratic management and democratic supervision, prevention and control of

Political Participation and Institutional Innovation:
A Case Study of Zhejiang

corruption at its source, which promote the harmonious relationship between cadres and the masses in grassroots governance to a certain extent, and reduce the pressure on petition departments of all levels, as well as promote local economic and social development and stability.

2.5.2 Innovation of democratic governance at the grassroots level is the practice of people's democratic idea in contemporary China

Etymologically, democracy is derived from the Greek words *demos* (people) and *kratia* (rule or authority), the most direct meaning of which is "rule by the people", which seems to be the most obvious. In modern history, people's sovereignty is a basic principle of the state and its politics, and the democratic ideal is generally accepted by people in the form of people's sovereignty. It is the idea of people as sovereign that inspires them to devote themselves to the revolutionary struggle against the absolute state. It can be said that in the process of modernization, democracy as a value orientation has gained unprecedented high degree of recognition in the development of human politics, and almost every country has accepted democracy as an ideology. However, since the 1950s, there have been growing doubts about democracy in Western countries, which have culminated in today's world with globalization, democratization, the popularization of the Internet and information technology. Actually, it is also an objective result of a decisive victory in democratic ideology in the whole world: The practice of democracy seems to have lost its way forward. On the other hand, with the gradual transformation of human society from the industrial society to the post-industrial society, as an industrial civilization, democracy and the way of thinking and construction are facing the possibility of "deconstruction" in an all-round way. Motivated by the need to seek governance solutions for post-industrial societies, prospective scholars are sceptical about democracy.

The people as the masters of their own affairs is the essence and core of socialist democratic politics. Socialist democracy is rich in

Chapter 2　From Election to Governance: New Development of Grassroots Democracy in Zhejiang Province

connotation, which is direct democracy in form, and essentially, people are the masters of their own affairs. Socialist democracy is embodied not only in the constitution and the law, but also in every aspect of daily life. Therefore, democracy is not an ornament, not a decoration, but a solution to problems. Under China's socialist system, the true meaning of people's democracy is to seek the greatest common divisor that conforms to the will of the people and social demands through public consultation. Innovation of democratic governance at the grassroots level in Zhejiang is the concrete interpretation and vivid practice of socialism with Chinese characteristics and the concept of people's democracy.

Innovation of democratic governance at the grassroots level in Zhejiang aims at adhering to the leadership of the CPC, improving the leadership level of the CPC, implementing leadership of the CPC effectively, constantly supporting the people as the masters of their own affairs and implementing rights of the masses. Through innovation practices such as democratic talks and democratic hearings to promote communication between officials and the masses, online forums and television governance to expand channels for citizens to participate in political affairs, and village affairs supervision committee to strengthen the balance of power at the grassroots level, the masses are included in the grassroots governance system in an orderly manner, and the ordinary citizens work effectively in the management of public affairs and power supervision of ordinary citizens. For example, the democratic talk in Wenling opened up an institutionalized channel for villagers to participate in public affairs and realize individual interests, enabling people to express their interests fairly and equally. This mechanism has the advantages of low cost, good efficiency, simple operation, and brings certain pressure on village cadres, which makes two committees of the village play a good role in serving the people and puts public power under the supervision of the broader masses, so that the hot and difficult problems at the grassroots level are solved on time. In Ningbo, a foreign businessman once planned to invest in a paper mill in Tengtou Village of Fenghua, which could bring a profit of at least three million yuan annually to the village after completion. According to the democratic decision-making system of the first discussion among party members and discussion system of villagers' representatives, the village party committee and villagers' committee convened meetings separately to discuss possible benefits and consequences of the investment for Tengtou Village. In the discussion, most representatives believed that the paper project, although profitable, would cause serious environmental pollution in the village and hurt the interests of future generations. Finally, according to the "referendum system of important village affairs", all the villagers voted down the project.

From the dimension of democracy, citizen supervision is undoubtedly the inevitable requirement for citizens to realize democratic rights and ensure the publicity of public power. Power without supervision is bound to become absolute power, and absolute power will definitely lead to absolute corruption, which is the logic of power operation. The essence of democratic politics is that all public powers must be realized on the basis of people' interests, accept powers of the people, use them according to people's wishes and demands, and accept people's supervision on exercise of the powers. The practice of democratic governance at the grassroots level in Zhejiang shows that the important purpose of citizen participation in the operation of democratic politics at the grassroots level is to realize supervision of public power, and on this basis, to perfect the supervision and restriction mechanism governance of public affairs. The innovation of village affairs supervision system in Wuyi County is to solve the problem of villagers' supervision over the villagers' committee. In former governance system arrangements at the village level, democratic supervision is mainly exercised by villagers' meeting. According to the regulations of villagers' autonomy, the villagers' meeting shall be convened and presided over by villagers' committee. This kind of system arrangement in which the meeting of supervisors is convened

Chapter 2 From Election to Governance: New Development of Grassroots Democracy in Zhejiang Province

and presided over by the supervised people will inevitably result in the weakness of power supervision at the village level, which can easily lead to violation and anomie of the power at the village level, and then lead to corruption. Although some villages have also set up financial supervision groups or similar democratic financial management teams, the main leaders of the two village committees often ignore them in their practical work; as a result, these groups find it difficult to impose effective restrictions on the two village committees. Compared to the village financial supervision groups and financial management groups that were established in other places before, the "village affairs supervision committee" in Wuyi County is more reasonable and perfect in system design and arrangement, the core significance of which lies in independence and detachment of the supervision committee. It can be seen in Houchen Village, birthplace of the village supervision committee in Wuyi County, that financial disclosure projects are very detailed in content, every expenditure in the village (such as a packet of cigarettes or a bottle of mineral water purchased for entertainment) must be disclosed truthfully, as well as signed and sealed by the village affairs supervision committee after examination and verification. All invoices shall be checked by the members of the village affairs supervision committee, and the village supervision committee shall be directly responsible for the villagers' meeting, which effectively solves the supervision difficulties existing at the village-level governance for a long time.

2.5.3 Development of democracy at the grassroots level in China "one step ahead"

At present, China is in the process of transition to modernization, so the political construction and the construction of the whole society in the future need to promote democracy and the rule of law. However, China is a country with deeply rooted political tradition of autocracy. Democracy, freedom and the rule of law have not stood still in politics and society, thus the development of democracy in China is a new pioneering undertaking. Therefore, the development of democracy in China is by no means just a simple copy of any existing democratic model in modern times. There is no ready-made experience in history or any model in the world that can be copied without changes, which requires us to explore in practice continuously, to seek democracy that can truly be transformed into practical actions. Although the principle of people's sovereignty is included in constitutions of most countries, in the practice of social governance, it is difficult to transform it into a direct governance scheme, and in the specific process of governance, it is impossible to make it directly appear in the form of democratic governance. The ways to realize democracy must be explored so that it exists not only as an ideal. Since the reform and opening-up, Zhejiang has made fearless innovations closely around the construction of socialist system with Chinese characteristics, and creatively combined with the reality of economic and social development in Zhejiang, forming a "Zhejiang sample", which includes Zhejiang's economic miracles with the development of private economy as the leading factor, and government's governance innovations with democracy and harmony as the main theme, making an exploration for the development of democratic politics with Chinese characteristics.

Achievements in the development of democratic politics at the grassroots level in Zhejiang include not only construction of the political system, but also orientation of the core values of political ideas. A broad consensus has been formed in society on modern political awareness and political concepts such as democracy, freedom, the rule of law and so on, which has become the basic criterion to guide and promote citizens' orderly political participation. With the continuous innovation of democratic governance and citizen participation mechanism at the grassroots level, the grassroots governance system and the governance ability of the grassroots government are obviously improved, and the democratic participation mechanism can resolve all kinds of contradictions and conflicts more and more effectively.

Chapter 2　From Election to Governance: New Development of Grassroots Democracy in Zhejiang Province

The practice in Zhejiang shows that democracy is not only about election and participation in procedure, but also a kind of political life status in which people control their own destiny, a way of life and a kind of substantial social existence. With the advent of the modern network society, governments at all levels in Zhejiang actively comply with the development trend of the times, make full use of the development and popularization of the Internet, which promotes the rise of network democratic participation forms, such as Zhejiang Internet Forum, E-government affairs and television governance. Compared with the traditional democratic model, network democracy has its unique instrumental attributes, which is fictitious, restrictive, more equal, more direct, more interactive and open, and can actively promote the rights of the citizens to political discourse, expand the space for political participation of the citizens, develop participatory democracy, create new ways of citizen supervision, promote the interaction between the officials and the masses, improve public governance and promote the breadth and depth of democracy. Meanwhile, network democracy reduces the cost of citizen participation and the cost of communication and interaction between officials and citizens, which stimulates participation interest of the citizens, promotes flattening of power structure and positive interaction between officials and citizens, innovates supervision mode of the citizens, and greatly encourages local governance reform. It can be predicted that with the development of network public domain, modern discourse democracy based on network technology can become more mature and active, and a new starting point for the development of democratic politics.

The practice of democratic innovation at the grassroots level in Zhejiang also shows that "positive actions" and "good deeds" of the government are the important driving forces to promote the transformation of local governance. From the current political reality in China, the dominant position of the government in governance at the grassroots level cannot be changed, and may be further strengthened with the promotion of comprehensive administration of the party and

Political Participation and Institutional Innovation: A Case Study of Zhejiang

anti-corruption measures. In the reform of governance at the grassroots level in Zhejiang, system construction is always put in the primary position. The government sets up rules and regulations in many aspects, such as organizational construction, financial management, comprehensive management and so on, and makes specific and practical provisions on rights and obligations of the villagers, relations between various organizations at the village level, contents and procedures of democratic management and democratic supervision, so that grassroots governance models such as democratic hearings, democratic talks and village affairs' supervision can be smoothly carried out in a normative and orderly system environment. In addition, the democratic consciousness and positive attitude of government officials often determine the origin and system performance of governance reform. From the practice of democratic governance at the grassroots level in Zhejiang, it can be seen that many system innovations are inseparable from the democratic consciousness and positive actions of government officials. The implementation of some innovation systems will also show different system performance due to the attitude of government officials. The democratic talk is a model of democratic participation at the grassroots level developed by local government leaders through active exploration and continuous innovation on the basis of accidental innovation.

Generally speaking, the starting point of modern democracy is to inquire into the legitimacy of power source of the government in the exercise of the people's sovereignty, and democracy has become an instrumental means to restrict power of the government. If the reason why rulers possess power constitutes the logical starting point of modern democratic politics, then the reason of government's monopolization in the supply of public goods inquired by the governance theory becomes the logical starting point for further development of democratic politics. The true essence of democracy lies in how to truly realize people's control over their own lives and how to exert their due influence and function on social public life, which is a set of system practices that can bring good governance to the

Chapter 2　From Election to Governance: New Development of Grassroots Democracy in Zhejiang Province

country and the society. The practice of democratic innovation in local governance in Zhejiang shows that democracy at the grassroots level, as a social governance mechanism, should be a kind of all-directional and diachronic process democracy, which penetrates into all phases and main links of governance at the grassroots level. Democracy at the grassroots level includes the right to know, to participate, to propose in advance, to make decisions, to supervise during the process, and the right to supervise and deliberate afterward in terms of all major local public affairs. Only by fully implementing these diachronic powers, allowing the people to be the masters of their own affairs and to participate in and take control of grassroots social and public affairs, and improving local governance, can corruption, which is increasingly rampant at the grassroots level, be eliminated and critical crisis of the local society be overcome.

In terms of citizens' political participation, different participation systems in various fields have different system effects, and any single system option is not enough to provide practical guarantee for the development of democratic politics. System innovations of democratic governance at the grassroots level in Zhejiang such as democratic talks and democratic hearings focus on the system supply of villagers' right to know in advance and the right to deliberate in terms of village public affairs; while for the villagers' right to participate and supervise during the process, as well as the right to supervise and deliberate afterward, the case of the supervision committee in Wuyi County provides a good example of system guarantee. The popularity of the Internet, the rise of microblogs, WeChat and various network participation platforms provide the best carriers for the orderly and efficient participation of the masses in the context of the Internet and informed society. Of course, due to the vast territory of China, regional differences, ethnic differences, cultural and religious differences are huge in eastern and western regions, coastal and inland areas; thus, local democratic governance shall also have the characteristic of diversity. As to the innovative practice of promoting citizens' orderly participation in

Political Participation and Institutional Innovation:
A Case Study of Zhejiang

the system in Zhejiang, obviously, it is impossible to cover all the development models of democratic governance at the grassroots level in China; on the contrary, the successful experience of democratic governance in Zhejiang is a successful example that governments at all levels in Zhejiang have explored according to the reality of local democratic governance. In the process of drawing lessons from Zhejiang's experience and promoting democratic governance at the grassroots level, other areas shall take measures adapted to local conditions, actively explore and form a democratic participation model suitable for local governance practices at the grassroots level, and constantly enrich and develop socialist democracy with Chinese characteristics.

Chapter 3

Democratic Consultation: Deliberative Democracy and Local Public Policy

Political Participation and Institutional Innovation: A Case Study of Zhejiang

With the rapid development of industrialization, marketization and urbanization, the social structure and social stratum of contemporary China have undergone great differentiation and reorganization. A number of new social strata, especially the private enterprise owners, appear and form, which inevitably brings about the diversity of interest demands and the complexity of interest differences among different social stakeholders. How to achieve a compromise and balance between pluralistic interests in a pluralistic and diverse society to achieve a win-win situation among all social classes and groups? In this regard, the primary-level democratic form with village committee election as the main content cannot meet the needs of local governance. The problems arising from the democratic election and rural society in various regions highlight the difficulties faced by rural governance and the development of grassroot democratic politics. Deliberative democracy between the government and citizens and other social organizations will bridge the differences and find the balance between the multi-stakeholders, providing a new idea for deepening the development of democracy at the grassroots level and responding to the new problems and new challenges in the process of grassroots social and political development in China. More and more scholars and local officials have realized that to develop China's grassroots democracy, the first is to acknowledge the fact that China's contemporary social interests are highly polarized, recognize the right of different groups to express their interests and make corresponding institutional arrangements for them to exert pressure on the government for pursuing their own interests. The role of the state is to act as a rule-maker and arbiter of conflict. Similarly, in the process of formulating relevant policies to carry out the authoritative distribution of social values, the state must conduct extensive communication and consultation with the social pluralist subjects to strive for consensus. This means that in a society with diversified interests, it is normal for different social groups to have different interests and conflicts of interest. It is also because of this that deliberative democracy is inevitable in social life.

Chapter 3 Democratic Consultation: Deliberative Democracy and Local Public Policy

Just as Jeremy Neill points out, deliberative democracy is an account of legitimacy and participation whose purposes are to produce justifiable political outcomes and to involve the citizens in productive conversations with each other.[1] Although deliberative democracy is of great significance to consolidate and improve the party's leadership, promote scientific and democratic decision-making, promote broad political participation, exercise and cultivate the spirit of citizenship, the British scholar Ian O'Flynn also points out that deliberative democracy provides normative standards that can inform the design of consociational institutions in ways that encourage political leaders to focus on the interests of everyone in society, rather than merely on the interests of their own ethnic group.[2] But how can public consultation mechanism be generated in local governance? What are the problems faced by democratic governance, which is centered on consultation? In the face of the practice of grassroots democracy in China, the application or explanatory power of deliberative democracy is a problem that we need to focus on and discuss in depth. Democratic consultation in Wenling of Zhejiang Province provides a good case for this purpose.

---

[1] Neill, J. Deliberative institutions and conversational participation in liberal democracies. *Social Theory and Practice*, 2013, 39 (3): 7.
[2] O'Flynn, I. Deliberative democracy, the public interest and the consociational model. *Political Studies*, 2010, 58: 572–589.

3.1 Wenling's democratic consultation: Deliberative democracy in local governance

3.1.1 Background introduction

Wenling is located on the southeast coast of Zhejiang Province, the south wing of the Yangtze River Delta region, and the land area of the city is 926 square kilometers. Wenling City is a county-level city with five sub-districts and 11 towns. At the end of 2013, the registered population of Wenling City, which was one of the most densely populated counties in China, was 1,211,000, with 105,000 as agricultural population and nearly 206,000 as non-agricultural population. In March 1994, approved by the state council, the county was set up as Wenling City.

Since the reform and opening-up, Wenling has been developing continuously, rapidly and healthily with a flexible mechanism and enterprising spirit. The comprehensive strength has been continuously strengthened. It has been

Chapter 3　Democratic Consultation:
Deliberative Democracy and Local Public Policy

rated as the National Rural Comprehensive Strength Top 100 County (City), China Star County (City), Advanced County (City) of National Farmers Income and The First Batch of Fairly Well-off County (City) in Zhejiang Province successively. In recent years, township enterprises have gradually become the main force of the whole city's rural economy, and have created the employment opportunities of "leaving the land without leaving hometown, entering the factory without entering the city" for farmers, which has become an important way to solve the problem of surplus rural labor force and increase the peasants' income. In recent years, 4/5th of the total output value of the whole city's rural society, 2/5th of the gross national product, 3/5th of the fiscal revenue, and half of net income increase of the farmers have come from the township enterprises. In the economic form, Wenling is the main subject of the joint-stock cooperative system between individual private and the "independent union of the laborers", and the degree of privatization and marketization is higher. In 2012, the total GDP of Wenling was 70.595 billion yuan, which remained the first among nine counties (cities) in Taizhou in terms of the total GDP. When calculated at comparable prices, it was 7% higher than in 2011. The per capita disposable income of urban residents was 34,444 yuan, a 10% increase over 2011. The per capita net income of rural residents was 16,639 yuan, an increase of 11% over 2011. In 2013, the total output value of Wenling City reached 74.828 billion yuan. In 2013, the total revenue of the city was 7.86 billion yuan, an increase of 8.9% over 2012. Among them, local fiscal revenue was 4.385 billion yuan, an increase of 12.8% over 2012. Local fiscal revenue accounted for 55.8% of total revenue, an increase of 2% over 2012. By 2015, Wenling's GDP reached 83.437 billion yuan, ranking 40th among the top 100 counties (cities) in China in terms of comprehensive strength.

　　In the process of social transformation from traditional agricultural society to modern agriculture and modern industry, the folk customs of Wenling society also show the intersection of modernity and tradition. With the development of the rural market economy and the gradual progress of urbanization, Wenling has an atmosphere of urbanization everywhere, such as highways, luxury residences and majestic buildings. The rapid economic development has absorbed a large number of migrant workers in Wenling City and added new content to local governance. The rural areas of Wenling are not traditional "farming" villages, and the development of market economy has led a small number of villagers to engage in traditional agriculture. Only about a third of the people in Wenling's countryside are engaged in agricultural production, many of them are elders, and the rest are working at home or into business. People are generally engaged in family-owned industrial production. However, there are still some traditional local customs, such as going to the temple on the first day of the New Year to burn incense to worship Buddha and obtaining blessings for the New Year.

3.1.2 The main form and its evolution process of Wenling's democratic consultation

The system of Wenling's democratic consultation initially had different names in various towns and villages, including "civil affairs", "villager democracy day", "farmer's platform" and "civil affair express".

(1) *Emergence of democratic consultation*

In June 1999, in order to implement the spirit of the 15th CPC National Congress and the Third Plenary Session of the 15th CPC Central Committee, according to the arrangement and deployment of CPC Zhejiang Provincial Committee, Taizhou Municipal Party Committee and Municipal Government, Wenling City decided to carry out education activities in agriculture and rural modernization throughout the city. As a pilot, the Publicity Department of Taizhou Municipal Party Committee and the Publicity Department of Wenling Municipal Party Committee jointly held the first session of "agricultural rural modernization forum" themed with "social security" in Songmen Town. The original intention was to avoid the traditional "didactic" propaganda. At that time, the agricultural and rural modernization

Chapter 3   Democratic Consultation:
Deliberative Democracy and Local Public Policy

education (i.e. the farmer's centralized education) had been carried out in Zhejiang Province for 12 consecutive years. Despite the different education content in different periods, it basically held the mobilization meeting first, and then invited some experts or officials to give lessons to the masses. This education method was boring for the masses, and it was difficult to achieve the effect of education. The pilot project of the Publicity Department of Taizhou Municipal Party Committee and Wenling Municipal Party Committee in Songmen Town which was aimed at this problem, tried to "jump out of education but focus on education", hoping to draw the party committee, government and the people close in the way of communication, dialogue and practical affairs. On June 15, the party committee and the government of Songmen Town held the first session of "agricultural and rural modernization education forum", which aimed to "promote the construction of villages and towns and improve the appearance of towns and villages". What the local government did not anticipate was that in contrast to the villagers' resistance and indifference in the ideological and political work in the past, the enthusiasm of the masses was very high in this education forum, which received unexpected good results. More than 150 people spontaneously came to participate in the forum to express their own views or requirements on the investment environment, the construction planning of villages and towns, the price of liquefied gas and the neighborhood disputes. The town leader answered more than half of the questions on the spot, gave detailed explanations for the problems that were not solved on the spot, or promised specific solutions and time. This new way of communication has received enthusiastic response from the masses. Subsequently, the local government held another four education forum activities. The total number of people who volunteered to participate was more than 600, with more than 100 questions raised, of which more than 80 were explained and answered on the spot, and more than 20 were committed to be handled. The "Education forum" was also called the "focus interview" by the local people.

Political Participation and Institutional Innovation:
A Case Study of Zhejiang

The "agricultural and rural modernization education forum" in Songmen Town was the embryonic form of the democracy in Wenling City. In essence, it was a dialogue mechanism between the government and the villagers, and the public commented and made suggestions on the work of the government, or requested for solutions to the problems of the individuals and individual enterprises. During this period, the scope of the issues discussed was broader. The development problems of agriculture, fishery, industry, primary industry, secondary industry and tertiary industry were mainly discussed. Urban constructions, road traffic, environmental hygiene, social security, school education, family planning and so on were also frequently discussed by villagers.

In August 2000, the municipal party committee held a meeting in Songmen Town, and organized various townships, sub-districts and municipal government departments to inspect and learn, required the whole area to promote the experience of Songmen, and extend the range of activities to non-public enterprises, urban communities, public institutions and municipal government departments. The success of the "agriculture and rural modernization education forum" in Songmen Town has greatly inspired the democratic innovation practice in other towns and villages in Wenling, thus mobilizing the enthusiasm of ordinary people to participate in the political affairs. After the promotion of the Publicity Department of Wenling Municipal Party Committee, there were various forms of democratic communication and democratic dialogue in the whole city, including "civil affairs", "referendum system of village affairs", "people's night talks", "convenience service platform", "rural democracy day", "farmers' platform" and "grassroots democracy forum". Although the names were different, the form and the content were similar to Songmen Town's "agricultural rural modernization education forum", which adopted the method of face-to-face consultation between leading cadres and the people, made decisions or commitments on issues of interest to the masses, and solved the practical problems of the masses. In order to further standardize and deepen these forms of deliberative democracy,

Chapter 3 Democratic Consultation: Deliberative Democracy and Local Public Policy

the Wenling Municipal Party Committee decided in 2001 to refer to it as the democratic consultation.

A review of the generation process of Wenling's democratic consultation can reveal a fact that is easy to be ignored or misread. That is, Wenling's democratic consultation was not a deliberate innovation by the local government to develop grassroots democracy. In particular, prior to the unification of various forum innovative forms by the Wenling Municipal Party Committee, the word "democracy" didn't come up very often, either from the minutes of the meeting or from the government's publicity language. Therefore, unlike other forms of the construction of democracy at the grassroots level to explore innovative form, the original intention of democratic consultation was only "an innovative carrier of the ideological and political work", and it's local government's response to the situation in the grassroots governance. As for democracy, it was soon combined with democracy at the grassroots level, which could be regarded as being conformed to the trend by the local government in the grassroots political work.

(2) Development of democratic consultation

If the primary focus of democratic consultation was the word "consultation", in the course of the following development, the focus on democratic consultation began to shift to "democracy". From December 25 to 26, 2000, Wenling Municipal Party Committee, Zhejiang Provincial Party Committee and *Zhejiang Daily* newspaper jointly held a "seminar on strengthening and improving rural ideological and political work with democratic methods". After attending the democratic consultation meeting in Songmen Town, the experts' attention to democracy and the excitement at the same time shifted from rural ideological and political work to grassroots democracy, giving democracy a new value and meaning.

The deepening of democratic consultation has preserved the initial form of dialogue, focusing on exploring how to expand democracy at the grassroots level, organizing and guiding the broad participation of the masses in decision-making, management and supervision of public affairs. For example, in June 2001, the democratic consultation on the theme of "Muyu Park construction" was held in Muyu Town. More than 80 people discussed the construction plan of Muyu Mountain Park and put forward 35 valuable opinions and suggestions, which involved the park's architectural style, scenic spot setting and layout, main buildings and supporting facilities and other important issues. The township government invited experts from the Urban Construction Planning Institute of Wuhan City, Hubei Province, to discuss and demonstrate the proposals and adopted 17 rules, which have greatly improved the park construction plan. For purpose of procedures, democratic consultation is generally chaired by the party committee, inviting local people's congresses, relevant social interest groups and people involved in decision-making matters, with other people voluntarily participating. Preliminary views and proposals were put forward by the government. After listening to the opinions, views and demands of the masses, the party committee and the government made preliminary decisions through collective research, and then gave feedback to the public to solicit public opinions again. For matters on which the majority of the masses objected or disagreed, they reproved or postponed the decision; after further investigation and research, they fully considered and absorbed the reasonable requirements and suggestions of the masses, and made corresponding changes or adjustments before making the decision. The implementation process and results of the decision were supervised by the presidium of the town people's congress.

With the continuous improvement and perfection of the practice of democracy, the new form of democratic politics was gradually developing from general communication focusing on individual interests and specific issues at the beginning into centralized consultation concerning some problems of public interests locally; from the one-way publicity of the ruling party's guideline and policies to the interactive exchanges between the local party committee, the government and the

Chapter 3 Democratic Consultation: Deliberative Democracy and Local Public Policy

public, then developed to consciously guide the masses to change their ideas, strengthen the democratic consciousness of the masses, and cultivate the people's participation in politics and consultant activities. On the whole, the further development of Wenling's democratic consultation was mainly embodied in the following aspects: First of all, democratic consultation was conducted at multiple levels and in an all-round way. After the unification of grassroots democratic innovation carriers with different names and forms into "democratic consultation", it began to extend vertically and horizontally across all levels and fields of Wenling. Not only were the towns, sub-districts, villages and residents' communities in full swing, but grassroots institutions, party and government organs, and mass organizations have all made vigorous efforts to promote democratic consultation. Second, the theme of the consultation was centralizing, and the discussion was more in-depth. In the early days of democratic consultation, the themes of the talks were generally broad, and they could be discussed on the spot as long as they were of concern to the masses. However, it was not possible to solve all the problems at one time, and many of the subjects that really needed to be discussed were easily ignored. After Wenling Municipal Party Committee issued A Number of Provisions on "Democratic Consultation" (Trial), there were clear rules on the scope of democratic consultation issues, including economic and social development planning, government investment of large construction projects, public welfare undertakings, community culture construction, villagers' contracted land changes and other local major matters or matters involving the interests of the broad masses. The clarity and centralization of the issue became a platform for communication between the masses and between the masses and cadres, so that the discussion among the participants would focus on solving a certain issue. Sometimes the government would investigate and study the issues, put forward several alternative preliminary schemes, and then submit to the conference to discuss, which had strong pertinence, effectiveness and improved citizen participation. Wenqiao Town of Wenling City, in 2001, adopted a form of consultation, which was mainly about the following: "the masses propose issues and the government focuses on implementation". The content of the consultation was mainly the focus of local work and various outstanding issues as well as the hot issues of special attention and social response. After deciding the issues, the government should, prior to the first week of the conference, publish the theme, time and place of the consultation conference and the precautions of the meeting in a proper form. The masses volunteered for participation, free discussion and free questioning. The leading cadres of the relevant departments in the town should give replies, solve or explain on the spot, and the matter that could not be decided on the spot should be clearly committed with the deadline.

From the perspective of the form and efficacy of democratic consultation, it could be said to be a kind of "consultative inquiry" democratic consultation in this period. The focus was on consultation, discussion and questioning. The main aim was to obtain relevant information and listen to the public. The main characteristics of the "consultative inquiry" democratic consultation are as follows: (1) The procedure was relatively simple. After the speaker briefly introduced the topic, the villagers discussed the issue or questioned the leaders. (2) The form was flexible and could be held at all levels, with fewer restrictions on the number of participants. (3) The result of the consultation was uncertain: Public opinion representativeness of participants was difficult to determine; there was a lack of quantitative analysis tools for controversial issues; there was a lack of guarantee mechanism to discuss the results, and the presider has the final decision on whether to adopt the results or not.

(3) *The deepening of democratic consultation*

The essence of Wenling's democratic consultation was a form of public participation in public affairs under the leadership of the ruling party. Its purpose was to establish effective democratic decision-making, democratic management and democratic supervision mechanism, and realize the transformation from "government sovereignty" to "citizen

Chapter 3 Democratic Consultation:
Deliberative Democracy and Local Public Policy

sovereignty". The deepening process of democratic consultation was the process of deepening the democratic governance at the grassroots level. As a form of grassroots democracy, democratic consultation was mainly derived from the democratic demands of grassroots people and the practice and innovation impulse of grassroots officials. It was the natural growth of institutional arrangements outside the system lacking support of realistic legal basis. This related to the coordinations between democratic consultation and the laws, regulations and existing specific systems of the state. The main problem is how to coordinate with the grassroots legal power structure such as the people's congress system and the villagers' representative system.

How to integrate citizen participation into the existing political system and improve the political validity of citizen participation? This is the main problem faced by democratic consultation in its development. The successful experience of Wenling's democratic consultation in practical exploration was to combine democratic consultation with the decision-making mechanism of grassroots people's congresses. The Constitution of the People's Republic of China stipulates that the people's congress is the supreme organ of power. The Organization Law of Villagers' Committee stipulates that the villagers' assembly is the highest decision-making organ of villagers' autonomy and the supervision organ of the village committee. If the public consultation is not involved in the existing political system, it can only stay in a "public opinion research" approach. In the deepening process of democratic consultation, Wenling actively seeks the combination with the grassroots people's congress or the villagers' congress. The results of democratic consultation may be submitted to the villagers' congress or the people's congress at the same level for a vote. Typical example is the town construction pre-election democratic consultation held every year since 2005 in Zeguo Town. After thorough consultation and discussion of the villagers, the urban construction budget plan of the year was formed. The town government directly presented the proposal of the democratic consultation as a bill, and submitted a vote in the subsequent town council.

Political Participation and Institutional Innovation:
A Case Study of Zhejiang

Since July 2005, the financial budget review consultation conference of the people's congress in Xinhe Town, Wenling, has directly brought democratic consultation to the people's congress's deliberative process. From 2005 to 2015, Xinhe Town's "deliberative democracy" consultation had been continuously developing, formed the people's congress's budget financial group, and delegated the right to amend the bill when there were more than five people's congress deputies. In February 2008, this "democratic deliberative" democracy began to be popularized in many of the people's congresses in the townships and towns of Wenling. Therefore, it integrated democratic consultation outside the system into the existing institutional framework, and gradually moved toward institutionalization, routinization and standardization.

3.1.3 Democratic meaning of democratic consultation

The practice of Wenling's democratic consultation shows us the democratic meaning of local governance.

The first is to make democratic decisions in the expression and aggregation of public opinions. In order to realize the full expression and aggregation of public opinions, it is crucial to ensure the fairness, justice and authenticity of the civil consultation process in the decision-making process. From the perspective of liberal theory, the process of the formation of democratic opinions and wills manifests itself only as a compromise among different interests. They should ensure the fairness of the outcome through universal suffrage, representative system and its operational procedures. The republicanism theory emphasizes that the process of the formation of democratic opinions and wills should be expressed as a moral self-understanding. The mode of deliberative democracy has absorbed some elements of liberalism and republicanism, and it seeks to combine realistic compromise with the moral self-discipline of the subject with an ideal negotiation and decision-making process. This means that the formation of democracy

Chapter 3 Democratic Consultation: Deliberative Democracy and Local Public Policy

is based on consultation and engagement rather than power and closure. At the same time, as a democratic decision, it is not just to point out the interaction between citizens and government in the decision-making process, but also to solve the problem of how to interact. Therefore, the major problems to be solved in the development and perfection of democracy in Wenling are how the government interacts with society and how to maximize the objectivity, fairness and authenticity of civic participation, that is, to solve the problem of content, method, degree and magnitude of interaction. Wenling's democratic consultation conference has the characteristics of broad content, many subjects and large amplitude. Not only do the townships, towns and villages, but also the residents' committee, the functional departments of the government, enterprises, public institutions and so on carry out various kinds of consultation activities. The topics include politics, economics, society and education. For example, the consultation of Wenqiao Town regarding "school network adjustment", "site selection of the cremated remains", "Qianyang block planning and revision", "democratic hearing of town general planning and revision", "democratic hearing of school network adjustment" in Songmen Town, "outdoor market relocation democratic consultation" and "democratic consultation for public budgets of town construction" in Zeguo Town and "democratic consultation for public finance budgets" and so on in Xinhe Town. Through multiple forms of democracy system provided by the democratic consultation, ordinary villagers' opinions and interests can be expressed, and the problems reflected could be solved on time or noticed by the government. People can participate in multiple levels of the democracy, and realize their needs through multiple channels and varying degrees of participation. If it is a question of universality, they can choose to make the same voice in a collective way, which reflects more intensity and is more likely to receive the support of other people and the attention of the government.

The core and key points of Wenling's democratic consultation are the important issues involving the people's livelihood, the most important of which is the rural major public affairs at the town and village levels. Democratic consultation at the village and town levels has become necessary and is required for the democratic decision-making of important government and village affairs. If the issues or plans proposed by the government or the village committee are opposed by the majority of the people, or there are more different opinions, or the conflict of views is more serious, the two committees of the local government or village will generally take a temporary suspension, postpone the determination or decision, and hold the meeting again after adjustment and improvement to make corresponding determination or decisions. For example, in 2002, at the democratic consultation for school layout adjustment in Songmen Town, the local government made greater adjustment to the original plan based on the deliberative democracy, which reflects the important role of public opinion in government decision-making. By presenting important matters to the public for discussion or decision, the previous decision-making process by a few leaders has been changed, making government decisions more transparent. The participation of the masses in the demonstration or vote for the outcome of the meeting is an effective way to reflect and represent the interests and wishes of the majority of the local people.

How to deal with the relationship between the interest of the government and that of the people in the democratic decision-making is another important question facing Wenling's democratic consultation. That is, the degree of the benefits expressed by the people could be brought out by the exchange of interests between the people and the government. Although, from the point of view of what it should be, except for the interests of the people, the government has no special interests of its own. The contradiction between the interests of the government and the interests of the people can be regarded as the contradiction between the long-term interests of the people themselves and the present interests, the overall interests and the local interests. But the reality is far from simple, the conflict of interests between local government and the people is an undeniable fact. A large part of

Chapter 3 Democratic Consultation: Deliberative Democracy and Local Public Policy

the contradiction is between the special interests of the government departments and the interests of the people, because local government occupies the dominant position in the rural social power structure, while the people are always on the weak side in the game of interest. Therefore, it also determines the recurrence and long-term nature of this interest game. Democratic decision-making is made in the form of democratic consultation, and the decision of important matters is changed from the original black box operation into a sunshine decision. To some extent, it can restrain the interests of power and privilege, make the decision-making process of government implement the spirit of democracy, and realize the exchange of interests between the government and the people in the decision-making of the government. Such decisions are more likely to strike a balance between the interests of the government and the interests of the people. From the wishes of the people, of course, it is hoped that each transaction can achieve its own interests to the maximum extent, but in fact it is very difficult to realize. In the exchange of interests embodied in democratic decision-making, it is impossible to achieve the interests of the people by a large margin each time. At the same time, it is not possible for governments to completely lose their special interests. One of the aims of democratic consultation is to effectively restrict the special interest orientation of government departments. By establishing a relatively smooth people's condition, public opinion channel and civil service network between the government and the public, the people's interest demands can be realized in administrative villages, towns and other levels.

Second, it shall realize democratic management in the primary exploration of multi-center governance. Since the World Bank first used the term "governance crisis" in its report in 1989, the term "governance" has been widely used in political development studies. In modern political theory, governance is different from ruling, and governance emphasizes the positive interaction between state and society through democratic participation. It is a kind of activity supported by common goals, and the participants of these activities are not necessarily the

Political Participation and Institutional Innovation:
A Case Study of Zhejiang

government, or not only the government, but also not realized mainly by the coercive force of the state. Since the 1990s, due to the dual dilemma of market failure and government failure of allocation of social resources, the theory of government governance has gradually replaced the traditional theory of political governance and gained wide attention from the international community.

The development goal of social governance is "good governance". As political power shifts from political to civil society, government power will be limited and national functions will be reduced gradually. But that does not mean the disappearance of public authority. It is only that this kind of public authority is increasingly based on the good governance of the cooperation between government and citizens, which is the necessary result of the process of social democratization. Good governance shows the nature and state of social order and authority being consciously recognized and obeyed. In this state, national policies have very high political legitimacy. And this legitimacy is based on the timely and responsible response of public administrators and management agencies to citizens' demands, the disclosure of political information, the degree of accountability of managers for their actions and the general participation of citizens in the process of social governance.

Wenling's democratic consultation is an active exploration for the realization of a society with good governance. Its implementation is to change the traditional way of political control. In "consultative inquiry" democratic consultation, the villagers can question the government about their concerns, ask the government to give explanations, and offer their own views and opinions on rural public affairs. And the government seeks the villagers' understanding and support in the consultation and interaction with the villagers. In "Public opinion polls" democratic consultation, the government of Zeguo Town has directly selected the villagers' consultation results as the selection criteria for the urban construction pre-selection project, which reflects the important

Chapter 3 Democratic Consultation:
Deliberative Democracy and Local Public Policy

value and role of public opinion in the governance of rural public affairs.

In the concept of democratic consultation, it regards good social governance as a cooperative process between government and social forces, tries to build a democratic process for managing public affairs, regards the participation of citizens in public policy as a new realistic form of contemporary democracy so as to overcome the inevitable deviation in the traditional principal–agent relationship. With the advance of democracy, some third sector organizations also began to play a certain role in local governance. For example, the union and the government of Xinhe Town held a labor democratic consultation regarding disputes between local workers and enterprises. Through an equal, free debate and negotiation process, the general will of citizens can influence government decision-making to a certain extent, thus enhancing its position and function in local governance. At the same time, democratic consultation implements public affairs management mainly through cooperation, consultation, partnership, establishment of common goals and other means. Therefore, the running of public power and civil rights is diversified and mutual, which is a management process of top–bottom interaction and multi-directional communication. All these are the preliminary exploration significance to the formation of the rural multi-center governance system.

Finally, the democratic supervision function can be realized by improving the transparency of public power operation. The political foundation of democratic supervision system is the power of civil rights and the formation of civil society. It is of vital significance to the citizens to enjoy the necessary political rights and political means. For various reasons, individual participation and decentralized participation are the main forms of political life for ordinary citizens in traditional Chinese citizens' political participation. On the one hand, the government is struggling to deal with various interest demands, but cannot accurately grasp the true orientation of the public opinion, thus,

Political Participation and Institutional Innovation:
A Case Study of Zhejiang

the interests of the people cannot be targeted. On the other hand, the influence of lack of collective participation by individual forces is also extremely weak over government decisions. Especially in the "state-social" structural system, which is in the contrast of power, it is difficult for such decentralized citizens to participate in democratic participation. In a certain sense, democratic consultation will bring together the individual strength of citizens, and through institutionalization, the effective restriction and supervision of citizens will be formed. Democratic consultation listing system requires green express personnel to conduct classification, numbering, registration, summarizing and sorting out, and submitting to the main leaders of the town on the day of delivery for opinions for issuance and listing the questions proposed by the people for solution over democratic consultation, matters reflected through green express for implementation, letters from the masses, calls, visits, matters referred by higher authorities and other issues reflected through other means. The contractor should deal with the matters accepted seriously, promptly and impartially. The result will be transmitted to the person concerned and signed by the relevant parties. If the party concerned expresses satisfaction with the result, it will cancel the number, otherwise it will reschedule the case as dissatisfied until satisfied. Some departments also report to the public opinion representatives on the implementation of the results of democratic consultation in the form of letters. Through the implementation of this series of democratic consultation supporting systems, the democratic supervision function of democratic consultation was implemented to some extent.

The outcome of democratic consultation concerns the question of how the public views the issue of democracy, as well as its effects. That is, whether citizens can effectively realize the restriction of government and the satisfaction of their own interests in the activities of deliberative democracy. It is necessary to strengthen the construction of the democratic supervision system to realize the effective restriction of citizens to the government, and carry out the system and measures

Chapter 3　Democratic Consultation: Deliberative Democracy and Local Public Policy

of democratic supervision to the whole process of power operation, establish a coordinated and interactive mechanism for democratic supervision and other forms of decision-making and give full play to the overall function of the supervision system. In the process of Wenling's democratic consultation, the realization of villagers' right to participate and the right to know is in essence the necessary guarantee for the effective supervision and restriction of the villagers. Democratic supervision can guarantee the effective exercise of power according to the will of the people and prevent the corruption of power. However, the successful implementation of democratic supervision is not easy. It involves various factors, such as the national political system, the operation mechanism of local governments and the degree of social organization. To implement effective democratic supervision, it is necessary to improve China's existing people's congresses, judicial supervision and administrative supervision, strengthen the restriction of power, strengthen the restriction of the people's power and make the people's regular democratic supervision of the government become scientific and institutionalized. Over the consultation, the villagers' comprehensive and extensive questioning of the government's work can make the public power transparent to a certain extent. Especially in the "deliberative" democratic consultation, the people's congress's deputies can ask the government to elaborate on the budget and adopt the financial group to implement the regular supervision of the government's financial operation. In order to implement democratic supervision function of democratic consultation, Wenling has also further improved the normal mechanism of democratic consultation activities and established the working system of the green express, the listing system of democratic consultation, engineering supervision group and other democratic feedback supervision mechanisms. Through the implementation of this series of systems, the democratic supervision function of democratic consultation is embodied, and democratic consultation becomes a new form of democratic supervision.

3.2 Participative budge consultation: Exploration of practice of deliberative democracy in Wenling

The contradiction between the growing awareness of citizens' desire to participate in social governance and the lack of channels for participation within the existing system have led to democratic consultation system in Wenling. After years of practice, the democratic consultation system has encouraged grassroots officials to abandon the traditional paternalistic leadership and work style. At the level of governance, the one-way management mode of "I command you to execute" is being transformed into a new type of grassroots social governance model with the masses, common management and two-way interaction. At the same time, with the awakening of civil rights consciousness, when people's participation demands cannot be legally satisfied, many will turn to non-institutional involvement outside the system, which could threaten social stability. How do we promote citizens' orderly political participation, and

Chapter 3　Democratic Consultation: Deliberative Democracy and Local Public Policy

let citizens participate in local public affairs and social governance? This is a major issue for governments everywhere, especially in economically developed regions. It has been adjusted and improved for nearly 10 years since the establishment of democratic consultation. It has been proved that Wenling's democratic consultation plays an indispensable role in the local democratic politics. Democratic consultation has become an important link between the government and social interaction in Wenling City and the whole Taizhou area. It is also widely believed by domestic scholars that democratic consultation provides a new platform for the masses to participate in the democratic management of grassroots social affairs. With the help of the new carrier of democratic politics, the masses have participated in various forms of political participation and consultation, and the democratic management ability of their own affairs has been gradually improved. But we should also see that, due to various reasons, for the new grassroots governance mode in practice, there are many bottlenecks, and in the further development, there are many insurmountable institutional obstacles.

First, how do we implement the fruits of democratic consultation and prevent it from becoming the democratic show of the government? How to prevent some grassroots party and government leaders from becoming an ornament and a cover for assessment? At the same time, the issues and agendas that are often determined by democratic leaders are easily influenced by the preferences of the organizers, which will make democratic consultation uncertain. In addition, democratic policy-making procedures need to be standardized. For the issues raised over democratic consultation, the organizer can make decisions on the spot, or not. When making a decision, how does the organizer absorb the public opinion of the conference, and decide by individual judgment or group discussion? There are no specific rules.

Second, how do we identify the function of democratic discourse? To develop democracy, we must correctly identify its function. Some scholars believe that the function of democratic consultation cannot be overrated, and it should be defined as "a mechanism for improving the inadequacy of public opinion". That is, to position it at the governance level. But some scholars argue that democratic consultation essentially gives rural autonomy a democratic component. To some extent, it is a realization form of grassroots democracy, and it needs to identify its function from the perspective of improving grassroots democracy. The differences in the functional orientation of democratic consultation will have a substantial impact on the content and procedures of democratic consultation. As a kind of innovation outside the system, when positioning too high, it is obviously not in line with the practice of grassroots management; when positioning too low, it is easy to overlook the value that it should have.

Third, how do we better realize the combination of democratic consultation and the existing system so as to avoid the phenomenon of "politics disappears when someone is gone"? Although Wenling's democratic consultation has been practiced for many years, its development and improvement are largely dependent on the innovative ideas and democratic consciousness led by the grassroots government. But the promotion by partial leadership cannot last. A realistic problem is that some towns and villages have been silencing their democratic consultation with the change of leadership. In particular, some grassroots practitioners are accustomed to using simple methods to make decisions in long-term political practice. The standard procedural democratic consultation is barely existent due to either lack of motivation or lack of practical experience. As a result, grassroots practitioners need more training to master and skillfully use the democratic consultation approach.

Fourth, how do we further improve democratic consultation technically? How to enhance the representativeness of the public opinion and the scientific nature of the choice of the representative? In the process of democratic consultation development, there is always

Chapter 3 Democratic Consultation: Deliberative Democracy and Local Public Policy

a difficult choice: The increase in the number of public opinion representatives means a reduction in the time and opportunity for each representative to speak. In general, there are a few dozen or many hundreds of people participating in democratic consultation. It is difficult to ensure that all delegates, or most delegates, are fully represented in a short half-day or one-day agenda. Through the observation of democratic consultation in Songmen and Ruoheng, it can be found that due to time constraints, on average, only 10–20 representatives of the democratic consultation have the opportunity to speak. Therefore, an urgent problem is how to increase the opportunities for expression of public opinion as much as possible during the limited discussion. In addition, the choice of participating in democratic consultation activities is also a problem that cannot be ignored. The main traditional way is voluntary participation. This has had a negative effect in practice. That is, the participants are basically those who have a close interest in the content of the consultation, thus it is easy to form a one-sided trend of the interests of the minority and distort the public interests. For example, over the school network adjustment consultation in Wenqiao Town, most of the objection came from the vendors and the owners next to the Qingyu Middle School. They urged other parents to oppose the adjustment on the basis of their own narrow self-interest. In this case, the government's timely and flexible decision avoided the possibility of confrontation or even conflict between the government and the villagers, but how to ensure the universality, scientificity and authenticity of the delegates to the democratic consultation is a question that the organizers must face.

In order to solve these problems in the development of democratic consultation, some villages and towns in Wenling City have actively explored and innovated. Among them, the most notable is the recent democratic consultation practice of Zeguo Town and Xinhe Town. A comprehensive analysis of the typical cases of the two places will be conducted, namely democratic consultation of Zeguo Town pre-selection project for urban construction and democratic consultation of Xinhe Town finance budget.

3.2.1 Democratic consultation of Zeguo Town pre-selection project for urban construction in 2006

Zeguo Town is located in the northwest of Wenling City. The town covers an area of 63.12 square kilometers, with jurisdiction over 97 villages, a permanent population of 120,000 and a floating population of over 150,000. In Zeguo Town, industry development was relatively rapid. In 2005, the total industrial and agricultural output value of the whole town was 15.77 billion yuan, of which the industrial output value was 15.502 billion yuan, and the per capita net income of farmers was 10,551 yuan. It ranked 145th in the country's 20,000 small towns in terms of comprehensive development.

(1) Basic process of democratic consultation of Zeguo Town pre-selection project for urban construction in 2006

The topic and task of "Democratic Consultation of Zeguo Town Pre-selection Project for Urban Construction" was to organize public representatives with broad representation, conduct full dialogue and consultation with the government and relevant experts and assist local government to make rational decisions on the selection of urban construction projects in 2006 on the basis of the collected representative public opinions. The consultation was to focus on the 38 projects of seven categories for the town building in 2006, including urban and rural planning, road, bridge and environmental construction. These projects were expected to require a total of 98.96 million yuan. However, in 2006, there were only 50 million yuan budgeted for the construction of the above projects. So it was needed to hear the public opinion on these projects through this democratic consultation and 5–10% of the money was drawn up for projects that the public opinion was strongly demanding. On the morning of March 20, 2006, the consultation was held in the great hall of the Second Middle School in Zeyang Town, Wenling City. The main leaders of the town, the leaders of the relevant functional departments, 249 villagers' representatives, and many experts and scholars who were invited attended the consultation. Among the 249 villagers, 237 were selected from the permanent resident population of the town by random

Chapter 3 Democratic Consultation:
Deliberative Democracy and Local Public Policy

sampling based on 2% proportion and the other 12 delegates were randomly selected from migrant workers. Specifically, there were three stages in this democratic consultation with duration of each stage explained.

Preparatory phase

(1) According to the development needs of the town, the village and township construction office proposed the next annual urban construction pre-selection project.

(2) The government had held symposiums in various aspects such as people's congress deputies and CPPCC members to listen to the opinions and suggestions of the next year's urban construction pre-selection projects.

(3) The town team listened to all aspects of the situation and prepared the preliminary plan for the annual urban construction pre-selection project.

(4) The village and township construction office invited professional personnel to conduct feasibility study on the primary plan, and provided the project cost budget and detailed instruction.

(5) The village and township construction office drew up a preliminary list of urban infrastructure construction.

(6) The democratic consultation team designed the first and second urban construction pre-selection project questionnaire according to the preliminary list of urban infrastructure construction. (The second questionnaire was basically consistent with the first questionnaire, but the latter part increased the content of the feedback to the democratic consultation.)

(7) According to 2% of the population of each village, the number of deputies to the village was generated. It compiled a list of villagers over the age of 18 and produced a representative in the form of random sampling; the representative was selected randomly among migrant

workers from the sized enterprise; the presidium of the town people's congress recommended five people's congress supervisors.

(8) The first public opinion questionnaire was printed and sent to the representative's house by the cadres of the village.

(9) An introduction to the background, practice and significance of the consultation was written. The introduction, urban infrastructure construction pre-selected project table, project description materials, and urban master plan were bound together and distributed to each public opinion representative and participative representative and field surveys were organized.

(10) Thirty-two teachers were selected from primary and secondary schools to serve as moderators and team members of the democratic forum, and relevant trainings were conducted for them.

(11) Drawing lots were printed.

Convening stage

The two-round group discussion program was adopted for this consultation. That is, including two cycles of meetings and group discussion. The entire agenda was as follows:

Duration		Content
Morning	7:50	Participants check in and take the number
	8:00–8:40	Consultation related to the meeting
	8:45–9:15	The preparatory meeting
	9:15–10:30	Hold the first consultation and carry out group discussion
	10:40–11:40	Hold the first meeting consultation and carry out the first meeting discussion
Afternoon	12:30–14:20	Hold the second consultation and carry out group discussion
	14:30–16:00	Hold the second meeting consultation and carry out the second meeting discussion
	16:00–16:30	Group discussion, fill out questionnaire

Chapter 3 Democratic Consultation:
Deliberative Democracy and Local Public Policy

During the group discussion, the chairman of each group shall bring their representatives to the panel discussion venue and the staff members shall distribute drawing lots to each group. The recorder shall record the statements of the representatives in detail. At the end of the session, the panel shall recommend three representatives who could focus on the views of the members of the panel at the meeting. The recorder shall fill in the speech drawing lots of the meeting and present to the host.

Subsequent stage

(1) According to the results of the questionnaire survey, the order from the most important to the least important was concluded for the urban construction pre-selection projects.

(2) The government office meeting is held and a preliminary project plan is made according to the questionnaire results.

(3) The town government shall form a representative bill for the primary plan to be considered by the people's congress. According to the vote of the people's congress, the general assembly resolution shall be formed.

(4) The democratic consultation feedback letter of the urban construction primary project shall be drawn up, which shall be distributed by each village cadre to the public opinion representatives to listen to the opinions of the representatives.

(5) The government shall organize implementation, and the town council shall elect five deputies as supervisors to supervise the implementation of construction projects, project quality and tendering procedures involved in the democratic consultation.

(6) The completion of the construction project shall be reported to each representative before the next democratic consultation.

Political Participation and Institutional Innovation: A Case Study of Zhejiang

(2) *Characteristics of democratic consultation in Zeguo Town*

This democratic consultation had great innovation in content and form, which was manifested in the following aspects.

First, full preparations had been made before the consultation. It could be learned from what the government had done in the preparation stage mentioned above, in order to get the villagers involved in the consultation to know about the pre-selection projects of the town construction in 2006, local government made a representative visit and distributed the basic materials to the public opinion representatives; held the pre-selected project explanation meeting, explained the project in detail, arranged the public opinion representative to conduct field investigation, carried out the questionnaire survey, etc., letting the representatives have sufficient time to understand the content and background of the meeting, so as to lay a solid foundation for improving the quality of the villagers in the consultation and provide the basis for the analysis of the comparison and summarization after the consultation.

Second, to implement a group discussion to address the limitations of speaking at the meeting. Two rounds of meeting and group discussions were held at the democratic consultation for the town construction pre-selection projects in 2006. Its main purpose was to solve the problem of the adequacy of consultations, so that each participant could get a better chance to express their views. In group discussions, the group host was a third-party neutral personnel (mostly Zeguo Town high school teachers), and trained in advance, to ensure that the host fairly, impartially and effectively organized the group discussion. The 16 groups were divided into eight "regular groups" and eight "rational groups", with 13–15 persons per group. In the group discussion of the regular group, the host was asked to play a secondary role. It would be freely discussed by the villagers and the atmosphere of discussion was more relaxed. For the rational group, the host was required to grasp the discussion process, consider the pros and cons, and ask the villagers to give reasons and grounds for their opinions.

Chapter 3 Democratic Consultation:
Deliberative Democracy and Local Public Policy

Third, the previous invitation and voluntary registration methods were canceled for the public opinion representatives, who were selected all by random sampling. In previous democratic consultation activities, the main participants were the invited people's congress deputies, CPPCC members, heads of various units, representatives of relevant interest groups and experts and scholars. As a result of the principle of voluntary participation, participants could actually fall into two categories: The invited representatives and the people who have a close interest in the consultation. To a certain extent, there is not enough representation of the participants, and it is difficult to reflect the general opinions of the broad masses of all strata in the society. Considering that the traditional invitation method may damage the representativeness and impartiality of the representatives, this democratic consultation selected delegates randomly in a similar lottery. The biggest advantage was that it was easy to understand and inexpensive. In the end, 249 public opinion representatives were selected from over 120,000 people in the town by random sampling. Therefore, its representativeness was more real and reliable.

(3) *Thinking over relevant issues of democratic consultation in Zeguo Town*

(1) Cost of democratic consultation. In total, the town spent about 80,000 yuan to complete the democratic consultation. Of course, because of the good economic development of the town, this expenditure did not constitute a burden to the town government. But for poor areas, especially those that are struggling to keep the government running properly, such a sum would be a heavy burden to the local governments and farmers, which would undoubtedly exacerbate the already struggling financial situation in towns and villages. The question of the cost is the primary issue facing the promotion of democratic consultation in the other regions. Thus, in terms of funding and workload, the democratic consultation approach can be used to address major issues such as budget formulation, environmental regulation and welfare distribution.

(2) Although the method of random sampling is fair, it brings the problem of low level of representation. It is likely to prevent those with enthusiasm and knowledge from joining the ranks of representatives. There is also the underrepresentation of relevant interest groups: When the subject of democratic consultation is concerned with a particular interest group, the group should have enough representatives, or it will be easy for the majority to disconsider the interests of the minority. Some democratic parties may have this situation: The real stakeholders do not attend the meeting, or only the stakeholders are present, and there is no objective neutral third party. Therefore, it is the key to balance between ensuring fairness and scientificity and avoiding bias and being manipulated by interest groups. To this, some scholars put forward that the generation of elected representatives should not be simply based on random sampling, and should use stratified random sampling, according to the representative's gender, age, occupation, education, etc.

(3) The difference in power structure is the main obstacle to the further development of Wenling's democratic consultation. After years of continuous development and improvement, Wenling's democratic consultation has preliminarily formed a network system and system carrier of grassroots democratic political practice. The change of social structure brought about by Wenling's democratic consultation is inevitably exerting the pressure and impact on the traditional political system and power structure. In turn, Wenling's democratic consultation about its own development is limited by the reality of traditional power structure. Democratic consultation has profound democratic values. To introduce such a method is to actually change the authoritative political culture of a long period of time, and create a change of the path of the political structure. At present, the main way adopted in democratic consultation in Wenling to remove this obstacle is to build the whole set of procedures and regulations, to ensure the fairness and justice of the democratic process, to reduce arbitrary interference and influence, and to promote the fundamental transformation of the traditional power structure. For example, two rounds of group discussions tried to ensure that each participant was deeply involved and allowed full expression.

Chapter 3 Democratic Consultation: Deliberative Democracy and Local Public Policy

Random sampling means that everyone has equal opportunity in a given community. However, we should also see that the democratic approach cannot directly change the political structure, and its impact on the traditional power structure is not fundamental and decisive. It can be seen from the democratic consultation in Zeguo Town that the democratic and open consciousness of government leaders and the motivation of democratic innovation are still the most essential elements for the smooth development of democratic consultation activities. And democracy is not a necessary part of government decision-making. The outcome of the discussion will be different depending on the government's consideration.

(4) To negotiate the relationship between democracy and civic culture, we need to improve the ability and quality of public opinion representatives. For China, a country with a system of autocracy for thousands of years and a political and cultural tradition based on the consciousness and culture of its subjects, how to improve the ability and quality of public opinion representatives of the town, and to make most representatives turn into modern citizens with a certain ability of independent thinking and analysis, from being farmers with a strong mentality of small-farm agriculture, is very important to improve the quality of democratic consultation. The practice shows that despite the fact that democracy has been practiced in Wenling for several years, the quality of public opinion representatives is uneven. Some people had a high level of articulation and spoke enthusiastically. Some people appeared nervous when it was their turn to speak: they had nothing to say, or they didn't know how to say, or they didn't know what to say. Most of them were women. There might be three reasons: First, they were not very familiar with urban construction projects; second, they were not used to speaking in public; and third, they were limited by their own qualities and could not really say anything.

3.2.2 Democratic consultation of financial budget of Xinhe Town in 2006

Xinhe Town, located in the northeast of Wenling City, is a town of 89 villages and six residential areas in the south of the Yangtze River.

Political Participation and Institutional Innovation:
A Case Study of Zhejiang

It has an administrative area of 71.4 square kilometers and a population of 120,000. It will be one of the five major blocks of Wenling's combined medium-sized city in the future.

(1) *Basic process of democratic consultation of financial budget of Xinhe Town in 2006*

On March 6, 2006, Xinhe Town of Wenling City held a democratic consultation during the people's congress session. Nearly 120 representatives of the town people's congress and attendance personnel held talks and discussions with the town government on the budget plan for the year 2006 and put forward suggestions such as increasing the cost of street maintenance and renovation and reducing the expenditure on tourism infrastructure construction. After the consultation, the government, the presidium of the people's congress and the budget review panel held a joint meeting to discuss the issues raised by deputies to the people's congress, adjusted the 13 projects including the increase of the 500,000 yuan cost of maintenance of the old city streets, involving a total budget of 8.28 million yuan. The town government revised the government's budget report and passed it on the next day's plenary session.

Generally speaking, the review of this budget could be divided into three stages.

First stage: Early work of the consultation

Five days before the formal meeting of the consultation, Xinhe Town posted notices to publish the time, place and key issues of the democratic consultation over the budget and required the public to be free to participate. The town government's budget report and budget details were sent to delegates two days in advance. Two days before the formal review of the people's congress, the budget consultation for the first review was held, where the social public of Xinhe Town could participate voluntarily. To improve the quality of this democratic consultation, before the consultation, experts from political science,

Chapter 3 Democratic Consultation:
Deliberative Democracy and Local Public Policy

law and finance in Beijing, Shanghai and other places had conducted a morning training session for the participants, which was the first time in the development process of democratic consultation in Wenling. The training included "how to review the budget", "the characteristics of the budget project", "the use efficiency of funds, and the way to use".

Second stage: Convening of consultation

On March 6, Xinhe Town budget democratic consultation was held under the chair of the town people's congress. The eight members of the financial group of the people's congress participated in the event as ordinary citizens, and many village officials and villagers volunteered to attend. The more than 110 participants in the democratic consultation were divided into three groups: agriculture, industry and social work. After the meeting, the budget review panel separately wrote the preliminary report on the budget of the three groups in agriculture, industry and social work, according to the participants' statements and discussions. On March 8, during the people's congress session, after the town government made the budget statement, the representatives of the three financial groups reported 56 opinions and suggestions on the 6-day budget preliminary review of democratic consultation. Subsequently, 110 deputies to the people's congress and 200 delegates raised questions on the government's leadership in the 2006 budget.

Third stage: The adjustment of the budget plan and the deliberation of the people's congress

In accordance with the preliminary report and the deliberation of the people's congress deputies, the presidium of the people's congress and the town government held a joint meeting to amend the draft budget, formed a "budget modification programme" and the budget review team participated in the revision process. The revised plan showed that most of the opinions expressed by representatives were reflected, and the entire budget had been revised in six major and 14 minor items. For example: the construction project of sanitation complex was changed to waste transfer station project; the drainage pipeline in the community increased from 50,000 yuan to 150,000 yuan; expenditure on tourism infrastructure construction decreased from 2 million yuan to 1.5 million yuan.

On March 9, delegates were divided into five groups to discuss and consider the government's "budget revision plan". According to the regulations, if the representative of the people's congress does not agree with the government's amendment plan, five or more representatives may propose a "budget amendment bill". On the morning of the same day, the presidium of the people's congress received more than 70 bills, including eight bills specifically targeted at the budget. But because six of the eight bills did not make any changes, only the remaining two could be put to the vote. The two bills were passed unanimously at a later plenary session of the people's congress. As a result, the draft budget report, which was revised by the joint meeting, was officially included in the 2006 budget of Xinhe Town.

(2) *The characteristics of the budget democratic consultation in Xinhe Town*

In the form of the democratic consultation, the public opinion will be connected with the government decision-making, which is the initiative of Wenling City in Zhejiang Province. The introduction of the system of "democratic consultation" to the government budget and the direct introduction of the agenda of the people's congress are the biggest innovation of the democratic consultation in Xinhe Town, which is also the first time in the development history of Wenling's democratic consultation. In particular, the characteristics of the budget democratic consultation in Xinhe Town include the following:

First is the "two-round grouping" discussion adopted at the 2006 democratic consultation for urban pre-selection construction projects in Wenling. The financial budget democratic consultation of Xinhe Town also adopted the way of two groups and two centralized deliberations. What was different was that the two groupings in Xinhe had a larger and more extensive time span, which greatly increased the opportunity

Chapter 3 Democratic Consultation:
Deliberative Democracy and Local Public Policy

for participants to express their opinions, and also made the discussion more in-depth and more qualitative. At the same time, the sub-group discussion was set up to make the group discussion focus on the interaction between participants. Each participant had a better chance to express their opinions by colliding and confronting various opinions.

Second, the people's congress deputies could jointly propose the "budget amendment", which was the most important system design in the process of the review of the Xinhe budget. After the discussion of the "budget modification plan" proposed by the government based on the discussion and deliberation of democratic consultation of the budget by the people's congress deputies, if there was any objection to the "budget amendment" of the town government, the "budget amendment bill" may be jointly proposed by more than five people. Its budget amendment rights include cutting or increasing the amount of a budget and denying a budget. After the examination of the presidium of the people's congress, the "budget amendment bill" shall be submitted by the presidium of the people's congress to the vote. A total of eight "budget amendments" were submitted by representatives of the people's congress deputies in Xinhe Town, six of which could not be put to the vote because they did not raise the specific amount of the budget expenditure items and the other two were approved by the presidium of the people's congress for approval. The two "budget amendments" adopted by the vote were: (1) Expenses for four operations in the family planning and for investigation were reduced to 0.5 million yuan from 1 million yuan and the investment in the village renovation in the capital construction expenditure was increased to 2.5 million yuan from 2 million yuan. (2) The cost of urban maintenance was increased by 0.5 million yuan, and the reserve fee of 3.3 million yuan was reduced to 2.8 million yuan.

Third, it was the establishment of the "financial group", and the successful connection of democratic consultation—the first grassroots democratic political form of Wenling—with the local people's congress. The financial group was made up of the "budget review group" during the people's congress session, consisting of eight representatives of the people's congress, divided into three groups: industry, agriculture and society. After the preliminary review of the budget, the three financial groups wrote a detailed and objective preliminary report on the budget. At the people's congress session, representatives of the consultation may question the government leaders on the report and related issues raised by the financial group, and propose amendments to the draft budget. After a budget adjustment by the government, the people's congress deputies discussed and proposed amendments to the amendment. Finally, the amendments proposed by the deputies were submitted to the town people's congress for a vote after the review of the proposed amendments. If approved, it would be officially included in the 2006 budget of Xinhe Town.

(3) *Practical significance of the budget democratic consultation in Xinhe Town*

In this three-day budget democratic consultation in Xinhe Town, there were more than 410 people's congress deputies and other members of the public. In the discussion and consideration of the draft budget, there were 112 suggestions and opinions, including 66 related to the budget, and 8 "budget amendments". The town government adjusted 13 budget expenditure items, one new expenditure item, two modified items and adjusted budget fund of 8.28 million yuan. Among them, seven items were adjusted, and the amount was 4.14 million yuan; six items were increased and the amount was 4.04 million yuan; and one item was added and the amount was 100,000 yuan. Such a large budget adjustment will inevitably have an impact on the economic, social development and the improvement of people's livelihood and welfare in Xinhe Town. At the same time, in terms of the development of the democratic consultation system in Wenling City, the symbolic meaning and theoretical value of the financial budget democracy in Xinhe Town should not be underestimated.

Chapter 3 Democratic Consultation: Deliberative Democracy and Local Public Policy

(1) Xinhe budget democratic consultation was a bold reform of the Chinese government budget review process and a bold attempt to reform the budget preparation and review procedures of the town government. According to the constitution, the power of budgetary review and approval is a very important power of the people's congress. Only by performing the right of this power in accordance with the law can the people's congress truly control the budget of the government. However, since there is no corresponding reform in the budgetary system, in most places, the budget review conducted by the people's congress during the budgeting process is actually a formal review or procedural review rather than a substantive review. Budget democratic consultation in Xinhe made all the government's revenues and expenditures under the supervision of the people and their representative bodies through the government's open budget plan and the public's full consultation on the budget plan. Li Fan, an academic, thinks that while some local governments in China are making public budget reforms, they are still dominated by the government. The budget reform in Xinhe Town was a major breakthrough in the reform of the public budget of local governments in China. Some scholars point out that Xinhe required five or more people's congress deputies to submit a budget amendment bill. After examination by the presidium of the people's congress, it was then submitted to the general assembly for a vote. They passed two budget amendments this time, which was a big step for a town-level government. In fact, this was also the first time for the people's congress to exercise the right to revise the budget. Xinhe trial represents the direction of China's public finances.

(2) The openness of the process and the high degree of civic engagement. The openness and public participation of the government budget review process is the necessary requirement for the establishment of the public budget and the basis for the full expression of public opinion. The openness of the budget of Xinhe Town was mainly reflected in two aspects: First is the open budget. The disclosed content was not only a draft of the budget report, but the specific

sub-items of each expenditure were made public without reservation. This made the citizens of Xinhe Town be clear about how the government spends money this year, who spends it, and where it was spent.

The public's participation in the budget democratic consultation was of great breadth and depth. Five days before the meeting was held, the town posted a notice announcing the contents, time, place and other matters of the democratic consultation, calling on everyone to make active preparations and participate voluntarily. At the democratic consultation, where the representatives of the general public and the town people's congress participated, most of the participants showed great enthusiasm for participating in the government's budget proposal, and made dozens of comments, requests and suggestions to the town government and submitted eight formal amendments to the people's congress.

(3) Xinhe budget democratic consultation has realized the full expression of the people's congress deputies in the process of government budget review. Full expression of public opinion is the key to budget consideration. In regards to the process of democratic consultation and concrete implementation, there are some common points between the two models of Zeguo Town and Xinhe Town. The issues for democratic consultation were concerned in the government's financial budget and the agenda adopted the approach of combining group discussion and meeting. But they also had many differences, such as the Zeguo Town government's individual budget, and Xinhe Town government's entire budget. In the way of the generation of the public opinion representatives, Zeguo Town adopted the strict random sampling method to select all the public opinion representatives, which was of a strong scientific nature. However, the disadvantage was that the overall level of consultation of the elected representatives was low, and the representatives paid less attention to the issues and lacked the necessary interest. For the consultation by the people's congress deputies in Xinhe Town, as a result of the more professional government

Chapter 3   Democratic Consultation:
Deliberative Democracy and Local Public Policy

budget review, a thorough training of the representatives was conducted before the convening of the consultation, thus ensuring the quality of the consultation. On the whole, the innovation on deliberation procedures and methods in budget democratic consultation of Xinhe Town realized the full expression of people's congress deputies in the process of government budget review. The first was to increase the number of discussions, to take two groups and two sessions for deliberation, so that the opportunity for participants to express their opinions is greatly increased, which also made the discussion more in-depth and more qualitative. The second was to improve the discussion mode and set up the procedure of sub-group discussion. The meeting focused on a more formal discussion, and one person's speech was audible to all participants. This added to the weight of the statement, leaving the government unable to ignore it or prevaricate, prompting the government to take the matter seriously and absorb the reasonable opinions of the participants. However, there was limited time for each speaker over the meeting, with only a few speakers. Due to the small number, small range, and flexible way of group discussion, the participants were able to debate and negotiate directly, giving each participant an opportunity to express his/her views fully. Moreover, the participants were inspired by each other in the debate, and different opinions collided and clashed, making the budget deliberation more effective. The third is that, the people's congress deputies might jointly submit a "budget amendment". It could be submitted to the general assembly for a vote after a procedural review by the presidium of the people's congress. If passed, the town government must revise its budget accordingly. This is the most effective way to innovate the public opinion during the Xinhe budget review process. This has expanded the power of people's congress deputies in the government's budget proposals, which have made the will of the people reflect in the government's budget proposals.

(4) New growth points of the democratic consultation: Integration with the grassroots people's congress system. From the perspective of the grassroots people's congress, this democratic consultation has

changed the status of the grassroots people's congress to a certain extent, and activated the role of the grassroots people's congress as the local supreme authority. At the same time, democratic consultation, this grassroots democratic form with the help of grassroots people's congress, has been integrated into the power system of the state so as to have more profound realistic influence and broader development space. The financial budget democratic consultation of Xinhe Town integrated the democratic consultation, the system innovation outside the system with the existing system, included the democratic consultation outside the system into the existing institutional framework, and gradually made it institutionalized, procedural and standardized. For comments and suggestions made by the deputies of the local people's congress at the democratic conference, when the government changed its budget, it could accept or reject them. At this time, the government was actively modifying them; the "budget amendment bill" proposed by people's congress deputies would be approved by the people's congress, and the government must revise it. At this time, the government was passively modifying it, which was the internal rigid restraint mechanism of the democratic system and the fundamental cause of the integration of democratic consultation and grassroots people's congress system.

Budget democracy means that the public can restrain the government's fiscal expenditure, thus constraining the government's policy choices and other political behaviors. The NPC, the country's highest authority, can effectively restrict and supervise the government as long as it controls the government's budget. Therefore, the representative office of the people's congress can also create a very solid institutional platform for future political and democratic development. Therefore, the value of the budget democracy in Wenling City is not only limited to the reform of public budget, but also has profound significance and further development prospects. The budget democracy, which was carried out under limited political participation, can accumulate valuable groundwork for future expansion of political participation and institutional innovation.

Chapter 3 Democratic Consultation:
Deliberative Democracy and Local Public Policy

Ensuring that the participation of villagers is conducted in an environment of equality and freedom is one of the issues that has always been of concern in the development process of Wenling's democratic consultation. Because the democratic consultation is an innovation outside the system, decisions made by it have no legal status. In some cases, it is inevitable that the existing decision-makers will control the negotiation process, and that the interests of government departments or the personal preference of government leaders will prevail over democracy. According to the relevant provisions of the Organization Law of Local People's Congresses and Local People's Governments at Various Levels, the township people's congress has the right to choose, recall, supervise and decide on important matters of the local government. In fact, it is often the standing committee of the town party committee, or even the party secretary, who has the right to decide the important matters. This is against the law of the people's congress, and it is difficult to avoid making mistakes. The town's budget is the biggest "important matter". The democratic consultation for construction of Zeguo Town was only a part of the government's budget. However, the careful organization of the government has also ensured the quality of the consultation, ensured the authenticity of the public opinion, and prevented the government departments from controlling the negotiation process to a certain extent. The practice of the budget democratic consultation in Xinhe Town shows that the former has played a certain role in replacing the people's congress. It is now possible to activate the role of the township people's congress through democratic consultation and make it play its due role. At the same time, it also made the democratic consultation find a new growth point.

3.3 Significance assessment: Deliberative democracy and local public policy formulation

The formulation and implementation of public policy is one of the most important activities in government governance, and it is an important means of authoritative distribution of social value. Therefore, the formation of public policy in the democratic consultation is undoubtedly the core manifestation of grassroots governance. Under the modern democratic system, the essential requirement of public policy is that it should set the goal of promoting public interest. Civic participation is the inherent requirement of ensuring public policy's publicity and legitimacy. However, due to the complexity of the government process and the strong presence of national power, some scholars point out that authoritarian governments carry out elections to gain legitimacy. However, people in these regimes usually lack confidence in the managed elections and are reluctant to participate. Similarly, in the formulation and

Chapter 3   Democratic Consultation:
Deliberative Democracy and Local Public Policy

implementation of public policy, citizens are often unable to participate in the policy process to express their reasonable demands due to lack of public expression mechanism. At the same time, it is unavoidable for the government to understand the real will of citizens because of the unimpeded channels of communication with the citizens, thus the policy deviation inevitably emerges. Wenling's democratic consultation has made a positive exploration of this. It sought the communication and understanding between the citizens and the government through the rational consultation process as it's the main method for citizens' extensive participation in local public policy and promoted the cooperation between the government and the people. Based on the practice of deliberative democracy in rural China in recent years, we will analyze the experience and significance of democratic consultation and public policymaking in the innovation of grassroots governance in Wenling.

3.3.1 Technical requirements for democratic consultation

Modern society is a divided society. "Deeply divided societies need not just sound practical advice, but also clear normative direction."[3] In the practice of these consultations, which are widely carried out in the grassroots governance, different consultation methods have different influences on the development process of local public policy and the distribution of social interests. Studies have shown that local governments in China would promote different forms of deliberative democratic practices in the interest of maintaining policy legitimacy and political trust. The public consultation practice, which is sought by the government, can indeed improve the public's political identity. For Wenling's democratic consultation, the main practical way is "the innovation of the consultative mechanism of the local regulations". But in recent years, it has gradually expanded and penetrated into three other ways, such as the "democratic deliberative" consultation in the

---

[3] O'Flynn, I. Deliberative democracy, the public interest and the consociational model. *Political Studies*, 2010, 58: 572–589.

people's congress, and the practice of labor and capital consultation in enterprises. However, in any negotiation mode, it is important to realize the rationality and full consultation of citizens in the process of local public policy formulation. As can be seen from the democratic consultation in the formulation of the public policy in Wenling, these elements mainly include the following.

First, citizens' full understanding of public policy-related information. This is an important premise for citizens to participate effectively in the process of rural public development. Without comprehensive access to information on public policy, citizens' participation and consultative activities will lose their substantive value. Prior to the convening of the democratic consultation in Wenling, the organizer generally posted the notice 3–5 days in advance, which made public the time, place, topics and participants of the consultation. The detailed sub-items of each expenditure in the government's draft budget were made public in the budget review of the Xinhe Town budget consultation, which enabled the participants to effectively review the necessity and rationality of administrative expenditures, thus improving the quality of government budget decisions. For example, in March 2006, there were 15 budget expenditure items in the 2006 draft budget report submitted by the town government to the people' congress, with a total budget of 92.97 million yuan. The detailed description of its budget listed all the specific items contained in the 15 expenditure items, totaling 110 items, of which the "administrative management fee" expenditure was 15.87 million yuan. The detailed description of this budget meant the breakdown of this item into 17 specific sub-items. The representatives of the people's congress were clear about the administrative expenses of the town government, and could carefully examine the necessity and rationality of various administrative expenses. In 2006, the town party committee and the government held a number of office meetings to arrange the preparations for the democratic consultation for the pre-selection projects for Zeguo Town construction. Most of the town government departments and staff were involved in different tasks. In order to get the public

Chapter 3　Democratic Consultation:
Deliberative Democracy and Local Public Policy

opinion representative to know about the pre-selection project of the Zeguo Town, the town government made a visit to the public opinion representatives and distributed basic materials to them, held the pre-selected project presentation meeting, explained the project in detail, arranged the representative to conduct field investigation, carried out the questionnaire survey and so on to let the representatives of public opinion have sufficient time to understand the content and background of the meeting, thus providing adequate information resources for the full consultation among the villagers. And it provided the basis for the analysis of the comparison and summarization after the consultation. The implementation of public budget reform in Xinhe Town has passed 15 years. The budget estimate of Xinhe Town has also increased from three pages in the beginning to 25 pages today, with more and more information is available for public discussion.

　　Second, the elaboration of the consultation procedure, namely in the process of citizens' negotiation, shall ensure the participants have an opportunity to speak freely and sufficient time to think, and each participant has equal opportunities to comment. Moreover, there shall be time for free discussion between the participants and so on. In the process of the consultation, "public opinion poll" democracy is undoubtedly a more successful practice mode. For example, the democratic consultation for pre-selection projects of town construction in Zeguo and democratic consultation of financial budget in Xinhe since 2005 have conducted two rounds of group and meeting discussions, and each participant has a better chance to express views. In group discussions, the group host came from a neutral third party (mostly Zeguo Town's middle-school teachers), and was trained in advance, to ensure that the host would fairly, impartially and effectively organize the group discussion. The 16 groups were divided into eight "regular groups" and eight "rational groups", with 13–15 persons per group. In the group discussion of the regular group, the host was asked to play a secondary role. The issues would be freely discussed by the villagers and the atmosphere of discussion was more relaxed. For the rational group, the host was required to grasp the discussion process, consider the pros and cons, and ask the villagers to give reasons and grounds for their opinions. After the group discussion, the groups' spokespersons were drawn by lottery.

The democratic consultations for financial budget in Xinhe Town ensured that each participant could have the benefit of full expression and exchange opportunities more from the system design. Take the first annual consultation of the financial budget held in Xinhe Town in March 2015 as an example. On the morning of March 2, 2015, there were three main agenda items: To listen to the work report of the People's Government of Xinhe Town, to listen to the work report of the presidium of the People's Congress of Xinhe Town, to hear the implementation of the fiscal budget of Xinhe Town in 2014 and the report of the draft budget for 2015. In the afternoon, the delegations reviewed the draft budget and submitted a budget review report (draft). The delegation was divided into seven groups, including middle town service area, the east town service area, the south town service area, the west town service area, the north town service area, the Changyu service area and the Tangxia service area. The debate in each group was fierce, and many suggestions and opinions were put forward, mainly focusing on land revenue, firefighting, environmental sanitation, education and other aspects. Then the general assembly held its second plenary session, with delegations presenting a report on the budget review to the general assembly. Subsequently, the assembly adopted democratic consultation to focus on deliberation over the draft budget. Participants, including people's congress deputies and attendance personnel, made suggestions, comments and asked questions to the members of the town government who sat on the platform according to the Draft Budget for 2014. The government officials responded to the questions raised by the public and adopted a "question and answer" approach. On March 3, according to the opinions of delegations, the town party committee and the government held a joint meeting to discuss the opinions of the people's congress deputies. After a thorough preparation of the

Chapter 3 Democratic Consultation: Deliberative Democracy and Local Public Policy

discussion, the relevant content of the draft budget was revised to form a revised plan and submitted to the town committee for consideration. At the same time, the people's congress deputies jointly proposed two budget amendments, which determined the resolution of the two budget amendments. The final vote was that it passed both amendments. In addition, the people's congress deputies of Xinhe Town also voted on the resolution of the handling report. The resolution was a highlight of the consultation. The resolution said that the Proposal to Speed Up the Construction of Sewage Treatment Facilities in Rural Areas and Boost the "Five Water Co-Governance" put forward by five representatives including Lin Xianfang was set up as a bill; the remaining 19 representative bills were treated as suggestions, criticisms and comments. It was required that the handling of the bill of the general assembly be included in the important agenda and the responsibility for the implementation of the suggestions, criticisms and comments made by the representative be implemented.

Third, the selection of consultation representatives. The selection mode of the consultation representative actually determines which groups can enter the rural public space for expression and aggregation of interests during the development of local public policy. In modern society, large-scale civic participation is not only unrealistic, but also dangerous. In Wenling's democratic consultation, in general, the main participants were the invited people's congress deputies, CPPCC members, heads of various units, representatives of relevant interest groups and invited experts and scholars. As a result of the principle of voluntary participation, participants could actually fall into two categories: The invited representatives and the people who have a close interest in the consultation. To a certain extent, there is not enough representation of the participants, and it is difficult to reflect the general opinions of the broad masses of all strata in the society. Therefore, how to guarantee the universality and fairness of civic participation in the policy process becomes the problem that must be solved for civic participation. In 2006, the democratic consultation for pre-selection projects of Zeguo Town construction canceled the previous invitation and voluntary registration methods for selecting the public opinion representatives and adopted strict random sampling. Notably, 237 public opinion representatives were selected, amounting to 2‰ of the permanent population of the town, by random sampling. Therefore, its representativeness was more real and reliable.

Fourth, the appropriate introduction of quantitative scientific statistical methods. In most of the democratic consultation in Wenling, the villagers were involved in making a rough idea or suggestion on a certain issue, for which quantitative statistics and analysis could not be conducted. Therefore, the government often failed to grasp the true representation of the participants after the consultation. After the democratic consultation for pre-selection projects of Zeguo Town construction in 2006, the town government made statistics of the results of the questionnaire item by item, and concluded the results of the urban construction pre-selection projects from the most important to the least important order. Subsequently, the town government held an office meeting, after making preliminary plan report according to the questionnaire results of the town construction projects. It formulated the first 21 items of the second questionnaire (total investment of about 50.03 million yuan) as the urban infrastructure projects in 2006 and the seven projects listed from 22 to 28, with a total investment of about 10 million yuan, as the preparatory projects, which would be constructed when the government's financial resources allowed. At the same time, data statistics and analysis could be carried out due to the two public opinion surveys. Therefore, it could better understand the preferences and policy choices of public opinion representatives, and provided reference for government decision-making.

3.3.2 How does the deliberative democracy affect the formulation of public policy?

Nowadays, the diversity of society, culture, race, nationality and social groups is an indisputable reality, which is accompanied by the

Chapter 3 Democratic Consultation:
Deliberative Democracy and Local Public Policy

diversity of interests and differences among different subjects. Although "deliberative democracy is attractive not only because it could work, but also because it would be "good" for us and it might solve a lot of problems",[4] the pluralism and complexity of society challenge the theory of democracy: If the vast majority of citizens are excluded from the consultation, democracy will be the price of consultation. When the consultation is targeted only in the public domain, the loss will be the institutional requirement of effective decision-making. How to achieve compromise and balance among multiple interests, the traditional democratic theory with the election as the core is unsatisfactory. Due to the existence of social pluralistic interests and the differences in moral cognition, in the process of public policymaking, the relevant participants are often limited rational actors. Different policy subjects will have different cognitive orientations on public policy issues based on their different perspectives, and may affect the public policy process in different ways. Thus, for an effective consultative democratic theory, the key issue is how to combine the following three elements organically: consultation, decision-making and all citizens. The concept and values of deliberative democracy provide the basis and premise for the establishment of government policy and the democratic orientation of the implementation network. We will discuss how the public opinion expression can enter the government's decision-making in the way of deliberative democracy in democratic consultation of Wenling. How can this process be implemented and what are the factors that affect citizen deliberative participation in public decision-making in local governments?

(1) *The relationship between public policy quality and civic participation*

The effective consultation of citizens requires sufficient information, and for the government, sufficient information is also a necessary condition for its scientific and reasonable public policy.

---
[4]Chick, M. Deliberation and civic studies. *The Good Society*, 2013, 22 (2).

Political Participation and Institutional Innovation:
A Case Study of Zhejiang

Therefore, any public decision has a series of policies or administrative constraints related to its nature, including technical constraints, regulatory constraints and budget constraints so as to protect the quality of the decision and restrict the participation of citizens. On the other hand, in order to improve the quality of decision-making, policymakers need more information and need to know the most authentic public opinions. The government is also a limited rational actor. They are limited in knowledge, information and intelligence. If those who directly face the social problems are allowed to participate in public policy process, through a variety of ways to deal directly with the decision-makers, it will no doubt help policymakers to search and obtain more comprehensive information resources to improve the quality of decisions.

In the democratic consultation, the subjects of various parties have discussed and communicated with various parties in the process of interest game. All kinds of interest preferences can be adjusted to each other, and on this basis, the interest demands and citizens' wishes are transferred to the decision-making system, which will help reduce the distortion of policy information, reduce the cost of searching policy information by the government, and help the government formulate local public policy quickly and rationally. For example, in Wenling City, Zeguo Town adopted democratic consultation when formulating investment projects for urban construction and achieved good practical results. The use and arrangement of urban construction funds is an important public policy which is related to the economic development of the whole town and the residents' life. In order to understand the most authentic public opinion, Zeguo Town tried to carry out detailed system design in five aspects, namely representative selection, the role of experts, representatives' understanding of the content, the opportunity to speak, and the understanding of the representative opinions by the decision-makers. Thus, the public opinion was more representative and authentic, making the decision more consistent with the public opinion.

Chapter 3 Democratic Consultation:
Deliberative Democracy and Local Public Policy

Universality is an important guarantee for the government to obtain information, but the breadth and depth of civic participation are often reversed. In particular, some of the more formal, large and specific forms of participation challenge the government's ability to organize effective civic participation. In the original "consultative and inquiry" mode of democratic consultation, the way that all volunteers could participate expanded the range of villagers' participation. However, there is a lack of targeted institutional design for the limited number of speakers in the general assembly. The "opinion poll" democracy in Zeguo has solved the problem better by adopting the combination of the general assembly and the group discussion. Although the issues for the democratic consultation of the town's construction were only part of the government's budget, the meticulous organization of local government also ensured the universality of the information sources and the quality of democratic consultation, which guaranteed the authenticity of the public opinion.

(2) *The legitimacy value of the deliberative public policy formulation model*

Legitimacy and rationality of legitimacy of political rule shows citizens' recognition and acceptance of government governance behavior and national political system. Bourdieu thinks that the legitimacy is the right to obtain the right identity of social order, that is to say, trying to make social order a natural power. Max Weber points out that any rule attempts to evoke and maintain the belief in its "legitimacy". The development and implementation of public policy is the main way of government governance. Therefore, is public policy devoted to the realization of social public interests or is it only for the special interests of a few people and a few groups is the fundamental criterion for judging and evaluating the legitimacy of the government and its policies. "To the extent citizen participation advocates offer a normative justification for their proposals, they tend to appeal to democratic ideals, contending that increased citizen involvement lends enhanced legitimacy to the government's actions".[5] This means that only by allowing the public to fully participate in the administration of the government and exert effective influence on the government's decision-making can the government truly represent the public opinion.

In the view of deliberative democratic theorists, if the conditions for civil consultation are fully satisfied in the process of formulating public policies, such a public policy would be more legitimate than any public policy achieved through any other means because of its inclusiveness and equality. Inclusiveness means that in the formulation of public policy, no relevant individual should be excluded; equality means that the government considers the will of all participants without bias. Or, as Williams puts it, all relevant arguments, opinions and personnel are taken into account, and cannot be swayed by individual subjective moral positions.[6]

Although "public participation can be strengthened by working out more than one alternative proposal for consultations",[7] in reality, the impact of public discussion on the formulation of government policies is often very limited, and the public lack effective means to effectively restrict the government's behavior. In particular, the participation of Chinese citizens as well as democracy is still to be improved. Why, then, should local governments adopt the policy tools of democratic consultation in the formulation of public policy?

---

[5] Bull, R. T. Making the administrative state "state for democracy": A theoretical and practical analysis of citizen participation in agency decision-making. *Administrative Law Review*, 2013, 65 (3): 611.

[6] Williams, M. The uneasy alliance of group representation and deliberative democracy. In: Will Kymliika and Wayne Norman (eds.), *Citizenship in Diverse Societies*. Oxford: Oxford University Press, 2000: 129.

[7] Vestbro, D. U. Citizen participation or representative democracy? The case of Stockholm, Sweden. *Journal of Architectural and Planning Research*, 2012, 29: 5–17.

Chapter 3 Democratic Consultation: Deliberative Democracy and Local Public Policy

Studies have shown that the attributes of the policy tools that the government chooses in the decision-making process tend to be the main consideration. Wesley M. Cohen and Daniel A. Levinthal have a good summary of the attributes of policy tools: resource intensity, including administrative costs and operational simplicity; objectives, including accuracy and selectivity; political risk, including the characteristics of support and opposition, public awareness and the probability of failure; constraints on state behavior, including forced difficulties and ideological principles that limit government behavior.

The cost of using different policy instruments varies. In the process of the development of democratic consultation, Wenling's every democratic consultation meeting would inevitably have a certain cost, and the cost is often proportional to the size of the democratic consultation. In this regard, the "public opinion polls" of Zeguo Town were very complicated and involved a large number of participants, thus both the time cost and the economic cost were higher. For example, in 2006, the government spent more than 1 month on the consultation of the urban construction budget project, which cost more than 80,000 yuan. The traditional Chinese government's closed decision-making model can be favored by the grassroots managers, in part because for the grassroots government, the system is a policy tool that makes governance (management) less costly, or simpler and more convenient. Its traditional inertial characteristics also determine its minor political risk. However, in the period of transition and differentiation, the interests of social subjects are becoming more and more obvious. The interest demands of villagers also show obvious diversification trend, which leads to the deviation between the government and public opinion in the process of formulating public policy. This deviation often leads to civil discontent and even protests.

The democratic discourse provides a new way for government decision-making, which basically meets the requirements of the government in the context of the current social transformation: The operational feasibility, the controllability of the target, the political benefits brought by innovation, and the government itself has a smaller substantive binding. A US scholar Reeve T. Bull points out that, "These relatively modest reforms could be enormously beneficial in providing relevant public input to administrative agencies and quelling popular perceptions of a 'democracy deficit' in the workings of the administrative state".[8] In the case of Zeguo, it is not hard to see that the important purpose of making citizens participate in the decision-making process is to make a policy arrangement with a high degree of citizen acceptance based on widely listening to the expression of public opinion. Especially when the decision-making process requires the understanding and cooperation of citizens, it is very important to absorb citizens' participation decision in order to improve the acceptability of decision-making.

However, the participation of citizens is not always directly proportional to the quality of public policy, and the deliberative public policy formulation model has many target orientations. In particular, for a comprehensive and professional public policy such as government budget, the participation of citizens in decision-making is crucial to the implementation of decisions. There is no evidence of a direct causal link between them. Why is democracy so valued? It is clear that the government is seeking not just citizens' acceptance of decisions. The widespread practice of democratic consultation in the formulation of public policy has a sophisticated dynamic mechanism and value pursuit. This needs to be answered in the wider social context of public policy formulation.

Professor Hu Wei points out the following: "Throughout the process of government in contemporary China, the expression of mass

---

[8] Bull, R. T. Making the administrative state "state for democracy": A theoretical and practical analysis of citizen participation in agency decision-making. *Administrative Law Review*, 2013, 65 (3): 611–664.

Chapter 3 Democratic Consultation:
Deliberative Democracy and Local Public Policy

interests and the comprehensive interests on this basis have little impact on macro decision-making. This is because the channel of mass interests expression is not smooth enough... The process of government in contemporary China is not motivated by the expression and synthesis of mass interests, but based on the general public opinion of the party and government officials. This is a feature of contemporary China's interest expression, interest synthesis and policy formulation."[9] Therefore, the "mass line" in the formulation of public policy has its realistic political significance. Increasing the acceptability of public policy can support the legitimacy of the policy. As a public policy of authoritative distribution of social resources, its legitimacy is an important source of government legitimacy. In particular, the government's decisions have taken on greater importance and legitimacy as public political participation has increased. According to the system theory, the interaction between government system and social environment is divided into three stages: input, transformation and output. At the input stage, due to the imperfect election system in China, the participation effectiveness of citizens is restricted, thus affecting the political legitimacy of the government from the input end. Therefore, as the most important output end of the government, public policy is often burdened with the task of extracting political legitimacy while meeting its own policy objectives. So in the context of the current Chinese political reality, public policy is more affected by political, economic, social and other environmental factors, or even completely subject to the "extra" consideration. One of the important aims of the grassroots governance innovation in Wenling's democratic consultation and so on is to enhance the legitimacy of rural power institutions by inspiring the villagers to participate in public governance. This is also an important reason why the Chinese rural practice of deliberative democracy is valued and affirmed by the higher government departments.

---

[9] Hu Wei. *Government Procedure*. Hangzhou: Zhejiang People's Publishing House, 1998: 208.

Political Participation and Institutional Innovation:
A Case Study of Zhejiang

(3) *The integration of deliberative democracy and diversified interests*

In the democratic consultation, various stakeholders can influence the development of local public policy in the relationship of equality and freedom. As a public policy of authoritative distribution of social value, it is crucial to balance the interests of all parties. Therefore, in the process of public policymaking, it is necessary to ensure citizens' interest expression, interest integration, preference transformation, and benefit compromise. Although civic participation is an inherent requirement to ensure public policy and public interest orientation, in practice, the interests of the participants do not necessarily represent the public interest. They may represent the needs of existing organized groups, but may also express their special interests rather than the general interests of citizens. Therefore, public consultation is introduced in the process of government decision-making, so that citizens can participate actively and extensively. This process enables the pluralistic interests of various social subjects to be expressed directly and makes different interest demands and value preferences directly collide with each other.

Habermas points out that the important value of deliberative politics lies in that the participants, through mutual understanding and discussion of the process of the debate, ultimately form a consensus on the terms of the principle. Its success does not depend on all citizens with the ability to act collectively, but depends on the corresponding process of communication and the establishment of communication preset, as well as the common role of the deliberative process and the public opinion formed informally. To achieve full expression and convergence of public opinion, how to ensure the fairness and authenticity of citizen consultation in the decision-making process is undoubtedly the key. In this process, democratic consultation has been institutionalized in negotiations through the use of various forms of communication, and those forms of communication promise that all the results obtained in accordance with the procedure are reasonable. Wenling's democratic consultation tried to combine the

Chapter 3　Democratic Consultation:
Deliberative Democracy and Local Public Policy

realistic compromise with the moral self-discipline of the subject with a negotiated decision-making process. This means that the formation of consultation is based on negotiation and engagement rather than power and closure. However, as a democratic decision, how to ensure the balance and coordination between the objectives of government decision-making and the interests of citizens is not a simple question to answer. In the democratic consultation for pre-selection of projects for town construction's primary project in 2006, taking into account the possibility of divergence of interests, and the possibility of important projects not listed in the budget plan due to limited government rationality, the town government had set aside 5–10% of the 50 million yuan of urban construction funds to be used for projects that were strongly required by the public to prevent huge conflicts of interest and escalation of contradiction. Although this situation did not appear in the symposium, the preference differences among citizens emerged in the first round of group discussions. It was difficult for some participants to reach a consensus on the investment of supporting construction funds and the investment of urban reconstruction funds. Some villagers thought it necessary to increase the efforts on road reform, while other villagers insisted on supporting construction of industries based on the higher ratio of Zeguo Town's gross value of industrial output to fiscal revenue. After several rounds of negotiations, most villagers approved the investment in road reconstruction that was closely related to their interests. By comparing the results of two questionnaires before and after the democratic consultation, we can see that the rank of several major reconstruction projects has risen in the questionnaire after the consultation.

Cohen points out that the ideal democracy should not only let the citizens choose between Tom and Harry to participate in the management, but should let them within the scope of the power identify problems, put forward the proposals, balance the argument on all aspects, make clear the concept and clarify the position, in general, to promote and deepen the thinking. Democratic politics is the mechanism and process of constant game, adjustment and compromise of interest of multi-parties. The practice of Wenling's democratic consultation shows that the process of public consultation is the process of mutual adjustment and compromise. On the basis of mutual respect, rational consultation between free and equal citizens can effectively achieve mutual understanding and tolerance, rather than intensification and escalation of contradictions. Of course, an important prerequisite for the effectiveness of public consultation is that when the subject of democratic consultation involves a particular interest group, the group should have adequate representatives, or it would be easy for the majority to deprive the minority of their interests. If the real stakeholders do not attend the meeting, or if only the stakeholders attend the meeting, with the lack of objective and neutral third parties, they may lead to biased and unfair results.

(4) *The effective participation pattern of citizens in public policy*

For civic engagement in public decision-making, American scholar John Clayton Thomas proposes an effective decision-making model for civic engagement based on the analysis of the large number of new citizens' participation movements since the 1960s and the theories of traditional citizen participation. In this model, the quality and citizens' acceptability of policy are two core variables, and their relationship with civic participation is as follows: the higher the decision quality, the more restrictive the citizens' participation in the decision-making, the more likely it is for them to participate only in information acquisition; and if citizens are more receptive to decision-making, the degree of civic engagement will be greater. In decision-making with higher acceptability requirements, civic participation is divided into citizen participation with the objective of obtaining information, and citizen participation with the goal of enhancing policy acceptability and building a cooperative relationship between the government and citizens. In this way, public managers can realize participation in public policy by citizens through decentralized public consultation, integrated public consultation and public decision-making.

Chapter 3 Democratic Consultation:
Deliberative Democracy and Local Public Policy

The core focus of the Thomas model is to answer the question of when and how the government should engage citizens. The underlying premise is the existence of responsible government, active citizens and the diverse social participation mechanisms. Obviously, such a premise is not realistic in China's rural society. Therefore, the question of citizen participation in China's local public policy needs to answer the question of how citizens can participate and in what way. Wenling's democratic consultation is a new way of transforming the Chinese public decision-making mechanism by establishing the public decision-making mode based on the citizen participation on the basis of deliberative democracy.

For Wenling's practice model of participation in the local public policy based on democratic consultation, whether it is the traditional "consultative inquiry" or the "opinion polls" of Zeguo Town, or the "democratic deliberative" consultation of Xinhe Town, it is difficult to simply boil down to any of these three types of decision-making processes. With regard to the relationship between the quality requirements of policies and citizen participation, Thomas's attention to the quality of policy has much in common with the "deregulation outcome-oriented" administrative reform in Western countries. And in the process of China's grassroots governance, because of ordinary villagers' lack of effective supervision and restriction mechanism of grassroots government, and academia's emphasis on citizen participation in public policy is more embodied in a process of "regulation" administrative mode, the improvement of decision quality has become a by-product of the rational negotiation of citizens to some extent. As a result, local governments' demand for policy quality is often not a key factor in determining whether citizens are involved. It is the most important reason for citizens to participate in the decision-making process of the government, to supervise and restrict the government's centralization of power and realize the expression of citizens' interests. But under the current system, whether citizens will ultimately be able to participate in local public affairs depends on how well local governments respond to such demands.

In the context of China's reality, the local government's introduction of democratic consultation in the process of formulating public policy has its unique dynamic mechanism and target appeal. Local public policy in China is often a comprehensive reflection of multiple goals. Most importantly, it has the task of realizing the legitimacy of the government in the current political system, thus playing the role of "administrative absorption politics". In the case of Zeguo, the final decision based on the questionnaire is a good way to realize the acceptability of the policy and the legitimacy goal of government behavior. Thus, contrary to the Thomas model, in the formulation of local public policy in China, the acceptability of the policy is attracting more and more attention, taking into account the increasing interests and conflicts of citizens.

From the perspective of grassroots democratic political construction, the democratization of government decision-making is an important link. The deliberative public policy formulation is mainly in the rural area under administrative control, and by redesigning the civic participation structure, it makes an exploratory response to the change of institutional environment. This not only expands the public participation field in the village and township governance, but also expands the space of rural public governance. In Wenling's democratic consultation, the participation of citizens in public decision-making is a kind of participation in many phases, including providing information for government decision-making, deepening the villagers' understanding of the policy and building a good relationship between the government and the villagers. At the same time, it is also an important way to control the non-democratic orientation of public power in grassroots governance.

Chapter 4

Hearing: Interest Expression and Interest Integration Mechanism

4.1 The system of hearing: Concept and theory

4.1.1 Hearing, citizen participation and procedural democracy

Hearing, or public hearing, is a form of institution introduced from the West. Hearing system originates from the principle of Natural Justice in the Anglo-American legal system. As a formal legal system, it means a procedural legal system where affected interest parties of an organization may express their views and provide evidence, pleas, cross-examinations for the legislation and decision-making organizations (mainly governmental departments) to decide, to listen and accept the evidence before the final results. Hearing, as a set of normative procedural systems to protect citizens' participation in policy formation, corresponds to several types of hearings, including legislative hearing procedure, administrative decision-making hearing procedure and judicial decision-making hearing procedure.

Political Participation and Institutional Innovation:
A Case Study of Zhejiang

Gathering and integrating public opinion is a necessary part of the process of government and is a part of the process of making public decisions. A hearing is an important institutional way to collect and integrate public opinions, and it is a basic form of civic participation in public decision-making and government process. As an institutional arrangement, the hearing is, in essence, a procedural democracy of civic participation. It ensures that ordinary citizens take the initiative to participate in the public decision-making process of the government and influence it so as to maintain and realize the interests of the citizens. It is also conducive to improving the legal and political democratization of the government, keeping the government stable and strengthening political supervision. As a kind of procedural democratic system arrangement, the hearing has the characteristics of legal, procedural, organizational and institutional participation. "Legal" means that the law prescribes the procedure of hearing, and it is illegal to add, subtract or cancel at will. The policy or administrative decision made as such is illegal, and can be declared invalid by the court. "Procedural" means that the political participation of the hearing must be based on the procedure of the law, including the process procedure and the result procedure. The hearing procedure is the process of restricting the government's power to guarantee civil rights. "Organizational" means that the political participation of modern hearing is in the name of political parties, interest groups or other NGOs, in the form of group interest spokespersons. Participation in the system refers to the procedural nature of the hearing, and almost eliminates the possibility of participation outside the system.

4.1.2 China's development background and characteristics of the hearing system

In China, since the reform and opening-up, Shenzhen was the first to introduce the hearing system. In 1993, the first "Price Advisory Committee" was set up in Shenzhen, which was directly

Chapter 4　Hearing:
Interest Expression and Interest Integration Mechanism

involved in the consultation and decision-making process of water price adjustment, and was considered the embryonic form of the hearing system in China. After the Administrative Punishment Act was promulgated in 1996, hearings began to appear in some places. For the first time, the Act explicitly provided for the inclusion of the hearing system in the process of administrative enforcement, and it stipulated that in the process of administrative penalty, the relevant government departments should hold a hearing in accordance with the requirements of stakeholders if it involves some interests related to the interests of stakeholders. After the Price Act of 1998 introduced the hearing system into the field of price decision, hearings appeared one after another all over the country. In 2000, the Legislative Law, adopted by the Third Session of the Ninth National People's Congress, extended the hearing system from the field of administrative law enforcement and price decision to the field of legislation. The concept of "hearing" has been widely known since the national railway price hearing was held in early 2002, with the help of the dissemination of the news media. The hearing system and political participation in hearings in contemporary China have since entered a new stage of development.

In today's China, a hearing is regarded as a civil procedure of deliberative democracy. Professor He Baogang advocates to understand the hearing and highlights the meaning of citizens' negotiation, that is, the value of citizens' influence on the decision-making of government from the perspective of deliberative democracy. After investigating a series of hearings held throughout China in the early 21st century, Professor He points out the following: "There are more and more public hearings in some places, and only 27 people have the chance to speak in a hearing of hundreds of people. That is not a hearing at all. For the participants, the hearing is actually a 'hearing of witness' and there is no 'negotiation'. ... The hearing must have a discussion on politics, must repeatedly discuss the argument and deliberate each kind of reason;

Political Participation and Institutional Innovation:
A Case Study of Zhejiang

that is deliberation".[1] Here, Professor He points out the civil nature of the connotation of the hearing, and emphasizes the consultative, deliberative and argumentative nature of the hearing.

4.1.3 Government process theory: An analytical perspective

Government process or process of government is an important concept or theory of modern government. It is essentially a political process. The core concepts of government process theory are interest expression, interest integration, decision-making, governance, and two auxiliary and safeguard mechanisms: the process of government information transfer and supervision process. Using the theory of government process, by examining the aspects of interest expression, interest integration, decision-making and information transmission system, we may have a more profound and unique understanding of the hearing system and its functions and characteristics in China today.

(1) *Interest expression*

Interest expression, also known as "opinion expression", is defined by Professor Zhu Guanglei as the process of making requests by different social interest groups on the basis of their specific interests.[2] According to Almond, the expression of interests is the request of various groups in society to express themselves.[3] In the process of modern government, groups are the main actors of interest expression. In addition to groups, the process of modern government does not exclude the expression of the interests of individual citizens.

---

[1] Chen Shengyong and He Baogang. *Development of Deliberative Democracy.* Beijing: China Social Sciences Press, 2006: 222.

[2] Zhu Guanglei. *Modern Government Theory.* Beijing: Higher Education Press, 2006: 243.

[3] Gabriel A. A. and G. Bingham Powell. *Comparative Politics: System, Process, and Policies.* Translated by Cao Peilin. Shanghai: Shanghai Translation Publishing House, 1987: 228.

Chapter 4 Hearing: Interest Expression and Interest Integration Mechanism

(1) *The main types of interest expression: Individuals' and groups' of expression of interests*

Individuals expressing interests can be divided into two groups: those who express general interests and those who express professional opinions. The individual of universal interest expression refers to the individual as a citizen who actively participates in the expression of the general interests of the society. At present, citizens acting strictly as individuals expressing their opinions are a small part of all citizens; the individual expressing professional opinion refers to the individual who is specially responsible for the expression of special interests of a certain group, such as the deputies to the people's congress.

The organizations expressing interests can be divided into institutional interest expressing groups, structural interest expressing groups and functional interest expressing groups. Institutional interest expression groups refer to those social groups, such as the Communist Party of China, the Democratic Parties and the Central Committee of the Communist Youth League, which are part of the basic organizational structure of China's political system. Structural interest expression groups refer to general people's groups or social groups. Although they are not the basic part of China's political system, they represent a certain aspect of contemporary Chinese society and a certain part of the masses. They reflect the specific interests and requirements of certain social interest groups in the expression of opinions. Functional interest expression groups refer to those who play a certain role in expressing interests, have a certain social influence, but are not part of the national system. They are social organizations that reflect the interests and suggestions of one or two social groups.

(2) *Channels of expression of interests: Intrainstitutional expression, non-institutional expression and functional expression*

The expression within the system is through the national system to express interests, such as deputies to the people's congress; non-institutional expression refers to illegal approaches, such as violence;

functional expression is in between the two, because while there are legal provisions, they are not always very clear. Functional expression refers to the government's non-institutional flexibility factors, such as hearings.

(2) *Integration of interests*

The integration of interests is called "combination of opinions", "convergence of interests" and "integration of interests". In the process of government, the integration of interests is the process where important political figures and representative political organizations combine interest demands through certain political mechanisms and channels, and form certain social interest goals. Almond believes the process of integrating interests is a process of bringing together demands into policy choices and mobilizing resources to support these policy options. Interest integration is based on the specific interests of different social interest groups and the expression of their interests. The goal of the integration of interests is that the policy choice of compromise between different interest groups can be promoted to law and government decision-making. The process of interest integration is that different social groups narrow the differences between different demands by competing with each other, and finally reach a limited communication process.

The integration of interests is only a series of policy choices for decision-makers. It is not a decision in itself. Integration is a social, consultative and more "bargaining" process. Decision-making is a strict legal process confined to the regime. Or decisions are made in accordance with legal procedures, and the integration of interests is a social process. At the same time, the main subject of government decision-making is the government; the subject of interest integration is broader, such as hearings, which can be hosted by various social organizations and groups besides the government.

(3) *Decision*

Decision-making is a key stage in the process of government, which is to transform effective political requirements into authoritative

Chapter 4 Hearing:
Interest Expression and Interest Integration Mechanism

decision-making processes. Before the decision, the expression of interests and benefits is the process of social "input" to politics, and the decision is the "output" process of government to society. There are two ways of transmitting information: single-channel information transmission system and multi-channel information transmission system.

(4) *Information transmission system*

In the modern government system, the information flow process is becoming more and more important in the government process, and the information transmission network, which plays the role of political communication, is called "the nerve of the government".

(5) *Hearings in the government process*

In the process of government, how to locate the hearing? First of all, the hearing is an institutional way to express interests in individual or group system. Second, the hearing is one of the political mechanisms and channels to integrate various interest demands, but it is not a decision in itself. Third, the hearing has a stabilizing effect on the political system, which plays a role in bridging the decision-making process and plays a substantive role in decision-making. Fourth, the hearing is one way to advance the information transmission system. Hearing is one of the preconditions and bases of decision-making. It plays an important role in several aspects of government process. In this book, the present situation and problems in the process of government such as interest expression, interest integration and information transmission channel in Zhejiang are investigated and discussed.

Based on the theory of modern government process, this chapter will look into the following research and analysis of today's Chinese citizens' political participation of the hearing germinal mechanism and the hearing function of political participation by considering the cases of several typical hearings in the legislative, administrative and judicial

Political Participation and Institutional Innovation:
A Case Study of Zhejiang

aspects of Zhejiang Province. The analysis of relevant cases mainly focuses on the process of hearing political participation and citizens' interest expression and interest integration, the effectiveness of the hearing system, the problems of hearing political participation and its causes. On the basis of case analysis, this book analyzes and reveals the institutional defects and negative effects of contemporary China's hearing system, and then discusses and proposes the feasible path of improving citizens' political participation.

4.2 Three case studies of the hearing

In this section, we take the three hearings held in Zhejiang Province in recent years as examples to specifically investigate the actual operation of citizens' use of the hearing for political participation and expression of interests. The scope of our review includes two aspects: interest expression and interest integration. The content of the inspection is as follows: The first is the hearing effect; the second, the problems and causes of the process of hearing participation and interest realization. Three hearings, including legislative hearing, administrative hearing and judicial hearing, are included in the case analysis. Among them, the first case is the legislative hearing, namely the legislative hearing of the Property Management Regulation (Draft) of Zhejiang Province. The second case is the administrative hearing, namely the hearing of Hangzhou taxi price adjustment. The last case is the judicial hearing, which is the case of the

Political Participation and Institutional Innovation:
A Case Study of Zhejiang

execution of Wu Shizhong outside prison by the court of Ouhai District in Wenzhou.

4.2.1 Legislative hearing case

Case 1: Legislative hearing of the Property Management Regulation (Draft) of Zhejiang Province

On February 28, 2006, the legislative hearing of the Property Management Regulation (Draft) of Zhejiang Province was held in the multi-function hall of Hangzhou Xinqiao Hotel. This was the third legislative hearing held by the Standing Committee of the People's Congress of Zhejiang Province.

(1) *Brief introduction to the hearing process*

(1) *Participation subject composition*

The Legal Committee of the Legislative Affairs Committee of the People's Congress of Zhejiang Province, the Financial and Economic Commission and the Legislative Work Committee of the Standing Committee of the People's Congress of Zhejiang Province jointly held the hearing. The representatives of the hearing were 16 people from Hangzhou, Ningbo, Jinhua and Shaoxing, including four owners; two representatives from the residential property and non-residential property owners committee; two representatives of the early property service enterprises and ordinary property service enterprises; two representatives of real estate development enterprises; two representatives of relevant professional units such as water supply and power supply; one representative from the neighborhood committee; one representative from the property management department; and two lawyers. Lu Wenge, Deputy Director of the Standing Committee of Zhejiang Provincial People's Congress, was the host of the hearing. Multiple media got involved in the coverage. There was a total of 28 media at all levels shooting and broadcasting. The hearing was attended by 30 members, including the hearing specialist Cui Yansheng.

Chapter 4 Hearing: Interest Expression and Interest Integration Mechanism

It can be said that the participants in this hearing are quite extensive, with both general interests expressing individuals (listeners, etc.) and professional interests expressing individuals (representatives of property and real estate company), but also institutional interest expression group (people's congress) and functional expression group (media).

(2) Perspective of the contents of the hearing

Targeting at three main issues in this hearing, namely the handover and maintenance of facilities and equipment such as water supply and power supply, the question of property decoration and the decision procedure of the owners' congress, 16 representatives of the hearing spoke at the hearing and had a heated debate.

Regarding the handover and maintenance of facilities and equipment such as water supply and power supply, the owner was willing to hand over the property rights of the water and electricity facilities, but the water supply and power supply units required conditional acceptance.

Articles 31 and 50 of the draft stipulate that the construction units shall hand over facilities such as water supply and power supply to the relevant professional units within 3 months after the completion and acceptance of the property by the construction units and determine its care and maintenance responsibility according to the ownership principle of property rights. The transfer of maintenance and repair management right of water supply and power facilities to relevant professional units is the consensus of representatives participating in the hearing. The discussion focused on whether the water supply and power supply units should obtain the relevant property rights and how to obtain them. Most speakers agreed with the idea that ownership of water and power supply facilities would be handed over along with management.

Political Participation and Institutional Innovation:
A Case Study of Zhejiang

According to Li Jinlin, a teacher at Zhejiang University, relevant professional units should assume responsibility for maintenance and at the same time property rights should also be transferred to relevant units. According to Cai Jianqiang, representative of the water supply unit, the transfer of property right and maintenance responsibility is not only in accordance with the principle of equal rights and obligations, but also in the fundamental interests of owners. "If the property right is not transferred, the water supply enterprise will not be able to depreciate the fixed assets as required, and the renewal and transformation of these assets in the future will lose the source of funds and increase the burden on the owners". According to Han Xiaohan, Deputy Director of marketing department of provincial power company, if the property rights of the owner of the water supply are accepted, according to the current legal policy, the relevant units need to pay the enterprise income tax of 33%, so it is urgent for the government to issue a supporting tax exemption policy.

With regard to the decoration of properties, it is safe for the owner to take precautions and adopt measures of "Better late than never".

Articles 51, 52 and 53 of the draft regulate the decoration of the property and make clear provisions on the prohibitions on property decoration. They strengthen the in-process supervision and post-supervision management, and give full play to the social power supervision function of the neighboring households, that is, the people who are strongly related to them without setting administrative licenses. It is the common opinion of the participants in the hearing to make a prohibition regulation on the behavior that endangers the building safety in the property decoration, but some representatives have raised their objection as follows on the question of whether to establish the administrative license or not.

Pan Xiaojun from Ningbo Meiwu Property Management Co., Ltd.: "As for the problem of property decoration, I don't think it is necessary to set the administrative license, but it is appropriate to make the

Chapter 4 Hearing:
Interest Expression and Interest Integration Mechanism

prohibition provisions. Since the existing laws and regulations have stipulated that it is not allowed to destroy the main body and the bearing structure, it is unnecessary to set administrative license in terms of the legal relationship". Tang Zhixin, Director of West Lake Home Owner Council: "Administrative licensing and prohibitive regulations should be carried out simultaneously. The most important thing is to implement compulsory measures. Destructive and barbaric decoration cannot be resolved through general ideological work and persuasion, and it is difficult to achieve a certain effect without enforcement". Han Nansheng, Deputy Director of Zhejiang Law Firm: "House decoration is the proprietor's disposition to own private property and does not need to be brought into the administrative license. It is suggested that the original house design drawings and the newly decorated design drawings should be submitted, including the developer's opinion on whether the decoration affects the safety. With this proof, the property management committee or the residential area shall first review the materials, and send to the urban construction management department for the record".

On the decision procedure of the owners' convention: "If the owner fails to participate in the voting, he shall be deemed to agree with the majority". Focusing on this provision, the parties to the hearing held their own views and launched a heated debate.

According to the Regulations on Property Management under the State Council, a decision of the owners' meeting must be approved by more than half of the voting power of the participating owners. Decision to formulate and modify the owner convention, rules of procedure of owner congress, hiring and firing the property management enterprise, use and raising plan of the special maintenance funds must be approved by more than two-thirds of all the voting rights held by the owner. Owners who do not vote are deemed to agree with the majority opinion. This was one of the most divisive issues among delegates at the hearing, and 16 presenters debated on it intensely. At the same time, many representatives also put forward many good methods on how to attract owners to participate in decision-making, how to protect the interests of owners who do not participate in voting, and how to clarify the main subject of conveners of owners' congress. The following are some examples.

Xu Chunzhou, Director of Owner Committee of Jinhua Liangjie District: "The majority of owners are concerned about what they propose, and the key is how to express their opinions. For a community with a large population, it is normal to have a long voting cycle and great difficulty. The more people a community is related to, the more manpower and material resources should be invested". Si Limin, the Party Secretary of the Party Committee of Jingduyuan Community in Xiacheng District: "'If the owner fails to vote within the time limit, he or she is deemed to agree with the opinion of the majority'. It is appropriate and feasible. At present, some owners do not come to vote for work or other reasons. If you wait for them, the reality is that the election cannot go on. So it's important that prior to the formulation of this provision, the owners must be informed in writing of the form and the relevant contents of the election and be endorsed by the owner's signature". Retired worker Li Jinlin: "'If the owner fails to vote within the time limit, he or she is deemed to agree with the opinion of the majority'. It has little effect on the majority opinion. Most people are not present at this time, so how can there be consent to the majority?" Lawyer Jin Ying: "It is also a way for owners to participate in community affairs and not to vote. 'If the owner fails to vote within the time limit, he or she is deemed to agree with the opinion of the majority'. It is contrary to the legislative regulations of the State Council, and it will also bring serious negative effects in future law enforcement practices. The result of such a vote will be hard-pressed to become the majority owners' conscious action".

After the hearing, the legislative committee of the provincial people's congress would compile the hearing report according to the records of the hearing. The hearing report would be submitted to each

Chapter 4　Hearing:
Interest Expression and Interest Integration Mechanism

of the members of the standing committee of the provincial people's congress as the basis for the second consideration of the draft by then.

(2) *Characteristics and effect analysis of the legislative hearing*

From the legislative hearing of the Property Management Regulation (Draft) of Zhejiang Province, it can be found that there are some characteristics of citizens' political participation and interest expression during the legislative hearing.

First is professional, that is, representative and expert integration. Many representatives themselves are experts in property management, giving people the impression that they are experts rather than representatives. Except Zhejiang University teacher Li Jinlin, retired workers Li Jinlin and Pan Jinkang, and college student Du Wangtong, others are business leaders from property companies, property management or hydropower professional units or law firms, with a strong professional background.

Second, the topic is concentrated, with the point of view collision more prominent, and there is a certain degree of debate. The hearing focusing on three major issues, with both democratic atmosphere and a certain depth of issues, can solve the need for improvement in the regulations. In the course of the discussion, 16 delegates engaged in a heated debate, especially the hydropower department, property management department and owners.

Third, strong openness. The whole process of the hearing is open, from the public solicitation of hearing representatives to the three focal issues to be discussed publicly by the public hearing process. And the 21st meeting of the Standing Committee of the 10th People's Congress of Zhejiang Province first reviewed the Property Management Regulation (Draft) of Zhejiang Province in November 2005 on the property management regulations of Zhejiang Province submitted by the provincial people's government. According to the decision of the Chairman of the Standing Committee of the People's Congress, the draft regulation was published in the full text of *Zhejiang Daily* on December 19, 2004, which makes the Property Management Regulation (Draft) of Zhejiang Province well known.

Fourth, the free participation of the press. In this hearing, dozens of media and networks participated in a comprehensive way, and many of the media conducted live interviews, shooting and broadcasting. The journalists from 28 media outlets in and out of the province went on the scene, and even the leaders of the well-connected Zhejiang Provincial People's Congress and other relevant departments marveled at the rare sight.

From the perspective of interest expression and interest integration, the hearing of the Property Management Regulation (Draft) of Zhejiang Province has basically reached the hearing participation and interest expression requirements of all parties.

From the point of view of interest expression, the elements of hearing participation in interest expression are basically complete and belong to normal interest expression. (1) The representatives' quality and ability are relatively strong. The 16 hearing representatives in this hearing are basically the elite of the property industry or the professional industry closely related to the management of the property industry, who have a strong professional background and there are no problems in information acquisition and property management. (2) Equality of rights and obligations. The speaking time of each representative is 8 minutes, and the statement is supplemented by 3 minutes, which ensures the fairness of expression; at the same time, the hearing is a more noticeable debate, not only are the interests of the various interest groups presented, but through the debate and in-depth comparison, these will also be specific and clear, making interests expression more accurate. (3) The delegates have a departmental interest tendency. The 16 representatives have the opportunity to make profits for themselves by taking advantage of this opportunity, which is also the nature of

Chapter 4 Hearing:
Interest Expression and Interest Integration Mechanism

the game of interests of the hearing. For example, the hydropower department of this hearing is not willing to accept the property rights of hydropower equipment in the property community, but bargains for more interests; property managers advocate that the owners' assembly vote implement "not voting is considered a majority opinion", ignoring the owner's democratic rights. Even if representatives have an interest tendency, their claims are more in line with the actual needs of real estate management. From these points of view, the hearing is basically able to accurately and fully express the interests of the majority of the owners, which is the reason for its success.

From the perspective of interest integration, through this hearing, the interests of various stakeholders have been basically coordinated or integrated. Interest coordination or integration requires equal hearing coordination mechanism and organized resources of various interest groups. (1) The coordination mechanism comprises at least four areas: First, the public system of hearing process from the solicitation of representatives to the hearing to the results of the aftermath; second, the hosts' neutrality; third, the media's free participation; fourth, the experts' neutrality. These aspects are ready to be a complete system of coordination of interests. These several points of this hearing have been basically available. (2) Interest game. There are several interest game subjects in this hearing. They are owners, hydropower departments, property management departments, hosts, lawyers, people's congress as the representatives of the neutral forces. (i) The interest competition among the stakeholders is obvious. For example, owners demand that all interests be maintained on the basis of property rights, and hydropower departments hope to get more benefits from the property industry. The property management department hopes that the management difficulties will be minimized, that the owners will give up some rights such as the right to vote and decorate, and that the hydropower department will assume more responsibilities to reduce the pressure on property management. (ii) Neutrality. For example, the neutrality represented by the host, the hearing sponsor and the lawyer who wanted to establish a property management regulation that would rationalize the interests of all parties, which is convenient for the government to enforce the law, and also to conduct business for the lawyers. It has legal basis to deal with the property disputes, so as to stabilize the property dispute revenue of the law industry. (iii) The degree of organization determines the position of the game. The hydropower department and the property managers get interests from the department and the industry. Their strength is concentrated, with high organization degree and they occupy the obvious superiority in the game; however, the owners are decentralized and unorganized, and play an interest game with hydropower and property management departments of high degree of organization, so their disadvantages are prominent. As Olsen puts it: "A small group can ignore the inevitable hitchhiker behavior of a big group,"[4] which is beneficial to develop a property management system that is operable and can make interests of all parties balanced. Therefore, this position of the people's congress, the open procedure of the hearing and the participation of the news media and the Internet are conducive to the integration of the interests of various interest groups.

(3) *Problems existing in the political participation and interest expression process of legislative hearings*

First of all, the elite of the existing hearing representatives affected the representativeness. Most of the participants in the hearing of the Property Management Regulation (Draft) of Zhejiang Province came from the elite of the society. The hearing, especially the legislative hearing, should be a framework of democratic participation, and its function is to meet the needs of the interests expressed and balanced. Public participation in the hearing is to let the participants understand their own interests and the other sides' needs. The participants in the hearing were indeed very professional,

---

[4]Olson. *Logic of Collective Action*. Translated by Chen Yu. Shanghai: SDX Joint Publishing Company and Shanghai People's Publishing House, 2004: 111.

Chapter 4 Hearing:
Interest Expression and Interest Integration Mechanism

and most of the participants were of expert origin. But it is hard to say that the conclusion of the hearing must be in the interests of the owners who have a stake in the matter but do not know much about the requirements of property management. Property management is only heard by property management experts, so it is difficult to ensure whether such hearing process ignores the interests of ordinary owners. The representative elite and specialization of this hearing are highly concentrated, and the ordinary owners can't form a fair benefit game even if they participate in the lack of equal benefit expression guarantee, and to some degree the ordinary owners belong to those being represented. We emphasize that legislation should protect the legitimate interests of the private sector and realize the interests of the majority in the legislation. However, we should emphasize that the unfairness of the original legislation of the original government should not be taken into account, and it is not fair to jump into some interest groups to use the democratic form of hearing to conduct the rough representation of the other interest groups. It is the balance of interests of all stakeholders that should be reflected in the hearing.

Second, the homoorganicity of the host, the organizer and the decision-maker will influence the impartiality of the legislation. This legislative hearing, the hearing person, the host and the organizer are all the provincial people's congress office, so this arrangement will affect the authority of the hearing. No matter how the people's congress tries to show how fair it is to listen to the views of various interest groups in society, due to the fact of the homogeneity of the host, the sponsor and the decision-maker of the hearing, there is a lack of power restriction and supervision among them, which makes the public doubt the fairness of the hearing process. In theory, no matter how hard it tries to ensure justice for power, as long as it is highly concentrated, it is suspected of being unjust. Acton believes that power corrupts and absolute power corrupts absolutely. Moreover, in practice, each country's hearing system seeks the balance of power of the participants. In the United States, Britain, Germany and Japan, the hearing system structure seeks to balance and restrict the power of the hearing system within the hearing system, including the supporting person, the organizer, the hearing person, the applicant, the witness (that is, the hearing representative), and so on, forming a hearing system cluster structure with mutual restraint and supervision. In their institutional structure, especially in the United States, the host has a special independent legal status. It is not a unified relationship with the organizer of the hearing. The hearing person is also separated from the organizer. The organizer is not the hearing person, and the hearing person is not the organizer.

Third, there is no arrangement for the representatives to speak, which is not conducive to the expression, coordination and integration of the interests of citizens. The hearing did not arrange for the audience to participate in the speech and debate, which was obviously detrimental to the interests of various interest groups, especially the owners. The owner fails to achieve the interest expression through the hearing representatives, nor can he/she make up for it by the audience, which is a lack of political participation in the whole legislative hearing. This lack of procedure is not conducive to the interest expression of each hearing interest group, but also affects the coordination and integration of the interests of all parties.

4.2.2 Administrative hearing case

Case 2: Hangzhou taxi fare adjustment hearing

On the afternoon of November 8, 2005, the hearing was held at Hangzhou Huachen International Hotel in Hangzhou. Twenty official representatives attended the hearing.

(1) *Brief introduction to the hearing process*

The following is the application plan for taxi fare adjustment submitted by the Hangzhou Transport Bureau: (1) The starting price of ordinary taxi is adjusted from 10 yuan/4 km to 10 yuan/3 km; (2) the charge for

Chapter 4 Hearing:
Interest Expression and Interest Integration Mechanism

the empty return for above 8 km will be adjusted to 50% from 20%, i.e. the empty return will be adjusted from 2.4 yuan/km to 3 yuan/km; (3) the night rental price is restored, but the price is increased by 20% from 10 p.m. to 6 a.m.; (4) the starting price of luxury taxi is adjusted from 12 yuan/4 km to 10 yuan/2.5 km. The rental price of 2.5 yuan/km is the same and the adjustment of empty return fee and night rate adjustment are the same as those of ordinary taxis. At the same time, according to the application plan, the linkage mechanism between freight price and oil price will be set up. When the price of oil breaks through a reasonable range, the price is adjusted by adjusting the mileage or the fuel surcharge.

In the proposal to the Transport Bureau, 11 representatives affirmed the application of the price adjustment of the Municipal Transport Bureau and believed that the full plan was feasible. Seven representatives agreed to adjust the price, and found that the scheme was basically reasonable, but the empty return fee was charged above 8 km, which was not suitable for the current situation of the expansion of the city in Hangzhou. Most representatives suggested that the empty return fee should be at least 10 km or more, while some representatives also said that the time limit for night overtime should not be too long. Two representatives objected to the price adjustment, saying that the price adjustment was not an effective way to solve the drivers' low-income problem. The municipal government should apply the special funds collected from the taxi license fee for special use to solve a series of problems. Finally, there were 18 votes of assent and two dissenting votes approving the fare adjustment application of the Transportation Bureau.

According to the result of the vote, Hangzhou Municipal Government fully recognized the request of the Transportation Bureau to apply for the price increase plan. On February 21, Wang Zhongguo, Director of the Administrative Department of the Administration of the Commodity Price Bureau of Hangzhou, announced that the city would raise the rate of taxi fares from the 22nd, after the Hangzhou Municipal

Government agreed. The specific plan for the price adjustment is as follows: The starting price of the luxury taxi represented by Mercedes-Benz is 10 yuan/2.5 km from the current 12 yuan/4 km. The rental fee is 3 yuan/km within 8 km, and 5 yuan/km for more than 8 km. In addition to luxury taxis, the starting range of most premium taxis is 3 km from the current 4 km, and the starting price is 10 yuan. The compensation fee for the empty return shall be adjusted to 50% of the above 10 km or more, i.e. 3 yuan/km. That is to say, the result of this hearing is fully accepted by the government and established by the policy.

(2) *Analysis of reasons for hearing*

There was a direct, deep-seated reason for the hearing: The immediate cause was a surge in international and domestic fuel prices. The basic reason is that the upgrade of taxi grade leads to the increase in the cost of taxi management fees, repair fees and insurance premiums, which in turn leads to the high operating costs of the taxi industry. Taxi owners and drivers are unable to continue their work, because many of the high-end vehicles are idle, and there is also a drivers' collective escape event.

Second, the upgrade of taxi grade. In June 2003, Hangzhou Municipal Government issued a policy, except for Xiaoshan and Yuhang. If the city taxi is updated, its displacement must be above 2 liters and the price is above 200,000 yuan. Later, 98% of Hangzhou's more than 7,000 taxis were replaced with high-end models such as Passat, Red Flag and even Mercedes-Benz. As a result, Hangzhou has become the city with the highest taxi grade in China.

The increase in grade leads to a sharp increase in taxi operating costs. How much do the high-grade taxis cost compared with the mid-grade car? Chen Jianhe, Marketing Director of Zhejiang Baotong Automobile Co., Ltd., who has 16 years of experience in automobile sales, made a detailed list at the hearing. *Price*: for ordinary Santana in 1996, including the surcharge, the total price is 150,000 yuan.

Chapter 4　Hearing:
Interest Expression and Interest Integration Mechanism

Currently, for Passat, Red Flag, Sonata, and other taxis in Hangzhou, an average price (inclusive of tax) is 210,000 yuan. *Oil fee*: in 1996, mid-grade taxi used 90 octane gasoline, and oil price was 2 yuan more. At present, the premium cars are using gasoline at either 93 or 97 octane, which has risen to 4.4 yuan due to the rise in international oil prices and the increase in the price of oil in China. And the premium taxi fuel consumption is much higher than that of the mid-range car. *Maintenance cost*: after the upgrade of the vehicle class, the maintenance cost has also been greatly improved. For example, the most commonly used oil is 50–60 yuan per barrel, but now Passat is using 84 yuan per barrel of oil. The price of front brake pads used earlier for Passat was 201 yuan per set, but now the price of front brake pads for Passat is 390 yuan per set. In addition, insurance premium is also a significant cost in taxi operation, and the increase in insurance costs caused by the upgrade of the taxi has made the situation worse for operators.

The taxi owners were unable to continue operations. Fang Kai, Deputy Secretary-General of Hangzhou Urban Taxi Association, gave several figures as an industry representative: Now taxi operators mainly bear the vehicle price, business license fees, insurance and so on. Compared with the situation in 1996, the monthly cost per car is 2,600 yuan more, and most of the profits of enterprises are consumed. General manager of Volkswagen pointed out the following: For a Mercedes-Benz, its 1-month depreciation expense is 5,233 yuan, the car insurance is 1,016 yuan, the financial fee is 1,140 yuan, the repair fee is 3,000 yuan and the total cost is 12,805 yuan. After deducting the cost and deducting the income tax of 33% from a rental fee of 13,200 yuan (one car and two persons), the company can only earn 265 yuan per vehicle per month. At the end of September 2005, Hangzhou Foreign Affairs Tourism Taxi Company and Hangzhou Sifang Passenger Transportation Company launched advertising, and began to voluntarily reduce the rent of "Mercedes-Benz taxi", but no one was willing to contract. Thirty five of the 50 Mercedes-Benz taxis of a Hangzhou taxi company were still in the warehouse.

Political Participation and Institutional Innovation:
A Case Study of Zhejiang

The taxi drivers were unable to operate, resulting in a collective escape. For example, Lu Yang was a Passat taxi driver in Zhejiang, and has been driving in Hangzhou for 5 or 6 years. He drove a taxi a few years ago, earning 7,000–8,000 yuan a month, and at that time, it was a high income. And after the upgrade, he earned less than 1,500 yuan. In the early hours of January 9, six Henan Xihua taxi drivers of Hangzhou Volkswagen Taxi Co., Ltd. drove out of Hangzhou with the contracted Mercedes-Benz taxi, and drove all the way back to their hometown of Ai Gang, Xihua County, Zhoukou City, Henan Province.

(3) *The effect and existing problems of the hearing*

For taxi operators, the interests of taxi operators and drivers are well expressed over the hearing. And then the vote and the government decision made their interests secure. For taxi operators, the aforementioned reasons are enough to justify the price hike. This is why previous hearings have been held for 8 hours for statement by the applicants and 8 minutes by the hearing representatives. For a hearing representative, such a short time is not sufficient to express interest. At this hearing, some representatives spoke for less than 3 minutes, and believed that the operators and drivers had a large workload and low income, and the price increase should be justified. And the hearing endorsed the price increase by a vote of 18:2. The result of this vote was adopted directly as the basis of decision-making; thus, it can be seen that the interests of taxi operators and drivers were fully expressed during the whole hearing process.

For taxi consumers, the representatives present at the hearing did not represent their interests very well, thus leading to the insufficient expression and integration of consumers' interest demands. This is one of the most prominent issues of the hearing. In protecting the legitimate interests of taxi operators and drivers, it should not be done at the expense of other groups. As defined in the distribution principle of Rawls's theory of justice, it should not be at the expense of the interests

Chapter 4　Hearing:
Interest Expression and Interest Integration Mechanism

of the minority for the satisfaction of most people, let alone meeting the interests of the minority at the expense of the interests of the majority. In order to solve the problem of legitimate interests of taxi operators and drivers, it should be based on the principle of fairness and justice rather than transferring the cost to consumers. The result of the hearing was that the interests of consumers which should not be sacrificed were sacrificed. This hearing had problems in the expression of consumer interests, which can be explained from the perspective of interest expression and interest integration.

From the point of view of interest expression, there is a lack of participation of elements in the structure of the hearing. This kind of hearing does not really reflect the interests participation and appeal of the missing elements. This hearing has two aspects of the absence of factors, one is the absence of consumers. Many people believe that consumers were not actually present at the hearing. Without the presence of consumers, the service providers pass on their losses to consumers, and the interests of consumers are not really expressed. Although representatives are produced through public solicitation, a limited number of nine official consumer representatives do not adequately represent more than 6.5 million Hangzhou residents. And during the hearing, 20 representatives at random sacrifice the interests of the entire consumer group regardless of consumers' doubts and objections. The following were the media reports at the time: The 20 hearing representatives represented 6,516,800 Hangzhou residents, while one person raised hands and more than 300,000 people paid the bill. The other is the government; as an important independent factor, it should have participted, but did not. It is widely believed that one of the responsibilities of the taxi operation dilemma is the so-called image project planned by the government by upgrading taxis rather than increasing fuel prises. The government should take on this responsibility, should reduce management fees appropriately, standardize enterprise's recruitment, unleash the taxi industry, rather than transferring the burden on to their customers, but the government did not appear at the hearing. The representatives believe that the rising cost of taxi operation is not a problem that can be solved by price adjustment alone. In fact, the taxi operating warrant system in Hangzhou is the source of unreasonable costs for drivers. It is unreasonable to adjust the freight rate just to pass the operating cost to the market.

From the perspective of interest integration, the interests of various interest groups in the hearing process are not balanced. The interests of the government, the Transport Bureau and the taxi companies are best integrated and they are the largest beneficiaries. The aggregate of consumers is the least sufficient. The representatives at the hearing do not fully represent the interests of consumers, and at most represent their personal opinions. Because of the absence of consumers at this hearing, their interests were not expressed and they were not coordinated. As a result, the interests of the government, the Transport Bureau and the owners, as well as the drivers are highly and fully presented to the decision-makers, and are the most widely understood parts by the policymakers. In the means of the integration of interests, the Transport Bureau and the owners can mobilize the maximum political resources support. Due to the lack of consumer interest expression and integration, the restriction of media participation, the result for consumers in the hearing is bad. The reason why the interest integration is so unbalanced lies not in the lack of media participation, but in the lack of free participation, not in the public hearing, but in the non-neutrality of the presiding organ of the hearing. The host of the hearing is dispatched by the organizer and has no independent legal status. The host of China's hearing often has close relationship with the government department, which is the relevant party of interest. The close relationship between the organizer and the government makes it difficult to ensure that the host of the hearing remains neutral, which affects the expression of hearing interests and the function of interest integration.

Chapter 4 Hearing:
Interest Expression and Interest Integration Mechanism

4.2.3 Judicial hearing case

Judicial hearing is different from legislative hearing and price hearing. It is not a massive hearing concerning a large general public decision where the citizens influence government. Instead, it is a hearing where the relative person of the specific judicial action will influence the specific judicial acts of the judicial organs in the field of legal system, in order to protect their own rights and interests. In the following case, we will examine how citizens can realize their own interests in the judicial hearing and apply the judicial hearing system to influence the judicial organs, so that the court can make decisions in favor of them, so as to protect the legitimate rights and interests of the citizens themselves.

Case 3: Hearing on serving sentences outside prison of Wu Shizhong, Ouhai District Court of Wenzhou

In 2003, Wu Shizhong was sentenced to 3 years' imprisonment by Ouhai District Court of Wenzhou for killing a person in a traffic accident. Wu made a request for serving sentence outside prison to the Ouhai District Court on the grounds that he had Hepatitis B. On July 5, 2004, the Ouhai District Court held a hearing on Wu's application. Li Jianping, President of the trial supervision court of Ouhai District Court, was the presiding judge of the hearing. Ouhai District Court invited Wenzhou Ouhai's district attorney to participate in the hearing. This was the first case of serving sentence outside prison in Zhejiang Province, which aroused strong reaction from the society. The specific case and hearing process are as follows:

(1) *Brief introduction to the hearing process*

In early August 2003, Wu Shizhong, in Xianyan Town, Ouhai District, Wenzhou, drove an overloaded truck with a fake plate and killed the driver of a farm truck on the spot. Then, he was arrested on suspicion of traffic offences by police. During the period, he was diagnosed with Hepatitis B and was granted a guarantor pending trial

**Political Participation and Institutional Innovation:
A Case Study of Zhejiang**

by the public security organ. On June 8, 2004, Ouhai District Court sentenced Wu to 3 years in prison for traffic offences. On June 28, before delivery, Wu Shizhong applied to the court for temporary service outside prison on the grounds that he was suffering from infectious diseases, and issued a medical appraisal issued by the People's Hospital of Ouhai District and the First Affiliated Hospital of Wenzhou Medical College. Wu Shizhong was identified with chronic active Hepatitis B in the medical appraisal record. Ouhai District Court heard the case before the trial supervision court. On July 5, 2004, Ouhai District Court held a hearing on whether Wu could serve his sentence outside prison. Local prosecutors also took part in the hearing. At the hearing, Wu's representation stated the reason for serving sentences outside prison. The prosecutor asked about Wu's medical history, treatment, family prevention and so on, and Wu answered and presented the relevant materials. The court held that after the traffic accident, Wu had a good attitude toward financial compensation and confession of guilt, and provided materials to prove that he was no longer socially harmful. According to Wu's medical appraisal and written materials, such as medical treatment and medication due to Hepatitis B in the early stage, the disease accorded with the relevant regulations of "the range of illness and disability of criminals seeking medical parole". On July 6, Wu Shizhong was sentenced to serve sentence outside prison for 1 year. According to the regulation, in the following year, Wu Shizhong would seek medical advice in his residence and regularly report to the police station. If there is a special condition to leave the residence temporarily, it must be approved by the police station; if it is necessary to seek medical treatment outside the province, it shall be approved by the county public security organ.

The hearing on Wu Shizhong's serving sentence outside prison was considered to be of great significance to judicial justice and protection of human rights. Li Jianping, presiding judge of the trial court of Ouhai District Court, said: "It is an attempt to hold hearings on serving

Chapter 4 Hearing: Interest Expression and Interest Integration Mechanism

sentence outside prison. This reflects the seriousness of criminal law and the spirit of respecting human rights". He believes that the serving of sentence outside prison is a change to the content of the execution of the penalty, and also has the nature of the exercise of the jurisdiction, which should be made jointly by the participation and negotiation of the public prosecution organ and the punished person. "This is the direct reason for our hearing", Chen Guanghua, Director of the Political Department of the Ouhai District Procuratorate, said. Prior to the trial of whether or not to grant serving of sentence outside prison, it was generally conducted in writing. The court has a large discretion, whose transparency is not high, affecting the credibility of the judicial organ. The court offered to hold hearings and invite procuratorial organs to participate, which is conducive to strengthening mutual supervision and restriction between judicial organs. Li Jinsong, a lawyer from Zhejiang Junan law firm, has a positive attitude toward serving a sentence outside prison. In his view, changing the written review to the hearing review is an opportunity for the convicted offenders to refute, which is conducive to the elimination of the black box operation of the law enforcement department and the openness of the law enforcement power. "This has positive significance for protecting the human rights of criminals and safeguarding judicial justice."

(2) *Analysis of the effect of the hearing*

This hearing is the first one in the history of Zhejiang Province on serving a sentence outside prison, with the following characteristics:

First, the transparent hearing provides sufficient information for the offender to openly refute and maintain his own interests. In this hearing procedure, the offender fully understands and grasps the requirements of applying for serving a sentence outside prison, and has more comprehensive information for serving a sentence outside prison. In the past, few courts had told prisoners under what conditions they could apply to serve their sentences outside prison. Citizens did

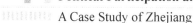

Political Participation and Institutional Innovation: A Case Study of Zhejiang

not know the law, and judges did not inform them, thus monopolizing information. Even if a prisoner has access to legal knowledge and information about serving a sentence outside prison from a lawyer, the court often has a great deal of discretion. Usually, when the information is not open to the public, the judge's will and interest decide whether to serve a sentence or not, and citizens often lose the opportunity to argue and defend their own interests because of the lack of relevant legal information. As for the legal provision of serving a sentence outside prison, very few prisoners will use it as long as the court does not give notice, and the court will often use its discretion to nullify this provision. So unless the court supports a prisoner's application to serve a sentence, few citizens would want to use these rights.

Second, consciously accept the power restriction and supervision of the procuratorate to ensure the legitimate interests and interests of prisoners. The court gives the offender the opportunity to plead, but in the hearing, if the court's power is not supervised, even if the court decides in full accordance with the law, the power is not subject to the restriction and supervision of relevant authorities, and it will give the impression of injustice. The hearing was no longer a behind-the-scenes ruling by the court alone, in accordance with past prison sentences, but instead invited prosecutors to participate. In essence, it is to accept the power supervision and restriction of the procuratorate in judicial practice, and limit the abuse of discretion in judicial proceedings, forming an external environment that is fair to prisoners' interests.

Third, to give criminals the opportunity to use all possible political resources to influence judicial decisions. The hearing gave the offenders an opportunity to express their interests and to provide a reference for the judge's decision. At the same time, it is helpful for the criminal to use a variety of political resources to influence judicial decisions, and further promote the judicial hearing to facilitate the expression of the

Chapter 4 Hearing: Interest Expression and Interest Integration Mechanism

interests of citizens and the integration of interests. In this hearing, the judge of Ouhai District Court not only provided the argument for his sentence, but also told Wu which elements should be given if he was to serve out of prison and the authority of which institutions should be recognized and supported. The court also requested the procuratorate to participate in the hearing on its own initiative. In fact, it was the Ouhai Court that requested supervision of the procuratorate on its own initiative, which objectively limited the discretion of the court and prevented the black box operation in the aspect of serving a sentence outside prison.

(3) Problems and improvement of judicial hearing

The hearing was the first in Zhejiang Province for serving a sentence outside prison. There are still some imperfections in the procedure. The hearing person, the host, the attendee, the media and other parties involved are still at the exploring stage. The whole hearing is not much different from the trial procedure, even the host is not called as the host but the presiding judge. However, the procedural requirements of the hearing are different from those of the court. Although called hearing, the mode is still a judicial trial one, reflecting the obvious deficiencies. Specifically, we need to consider the following aspects, in order to truly benefit the expression and integration of the interests of citizens.

First, open process. The hearing was only a limited form of publicity. Compared with the previous closed court trials, this hearing has brought in the participation of other organs in the field of judicial power, such as procuratorates, which means a kind of transparency and openness. This made it possible for the court to share power with other judicial power units, which would otherwise have belonged to the discretion of the court, making black box operation impossible in power constraints. But we said the hearing was very limited. The news prior to the hearing was not published in the media and did not give citizens other than the perpetrator the right to know; despite its significance, serving a sentence out of prison is in the interest of millions of citizens. The hearing was not conducted in public, with involvement of the procuratorate in court trials, which was not known to citizens outside of the proceedings. The results of the hearing were also closed to the public. Their awareness of such a significant hearing was the result of subsequent media reports and revelations by the judge.

Second, open access. The hearing may have been a limited disclosure at the outset, and it was not intended to involve too many people, so it did not attach importance to the arrangement of the attendees. For a hearing, an important element is that there must be an attendee who not only participates as a representative of an interested person but also supervises the judicial power on behalf of the social power. The presence of an audience means that judicial power is made public, and that the black box operation under power of judges can be reduced. Hearing audition is also a witness of the public hearing. Without audition, the hearing is not a complete one. Hearing is called "public hearing" in English. One of the meanings is to hear and witness, not the testimony of the prosecution, but the witness of the listeners.

Third, open media participation. Hearings mean openness and the free participation of the media. Once the court adopts the form of hearing, it means that it must accept the participation of the media, give interviews and broadcast the information of the hearing to the public in time, facilitate citizens to pay attention to and comment, and accept the supervision of citizens. However, the whole process of the judicial hearing, including the preparatory process before the hearing, the formal hearing process and the announcement of the results after the hearing, had no media participation. Media coverage of the hearing was "old news" of interviews with judges and prosecutors days after the hearing, rather than live coverage. Without media participation, citizens' right

Chapter 4　Hearing:
Interest Expression and Interest Integration Mechanism

to know is restricted, which inevitably affects citizen participation and interest expression.

Fourth, the host of the hearing should be neutral and impartial. If the hearing is not a trial, it should not be conducted in accordance with the trial procedure. In particular, the host of the hearing should be neutral, because then the results of the hearing can have more authority and fairness. The court wants to hear, and the presiding judge of the hearing is acting on his own, so it is easy to leave an impression of injustice. The hearing authority of the court should come from the restriction and supervision of the hearing power. In terms of judicial power, organizations such as the procuratorate and the judicial committee of the people's congress act as hosts more impartially and credibly than judges themselves.

Fifth, the court, procuratorate, people's congress, judicial organs and other units should form the power of restriction and supervision. The hearing of the court is the product of the restriction and supervision of judicial power, and any organ with jurisdiction can exert authority over the hearing result. Therefore, the court hearing is not just for the procuratorate—the entire public security bureau, the procuratorate, the court system as well as the large judicial committee and even the legal institutions can participate in the hearing and conduct supervision. This will make the results of the hearing more fair and authoritative.

Sixth, the restriction and supervision of judicial power by social power represented by citizens, public opinion and lawyers. The restriction and supervision of public power by social power of citizens, public opinion and lawyers is formed over judicial power beyond the power supervisory system of government departments. Of course, social power cannot interfere with the court's independent hearing, nor can it interfere with the court's judgment in accordance with the law. But society and the public have the right to know

Political Participation and Institutional Innovation:
A Case Study of Zhejiang

how the courts hear and whether the hearing proceedings are in accordance with laws, and to comment on the hearing. The judicial hearing did not invite citizens to attend the hearing without the direct participation of the media. It is difficult to ensure the objectivity and impartiality of judicial hearing without the effective supervision of the judicial power of the court.

4.3 Functional analysis of the hearing system

Modern government theory is based on behaviorism methodology and structure–functionalism theory, forming the theoretical framework of supporting and safeguarding the mechanism of governments' information transfer system and supervision process with the interest expression (opinion expression), interest integration (opinion synthesis), decision-making and governance as the core. Structural functionalism represented by Almond believes that the function of the political structure is carried out in the political system, the political process and the political policy process. The system, the process and the policy should be analyzed from the perspective of structure. The hearing is a way and a political structure to achieve the objectives of the political system. The function of this approach and structure can be viewed from the political system level, governmental process level and public policy level. Following the hearing cases in

Zhejiang, we will examine and discuss the functions of hearing political participation according to the government process theory.

4.3.1 From the level of political system
(1) *Enhance the political legitimacy of local government decisions*

The hearing is an institutional innovation to promote citizens' orderly political participation, which provides opportunities for citizens to participate in local public affairs, approach the government officials and directly influence government decision-making. Through the political participation of the hearing, communication and contact between local governments and citizens have been promoted. Through the public consultation formed, it can not only effectively resolve the contradictions and conflicts between citizens and government, but also improve citizens' approval of the government public power and the sense of belonging, so as to enhance the public opinion legitimacy of the government.

(2) *Promote social stability*

The political participation of the hearing has the function of the decompressor. The introduction of the hearing system as well as a series of hearings in the administrative, legislative and judicial processes provide citizens with the available functional channels for the expression of interests and the integration of interests, so that the interests of citizens have the opportunity to enter the public decision-making of the government. Thus, it can help alleviate social contradictions and even eliminate contradictions and conflicts in the embryonic stage.

(3) *Promote grassroots democracy and local governance*

The cases of Zhejiang hearing show that the hearing impels the rise of democracy, equality and public spirit in China. While the general public is rushing to sign up for or attend various kinds of hearings, and the representatives of all parties in the hearing are ready to speak up before the meeting, all kinds of news media's enthusiastic participation

Chapter 4 Hearing:
Interest Expression and Interest Integration Mechanism

and the extensive concern of social public opinion suggest that the hearing system has the positive effects of promoting citizens' orderly political participation and enhancing democracy at the grassroots level and local governance. From the cultural aspect of the political system, the hearing has a positive effect on the cultivation of China's participative citizens and the formation of participatory political culture, which reflects the new atmosphere of democracy development at the grassroots level.

4.3.2 From the level of government process
(1) Function of interest expression

The function of interest expression is the primary function of the hearing system. The political participation of the hearing is the functional means for the citizens to express their interests, protect their legitimate rights and interests, and play the function of benefitting expression. For example, in the legislative hearing on the urban and environmental hygiene regulations of Hangzhou City held on November 20, 2004, Lu Jiangtong, Deputy Director of the Legislative Affairs Committee of the Hangzhou People's Congress pointed out that, "The participants in the hearing are all voluntarily signing up for the meeting, because the content involves their own interests. Its purpose is clear, that is, to fully express their views, so that the hearing person accepts their own point of view. Sometimes it is necessary to argue with the holder of a different view in order to achieve the goal."

(2) Function of interest integration

In the government process, a perfect integration of interests involves the following elements: (1) There must be a wide participation of interested parties or their representatives; (2) the free and equal expression of the interests; (3) the interests must be treated equally; (4) a set of mechanisms or channels to guide the integration of interests in the public interest; (5) aim to be promoted to legal and governmental decision-making. The hearing system established in Zhejiang has preliminarily satisfied a series of elements of the above-mentioned interest integration. First of all, from the perspective of stakeholders or their representatives, whether it is a legislative hearing, a judicial hearing or an administrative hearing, stakeholders and representatives are broadly representative. Second, from the free and equal expression of interests, the hearing itself is the platform to listen to public opinion, whether in theory or practice, and it is to achieve the free and equal interests of groups. Third, from the perspective of equal treatment of interests, although the various interests of the program are treated fairly, this fairness is not reflected in the operation. Fourth, from the perspective of the mechanism of interest integration and its guiding principles, the hearing itself is a mechanism of interest integration. At the same time, the public interest as the guiding principle is also reflected in the hearing system. Fifth, judging from the impact of the hearing on decision-making, the consensus of the hearing and the public opinion reflected in the process of the hearing have influenced the decision-makers and decision-making to some extent. It can be seen that the hearing system established in Zhejiang Province and a series of hearings held in recent years, although there are still some problems and deficiencies, serve the function of the integration of interests to some extent.

4.3.3 From the level of public policy
(1) *Information feedback function*

In the modern government system, the information flow process plays the function of "government nerve". For a long time, China has implemented the single-channel mode of information transmission, and the information channel could not play the function of "government nerve". In recent years, a series of legislative, administrative and judicial hearings have been held in Zhejiang Province, which have increased the function of the government information transmission channel and information feedback. This indicates that the establishment of China's hearing system increases the channels of government information transmission. Hearing is both the input channel of

Chapter 4 Hearing: Interest Expression and Interest Integration Mechanism

government information and the output channel of policies. It alleviates the pressure of the traditional single-channel information transmission system, expands the transmission mode of government information, and facilitates the transition of government information from single-channel to multi-channel.

(2) Social supervision function

The closure of traditional single-channel information transmission system has weakened the social supervision function in the process of government. The implementation of the hearing system provides the channel of information transmission for social supervision. In Zhejiang, the application and implementation of the hearing play a role in the social supervision of the government process, for example, the administrative hearing on the adjustment of water supply price and sewage treatment fee in Wenzhou City. The fact that the water supply consensus reached 8:2 in the hearing was distorted in the later decision-making process caused a great social response, prompting the government to reflect on its decision. Undoubtedly, this social response itself is also one of the social effects of the hearing, which helps improve the supervision of the decision-making process of the government.

4.4 Institutional defects in the participation of political citizens

4.4.1 Defects and system "deviation" of the hearing system

(1) *Participants*: *Representativeness and neutrality*

First of all, the solicitation is not normative and representativeness is not organized. Except for cases we have investigated, the political participants in the hearing tend to be citizens in the name of individuals and less in the name of organizations or associations. In addition to "permanent representatives" such as deputies to the people's congress and members of the CPPCC, other representatives participated in the name of individuals in the hearing. The "potato" nature of this participation caused no necessary connection between the representative and the interest group. These representatives without organizational or group background are not necessarily representative, nor are they able to express the interests and demands of their

Chapter 4　Hearing:
Interest Expression and Interest Integration Mechanism

representative groups well during the hearing process. That is why the consensus at the hearing was widely denied and rejected outside the venue. Political scientist Huntington points out that institutionalized trade unions, the Communist Youth League, and women's federations are understood as extensions of government due to their innate quasi-official nature. Those highly organized groups have a strong political dependency and a weak free expression function, and the political space for the existence and development of independent groups that can truly represent the public interest is limited.[5] Undoubtedly, the non-standard and non-organizational representation collected by the hearing representatives has influenced the full expression of the public opinion and weakened the influence of the political participation of the hearing on the government's decision-making.

Second, it is the role positioning of local government. According to Max Weber's theory, the government itself has special interests and is not a natural representative of the public interest. When the content of the hearing is directly related to the interests of the local government, the government should also participate in the hearing as the party concerned. In any case, assuming that the government does not have its own interests and acts as a referee should be avoided.

Third, it is the neutrality of the host. The host of the hearing should be relatively independent in legal status. If he or she cannot be in a more detached position, he or she is bound to find it difficult to judge right and wrong objectively and fairly, therefore weakening the objective fairness of the hearing process. As with the decisions of the judges of the courts, the decisions of the administrators at the hearings must be made by impartial, non-partisan interrogators. China's current laws, regulations and rules are too simple for the hearing host, and the legal status of the hearing host is not involved. In

---

[5] Samuel Huntington. *Political Order in Changing Societies*. Translated by Li Shengping *et al*. Beijing: Huaxia Publishing House, 1988: 41.

order to ensure the relative legal independence of the presiding officer, the non-unit dependency system of the host is generally implemented in the international community. For example, some countries give the administrative judge the independent status of the administrative organ where the hearing is conducted. And this is a weakness of the current Chinese hearing system. The current legislation stipulates that the presiding officer of the administrative hearing is subordinate to the administrative organ, and the unit of the presiding officer of the legislative hearing and the judicial hearing is more dependent. The organizational background of the host often leads to the preemption of the interests of the unit over the interests of the parties in the process of conducting the hearing, and it is difficult to maintain justice in the hearing. Even if the host does not take the interests of the unit as the first priority, as long as the fact that the host belongs to a certain unit exists, the citizens will also be under pressure and unable to participate equally to express their interests.

Finally, it is the non-neutrality of the hearing organizer. In today's China, it is difficult for the holding organization of the hearing to get rid of the conflicts of interest and achieve objective neutrality, which affects the impartiality of the hearing process. Among them, the administrative attachment of the organizer and the government may become the "hearing show" of the organizer to use the hearing to carry out the government's intention. The government also has its own interests, and the behavior of government officials is not exactly the manifestation of the public interest. Wenzhou water price hearing is a proof of this. There is a gap between the consensus reached by the hearing and the government's intentions. As a result, in later decisions, the functional departments gave up the water intake ratio at 8:2, but implemented the water ratio at 7:3 already decided by the government.

(2) *Hearing procedure*: *Transparency, legal and procedural issues*

First, the public transparency of the hearings is not enough. From the case analysis of Zhejiang's hearing mentioned above, it can be seen

Chapter 4 Hearing:
Interest Expression and Interest Integration Mechanism

that the solicitation of social representatives is still open. It's just that sometimes public channels are too narrow and publicity is not enough, so there are not many people who know and the effect of participation is very poor. The results of the administrative hearings are not made public, and the results of the price hearings are usually not announced. For the opinions represented at the hearings, especially those that were not adopted, the relevant functional departments did not provide the necessary explanations and were not questioned. It appears that the hearing is the hearing while the decision is the decision: The two are not intrinsically connected. For example, after the adjustment of the water price in Wenzhou City, the ratio of water decided on was not the one announced as 7:3, and there has been no explanation, which will affect the enthusiasm of citizen participation and weaken the performance of political participation, interest expression and interest integration. Second, the hearing has a low degree of legality. In addition to administrative penalty and administrative license, there is no standard hearing procedure law in legislation, price and judicial hearing; whether or not to hold a hearing depends entirely on the will of the government and the decision-makers, not on the legal procedures that the administration, the legislature and the judiciary have to go through, which is bound to weaken the participation of the hearing. Third, the hearing procedure is not standardized enough. From the hearing practice in Zhejiang, the selection of issues to hear, and the selection of people to participate in the hearing, it can be gathered that the process lacks basic legal procedures, and it is entirely up to the subjective will of the hearing organizers. For example, the participants in the legislative hearing of the Property Management Regulation (Draft) of Zhejiang Province are only professionals; Hangzhou's taxi price adjustment hearing has been accused as a hearing with absence of consumers. Some people suggest that Zhejiang's legislative hearing specially formulated procedures for the hearing, some of which are legislated and some are based on the work system, and Hangzhou's People's Congress reports plans in advance. There are procedural provisions, mainly specific provisions on the hearing person, hearing statements, speech procedures, hearing notes, hearing reports and other content. These provisions are binding upon all those who attend the hearing after they have been approved by the Council of Directors. This makes the hearing procedure more standardized and rigorous. Finally, the cost of the hearing is relatively high. The organizers' pursuit of the form is better than the essence of the hearing in the current hearing practice. Hearings are often held in hotels, so advertising is also needed, and the pursuit of symbolic democratic participation in publicity results in the cost of hearings being too high. The restrictions on civic participation and the burden of government have limited the regularity of the hearings. For example, before the legislative hearing in Zhejiang, the Zhejiang Provincial People's Congress would use a lot of manpower and material resources to prepare for the hearing. Originally, it was only half a day or a day of legislative hearings, which turned into a big and lively event, as if it were a "festival". This may have a good temporary social effect, but it is also likely to become a burden for the system.

4.4.2 The negative effects of defects in the hearing system

First, formalism undermines the government's image. An official of the Ministry of Civil Affairs believes, in many places, democratic hearings are often formalized, and the organizers of the hearing have a relatively mature plan before the hearing. It can be said that the decision was made and the hearing was a formality. The government had already determined the water intake ratio of 7:3 for the Wenzhou water price adjustment hearing, and Hangzhou taxi pricing decisions were exactly the same as required by applicants. Participation experience shows that participation does not serve their interests, and citizens will be turned from active participation to apathy so that they no longer participate. Thus, the degree of recognition of the government is reduced and the legitimacy of local government decision-making is affected.

Second, a hearing that ignores the interests of citizens will lead citizens to distrust government decisions. Citizens' enthusiastic participation in the hearing is a result of the belief that the government

Chapter 4 Hearing: Interest Expression and Interest Integration Mechanism

will listen to the public and respect the public opinion. In fact, many of the hearings do not give enough respect for the citizens, even ignore the result of the hearing, which seriously frustrates the enthusiasm of citizens to participate in the hearing. The practice of each country's hearing system proves that the hearing is not only "listening", it is not to hear without decision, and the final purpose of the hearing is to make better decisions. Since the practice of hearing cannot waste manpower and material, it must embody the authority of the hearing and the non-deceptive nature of the public opinion. In the real hearing, it is the obvious and correct opinions that are reflected in the public hearing that are often ignored, which arouses the dissatisfaction of the citizens with the hearing. If the government does not pay attention to this phenomenon, it will deepen the public's distrust of government decision-making, which will affect the political legitimacy of local governments.

Finally, the non-standard hearing system also affects the authority of public decision-making. In the actual operation of the hearing, because the hearing does not have the legal status of decision-making, some government departments hold the hearing only to deal with it. As a result, the public decision-making after the hearing not only cannot improve authority but also affects authority in many cases. For example, although the Wenzhou water price adjustment hearing reached 8:2 water intake ratio, the decision was made to implement a ratio of 7:3 that the city government had decided 2 months before the hearing. Such decisions always give people the impression that the government disregards public opinion.

4.5 Discussion and summary

    Based on the investigation of Zhejiang hearing cases and from the perspective of political process, as a kind of procedural democracy, the hearing system provides a new way for China to promote its citizens' orderly political participation. The legislative hearing has promoted local people's congresses to make laws and regulations more in line with local people's feelings and better care for the interests of all parties in the society. Administrative hearing is a platform for promoting administrative democracy, guaranteeing citizens' legitimate rights and interests and providing public consultation. Judicial hearing makes the trial and execution of judicial cases more consistent with the principle of fairness and justice. At the same time, there are still many problems and confusions that need to be considered carefully.

Chapter 4 Hearing:
Interest Expression and Interest Integration Mechanism

4.5.1 Hearing participation and the participation ability of contemporary Chinese citizens

To view from the political process, civic participation is essentially a game of interest. As rational actors, participants have a clear interest in participating in the act, and the goal is to maximize their own level of payment by selecting actions (or strategies). The quality and participation ability of the hearing representatives in China is always a controversial issue in academia. How to view the hearing ability and quality of Chinese citizens today? What factors influence and determine the hearing participation ability of Chinese citizens? The citizens' hearing participation ability undoubtedly depends on the participants' participation interest awareness level and the interest calculation need. The correlation degree of the realization of interest affects the quality and ability of citizen participation. If the interests are not clear, the participants are indifferent and random; if the interests are clear, the participants are enthusiastic and have a strategy. Questioning the ability of Chinese citizens to participate in the hearing is in essence interrogating Chinese citizens' cognitive and action strategies for hearing. We sometimes see the hearing representatives at the hearing lack ability and the interest expression and the interest integration ability is low. Often the participants lack confidence in the hearing, or they don't know how the hearing will benefit them. And many citizens with high quality and ability to participate usually do not want to waste time and energy on the hearing. Once they realize the connection between the hearing and their own interests, they will have more trust in the hearing, be more willing to participate, and their interest calculation instinct will be stimulated. With the awakening of democratic consciousness and right consciousness of Chinese citizens, the enthusiasm of participation will be aroused. They will also increasingly actively intervene in the government's hearing activities and make the hearing an important field of their game of interests.

The sense of right and interest calculation are the keys to analyze the hearing ability of Chinese citizens. If the awareness of rights and

Political Participation and Institutional Innovation:
A Case Study of Zhejiang

interests is clear, the participants would have great motivation to improve and show their participation quality and they appear to have the ability and quality. Otherwise, participants appear to show poor ability and quality, while participation shows coping and randomness. From the practice of hearing in Zhejiang Province, in 2006, the legislative hearing of the Property Management Regulation (Draft) of Zhejiang Province was mainly attended by elite representatives, while a few ordinary representatives participated. The government needs to mobilize the ordinary citizens to participate in the hearing. But several years later the situation changed, there was no need to mobilize, and a large number of people appeared to participate in a hearing. The key is that the hearing representatives' hearing rights consciousness and interest calculation are quite clear. It can be said that the development of China's hearings in the past two decades is increasingly closely related to the interests of citizens, and has constantly stimulated citizens' consciousness of rights and the ability to calculate their interests. This has led to a growing number of qualified and competent citizens involved in the hearings, which made them improve their ability to participate in the hearing in the process of participation, know how to use the hearing to express their own demands, and strive for and protect their legal rights and interests.

4.5.2 Improve local governance or officials make a show?

With regard to the evaluation of the hearing in China and the future development of the hearing, the opinions of the academic circles are very different. Pessimists believe that China's hearing is only a hearing show, while optimists believe that the political participation of the hearing promotes and enhances local governance, especially at the grassroots level. In fact, in China, the hearing show is an objective phenomenon, and it is also a fact that the hearing promotes and enhances the quality of grassroots governance. This is a paradox. How should we understand it? We may need to examine the inner connection between the two to make a factual and logical judgment. On the one hand, it is unrealistic to completely avoid the official's hearing show

Chapter 4　Hearing:
Interest Expression and Interest Integration Mechanism

under the current government system. "Every hearing increases the price" is the impression many people have of China's price hearing. It means that when the government needs to raise the price of a certain kind of public good, it usually avoids the direct price increase, which will cause the public to question and affects the execution of the price decision. The government tends to hold a decent hearing. It seems that the government is listening to the public, and as soon as the hearing is over, it will quickly roll out and implement decisions based on the price plans already set by local governments. In fact, local governments may reject hearings based on the scarcity of government resources and the simplicity of administrative action. Yet the government cannot resist the growing demands of citizens for hearings. At the same time, the government needs to use the legitimacy of the hearing to promote administrative efficiency. This explains why, in many cases, local governments do not really hold hearings, but are often forced to hold hearings in the face of public pressure and the desire to use the legitimacy of public opinion. Such a hearing would undoubtedly be a formality, making the hearing show a popular phenomenon in local governance. Several hearings in Zhejiang Province more than a decade ago have provided examples, there is no exception.

On the other hand, it is also true that the hearing improves the basic social governance, which is the inevitable result of the development of the political participation in the hearing. Without a hearing, the public will question and challenge the government's policies concerning people's livelihood. It not only affects the implementation of government policy, but also increases the crisis and risk of damage to administrative efficiency and government image. At the same time, the state compensation caused by petitions and mistakes made by the public will greatly increase the expenditure cost and time cost of subsequent administrative expenses, which will become unbearable for local governments. After the hearing, if the hearing is not always the decision, and the decision and the hearing are two pieces of skin, then the citizens will lose patience and attraction to such a hearing. The government's image, government trust and authority will fall into crisis, and the hearings will go to the opposite side of the expectations of local governments.

At the same time, after the education of democracy and rule of law for 40 years since the reform and opening-up, and the training of hearing for many years, the public regard the hearing as the field of interest game; in the meantime, the consciousness of people's rights has been activated, and the ability of hearing participation has been greatly improved. It's more difficult for the local government to make the hearing show. The hearing show has lost the market because the improvement of the space for government officials to make a hearing show is increasingly compressed, and the government either has to choose not to have a hearing or can only hold a true hearing. Otherwise, the pressure from the assessment by the higher level government of bureaucracy and the participation pressure of grassroots people will make the hearing show have no market. From "hearing show" to "hearing" is an unquestionable trend. Generally speaking, so far, the primary democratic governance in China has mainly included two aspects: First, the public affairs at the grassroots level should be implemented in a democratic and open stage, and the second is the stage of democratic decision-making and democratic election in the grassroot public affairs. On the basis of the public practice of local government affairs, citizens have accumulated rich experience in democratic management and democratic supervision. They will no longer be satisfied with the grassroots level of government affair and financial disclosure. They will also require direct interest expression and participation, and directly participate in democratic decision-making and democratic elections in local public affairs. Based on this, Hangzhou has launched an open-plan decision to promote people's livelihood through democracy. For some major projects, especially for public works, they are required to be based on adequate public opinion, and to ensure the full right of citizens to know, to participate and to supervise. This has contributed to the widening of the scope of application of the hearing system and an increase in the authenticity of

Chapter 4 Hearing:
Interest Expression and Interest Integration Mechanism

the hearing and the game of interest. All in all, after early hearing of imitation and adjustment of hearing show stage, a growing number of local officials have recognized that the after-hearing decision may be the one with the lowest cost and minimum resistance. With the improvement of governance capability, government officials will be tired of the "hearing show", which will make the hearing and public consultation more and more standardized and realistic. The scope and matters of the hearing will also be expanded to bring about the progress and improvement of grassroot social governance.

4.5.3 The transformation of the target of the political participation in the hearing

From the practice of Zhejiang hearing cases, in general, China's political participation in hearings has low target positioning, which is mainly a kind of institutional innovation driven by local governments on the basis of the legitimacy of public opinion. The formal arrangement of the hearing is obvious, and the setting of the hearing target may require a considerable degree of adjustment and transformation. From the perspective of political process, the key system design of citizen participation lies in the information input and output of the political system. In other words, the interests of citizens and organizations and the government's response and decision-making to the information input of the political system are expressed, coordinated and integrated. The key is undoubtedly the relationship between the government and citizens. However, the target transformation of political hearing participation may need to be considered from the following four aspects.

(1) *Change from consultative hearing to game hearing*

The hearings held so far have been mostly opinion consultation hearings. The hearing is only a supplement to the insufficient information of decision-makers. The relevant design of the hearing system theoretically assumes that the subjects involved in the hearing do not have independent pursuit of interests and there are only differences of opinion among the government, experts and representatives at the hearing, and there are no differences of interests. The system design of this kind of opinion consultation hearing has produced various problems in practice, which has restricted the normal interest expression, interest game and interest integration of civil society. The so-called game-based hearing advocates that the hearing is only a fair system platform. It respects and provides equal opportunities for all parties to participate in the hearings to realize equal, open and fair expression of interests and interest integration. All individuals and organizations must comply with the procedural requirements for hearing participation. Within the framework of the hearing system, only the participation of interests in accordance with the legal procedures is recognized, no predetermined authority is assumed, and the government should not be an exception. Under the pattern of interest differentiation in the Chinese society, the hearing system needs to change from opinion consultation to interest game. So far in the hearing practice, there have also appeared some interest group game. For example, Hangzhou hydropower price hearing has the characteristics of game hearing. The power sector and consumers are playing a game for their own decisions; moreover, the final decision of the Price Bureau of Hangzhou Municipality is at the higher level of the Provincial Price Bureau. There is also a clear game between the municipal and the provincial price bureaus. The following principles must be followed in order to realize the transformation from the opinion consultation-type to the game-type in the hearing political participation: First, the government, experts, hosts, organizers, hearing representatives, hearing applicants and hearing attendees are all regarded as participants with their own interests. Second, there is a clear legal procedure of hearing. Third, everyone is equal before the hearing, and the government must obey the legal procedure of the hearing.

(2) *Change from individual participation hearing to group participation hearing*

In the current practice of hearing, the political participation of the hearing is mostly in the name of individuals, and hardly in the name of groups. The determination of the participants in the hearing shall

Chapter 4 Hearing:
Interest Expression and Interest Integration Mechanism

generally be given a certain number of places by the organizers or functional departments of the government according to the industry, sector, class and occupation involved in the hearing. The arbitrariness of the confirmation procedure of the hearing participants leads to the exclusion of stakeholders from the hearing. As a result, in the national railway freight rate adjustment hearing in 2001, there was not a single representative of the student community. For the legislative hearing of Hangzhou City Appearance and Environmental Health Management Rules, there were two student representatives from the City College of Zhejiang University attending the hearing, which led to the other extreme and affected the representativeness of the hearing. The arbitrariness of the selection of hearing representatives in the two hearings has something to do with the lack of group participation in the hearings in China. If a group participates in the hearing, it is easier to solve such problems based on the representativeness and participation ability of participants and the information asymmetry of the hearing. At the same time, in the case of organized participation, the hearings are open to all operations. Open procedure, public solicitation of social representatives, public hearing process and open results after the hearing can effectively prevent any party from manipulating the process of hearing at will, avoiding the polarization phenomenon of interest participation. The hearing system is the game field of different interest groups. The transformation of political participation in the hearing from individual participation to group participation is a necessary step to improve and perfect the hearing system in China. It is also an inevitable trend of the development of democratic politics under the pattern of marketization and diversification of interests.

(3) *Change from government-led hearing to third-party led hearing*

China's current hearing system is government-led hearing. Since China's market-oriented reform is not complete, the government still controls the power of resource allocation in many areas. While state-owned enterprises occupy a monopoly position in many industries, this government-led hearing system has many drawbacks: for example, the organizer, the host and the expert cannot be neutral. The government is part of the market. Although it could not appear at the hearing as a member of its own interest, it acts as both a referee and an athlete, which is not conducive to the normal interests expression and interest integration of civil politics. Professor He Baogang points out that pure government dominance tends to give an unconvincing impression: "The British also had a hearing, but people didn't believe it, so the government took a strategy, that is, to let civil society do it, or find intellectuals to do it, which is neutral, which increases its legitimacy. There is a state in the United States that also allows people to hold hearings. Another way to do it is to have random sampling. Random sampling overcomes artificial control, brings credibility, and the result is convincing. If the government decides who's going to be there, people will think you're going to get the people you want, and they won't believe it."[6] The establishment of a diversified leading system of hearing can overcome some disadvantages of government-led hearing to a certain extent.

Under the situation of the diversification of the main subjects of interest, the trend of diversification of the expression of social interests is becoming more and more obvious. Therefore, we should explore the establishment of a diversified hearing leading system. That is, the hearings may be initiated and organized by third parties outside the government, such as CPPCC committees at various levels and even non-governmental organizations, in order to break the situation where the competent government departments initiate and organize hearings themselves, thereby improving the legitimacy of the hearings and the performance of political participation in the hearings.

(4) *Change from power-dependent hearing to power restriction and supervision hearing*

Hearing is a kind of procedural democracy and a legal system structure. In this framework, the subject of participation is equal in

---

[6] Chen Shengyong and He Baogang. *Development of Deliberative Democracy*. Beijing: China Social Sciences Press, 2006: Appendix.

Chapter 4 Hearing:
Interest Expression and Interest Integration Mechanism

principle, and the hearing must embody the principle that everyone is equal before the hearing. In the hearing, if there is inequality of power and status of the participants, whether it is explicit inequality or implicit inequality, as long as some of them are dependent on the power and interests of others, it is possible for the participants with a strong position to impose their will on the subjects with the weak position, and the vulnerable subjects have to submit to the strong subjects. Under such circumstances, the hearing cannot be a fair democracy of the legal process. The hearing process is easy to manipulate, and the hearing may end up as a democracy show and performance show. In the past 10 years, the hearing system of China has developed rapidly and made great progress. At least in theory, the hearing gives citizens the opportunity to express and integrate their interests in public decision-making and administrative actions involving their own rights and interests, which is a progress in China's political history. It is a breakthrough in the political tradition where the masses have no right to intervene in politics under the bureaucratic system of imperial power supremacy.

However, we should also note that there are still a lot of problems in China's hearing system, such as assigning delegates, arranging beforehand, the status of the participants in the hearing being unequal, one-sided meeting, ending up with nothing definite after the meeting, unanimous agreement at the meeting and an uproar outside the meeting and other strange phenomena. There are even "public opinions" being replaced, as in the case of Wenzhou's water hearing. Of course, there are many reasons for these irregularities, but one of the most fundamental reasons is that the power system has not been straightened out, and the participants in the hearings have a relationship of power dependence, and they cannot achieve the equality of everyone in the hearing, which provides an opportunity for false hearings that create so-called public opinion to the detriment of the public interest. In other words, the root cause of these problems is that local hearings are not yet a statutory independent institutional framework.

Strictly speaking, the hearing system is a constitutional power structure, where the political power has clear boundaries, clear functions of restriction and supervision, and all parties involved in the hearings are equal and independent and the powers of the participants in the hearings are derived not from other powers, but from the constitution and the law. Under this framework, the various branches of power restrict and supervise each other and do not depend on each other. Hearings are the epitome and application of such a power structure, and naturally there will be no dependent relationship between the participants. In this way, it is possible to achieve equality before the hearing. It is also possible for participants to be bold and speak the truth in the hearing without fear of some authorities. Only in this way can there be real interest expression and interest integration. In countries where power relations are constitutionalized, it is easy to participate in political hearings. As long as the power system is adjusted according to the constitution, all power departments respect and operate according to the power entrusted by the constitution, and the hearing system can be improved and operated effectively. Therefore, there are many problems of political hearing participation at present, and the improvement of the hearing system needs to promote the reform of political system and constitutional system, use laws to define the relationship between the state and its citizens, and between the state and society and its boundaries, clarify the power relations among the various organs of government, standardize the behavior of governments and officials at all levels by law, and promote the process of law-based administration.

4.5.4 Improvement of government process theory and political participation in the hearing

From the perspective of the governance structure of modern democratic countries, the hearing is an important link in the decision-making process of the government. From the theory of government process, we observe and consider the hearing system and citizens' hearing political participation. The problem we should be concerned

Chapter 4　Hearing:
Interest Expression and Interest Integration Mechanism

about is that, according to the theory of government process, the main function of China's hearing political participation is to improve the hearing participation links of interest expression, interest integration, decision-making and feedback. Based on the consideration of Zhejiang's practices and the theory of government process, contemporary China's political participation in hearings needs to be constructed and optimized from the perspectives of participants, hearing procedures and hearing costs, which can include the following aspects.

(1) *Improve the representativeness of hearing representatives and establish a neutral host system*

(1) Increase the representativeness of the hearing representatives. The hearing is a part of the government process, focusing on the interest of all parties, providing them with an open, fair and equal opportunity to express their views. The selection of hearing representatives at the hearing should as far as possible reflect different positions to ensure that all groups of interest are represented. Group representatives have the advantage of interest game and have more power than individuals to make their opinions and expressions be valued. Therefore, in order to ensure that all social diversified interest groups have the opportunity to express their interests and improve the representativeness of participants, we believe that hearing representatives should participate in the name of interest groups. Under the current situation of low organization of social interests, some people put forward the plan of establishing the "hearing representative database". It should be said that "hearing representative database" is a good arrangement for China to move from individual participation to group hearing. It is suggested that a fixed "hearing representative database" be set up to allow ordinary citizens to register on their own, or to be recommended by units, large clients, CPPCC, democratic parties, mass organizations, consumer associations, and community organizations, ensuring that the hearing representatives are from all levels. Furthermore, the hearing representatives should be selected randomly according to the hearing contents.

(2) Establish a neutral host system for hearings. The determination method for China's current hearing host is improper, which has the suspicion of injustice. For example, Article 8 of the Measures for Hearing Government Price Decisions says "The presiding officer of the hearing shall be the person in charge of the price department of the government", which often results in price hearings being conducted by the head of the government's price department. As Yang Zhongxin, Director of Qinhuangdao Price Bureau, said: "In terms of the organization of the hearing, we do not have a specific host for the hearing at present. It is mainly the director of the hearing, the director of the bureau in charge of the hearing." There is no neutrality of the host of the hearing who is suspected to be both an athlete and a referee in China. Measures should be taken to improve it and make it as neutral as possible. For example, an administrative hearing may consider establishing a system in which the host is independent from the organization and has a professional host team.

(2) *Standardize and improve the hearing procedures through legislation*

(1) Expand the scope of hearings. In general, the scope of China's hearings is still too narrow and suitable for expansion. For example, according to the Price Law enacted on May 1, 1998, in terms of public utilities, there is no precedent for hearings on postal services, telecommunications, urban water supply and drainage, and thermal power. As far as public welfare services are concerned, there are few examples of education hearings on fees, epidemic prevention, sanitation, greening, museums and public service advertising. For example, China's administrative hearing procedures are only applicable to administrative penalties such as ordering the suspension of production and business, revocation of licenses, and large amount of fines and other administrative penalties. This situation is not conducive to the protection of the legitimate rights and interests of the administrative counterparts, nor is it conducive to the realization of the just value of

Chapter 4 Hearing:
Interest Expression and Interest Integration Mechanism

administrative law. In particular, the Law on Administrative Penalties excludes administrative penalties that restrict personal freedom from the scope of hearings. Obviously, it is contrary to the legislative purpose of the administrative penalty law, especially the purpose of establishing the hearing procedure. It seems like you can hear everything, but in practice only important regulations are considered necessary. In terms of local conditions in Zhejiang Province, from the promulgation of the Legislative Law in 2000 to 2006, there were only three legislative hearings held.

(2) To push forward the hearing legislation and end the lack of unified legal norms. At present, China only has relatively complete legal norms on administrative penalty, including the content and procedure of administrative penalty. However, the legal provisions of price hearing and legislative hearing are not perfect enough, and even for the price hearing stipulated by law, the relevant legal norms are relatively general. The Price Law of the People's Republic of China, which came into force on May 1, 1998, defines the status of the hearing system in the form of legal provisions. Article 23 of the Price Law states the following: "A system of hearings shall be established for setting government-set and guided prices for public utilities, public welfare services, natural monopoly commodities and other goods that are relevant to the vital interests of the people." Presided by the government price authority, the government will solicit opinions from consumers, operators and other relevant parties to demonstrate its necessity and feasibility. It is up to the price departments of the government, not the citizens, to decide whether a hearing should be held, and it is only "ought" to be set up rather than necessary. It can be seen from the regulations that China's current laws and regulations have not yet formed a basic procedural provision for the hearings. Whether or not the hearings are conducted depends entirely on the will of the decision-makers. For example, for price hearings and legislative hearings, the right to decide to hold such hearings is entirely in the hands of the organizing unit. Either it "can"

or "should" hold hearings, none of them "must" hold hearings. In many cases, some localities and departments have taken advantage of this. In those issues where the masses are concerned and hearings are necessary, they refuse to do so. Therefore, the hearing legislation should actively promote the system construction and extend the hearing legislation to all fields.

(3) Improve the public hearing system. Public disclosure is an important means to prevent formalism and counter the manipulation of hearings. First of all, it should clearly stipulate that the news media have the right to participate in the reports of all links of the price hearing and play its role of public opinion supervision. As the "fourth right", mass media can use its technological and information advantages to form a powerful influence on society. Second, we should learn from the principles of Shenzhen to conduct hearings to further expand the scope of public matters and ensure that the hearings are open before and after the meetings.

(3) *Political participation in hearings and formulation of local public policies*

To improve the political participation of the hearing, it is necessary to make clear in law how the opinions reached during the hearing are connected with the procedures of local public policymaking. Therefore, we need a set of rigid restrictions, supervision and inquiry system. For those departments that regard the hearings as show venues, fail to implement the opinions formed after the hearings and make amendments to relevant policies, they must be restrained and regulated from the system. For example, make a public announcement, instruct the responsible party to explain, and accept the citizens' inquiry. Take the price hearing as an example. If the representatives attending the hearing fail to accept the opinions reached at the hearing or disagree with the final price decision, the relevant functional departments should be responsible for explaining the reasons to them, rather than merely informing the society of the final results of the pricing.

Chapter 4 Hearing:
Interest Expression and Interest Integration Mechanism

With regard to the influence of the outcome of the hearing on the formulation of public policy, the present hearing only has the nature of consultation and does not have the statutory function of the decision-making hearing, so the decision-maker can often put aside the hearing to make decision, and the hearing often becomes a kind of form. So, how can we strengthen the decision effect of the hearing? Some scholars suggest to promote the role of hearings in public policymaking through the transparency and openness of hearings. "The hearing is not mandatory. It's a judgment, not mandatory," says Sheng Hong, Director of the Tianze Economic Research Institute in Beijing. He suggests several ways to improve the process. Besides the consciousness of the officials, the hearings should be open and transparent, that is, all the opinions of the parties during the hearings should be made public very transparently. We shall establish a transparent and rational decision-making system for officials. Although the public have no decision-making power, they can use the hearing procedure to understand the evaluation decision, so as to restrict and supervise the behavior of the decision-maker and make the decision conform to the requirements of the public interest as far as possible.[7]

At present, some hearings held in various places have problems of gentrification and high cost, which restrict the participation opportunity of ordinary citizens and affect the enthusiasm of ordinary citizens to participate in the hearings. For example, legislative hearings can have simple hearing procedures, rather than excessive pursuit of large and noisy ostentation and extravagance, and should pay greater attention to the practical effects of hearings. Meanwhile, the news media pay more attention to such local legislation involving the civic and public interests, actively participate in the hearing process, and promote the information exchange between the public and the hearing process. At the same time, the cost of legislative or other hearings should be reduced. Local laws and regulations that involve the vital interests of the

---

[7]Chen Shengyong and He Baogang. *Development of Deliberative Democracy*. Beijing: China Social Sciences Press, 2006: Appendix.

people should be able to go through the hearings as much as possible, so that the process of making local regulations is no longer a closed door for legislators and the interests of all sectors of society can go through extensive dialogue and consultation between the stakeholders, especially so that the interests of stakeholders can be balanced. In addition, governments at all levels should appropriately increase their input in hearings. For participants from outside the hearing area, the government may consider providing appropriate transportation and accommodation subsidies to increase the passion and enthusiasm of citizens for participating in the hearing.

Chapter 5

"Our Round Table Meeting": TV Political Consultation and Public Consultation

Political Participation and Institutional Innovation:
A Case Study of Zhejiang

"Our Round Table Meeting" is a talk show that was launched by Hangzhou TV General Channel in December 2010 and continues to this day and is also an influential TV program of China's local TV stations. Since entering the 21st century, in the face of the pattern of differentiation of social strata and the pluralistic pattern of interest subjects formed due to the great transformation, the ruling party and the government have responded to the needs of the pluralistic society, and established the expression mechanism, coordination mechanism and integration mechanism of social interests, promoted political consultation, resolved the increasingly complex social conflicts through public consultation, coordinated the interests of all parties and promoted social harmony and stability. In the process, on the one hand, the pragmatic Chinese local government wants public consultation to play a dual role: to meet the needs of national governance and solve the practical problems faced by the society. On the other hand, with the awareness of civil rights and democratic consciousness, an increasing number of people are pressing for participating in public affairs and making their own reasonable demands. The common need of officials and civil society has created a new form of public consultation, namely TV political consultation.

The launch of "Our Round Table Meeting" as a TV political consultation platform was required by Hangzhou Municipal Party Committee and Municipal Government according to Implementation Opinions on the Establishment of a Democracy to Promote the Livelihood of the People, and is hosted by the General Office of Municipal Party Committee, the General Office of Municipal Government, the Publicity Department of the Municipal Party Committee, the Municipal Development Research Center, Hangzhou Culture Radio Television Group and Hangzhou Development Institute, and undertaken by

Chapter 5 "Our Round Table Meeting": TV Political Consultation and Public Consultation

Hangzhou Television General Channel and Life Quality Hall. The program tries to adopt multi-party interaction and cross-boundary communication through the cooperation of party, government, citizens, media, colleges and enterprises, expanding channels for democratic participation and improving people's livelihood in a democratic way.

TV political consultation is a platform for public participation and a new form of deliberative democracy, and its main feature is the creation of television programs by professional television programmers, selecting topics through a certain mechanism, collecting relevant information and selecting the consultation representatives to conduct consultation within a specific time and space. The consultative platform created by TV media has formal and authoritative features. The guidance of the professional host and the post-editing and directing also help this way of consultation avoid deviation from the topic or polarization in the argument and deviating from the original intention of the consultation. In this chapter, the analysis of the case of "Our Round Table Meeting" TV political consultation by Hangzhou TV Station is mainly based on the case interviews of more than 50 people, including the head of the organizers of the program, the host and the representatives of the participants of the program. In total, 696 sessions from December 1, 2010 to December 31, 2014 were selected as a case study of "Our Round Table Meeting" to inspect the realization mechanism of public consultation. In the case study that follows, we will examine the composition of the participants in the TV political consultation one by one, the generation of the participants, the generation and distribution of topics, the running process and the performance of TV political consultation. Finally, this chapter will discuss the contribution and limits of TV political consultation in the Chinese democratic process and local governance performance.

5.1 The rise of TV political consultation and "Our Round Table Meeting"

In present-day China, because deliberative democracy is compatible with the existing political consultative system, the traditional ideology and culture, it can improve the legitimacy of the ruling, and thus is regarded by the theoretical circles as an effective way to develop local democratic politics and improve governance performance. However, the practice of deliberative democracy is rooted in a particular political, social, cultural and technological environment. If it is incompatible with the local environment, it will be difficult to apply it in a larger space. China's complex political and social environment and the high cost of trial and error determine that the process of Chinese democratic politics may require a local experiment rather than advancing on the whole. Therefore, China's deliberative democracy is a tentative exploration process, which is uncertain in nature.

Chapter 5 "Our Round Table Meeting": TV Political Consultation and Public Consultation

This process emphasizes local adaptability to democratic practices. "Our Round Table Meeting", as a unique form of public consultation, embodies the above characteristics of local politics.

5.1.1 Development course from "TV political consultation" to public consultation

TV political consultation is a form of deliberative democracy, which combines the audience universality of mass media with the reality of live debate, in order to be widely accepted by the general public. As a result, such a combination of television and political programming has aroused widespread public concern. Since entering the 21st century, TV political consultation shows have became popular in China, among which the more influential programs are as follows: the Ningbo Network Dialogue Program started in 2002 (http://www.cnnb.com.cn/duihua/wsfbt/index.shtml), Lanzhou TV Station's "Leaders on TV" program in 2005 (http://www.lzbs.com.cn/zt/ybs/index.htm), Hubei Wuhan TV Station's "TV political consultation" program launched in 2011 (http://www.hb.xinhuanet.com/zhuanti/12four/dswz/) and Zhejiang Wenzhou TV Station's "TV political consultation" program launched in 2014. In addition, Luoyang, Zhoukou, Yueyang, Chenzhou, Lujiang and other city- and county-level TV stations also launched "TV political consultation" programs.

Since 2011, "TV political consultation" has increased rapidly. "TV political consultation" combines television media with public governance to make serious governance issues entertaining. Because of the dramatic emotional conflict between ordinary people and the government, the topic of discussion is closely related to the interests of the public, and many of these programs have achieved good ratings. What's more, on August 4, 2014, during the recording of Hunan's 8th session of "TV political consultation", there was an amazing event where the Hengyang City Mayor immediately suspended the county's Xidu timber checkpoint station chief and deputy station chief from their duties.

Political Participation and Institutional Innovation: A Case Study of Zhejiang

With the growing popularity of TV programs, the unsustainability of this public consultation model is becoming increasingly obvious. Restricted by the time of the program, "TV political consultation" is bound to have limited time, and it is often cyclical. Such interval cycles cannot meet the requirement of solving new problems in urban governance. In addition, the non-government participants in "TV political consultation", in the context of emphasizing conflict and drama, are more enthusiastic than rational. Government officials, who are also involved, are also under pressure to comment on the form of public consultation, which prevents the two sides from continuing to interact rationally. More importantly, "TV political consultation" has strengthened the public and media's ability to supervise, but it is difficult to form a collective consensus to promote the formation of a satisfactory solution for all parties. The cycle dislocation, participative mood disorders and biased governance effects have led to a single political consultation which cannot satisfy the actual needs of the multiple subjects who participate in public governance.

Television political consultation programs have gradually shifted to public consultation. The combination of a TV platform and public governance is inseparable from the effective participation of government agencies, officials, experts and scholars, and the general public, seeking common solutions to problems or seeking a consensus on public issues. The governance reform based on empirical practice is becoming a new trend of grassroots innovation. For example, as the pioneer of "TV political consultation" program, "Leaders on TV" was replaced by a new weekly show in 2009—"Talk about People's Feelings and People's Livelihood" (later renamed "Voices"). On the related topics of "TV political consultation", the government departments, social organizations, experts, scholars and netizens were selected by the program to interpret policies and solve public confusion through interviews conducted by the host. Hangzhou TV's "Our Round Table Meeting" program, as the original design of Hangzhou Municipal Government and media, is the successor to the concept of "TV political consultation".

Chapter 5 "Our Round Table Meeting":
TV Political Consultation and Public Consultation

5.1.2 The establishment of "Our Round Table Meeting" and the characteristics of public participation

Zhejiang has been one of the earliest and most developed areas of the private economy since China's reform and opening-up. In the process of industrialization, marketization and urbanization, party committees and governments at all levels have actively expanded the channels for expression of people's feelings, and the government has set up interactive platforms like "Government Reception Day", "Mayor's Hotline", "Citizens' Town Hall" and "Democratic Consultation" to encourage citizens to express their interests and participate in political affairs. In the process of urban governance, the Hangzhou Municipal Government encourages open decision-making and promotes the people's livelihood with democracy. Since 2000, Hangzhou has implemented a series of livelihood projects like comprehensive protection of the West Lake, Xixi Wetland and the Grand Canal, comprehensive improvement and protection of urban river courses, improvement of alleyways and improvement of old and dilapidated houses, and solved problems such as difficulty in employment, difficulty in medical treatment, difficulty in going to school, in housing, in parking, in handling affairs, and in cleaning and sanitation. In order to make these projects more effective in responding to the needs of the people, the Hangzhou Government has been promoting its citizens' participation and has tried to mediate the conflict of interests between the government and people in the city construction in a democratic way. In June 2009, Hangzhou Municipal Party Committee and Municipal Government issued the Implementation Opinion on the Establishment of a Mechanism for Promoting the Livelihood of People with Democracy, insisting on getting to know the public feeling, the public needs, listening to the public opinion and being subject to performance assessment by the public, upholding the principle of democracy in all aspects of improving people's livelihood. A democratic mechanism has been established, whether it is the determination of crucial matters, the policy choice to improve people's livelihood, the supervision of

Political Participation and Institutional Innovation:
A Case Study of Zhejiang

the implementation process or the assessment of the improvement of people's livelihood. Let citizens decide whether to do or not, choose what to do and propose how to do it, and let citizens assess "good and bad", effectively implement citizens' right to know, participation, choice and supervision, making development democracy an institutional guarantee for improving people's livelihood.

To implement the concept of democracy promoting people's livelihood, Hangzhou Municipal Party Committee and Municipal Government successively created "Hangzhou Assembly Hall" on Hangzhou Net network channel (http://hwyst.hangzhou.com.cn/) and broadcasted "Our Round Table Meeting" on Hangzhou TV General Channel (http://tv.hoolo.tv/hzzh/wmyzh/), using the "Hangzhou Assembly Hall" and "Our Round Table Meeting" as concrete measures and platforms for the implementation of democracy and the people's livelihood. "Our Round Table Meeting" program started on December 2010, with more than 700 sessions covering more than 400 topics as of January 2015 and more than 5,000 guests participating in the program. It takes "ask questions—discuss questions—make suggestions" as a clue, and "studio group talk" as the form, realizing the goal of "gathering people's wisdom, exchanging and communicating, promoting development, promoting harmony and improving quality" through consultation and exchange among party, government, intellectuals, industry and business circles, media and citizen representatives. Each session revolves around a topic, with discussions limited to 40 minutes and 1–2 sessions per week. The basic mode of the program is that the host leads the participants to exchange and discuss ideas in the studio and analyze the problems layer by layer; meanwhile, it is also interspersed with various interactive links such as off-site interviews, background information reviews, telephone hotlines, Internet observer comments, and investigation and release, making public consultation diversified and contextualized. "Our Round Table Meeting" is a practice of multi-party public consultation governance with three main features.

Chapter 5 "Our Round Table Meeting": TV Political Consultation and Public Consultation

The first is the diversity of the participants. The main subject of "Our Round Table Meeting" is "us", and "we" are inclusive, not exclusive. The main participants are representatives of the party and government organs, ordinary citizens, the media, the intellectual community, the business community and so on. These representatives are leaders of public affairs. They not only speak for their own groups but also adopt the "role complementary" approach, which constitutes a discussion model based on the "us" perspective. Among the more than 7,000 representatives who participated in the discussion, the representatives of functional departments were the heads of government departments concerned with the topic. The departments with the highest frequency of appearance were the environmental protection department, transportation department, urban management department, etc. Academic representatives were usually experts and scholars from universities and research institutes, and media representatives were well-known lawyers and commentators; in addition, people from all walks of life and CPPCC members also frequently appeared. Furthermore, the heads of social organizations were often involved, such as "Green Zhejiang" and "Drop of Water Public Welfare". At the same time, citizens concerned about public welfare actively participate in the discussion.

The second is the uniqueness of the communication channels. Face-to-face dialogue is the way participants practice public consultation. "Our Round Table Meeting" participants all gather around the round table to speak on the spot and talk impromptu. All the guests sit in front of each other and, guided by the host, communicate with each other on TV, listen to other people's voices and express their own demands. Due to the plurality of participants and the complexity of social contradictions, there is a lot of disagreement on the topic of social concern. This requires the voice of the representatives to be heard, the voice and advice of others to be considered, and then the original idea by the representative to be revised. "Our Round Table Meeting" seeks to present the demands of all parties through equal exchanges to find resonance and consensus in listening, creates a conversation space for mutual listening, mutual respect and equal exchanges in a relaxed atmosphere, promotes understanding through communication, enhances mutual trust through interaction and explores new ways to solve problems through cooperation.

The third is the diversity of topics. "Our Round Table Meeting" highlights publicity and universality of topics, pays attention to topics that are closely related to public interest and social groups, and seeks organic integration of the government agenda, the media agenda and the public agenda. As of January 2015, among 702 sessions of the program broadcasted, the topics have involved transportation, cultural and spiritual civilization construction, people's livelihood, social construction, environmental ecology and other public issues. The topics of the program focus on being close to reality, life and the public opinion, which will combine the improvement of residents' life with the promotion of economic and social development.

5.2 The composition and generation of the participants

The composition and procedures of selecting the citizen representatives of "Our Round Table Meeting" directly determine the quality and performance of public consultation. Who are the participants in "Our Round Table Meeting"? What principles or procedures do these participants follow?

5.2.1 Composition of the participants

The basis of citizen consultation is the citizens' participation in public affairs and the autonomy of civil society. A stable public life and a prosperous democracy are premised on the active participation of the majority. Different people have different backgrounds and different experiences. They have different interests, positions and values, and different resources. Participation representing citizens with different interests and values is the social foundation of public consultation. Of course, to a certain extent,

Political Participation and Institutional Innovation: A Case Study of Zhejiang

differentiated interest demands are the driving force for the sustainable development of public consultation.

In the analysis of videos from January to July 2014, a total of 676 guests participated in the discussion of "Our Round Table Meeting" (see Table 5.1). The ratio of participants ranged from high to low in the following order: citizen representatives, functional department representatives, CPPCC and people's congress deputies, experts and scholars, industry representatives and media commentators.

Citizen representatives: There were 250 person-times, accounting for 36.98% of the total number of participants. This was the largest group of participants in the program. They were representatives of Hangzhou citizens whose views were not authoritative or comprehensive. But they were the direct audience of social hot topics and difficult issues, and the details of each policy were closely related to their lives. So different groups of people have different feelings. Their appeal is the starting point and ultimate goal of "Our Round Table

Table 5.1. Participant classification.

	Number of participants	Ratio (%)
Citizen representatives	250	36.98
Functional department representatives	133	19.67
CPPCC and people's congress deputies	116	17.15
Experts and scholars	80	11.83
Industry representatives	51	7.54
Media commentators	46	6.80
Total	676	100.00

Source: According to "Our Round Table Meeting" video data analysis and sorting.

Chapter 5 "Our Round Table Meeting": TV Political Consultation and Public Consultation

Meeting" for public consultation and solving social problems. They are an essential part of the round table discussion.

Functional department representatives: There were 133 person-times, accounting for 19.67% of the total number of participants. Most of them were heads of government departments related to the topics of discussion. In the round table discussion, they represented the government and participated in the program to understand the practical problems of the society and explained the intentions and operational rules of government policies to the public in a timely manner. The government is the helmsman of economic society, the maker and executor of various policy measures. The public consultation platform of "Our Round Table Meeting" will help the government to collect public opinions, accurately respond to the demands of the people, provide the services needed by the people and solve the actual difficulties faced by the people.

CPPCC and people's congress deputies: They formed the most special group among the guests, and were the latest group that was added to "Our Round Table Meeting". They had 116 person-times, accounting for 17.15% of the total. They mainly appear in the monthly "CPPCC Viewpoint" or "NPC Window" program, and the regular "Our Round Table Meeting" also occasionally has the participation of CPPCC members or people's congress deputies. Members of the CPPCC and people's representatives are representatives of various industries in various fields. They come from the masses and go to the masses, observe the social dynamics in daily life, understand the difficulties of the masses, respond to the people's feelings with special political status, contribute ideas and exert effort. At the same time, they are representatives of the people who comment on the work of the ruling party and the government as part of their work. Therefore, they participate in "Our Round Table Meeting" to listen to the people, understand the public opinion and make suggestions to the party committee and government.

Experts and scholars: There were 80 person-times, accounting for 11.83% of the total. They were experts and scholars from universities and institutes of science, representing the intellectual community. Their degree of specialization is higher than that of other representatives and they can analyze the subject objectively and impartially. With rigorous attitude and thorough analysis, these experts and scholars left a deep impression on the public, and their voices are the most convincing.

Industry representatives: There were 51 person-times, accounting for 7.54% of the total. They are business owners, industry representatives or frontline workers who are closely involved in the discussion. Similar to ordinary people, these representatives are closest to hot topics and difficult issues. Their personal experience is the most expressed in the round table discussion, with information that other participants can't grasp. Their points of view add "real material" to the Round Table, which helps other participants to look at the topic in a comprehensive and objective way.

Media commentators: There were 46 person-times, accounting for 6.80% of the total. Such representatives are mainly composed of senior social commentators and well-known lawyers. Commentators and lawyers are representatives of the media, and the media, as the "fourth power", play a pivotal role in political life. In "Our Round Table Meeting" discussions, media commentators seek a critical perspective of the media from different viewpoints and integrate all voices to face up to the ugly facts and focus on the grievances of the people, while playing the role of supervision.

5.2.2 The generation of the participants

The representatives of "Our Round Table Meeting" are generated according to the "Interest-related principle" and "technology-relevance principle", and they are chosen and informed by the committee members. The members of the committee are composed of members of the program and the relevant staff members of the municipal party committee.

Chapter 5 "Our Round Table Meeting": TV Political Consultation and Public Consultation

Based on the concept of cross-border cooperation, the committee was composed of representatives of government functional departments, social organizations, enterprises and institutions, experts and scholars, citizens and special commentators. The total number of participants was increased from 6 in December 2010 to about 12 in 2015.

According to the classification of Professor He Baogang, this kind of public consultation group is a focus group. The number of participants in the focus group is generally relatively small and is subject to one or more thematic discussions by the participating representatives. The classical system design of this method is based on the "the interest-relevance principle", which leads to the more explicit negotiation by participants. They represent the interests of different groups, use public rational methods based on individual economic rationality, facilitate mutual compromise, reach consensus and form public resolutions. In "Our Round Table Meeting", different representatives have a common regionalism on topics, which gives the participation representatives common interests. The "technology-relevance principle" is balanced with the "interest-relevance principle" in the selection criteria for representatives, guaranteeing that public representatives based on different cognitions and standpoints can represent the demands of different groups and think about public problems in the way of public rationality.

(1) *Selection of indirect stakeholders*: *The principle of technological relevance*

In the consultative platform, representatives such as experts and scholars, heads of social organizations, special commentators and other non-stakeholders participate in the negotiation independently. The choice of independent representatives is based on technical relevance, and it is difficult to prioritize the appropriate representative portfolio. Therefore, the public consultation representative is non-specific, which also determines that the choice of representatives can only refer to the satisfaction principle under the relevant technical standards.

The committee has also played an important role in the selection process. Through the principle of technical relevance, independent representatives are generally selected in this network according to the order of familiarity to general strangers. In addition, the program of "Our Round Table Meeting" has also been devoted to the improvement of an "expert resource base" in the process of its operation.

(2) *Direct stakeholders*: *The principle of interest relevance*

The selection of citizen representatives, representatives of functional departments and representatives of enterprises shall be made according to the principles of interest relevance in the discussion. The government functions involved in different issues are often determined with highly consistent positions. The heads of these departments, of course, have become representatives of the government, with the demonstration effect of good discussion and the requirements of the General Office of the Municipal Party Committee, which is a supporter of the committee. The public is diverse, with goals and responsibilities relatively scattered, and public participation in public affairs is still relatively inadequate. Therefore, in the reality that the representatives of the citizens have relatively few choices, the committee hopes to inspire the public to enter the studio and participate in public consultation with enthusiasm inspired by interest correlation, and hopes that a few "star citizens" who can communicate and perform well in the process of discussion can play an active role in the demonstration.

In addition, in the representative selection process, "Our Round Table Meeting" committee also plays a fundamental role and constitutes the principle of technology-relevance selection for independent representatives with diffraction points of the members of the committee as the order of composite social networks. This principle, together with the interest–relevance selection principle generated by public representatives, constitutes the method of selection of consultative representatives. From the point of view of original design, these two

Chapter 5 "Our Round Table Meeting": TV Political Consultation and Public Consultation

principles can better bring together public rationality beyond personal interests, but there are still three problems. First, there is a lack of a corresponding system of accountability for selected representatives in public consultative meetings; second, due to the limited number of public consultation representatives, it is difficult to represent the interests of more groups and more areas; third, the choice of the guests, especially the independent representatives, lacks a more institutionalized and standardized way of selection.

5.3 The emergence and distribution of topics for consultation

The composition of the participants is directly related to the topic, so who sets it? What factors affect the setting of the topic? Is there a certain regularity in the distribution and change of topic? Below, we will analyze these one by one.

5.3.1 Topic setting
(1) *Role of the committee*

In "Our Round Table Meeting" consultative platform, the agenda enters the consultative process under the operation of the special committee. The public agenda is a general public concern about a social issue that begins with public interaction in the public sphere. The public agenda may not be on the government's agenda. "Our Round Table Meeting" is a way to get the public agenda into the government's agenda. Through this public consultation platform, we can form a collective consensus, which enters relevant

Chapter 5 "Our Round Table Meeting": TV Political Consultation and Public Consultation

government functions and is converted into the government's agenda. In the process of soliciting and establishing the topic, the committee is the only authority.

The topics of "Our Round Table Meeting" discussion were chosen by the committee through behind-the-scene selection. The committee has received telephone calls, letters and Internet comments for "Our Round Table Meeting", soliciting topics from the public domain that are of public interest and require discussion from the community as a whole. However, in the actual operation process, the topics are mainly collected by committee members through searching for hot topics for discussion. In addition, based on long-term good consultation practices, there are also a number of government departments that offer voluntary, imminent or already implemented public policies, which will be discussed on "Our Round Table Meeting" platform. The alternative topics discussed at the weekly meeting will be submitted to the TV station leader and the head of the municipal party committee, which will be reviewed by the two sides.

On the basis of the choice of topics, "Our Round Table Meeting" has the dual nature of TV program and public consultation. Audience rating is not the main factor affecting the selection of committee topics. The committee aims to find out the hot topics of public concern in the public domain. Therefore, the speed and urgency of social transmission, the scope and extent of interest influence, timeliness, controversy and so on constitute the criteria for the selection of topics. In addition, the social guidance factor and the government guidance factor, although nominally, not only constitute the basis for topic selection but also affect the choice of committee members.

As to the constraints of the choice of topics, the topics of "Our Round Table Meeting" program have no written rules and no formal systems. However, the topics are still subject to a series of "soft constraints", which mainly include the public consultation purpose, self-restraint and censorship constraints of "Our Round Table Meeting". Aimed at the orientation of life politics, it constitutes the purpose constraint of the topic selection. As the committee is solely responsible for setting up topics, it will consider options on the basis of its own values. Its value judgment becomes an integral part of self-discipline. Finally, at the stage of the topic review, the veto power of the executive director is also part of the soft constraint. Under these non-institutionalized constraints, "Our Round Table Meeting" committee has a very precise grasp of the scale of topics. Thus far, no issues submitted by the committee have been rejected in the review.

Generally speaking, the agenda setting of "Our Round Table Meeting" is operated by the committee, and the choice of collective rationality instead of public rationality is the obvious one due to difficulties in public rational expression and attempts to centralize public rationality. The committee's vague choice allowed them to dominate the topic setting under non-institutional constraints.

(2) *Several factors influencing the topic setting*

The setting of "Our Round Table Meeting" issues is also constrained by factors such as the urgency and timeliness of the topic and other factors. The topics of "Our Round Table Meeting" are decided by the committee, but they are still constrained by social factors and the party and government departments. Social factors and party and government departments should play a role through the judgment of the committee.

Among a number of factors, social factors are considered to play the most important role. They stem from the impact of major social events and exert influence over the administrative departments through more intensive media coverage, pushing the public agenda to change to the government agenda. Such social public opinion is an important source of hot issues that can be approved by the committee and passed quickly. Authoritative media coverage tends to focus on

Chapter 5 "Our Round Table Meeting": TV Political Consultation and Public Consultation

public events that attract more social attention. Social factors, therefore, are a response to both social concerns and to the realization of public consultations through "Our Round Table Meeting" program.

Food safety issues, for example, have been on the public agenda since China's dairy contamination in 2008, and have been widely discussed in the public sphere. The issue of "food safety" also became a topic of discussion in the first session of "Our Round Table Meeting" program in December 2010. However, in 2011, food safety related issues only appeared two times, accounting for 0.83% of the total number of issues in the whole year. Since then, the proportion of the issue continued to rise from 2012 to 2014, and finally reached 6.52% in 2014. It had become a hot topic in 2014 after environmental issues and traffic problems, which indicates that social public opinion guidance can have a lasting impact on the topic selection of "Our Round Table Meeting".

Party and government departments have also played an important role. Decisions made by major party committees will have an important impact on the selection of topics. For example, the discussion of the plenary session (enlarged) of the Hangzhou Municipal Party Committee is the most important source of "Our Round Table Meeting". Party and government guidance and social guidance have similar publicity paths and modes of action. Party and government guidance is closely related to the specific behaviors of government departments. Therefore, government functional departments can cause huge cumulative effect through public consultation.

Under the role of the same direction of social guidance and party and government guidance, the types of issues involved have gained great attention in public consultation on "Our Round Table Meeting". Since 2010, China has been plagued by frequent smog, and its natural environment and residential environment have attracted extensive attention from urban residents. The "Jiufeng waste incineration" incident in Hangzhou in May 2014 aroused strong public concern. The government raised the environmental issue to the same height as social stability. On the contrary, at the end of 2013, the Fourth Plenary Session of the 13th CPC Central Committee of Zhejiang Province put forward the strategy of promoting economic transformation and upgrading with "Five Water Co-governance". Guided by government and society, the issue of environmental protection, which was a hot topic in the past, became the hottest topic in the discussions of "Our Round Table Meeting" in 2013, accounting for more than 25% of the annual total.

5.3.2 Distribution and change of the topics

According to the information released from "Hangzhou Net Congress Hall" (http://hwyst.hangzhou.com.cn/), we selected the 696 sessions of program from December 2010 to December 31, 2014, to conduct statistical analysis on the topics discussed in "Our Round Table Meeting" and analyze the distribution and changing trends of public consultation topics from the micro level.

(1) *Distribution of the topics*

From the point of view of the fields of the topics, we have seven main topics: (1) Urban management, including urban comprehensive management, urban construction planning, public safety and crisis management in urban space; (2) the spiritual and cultural development, composed of the ideological and moral construction issues of citizens and the construction of cultural undertakings; (3) basic survival and development, including education, residence and property management, medical treatment and health, food safety, transportation, old-age care, handy service for the public and the impact of science and technology on life; (4) economic development, including macroeconomic issues of the overall economic situation and industrial development, as well as microeconomic issues of certain product prices or specific market specifications; (5) political development, including the interpretation of party and government documents, the construction of various party and government organs and the participation of citizens; (6) public welfare

Chapter 5 "Our Round Table Meeting": TV Political Consultation and Public Consultation

undertakings, including natural environment, living environment, charity and special vulnerable groups; (7) other topics, including summary programs and special programs that are broadcast at a specific time slot.

Among them, the topics concerning the basic survival and development of urban residents are most popular, reaching 41.38%. In second place is the topic of public welfare (17.10%), with the topic of spiritual and cultural development reaching 14.80%, ranking third, which is followed by urban management (11.35%), economic development (7.04%), political development (6.75%) and other topics (2.16%), as shown in Table 5.2.

Table 5.2. The distribution of "Our Round Table Meeting" topics from 2010 to 2014.

Subject	Topic	Session	Ratio (%)
Urban management 11.35%	Public crisis management	38	5.46
	Comprehensive urban governance	21	3.02
	Urban construction planning	20	2.87
Spiritual civilization 14.80%	Cultural undertakings	63	9.05
	Ideological and moral education	40	5.75
Basic survival 41.38%	Traffic	104	14.94
	Education	44	6.32
	Handy service for the public	35	5.03
	Living and property management	31	4.45
	Medical care and health	31	4.45

(*Continued*)

Political Participation and Institutional Innovation:
A Case Study of Zhejiang

Table 5.2. (*Continued*)

Subject	Topic	Session	Ratio (%)
Basic survival 41.38%	Food safety	19	2.73
	Science and technology and life	16	2.30
	Provide for the aged	8	1.15
Economic development 7.04%	Microeconomy	25	3.59
	Macroeconomy	24	3.45
Political development 6.75%	Party and government development	19	2.73
	The spirit of party and government documents	18	2.59
	Civic engagement	10	1.44
Public welfare undertakings 17.10%	Ecological environment protection	71	10.20
	Special groups	36	5.17
	Charity	12	1.72
Others 2.16%	Special topics	8	1.15
	Summary topics	7	1.01
Total		696	100.00

Source: According to the 696 sessions of the program selected from December 2010 to December 31, 2014, from "Hangzhou Net Congress Hall" (http://hwyst.hangzhou.com.cn/).

(2) Change of topics

As time has changed, "Our Round Table Meeting" consultation topics have also changed. With the "annual proportion" of the topic type as the main reference, through statistics on the proportion of topics discussed in the round table from 2011 to 2014, among the 23 topics discussed in each year, the top five topics are selected, and the annual and overall hot topics are obtained, as shown in Table 5.3.

Chapter 5 "Our Round Table Meeting": TV Political Consultation and Public Consultation

Table 5.3. The annual topic occurrence of "Our Round Table Meeting" from 2011 to 2014.

Year	No. 1	No. 2	No. 3	No. 4	No. 5
2011	Cultural undertaking 14.11%	Traffic 13.28%	Public crisis management 7.88%	Ecological environment protection 7.47% Moral education 7.47%	
2012	Traffic 15.13%	Cultural undertaking 7.56%	Education 7.14% Special groups 7.14%		Comprehensive urban governance 6.30% The spirit of party and government documents 6.30%
2013	Traffic 14.66%	Ecological environment 12.93%	Education 8.62%	Special groups 7.76%	Medical care and health 6.03% Public crisis management 6.03% Ideological and moral education 6.03%
2014	Ecological environment 26.09%	Traffic 14.13%	Handy services for the public 6.52% Food safety 6.52%		Cultural undertaking 5.43% Science and technology and life 5.43%
Total	Traffic 14.94%	Ecological environment 10.20%	Cultural undertaking 9.05%	Education 6.32%	Ideological and moral education 5.75%

Source: According to the 696 sessions of the program selected from December 2010 to December 31, 2014, from "Hangzhou Net Congress Hall" (http://hwyst.hangzhou.com.cn/).

Political Participation and Institutional Innovation:
A Case Study of Zhejiang

Through Table 5.3, it is not difficult to find out that the topic of public governance related to traffic is the hot issue of "Our Round Table Meeting", which comes in the first and second place for attention in 4 years and the first for total attention. The related issues of cultural undertakings and ecological environment protection have also received high attention. The former comes in first and second place in 2011 and in 2012, the latter receives the second place in 2013 and the first in 2014, and surpasses the former to third place in total attention. In addition, education, moral education and urban special group issues have also received more attention in many periods.

These hot topics have three characteristics: importance, universality and clarity. They are closely related to the daily life of all citizens, and also contain a complex and specific practical problem and corresponding policies. There is room for discussion on improving the performance of public governance. More importantly, these issues are at an appropriate distance from the basic political framework of local governance structures and their values. At the same time, these issues are widely recognized by the public, such as environmental protection and education. These specific practical problems make the content of public consultation difficult to extend or deviate from and it is easy to form a consensus.

From the changes of these hot topics, we can see the difference between overall planning administration and other public consultation systems or practice. Public consultation on television is more flexible and diverse. But the topic of "Our Round Table Meeting" focuses on issues of public interest in the area of life politics. These issues are seriously discussed because of their wide scope and wide policy coverage, and controversial issues are not on the agenda of "Our Round Table Meeting". We will use democratic consultation to promote public governance and improve governance performance.

5.4 The operational process of "Our Round Table Meeting"

The operation process of "Our Round Table Meeting" mainly includes government guidance, the host, citizen participation and constraint mechanisms.

5.4.1 Government guidance

"Our Round Table Meeting" is not spontaneous, but established and developed under the guidance of the government. In "Our Round Table Meeting" practice and exploration, the cooperation mechanism guided by the government mainly includes cooperation between party and government, citizens and media, as well as cross-boundary cooperation between party and government, universities, enterprises and media. This cooperation effectively integrates the resources of all parties.

"Our Round Table Meeting" program has established the leadership group for the construction of the interactive media platform for the democratic people's livelihood in Hangzhou. Under the working leadership group is the general planning

Political Participation and Institutional Innovation: A Case Study of Zhejiang

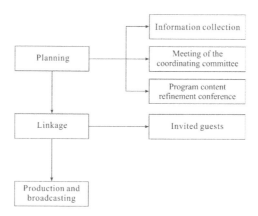

Figure 5.1. "Our Round Table Meeting" workflow diagram.

group. Under the guidance of general planning, the expert advisory group and the program working group have been established. Among them, the program working group is divided into planning group, linkage group and production and broadcasting group. The planning group is composed of the general office of the municipal party committee, the municipal development research center and Hangzhou TV Station, which are responsible for the screening, determination and planning of the program. The linkage group is responsible for inviting the experts, departments, industries, media and citizens involved in the program to interact with other media. The production and broadcasting group is the editorial staff of Hangzhou TV General Channel, which is responsible for the production and broadcasting of the program (see Figure 5.1).

The influence of "Our Round Table Meeting" also benefits from the "linkage" between the social subjects participating in the program. Citizens (subject), experts (support), party and government (guidance), media (propagation) and industry enterprises (participation or execution) are not only related to one another with clear division of labor but also constitute the network interaction, namely establishing the linkage mechanism for relevant functional departments of municipality, district and county (city), experts,

Chapter 5 "Our Round Table Meeting": TV Political Consultation and Public Consultation

scholars and research institutions, industry enterprises, citizens' representative work mechanisms and "people's good advice" solicitation work.

5.4.2 Host

Unlike the general host, in the long run, the host of "Our Round Table Meeting" public consultation has gradually developed a unique style of hosting. This approach does not emphasize the use of hosting skills to please the audience, but emphasizes that the host realizes two main functions on the basis of a full understanding of the general rules of procedure and the characteristics of public consultation: (1) to guide the consultation representatives to speak and (2) to distribute the right of discourse evenly and establish a proper interpersonal relationship between the speaker and the audience.

In public consultation on television, the host has the right to make a statement on behalf of one party, ensuring that each party gets the same amount of time. In the representative's statement, the host ensures that the participants understand the content of the speech well and avoids the distortion of the representative's speech. For the questions and doubts raised by the field representatives or other channels, one of the representatives is required to respond, which is conducive to the formation of the dialogue context. The moderator distributes the right of speech to all parties in a relatively balanced way, avoiding the "one alone has the say" of the strong representative, and guiding the ordinary people who are not good at talking to express their demands equally.

The implementation of the host's guiding role requires two mechanisms: support mechanism and constraint mechanism. From the support mechanism, the host needs to negotiate the respect and recognition of the participants, so as to ensure the effective implementation of the coordination function. "Our Round Table Meeting", through the form of TV media, has the authoritative and dominant position required by the host given by the TV media with solemn and formal features. From the constraint mechanism, to maintain the effectiveness of public consultation, the manipulation behavior of the host should be curbed, which might cause uneven distribution of the right of the discourse of the public consultation representatives, even suppress one side's view and promote the other's point of view. Therefore, it is necessary to ensure the fairness and justice of the host's conduct, and to control the host's right of speech within the necessary and minimum range.

The host is not only a necessary element in TV political consultation but also an important mechanism to create equal consultation space and promote effective dialogue and communication in the process of public consultation. The setting of "Our Round Table Meeting" gives full support to the host and ensures the approval of the representatives, but it lacks an effective restraint mechanism for the host. The committee plays the main role in the process of representative selection, and the television platform determines the fixed and close relationship between the committee and the host. Therefore, it cannot be ruled out that the private social relationship between the host and the public negotiator may affect the fair behavior of the host. This means that it is not only difficult to rely on the self-restraint of the host unilaterally to ensure that he does not exert excessive influence but also that there is a lack of expedient measures under institutional norms. The system of representative selection based on the committee's social network also calls into question the fairness of the host.

5.4.3 Citizen participation

Citizen participation is the premise of public consultation. In public consultation, citizen participation is not only the recognition of the members of the community of participants based on common interests but also a means to protect the rights of members and realize their interests. The basic elements of citizen participation in public consultation include the following:

Chapter 5 "Our Round Table Meeting": TV Political Consultation and Public Consultation

(1) *Equality*

Equality is the basic idea of building democracy and one of the core elements of deliberative democracy. First of all, as for the design of "Our Round Table Meeting", the round table design is a kind that has no advantages or disadvantages. This type of seating arrangement makes government officials, experts and scholars, media commentators, enterprise representatives and ordinary citizens remove identity and labels, regardless of high and low grade, in order to sit around a round table to have a face-to-face dialogue. The "round" design gives a sense of comfort of equality both visually and psychologically. It is conducive to mutual exchange and debate among different participants in the consultation process, as well as to the coordination of differences and promotion of mutual understanding. Second, equality is reflected in the equality of opportunity in the consultation process. If formal equality is to create a relaxed environment for citizen consultation, equality of opportunity in consultation is a key factor in ensuring equal participation of citizens. Before the round table discussion, participants invited to the discussion or invited guests can obtain relevant information on the discussion topics through various channels. The access to information is equal and there is no difference. In the consultation process, although the participants have different information resources and different abilities to express themselves, they have equal opportunity to participate in the discussion and express their demands.

According to the statistical analysis of video data, in the 50 sessions from January to June 2014, a total of 676 people went into "Our Round Table Meeting" studio to participate in the discussion. There were 478 person-times of male guests and 198 person-times of female guests (see Table 5.4). More statistics of guest speaking opportunities, including the number of statements raised by functional departments, experts and scholars, media commentators, enterprise representatives, warmhearted citizens and members of the CPPCC and people's congress deputies, are shown in Table 5.5.

Political Participation and Institutional Innovation: A Case Study of Zhejiang

Table 5.4. Gender classification of participants.

Sex	Participation person-time	Ratio (%)
Male	478	70.7
Female	198	29.3
Total	676	100.0

Source: http://hwyst.hangzhou.com.cn/.

Table 5.5. Statistics of guest speaking opportunities.

Number of statements	Total	Male	Female	Ratio (%)
Functional departments	433	375	58	26.4
Experts and scholars	395	338	57	24.1
Media commentators	112	90	22	6.8
Enterprise representatives	137	106	31	8.3
Warmhearted citizens	369	221	148	22.5
Members of the CPPCC and people's congress deputies	196	129	67	11.9
Total	1642	1259	383	100.0
Proportion		76.7	23.3	

Source: http://hwyst. hangzhou.com.cn/.

Different career representatives have different speaking opportunities as follows: representatives of functional departments, representatives of experts and scholars, representatives of ordinary

Chapter 5 "Our Round Table Meeting":
TV Political Consultation and Public Consultation

citizens, members of the CPPCC and people's congress deputies, representatives of enterprise industry and media commentators. This distribution is in direct proportion to the number of people participating in the discussion. At the same time, the number of male and female guest speakers is positively proportional (see Table 5.4).

The participants' views were considered equally in public consultation. Consultation is not a disorderly quarrel among the participants, but an equal opportunity to speak in an orderly discussion, as well as an opportunity to defend one's views. In "Our Round Table Meeting", civic participation is concrete and realistic, and consultation and communication are conducted around specific public issues. The characteristics of equality balance various viewpoints that are exaggerated or ignored because of their status, which is the concrete manifestation of deliberative democracy's pursuit of equality.

(2) *Rationality*

Rationality is the key and core of public consultation, and rationality can ensure that multi-party participants reach a consensus in the negotiation process and aim to realize public interest. On the basis of a more persuasive message, the parties involved in the process of "making an argument—accepting the consideration—justifying the argument—reaching a consensus" constantly review all viewpoints, perfect or revise existing knowledge and preferences. It is not enough to rely on skilled expression at the site, and the issue must be fully understood to maximize the rational utility in the process of consultation.

Collect topics related to issues in advance: All guests participating in the round table discussion, although their occupation, age and understanding of the social hot topics are different, will receive materials related to the topics from "Our Round Table Meeting" program in advance, which will help them to be familiar with the topic content. At the same time, participants can collect relevant materials through field research, visiting stakeholders, listening to ordinary people and even getting suggestions from netizens. Government departments should sort through the relevant policy documents so as to solve the problem. Experts and scholars should collate relevant data and survey data, and media commentators should collect various opinions from various perspectives. All participants strive to master the most comprehensive information and prepare for the consultation and communication.

Careful thinking and rational speech during the consultation process: Data information reserve is the basic condition for rationality to play a role. In the process of consultation, orderly expression and critical thinking are the keys to the realization of rational participation. Cohen points out that consultation must be rational because participants give specific reasons for supporting or criticizing an opinion. During the round table discussion, the participants should objectively present the information to other participants, and listen to the different views of others and their reasons. Coordination enables participants to look at the same issue from different perspectives and strive to maximize public interest.

Treat differences rationally: Consultation is to change preferences rather than an attempt to achieve the convergence of preferences. In the exchange of all parties, the views are diverse, and a basic consensus is reached through equal discussion among the participants. But not every participant's opinion can be integrated into the consensus. In the exchange of opinions, participants gradually understand different viewpoints and their rationality, and can view their opinions and reasons in an inclusive and rational manner, thus realizing compromise.

(3) *Legitimacy*

The legitimacy of civic participation is an important condition for ensuring effective public consultation. Legitimacy is mainly embodied

Chapter 5 "Our Round Table Meeting":
TV Political Consultation and Public Consultation

in the credibility of the participant's identity and the negotiation process. Legitimacy is manifested in citizens' participation in "Our Round Table Meeting" consultations: Participants get involved voluntarily through legal channels, and consultation procedures are legal.

Participants in round table sessions are selected via the Internet, telephone, on-site voluntary registration or are invited by the program team. Both voluntary applications and invitations are open and transparent. With the expansion of influence of the program, an increasing number of people actively contact the program group and ask to participate in it. On May 16, 2014, for example, most of the guests who participated in the discussion of "Mayor Talk about Water" were selected through the Internet, by phone or by means of on-site registration. Most of them were "civilian observers", who were members of the general public, concerned with social issues, actively observing, collecting opinions or suggestions from the masses, and participating in public welfare.

The legitimacy of the consultative process: James Berman and others point out that the legal consultative process gives each participant an equal opportunity to express themselves and listen to others. At the same time, it ensures freedom of opinion, equal communication and only follows the "power of best ideas". The consultation process is legal and its first element is the openness of the process. "Our Round Table Meeting" is open to the public in obtaining information, participating in discussions, expressing opinions and reviewing the whole process. The second is that the content is open and authentic, and the credibility is high. "Our Round Table Meeting" has a clearly defined program flow chart. Each step is announced in the program's charter, from program planning to topic selection, to guest invitation and program broadcast, especially in the guest discussion process, unlike many other TV interviews or communication programs with predefined guest lines, which will rehearse the whole process in advance, and guests only need to follow the procedure and recite lines on the real broadcasting stage. "Our Round Table Meeting" discussions do not have a pre-set standard line, nor do they require participants to say anything, let alone rehearse the entire consultation process ahead of time. The participants' statements and opinions are expressed in their real voice during the live discussion without any inducement or hinting in advance.

5.4.4 Constraint mechanism

Public rationality is the ability of the public to seek public interest. It depends on the rational ability of individual citizens and is higher than individual rationality. The scope of its application includes social community members or members of the political community who are concerned with public issues and facilitate public consultation and dialogue. Public rationality is an essential element of effective public consultation. In order to ensure public rationality, public consultation must have a certain constraint framework to regulate the consultation process and eliminate the interference of irrational factors.

In public consultation, the irrational factors such as personal interests and excessive emotions cannot be completely excluded. Public consultation is the process of exploring the distribution of benefits jointly. As the negotiator for the economic person, it is not because of the formation of the public consultation field that personal interests are not taken into account. For this reason, "Our Round Table Meeting" presupposes indirect stakeholders in the middle position, such as hosts, experts and scholars, to prevent public consultation from deviating from the track of public rationality. However, it is impossible to completely eliminate the irrational factors, because language carries emotional factors, and the influence of expression is often no less than the influence of effective information. Moreover, the more frequent the information exchange, the more likely it is to involve the emotional factors that represent it, and the more likely it is to lead the consultation to irrationality.

Chapter 5　"Our Round Table Meeting": TV Political Consultation and Public Consultation

If public consultation cannot completely remove the influence of emotion and interests on public rationality, then public rationality should be placed under the criticism and supervision of the public domain. In the form of "Our Round Table Meeting", television programs connect the public domain (party and government) and the dispersed civil society. Thus, such public domain forms have formed two constraints on the consultation process. Through the setting of the rules framework and the individual rationality of the participants, the self-restraint of the participants is strengthened to eliminate the influence of the irrational factors.

"Our Round Table Meeting" committee did not explicitly request a ban on the representatives involved in the consultation. However, in the long-term practice, "Our Round Table Meeting" contains a series of rigid rules, mainly with fixed statements and positions. In addition to the general rules of courtesy, the rules of speech also contain structural constraints, requiring participants not to speak at will, but to speak succinctly under the guidance of the host, which effectively reduces the influence of emotional factors in speech carriers and avoids unrestricted speech and excessive extension to the interference of topic formation. In addition, "Our Round Table Meeting" stipulates that the participants represent public interest rather than group interest, which is implied by the participants and constitutes a constraint on the negotiation behavior of the participating parties.

At the same time, "Our Round Table Meeting" also has a series of soft constraint mechanisms. These mechanisms mainly include the identity constraint and image constraint of the negotiators. The identity constraint is the trust placed by the organizer on the negotiators. It reinforces the participants' sense of ritual and formality, and strengthens the consensus of the negotiators on the hard constraints such as rules and positions, thus constraining the participation behavior of the negotiators. There is a wide spread of programs broadcast on

TV platforms, and in a way, participants will appear in the public domain, subject to public supervision. Therefore, in order to maintain their image in the public domain, the participation of the negotiators will also be restrained. These two kinds of soft constraint mechanisms enable the participants of public consultation to respect and abide by the rigid rules, thereby excluding the influence of irrational factors and the maximization motivation of personal interests on public rationality.

In short, "Our Round Table Meeting" has effectively combined the long-term and orderly participation of the public television media with the guidance of the committee to form a binding system of public consultation. This raises the self-monitoring of "Our Round Table Meeting", which limits the interference of non-public rational factors in the negotiation. The platform has acquired the ability to communicate, exchange and understand through the establishment of topics, selection of representatives and coordination mechanism of hosts. Its realization of the dialogue among multilateral representatives and consensus building will help it achieve scientific and democratic public policies.

5.5 The performance of "Our Round Table Meeting" TV political consultation

After years of practice, "Our Round Table Meeting" has enlarged the scope of citizens' participation, promoted the enthusiasm of citizens in participating in local affairs, cultivated the consciousness of citizens' public rationality and democracy, and shaped and expanded the public sector.

5.5.1 Cultivation of public rationality and democratic consciousness

Public rationality is the essential thinking tool and consensus foundation in public consultation. As an individual or a group of public administration units, the lack of public rationality makes it easy to form a collective action of "free-rider" or a "tragedy of the commons" phenomenon, leading directly to failure of public interest or damaged governance. The practice of public consultation on television political consultation has spread the values of democratic science and helped to cultivate public sense and democratic consciousness.

On the public consultation platform of "Our Round Table Meeting", participants focus on the specific social issues, and the relevant basic information is popularized in the form of expert consultation and a short film introduction to the background. Through expert explanation, the information is gathered into a logical chain, so as to show the public a specific rational judgment and a logical analysis process. Similarly, the television media repeatedly present the demands of the participants through consultation and argumentation from personal rationality to public rationality and public interest. Public viewing is also a process of learning democracy.

The process of public consultation cultivates citizens' sense of democracy. In "Our Round Table Meeting" discussions, ordinary citizens express their demands or suggestions based on their own experience or knowledge. The functional departments of the government should not only listen to the voices of the people but also make comprehensive and detailed explanations to the public. The experts, scholars and media commentators, respectively, give professional, scientific, objective and novel suggestions. All kinds of voices are treated equally in heated discussions. This kind of consultative process strengthens the democratic consciousness of the participants and viewers, promotes mutual understanding between stakeholders and contributes to the formation of public rationality and the realization of public interest.

5.5.2 The shaping of the public domain

The public domain is an element for public consultation. A stable and vibrant public domain can build a buffer between the government and the public, helping to maintain social stability. Habermas emphasizes the necessary conditions of the two aspects under the premise of the rule of law, that is, the relative independence of society and the state and that citizens should have certain property and receive

Chapter 5 "Our Round Table Meeting": TV Political Consultation and Public Consultation

education. A healthy public domain is the result of the cooperation between government, society and citizens.

The practice of "Our Round Table Meeting" provides an opportunity for multiple subjects to rediscover themselves and reposition their respective codes of conduct. In the practice of public consultation, "Our Round Table Meeting" promotes the initiative of the government functional departments to negotiate with all sectors of the society on an equal footing, and the two mayors of Hangzhou have participated in the Round Table many times in person. The influence of the Round Table participants will be sustainable. In a certain sense, the consultative system that continues to improve performance can dispel long-standing pessimism, such as "the policy stops as soon as the leader is gone". To a certain extent, the functional departments that participate in the negotiation as participants will abandon the prejudice of "site" complex and "officialdom bossism", and form an open attitude and an idea of cooperation. As providers of public goods, institutions and social organizations have a difficult time finding their own positioning in traditional administrative systems, and are often marginalized or become assistants to the government. Participation in public consultation helps social organizations find their own position and responsibilities. For citizens, the Round Table practice has gradually reversed the long-standing bias toward government functions. The practice of consultation and discussion of public affairs has produced a demonstration effect through the dissemination of television media, triggered the imitation of social members and formed the possibility of social cooperation in a wider space beyond the Round Table. Therefore, the effective Round Table practice enables the social pluralistic subjects to achieve positive interaction by means of participation.

5.5.3 Expansion of civic participation

The scale of the direct participation of "Our Round Table Meeting" is expanding. The early Round Table generally invited two representatives of government functional departments, two experts and scholars and two social representatives. In 2014, the number of participants reached 12 and they sat in the middle of the venue. The increase in the number of direct participants solves the problem of which department should be selected when a particular issue has been involved in the past, and also allows for greater flexibility in the selection of representatives. Since 2014, having 12 representatives has been more conducive to the average distribution of rights without affecting the consultative order, so that public consultation has avoided the situation of being dominated by the individual elite.

The most obvious change since the launch of "Our Round Table Meeting" was the attitude of participation by the government departments, from resistance at the beginning of the program to passive participation and then to the active participation since 2014. Government departments will listen to the voice of the people and understand the public opinion as normal before conducting work concerning the people's livelihood. The main leaders of the city government also pay increasing attention to the link of public opinion before making decisions. In 2014, for example, the mayor of Hangzhou walked into the Round Table three times, and consulted the public on the topic of "Five Water Co-governance", "Garbage Disposal" and "Ten Things for People's Livelihood".

The general public is increasingly concerned about the Round Table, and the number of people who actively sign up for the Round Table is increasing. The program set up a special "guest database", consisting of hundreds of experts and scholars and thousands of citizens. Every program has residents signing up for it. They are either insiders with detailed information of the topic, or direct stakeholders in the topic, or residents who are simply concerned with social issues in order to understand the real situation.

In Hangzhou, residents are increasingly commenting on the Round Table, and show hosts and regular attendees have become familiar

Chapter 5 "Our Round Table Meeting": TV Political Consultation and Public Consultation

stars to passers-by. From December 2010 when "Our Round Table Meeting" started to the end of 2014, the network's videos had more than 100 million views. In the program's microblog and discussion groups, the audience is increasingly active. At the same time, the program also received official approval from *People's Daily*, the state administration of radio, film and television, won the "2012 China annual TV applause award", was hailed as "a small step for the media, a big step for social democracy", and received praise from all sectors of society.

5.6 Discussion and conclusion

    The 21st century is a new century of globalization, the Internet and the post-Internet era. In today's world, democracy and democratization have encountered all kinds of problems and challenges, and we believe that the pursuit of democracy will not stop and democracy will remain the theme of the new century. Of course, unlike the democratic politics of the 19th and 20th centuries at the national level, democratic politics in the 21st century may be more focused on the general public. With the popularization of mobile Internet, citizens' direct participation in public affairs is likely to lead to their increasingly direct participation in local governance. From the practice of participatory democracy, democratic practices around the world are diverse. The practice of "Our Round Table Meeting" suggests that television is a way for local governments in China to try to learn new ways of governance in order to adapt and respond

Chapter 5 "Our Round Table Meeting": TV Political Consultation and Public Consultation

to the needs of society and the people. At the time of improving local governance, due to the properties of the media, this mode of political consultation also presents certain characteristics of entertainment. Thus, the public policy is affected by the results of public consultation, and the practice of democracy is difficult to deepen.

5.6.1 Local and global democracy

The forms and practices of democracy are diverse. In concept, democracy is global. In practice, democracy is local. In *The Third Wave*, Huntington points out that the transition from non-democratic countries to democratic ones is varied, such as change, displacement and transfer.[1] Defeat in the third wave of democratization and so-called color revolutions in recent years show that the democratization of a country must be rooted in the local land, which means that the democratic practice is endogenous and cannot be transplanted. But this does not mean that democracy is full of pessimism. On the contrary, in practice, the practice space of democracy is huge and diverse.

"Our Round Table Meeting" is a positive response and exploration of Hangzhou's local government to urban expansion. The urbanization rate in Hangzhou increased from 36.52% in 2000 to 69.50% in 2009, 74.3% in 2013 and 76.20% in 2016. The urbanization rate increased by 39.68% between 2000 and 2016.

During this period, Hangzhou City construction had successively experienced comprehensive protection of the West Lake, Xixi Wetland and the Grand Canal, comprehensive improvement and protection of urban river courses, improvement of alleyways and old, dilapidated houses, courtyard improvement, subway construction and other extremely complex problems. In this context, by solving complex social problems and promoting people's livelihood in a democratic way,

---

[1] Huntington, S. P. *The Third Wave: Democratization in the Late Twentieth Century*. Norman, OK: University of Oklahoma Press, 1993.

the Hangzhou Municipal Government was actively attempting to make reforms. The attempt is both a response to the government's "growth machine" and a response to the "urban regime".

In the age of globalization, the practice of democracy is diverse. Not only are there big differences between different countries, but even in one country, there are differences in the practice of democracy. In the practice of local democracy in China, the characteristic of the local democratization process is that democracy can only go from top to bottom, but cannot be promoted or expanded horizontally. For example, "Our Round Table Meeting" only applies to Hangzhou and the subordinate party and government organs and society. It can neither be promoted to the whole of Zhejiang Province nor can it be promoted horizontally to Ningbo City, Huzhou City and other cities parallel to Hangzhou, because there are unique local practices everywhere. Just as there are many types of democracies around the world, the type of local democracy that is transforming China is diverse and incommensurable. But the idea of getting people involved in public affairs is the same.

5.6.2 Government role of public consultation: Excessive or inferior

It makes no sense to discuss in general terms what role the government should play in public consultation, since the role of the government is determined by the specific governance environment. Compared to those countries or regions with a relatively high degree of democratization and relatively mature civil society, the government should play a more active role in public consultation, or even perform administrative intervention, in countries or regions where the degree of democratization is not high and the civil society is underdeveloped. Without active government intervention, public consultation would not have happened.

In China, which is in the social transition period, the role of government in different levels of public consultation is also different.

Chapter 5 "Our Round Table Meeting": TV Political Consultation and Public Consultation

The central government views deliberative democracy as a national strategy and the grassroots government has vigorously carried out varied and resourceful deliberative and democratic practices such as democratic consultation and TV political consultation. Prefecture-level governments at the middle level are more cautious, for example, Hangzhou's "Our Round Table Meeting". In the practice of public consultation, we should consider the political costs as well as the administrative costs and the social risks that social pressure can lead to, which cannot go too far. It is important to carry out tentative and adaptive governance innovation under uncertain conditions, and in this innovation, the prefecture-level city government is more circumspect.

This kind of adaptive governance innovation of middle-level government is the process of continuous learning by the government. The specific performance is in two aspects. One is the topic selection. In the system of "Our Round Table Meeting", the establishment of the issue is the responsibility of the committee. Selection of topics includes information summary, monthly topic preparation meetings, monthly topic planning meetings, weekly routine meetings for program production and broadcasting, and temporary planning of unexpected topics. Such a procedure is complex, but it can make the topic desensitized. However, this complex process of topic selection cannot keep pace with the updating of public issues in the process of rapid urbanization, nor can it meet the requirements of timeliness of television program production. Therefore, after 2014, the number of topics for "Our Round Table Meeting" increased. In addition to continuing to rely on committee members to actively collect public issues worthy of consultation and discussion, it is also emphasized that government departments should actively set up their own issues and Internet users could provide the topics by email or telephone. The second is the choice of representatives. For example, the choice of experts and scholars is mainly based on the principle of technical relevance. This lack of prioritization is mainly based on the establishment of an "expert database" by members of the committee through personal social networks, with a limited number of experts. Since 2014, the municipal government has sent invitations to universities in Hangzhou to expand the size of the expert database.

5.6.3 Similar entertaining nature of public consultation

Under the conditions of technological progress, using the form of TV programs, the serious social problems are presented in the form of entertainment, which is the necessary link of democratic politics from the design of the high-level system to life practice. Compared with the traditional black box consultation, "Our Round Table Meeting" in the form of a TV show is aired at 8:30 p.m. on every Saturday and Sunday on the Hangzhou TV General Channel and Hulu Network. Public consultation in the form of entertainment, not only for the participants in the immediate presence but also for the ordinary people watching the show, conveys the real experience of the scene. That's why the ordinary citizen involved in the consultations often feels like a movie star.

For the public consultation in the form of entertainment, it is required to keep track of the social hot topics, eye-catching social hot issues, the drama of the negotiation and the extensive communication of the consultation process. But, to some extent, does the public consultation in the form of entertainment not care whether the consensus of public consultation affects policies? Or does it not care whether consensus can be converted into policies? Because the public consultation in the form of entertainment has met the needs and objectives of all direct participants, the Round Table committee has completed a task and the government's functional departments have explained to the public the good intentions or difficulties of the policies and departments. Experts and scholars have engaged in a sharp debate on social issues. The public representatives have realized the star dream, and the audience likes watching a wonderful program. So what happens after public consultation? It is likely that everything is the same.

Chapter 5 "Our Round Table Meeting": TV Political Consultation and Public Consultation

Why does "Our Round Table Meeting" not include consensus in the policy process? "Our Round Table Meeting" is a loose collaboration between multiple functional departments of the municipal government. Its original intention is to realize the "dialogue, communication, exchange, understanding and win–win" platform of cross-border cooperation. In essence, this platform is a loose network of virtual platforms that do not have executive power. Even given the power to enforce it, the parallel government functional departments may not obey. In addition, "Our Round Table Meeting" plays the role of public opinion supervisor, whose main function is to focus on public opinion, and form public pressure and moral pressure on the functional departments involved. It is also unknown whether the government's functional departments will produce the promised results due to pressure from "Our Round Table Meeting". However, from the practice of "Our Round Table Meeting", the government departments in Hangzhou have not directly responded to the social pressure from TV political consultation. Therefore, it is worth our concern that this kind of public consultation in the form of entertainment may become pure entertainment.

5.6.4 Public consultation and local public policy

The representativeness of participants and the binding effect of public consultation on decision-makers are two difficult problems that are commonly encountered by television political consultation in all parts of China. It can be said that on these two points, "Our Round Table Meeting" has also not substantially advanced.

"Our Round Table Meeting" residents are mostly male retirees, while young people, office workers and women are underrepresented. Why? On the one hand, this is related to individual factors, such as the topics of the Round Table being mostly social and public. Women's interest in participation is not high, so the participants are mostly male. However, with the increasing influence of the program, the program topics are increasingly grounded. They are not only topics related to politics but also to the daily necessities of life. On the other hand, the lack of participation by women and young people is due to the conflict between the recording time and space of the program and their working time and place. It's recorded in working hours, during which most young people have to work. The program is recorded in a fixed studio, and there is a time and space conflict between the normal work of office workers and the program recording. Even young people with high levels of enthusiasm are unable to participate in live programs.

Does civic engagement really influence decision-making? In the theory of public consultation, the participation of citizens in the consultation process may not be able to reach a compromise and consensus. But, at least in the context of government involvement, has the consensus been translated into a part of government decision-making? "Our Round Table Meeting" has no breakthrough on the issue because from program planning and invitation of guests to production and broadcast, the program has no power or ability to require the government's functional departments to adopt the consensus reached. Moreover, after each discussion of the topic, the program did not arrange the opinions of the participants to be directly reported to the relevant government functional departments. It is only occasionally that the views of the discussion will be submitted to the municipal committee office in the form of internal reference. The lack of cohesion between consensus sharing, consensus building and government decision-making can easily dampen the enthusiasm of citizens. In the long run, it will affect citizens' prospects and confidence in democracy.

What are the boundaries of civic engagement in the context of public consensus that cannot be translated into decision-making? In other words, what areas should governments open to the public? To what extent? If a consultative consensus cannot be converted to policy, consultation is just like going through the working procedures. So, expanding the scope of citizen participation is bound to improve

Chapter 5 "Our Round Table Meeting": TV Political Consultation and Public Consultation

citizens' expectations of local public policy. This will undoubtedly involve some social risks. On the contrary, the views expressed through public consultation are not consistent with the government's intention in the short term, although they are in line with the needs of social development and the long-term interests of citizens. Should the government adopt, ignore or block such views? These problems exist not only in public consultations on television but also in other types of consultations.

Chapter 6

Citizen Participation Platform on Internet

6.1 Citizen participation and democracy in the era of Internet

About 20 years ago, political scientists had optimistic expectations of the relationship between the Internet and politics. They thought the Internet had unlimited potentials that could promote development of representative democracy and pure democracy, bringing about an open society and broadening public domain. However, in recent years, with more limitation on Internet usage, broadening digital divide and increasing risks of Internet populism, researchers have begun to doubt such optimism about Internet politics and review the relationship between Internet and politics. As a technological tool, Internet's relationship with democracy is not static. Such a relationship is restrained by many variables, including regime, government ability, governance situation and so on. Therefore, the relationship between the Internet and democracy shall be studied within the frame of national governance.

Political Participation and Institutional Innovation:
A Case Study of Zhejiang

The Internet today is not just a technology or just for business, but also exists genuinely for politics and society. Every citizen in modern times lives in an Internet era. In today's China, especially in Hangzhou of Zhejiang, where Alibaba Group is headquartered, a series of political participation has been innovated in governance. Governments of different levels collect popular will on the Internet; people's congress builds a representative duty performance platform; CPPCC builds an Internet liaison office; governments build government affairs service centers; public service sectors including public security bureau, urban management and civil administration build their own information service platforms one after another. Such platforms are upgraded continuously and integrated into a social management comprehensive information service platform, which allows different sectors to share information and cooperate with each other efficiently, so as to improve the local management. It is not a new thing that a technology is used for social governance. As early as late 1900s, adding machine, typewriter, punched-card machine and the decimal file management system were introduced into the government management, highly improving the work efficiency. That is to say, technicalization of public governance has been a trend for management in modern countries. People can participate in public affairs and express their interest demands on the Internet, making it possible to reach pure democracy. However, extensive use of Internet and mobile technologies as well as popularization of Internet political participation also bring many political, economic and social problems. While it benefits people, the Internet also brings problems including telecommunication fraud and Internet financial fraud, and the crisis that individual privacy is severely infringed. Political crises including "Prism", etc. show that risks of technology management have been raised in many fields in many ways. The Internet political participation in China develops under the aforesaid background.

There are two kinds of schools in terms of research on relationship between technology and governance: optimistic school and pessimistic

Chapter 6 Citizen Participation Platform on Internet

school. Researchers of the optimistic school deem that Information Communication Technology (ICT) in over the past 20 years has promoted cooperation among governments and sectors of different levels, improved service efficiency, responsiveness and trust of governments, increased channels for citizens to get information from, and encouraged participation of citizens, bringing local democracy and good governance. However, researchers of the pessimistic school deem that it is impossible for technology to realize self-contradictory goals at the same time. Technology, while improving efficiency, transparency and trust of governments, is also weakening policies and execution ability of local governments and local behavior bodies. Moreover, due to the lack of top-level design and being driven by sector interest, technology coordination will worsen the fragmented governance and cause more information-isolated islands, even public information disclosure, instead of enhancing cooperation and overall efficiency of different sectors.

The core of the dispute between two schools is whether technology is neutral or not? What relationship does technology have with its multiple functions during governance? The optimistic school deems that technology is neutral and it can obtain its multiple functions during governance. However, the pessimistic school regards that technology owns its value, social and political attributes, and technology cannot obtain multiple functions during governance. In fact, relationship of multiple functions of technology in democracy and governance cannot be inspected without referring to specific field and analysis levels. If so, different results can be obtained. In the following discussion, we will start from social and political attributes of the Internet and IT to inspect Internet political participation in current China while placing Internet political participation under the frame of national governance. We want to discuss influence of technological empowerment, system restrictions and government supervision on citizen participation through analysis of Internet citizen participation platform innovation in recent years in Zhejiang, including government affairs forums on government web

Political Participation and Institutional Innovation:
A Case Study of Zhejiang

portals, Internet discussion on government affairs, and microblog and WeChat governance. In our opinion, while the governments at different levels promote the construction of an Internet participation system, they also strengthen their supervision on citizen participation, leading to limited Internet participation in China. This is the interior logic of citizen participation in the Internet era in China.

6.2 Internet political participation: Forms and fields of participation

6.2.1 Forms of Internet political participation

Since the 21st century, with the popularization of computers and the Internet, developing communication ways and IT have empowered average citizens and developed citizen participation ways. However, this also brings new pressure and challenges to governance of governments. When the Internet and computers were introduced in China, governments at all levels started to adopt the Internet, promoted Internet technology, and built Internet participation and public negotiation platforms. On the one hand, citizens are encouraged to participate and their opinions are listened to. On the other hand, citizen participation is supervised and restrained to ensure an orderly Internet political participation and a stable society. The current Internet political participation in China has three alternative and interdependent forms, namely Internet

Political Participation and Institutional Innovation: A Case Study of Zhejiang

government affairs forums, Internet discussion on government affairs and participation anytime anywhere.

(1) *Government affairs forums on government web portals*

Internet Broadband Service (BBS) originates from America. In the spring of 1994, National Intelligent Computer Research Development Center built the first BBS in the mainland of China—Shuguang BBS. After that, Internet BBS developed quickly in China. Internet BBS includes the following categories: the first kind is the BBS built by some web portals. Almost all web portals in China now have their own BBS, such as Focus Comment of Sohu, Strong Country Forum of People. com.cn, Development Forum of Xinhuanet, News Discussion of Sina. The second kind is BBS of universities. All universities and colleges in China have their own BBS, among which the famous ones include SMTH of Tsinghua University, Weiming of Peking University, Yinshuisiyuan BBS of Shanghai Jiao Tong University, Riyueguanghua of Fudan University, and Freecity of Zhejiang University. The third kind is government affairs BBS of governments at all levels. In Zhejiang, from 2000 to 2005, governments at the provincial level, municipal level and county level all had such a kind of BBS, such as government affairs network of People's Government of Zhejiang Province—Government and the Public Interaction, Hangzhou China—Government Affairs Forum, and Quzhou Internet office hall—Inquiring the Public. Some cities and counties also build government efficiency networks and public situation networks, such as Tiantai efficiency network, Taizhou public situation network, Linhai efficiency network, Wenling efficiency network, Huangyan office efficiency network, Yuhuan efficiency network, Sanmen efficiency network, Jiaojiang efficiency network. Such BBS are fruits of practice of democratic politics at the grassroots level. They focus on politics, being forums for public opinion expression, interaction between government and the public, negotiating dialogue, and efficiency construction.

Chapter 6 Citizen Participation Platform on Internet

In recent years, with the development of information and communication technology, especially the maturity of 3G and 4G technologies and popularization of smart mobile phones, the number of people who visit government affairs forums is decreasing, leading to some government forums being closed or changed. For example, Hangzhou government affairs forum, and government and the public interaction on government affairs network of People's Government of Zhejiang Province (http://www.zj.gov.cn/) have modified their layout and set nine columns, including provincial governor mailbox, department mailbox, prefectural and municipal mailbox, government affairs microblog, live broadcast online, Internet investigation, open data, response to concerns and online interview. Government affairs network of Hangzhou Municipal Government has set eight columns, including secretary mailbox, mayor mailbox, efficiency complaint platform, Internet receiving room, live broadcast online, Internet hearing, advice collecting and Internet investigation.

(2) *Internet discussion on government affairs*

Internet discussion on government affairs is a way in which public managers collect opinions of the public on government affairs on the Internet. Through Internet dialogue between the government and the public, opinions of the public are adopted, ensuring that the government makes decisions in a scientific and democratic way. This participation method that allows an interaction between the government and the public meets demands of societal development and is the direct result of technology. Since 2000, TV discussion and Internet discussion on government affairs have gotten popular. In particular, TV discussion got popular before Internet discussion. Then with the maturity of 3G and 4G technologies and popularization of smart mobile phones, Internet discussion on government affairs soon became popular. Compared to government affairs forums, Internet discussion on government is more real time and controllable.

Internet discussions on government affairs in Zhejiang, including CNNB—Dialogue and Public Condition of Shaoxing, have some influence all around China. CNNB—Dialogue was launched in August 2001, with a purpose to build a platform for communication between the governing party and the government and the people. By the end of 2016, the program has been broadcast 767 times, making it one of the influential news interaction platforms in Zhejiang, even in China. During the broadcast, the average page view per day was always over 600,000, with the highest view being 3.3 million. Public Condition of Shaoxing originates from "interaction between the government and the public" set by Shaoxing network in August 2011. It changed its name to "Shaoxing public condition online platform" in July 2013. The column aims at listening to the public's opinions, collecting their advice and responding to their concerns. It has invited 88 municipal departments to propagate policies, answer questions, respond to appeals and listen to advice of the public, aiming to answer netizens' questions and implement policies in the fastest way.

Internet discussion on government affairs has a continuous influence because it has many participants and face-to-face dialogues, combines TV, media, Internet technologies and public governance, and presents serious and tricky governance problems in an entertaining way, which allows the public to experience it themselves. At the same time, Internet discussion on government affairs has flexible forms. Linking responsible persons of the party and government departments with ordinary people as well as allowing the government and the public to have dialogues face-to-face makes such discussion more controllable than government affairs forums.

(3) *Participation anytime anywhere*

Since 2015, Internet political participation has tended to happen anytime anywhere. This is promoted by two factors: one is the development of big data and the Internet of Things. Based on the 4G technology, big data and the Internet of Things have become possible and are widely used for manufacturing as well as for public service and social governance of government. The other one is new requirements of the central government. The Fifth Plenary Session of the 18th CPC Central Committee held in 2015 put forward the development idea of innovation, coordination, political environmental friendliness, openness and sharing, requiring governments to change from closed control to open shared governance and actively manage society in the way of Internet +. Participation anytime anywhere is one form of shared governance of society and aims at encouraging all kinds of power to participate in social governance, creating more values.

In Zhejiang, fields that citizens participate in are increasing. In politics, people's congresses at provincial, municipal, county and village levels all have set up people's congress deputies duty performance platforms, which allow ordinary citizens to contact such members anytime anywhere to express their appeals and participate in matters of people's congress. Internet CPPCC member liaison office extends the institution to the grassroot entities. In the meanwhile, the governing party consciously leads citizens from politics to public service and social governance. In public service, at the provincial level, Zhejiang Government Affairs Information Network is built to provide service for most departments, realizing online service; government functional bureaus including civil affairs bureau widely use an APP called Min Qing E Dian Tong (for knowing the public conditions quickly), and public security bureau has built an APP called Safe Zhejiang. Ordinary citizens can participate anytime anywhere without being limited by locations or time. In terms of participation methods, more new ways including microblogs, WeChat, APPs are appearing, which support flexible forms such as voice, pictures and videos.

6.2.2 Analysis of Internet political participation factors

Internet political participation has structural factors mainly including public platforms, topics, roles and information. Actually, it is due to the coupling of such structural factors that the interaction system of public platforms being created maintain the dynamic adjustment of structural relationship between the country and society.

Public platforms: Public platforms are built in a public virtual space, being a comprehensive service platform that provides individuals, governments, enterprises and organizations with business service and user management. With the development and popularization of information and communication technology and equipment, previous public platforms like BBS and government affair forums are gradually replaced by Internet discussion on government affairs, microblogs, official accounts, APPs or WeChat. Additionally, participation through public platforms is more diverse, namely live broadcast online, with microblogs, WeChat and APPs used at the same time and data exchanged through such platforms. For example, Hangzhou China—government affairs forum built in 2003—was closed in 2015 because participants were decreasing. Actually, each kind of public platform is a big space for communication and interaction. Public platform provides a shared "virtual" space for Internet interaction, which makes it one of the structural factors of Internet political participation.

Topics: Dialogue on public platforms essentially is a process of negotiation and communication. Such process will no doubt move on with a "topic". Information and communication technology can not only support complicated interaction with many participants, but also realize a special participation of only "reading" without any "speaking". Therefore, topics on public platforms come from the initiator. That is to say when a person talks, a topic is created, which is the foundation of interaction and dialogue. To some extent, "topic" is the core of interaction on public platforms. For example, on forums including government affairs forums, Internet discussion

Chapter 6 Citizen Participation Platform on Internet

on government affairs, WeChat and APPs, what we can mainly find are specific "topics" such as "public security", "traffic problem", "education", "housing", and "environment protection". Based on such "topics", these platforms can continuously have new information, viewing, comments and communication, which allows interaction to be continued.

Roles: Role is the key to connect individuals and structures as well as the core of interaction theory. According to Turner[1], actors build roles and tell others their roles during communication. People act based on this hypothesis. Because of the virtuality of public platforms, their participants are more like "self-presentation in the theater" said Goffman. But presentation on public platforms is in the form of words and pictures. If self-presentation in daily life is an unconscious role play, on public platforms people are playing specific roles consciously. There are four roles of interaction on public platforms. One is the speaker, namely the person who comes up with a "topic". This role usually uses some themes to attract others' attention to the topic. The second is the replier, namely the person who replies to the topic. This role usually uses the information to reply and participate in the discussion of such topic. The third is the reader, namely the person who reads the information without participating in the discussion. This role usually aims at obtaining the information. The last role is the manager, also known as forum moderator, group leader or platform manager. This role is to maintain the order of public platforms. It is because of the existence, interaction and management of such four roles that the interaction of diverse public platforms can be built.

Information: As one structural factor of public platforms interaction, information is the "courier" and "grantor" of interactors.

---

[1] Turner, J. H. *The Structure of Sociological Theory*. Homewood, IL: Dorsey Press, 1978.

It is due to the release, reply and reading of such information that the special interaction model of public platforms can be built. It is generally known that information communication not only endows one's action with meaning, but also understands or seeks to understand the meaning given by others, which allows real communication. During such a process, information is the "grantor" of virtual space. Achievements of net friends in virtual public space are based on the degree they recognize others and are recognized by others. The way to be recognized is through information.

6.2.3 Technological empowerment and system restraint: Logic of citizen participation in the era of the Internet

Professor Zheng Yongnian (2008) points out the following in his book *Technological Empowerment: The Internet, State and Society in China*: The Internet has empowered both the state and society, allowing both parties to benefit from Internet development. The Internet creates a fundamental structure for the state and society to get close to each other. Technological empowerment is important, but it is not enough to only know technological empowerment and development opportunities it can bring. We shall also review seriously how the state and society use technology, technology invasion and restraint features and potential risks they can bring to societal governance after technology has empowered the state and society.

Based on this, we deem that in specific governance situations, social attribute and political attribute of technology will usually present two different but interdependent features: the feature of production and empowerment, and the feature of invasion, restraint and opaqueness. The former feature can bring development opportunities, promote democracy process in specific environment, enhance efficiency of government and increase social welfare. The latter hides crises and disasters during social governance. However, it shall be pointed out that such features come from the social

Chapter 6 Citizen Participation Platform on Internet

attribute of technology and they are interlaced and interdependent. Development opportunities and governance risks brought on by such features are also interdependent.

Technology and technology platforms can empower both users and managers. Technological empowerment in countries such as Egypt can cause turmoil, but in countries like China it can enhance quality of public service and social governance, which can further solidify the governance system. Why does Internet participation in different countries bring about different results? Of course, whether to shock or to solidify the system, in essence, technology has input new meanings and values into social order. The problem shall not focus on whether technological determinism is right or not, but on to what extent, in which way and under what conditions can specific technology shape society in a more powerful way. This frame also supplements and clarifies human initiative: to what extent, in which way and under what conditions can specific groups shape their social technological system? Actually, technological parameters have been introduced into official system to distinguish the good and the bad, form the border of "acceptable" and "unacceptable", so as to form new recognition and knowledge, rationalize actions of actors, establish a new moral order for society, and develop "a set of knowledge system and power order". Also, the new public order will be reproduced through conduct code, enforcement system, identity and cultural system.

At least, similar to countries like Egypt, Internet political participation in China is also strictly restrained and supervised by the state. However, different from Egypt, Internet participation in China not only has the political attribute. Governments create legal platforms and widen participation channels for Internet political participation to include citizens into the political process, which increases tenacity of the system. Moreover, governments at various levels actively encourage citizens to participate in public service and social

Political Participation and Institutional Innovation:
A Case Study of Zhejiang

governance rather than just focusing on the political sector. Seen from this point, Internet political participation in current China presents features of order and stability under state's governance. Such kind of order is built under the impact of both technological empowerment and system restraint.

6.3 Technological empowerment: Examples of Internet participation platform and citizen participation

Empowerment is one important function of the Internet. Technology can not only empower users and managers, but can also supervise users. Just as what Marx said, technology can transform society. Advice of General Office of the State Council on Using Big Data to Strengthen Service for and Supervision on Market Subject (G.F.B. [2015] No. 51) mainly emphasizes functions of service and supervision of technological platforms. Service function of technological platform can mainly be presented in two aspects: one is to empower both users and managers to enhance their abilities; the other is that the service function of the technological platform is realized not only by the technology itself, but also by the innovative governance idea of governments (such as service, innovation, coordination, openness and sharing), innovation of traditional official systems, and adjustment of relationship between governments and society.

On the premise of technological empowerment, Internet political participation of Chinese citizens is tolerated and supported by the government system, especially people's congress, CPPCC, government functional departments which actively adjust to and require citizen participation and build technology platforms for such participation. For example, people's congress and CPPCC build Internet duty performance platforms, extending their work to grassroot entities and virtual space; governments collect opinions of citizens on the Internet; functional departments collect information through APPs. Through such ways, opinions of citizens are adopted and service level is enhanced.

6.3.1 Governments using Internet platforms to promote public negotiation and collect public opinions to provide service for people

Since the year 2000, governments at all levels in China have gradually opened policymaking processes, allowing ordinary people to participate in policymaking. Internet provides a possible way for them to participate in such processes. The development of Internet technology promotes governments' ways of collecting public opinions through Internet, namely changing from government affairs forums and Internet discussion on government affairs to allowing citizens to directly participate in decision-making through the Internet.

(1) Government affairs forums on governments' website

When the web portal of People's Government of Zhejiang Province was launched on June 28, 2003, government affairs forums were also built immediately, being the signboard of Hangzhou web portal. By August 11, 2006, there were 41,116 posts, 5,071 topics, and 8,204 members on the forums, with the most number of posts being 138 per day on June 13, 2004. The forums became places that listen to and collect public opinions besides "12345" and "96666" hotlines. They allow two-way interaction. In addition, they have 16 Internet receiving rooms.

Chapter 6 Citizen Participation Platform on Internet

One distinct feature of the government affairs forums is that they are channels allowing governments and citizens as well as citizens and citizens to have real-time communication. For the establishment of such a forum, two aspects are important: first, the coming of information age and e-government affairs age. Second, during the transformation of governments' functions, they need citizens to participate in decision-making. To deeply research Internet political participation, a post released on May 30, 2006 on Hangzhou government affairs forum will be analyzed as an example.

Example 1: Bus Rapid Transit research

On May 30, 2006, a net friend signed as "West Lake fisherman" posted a message on the website of Hangzhou government with the title of "Research on Bus Rapid Transit (BRT)". The topic of the post was "Hangzhou BRT has been put into use for some time, leave your opinions whether you have taken it or not".

First, policy and system basis for Internet political participation. Documents including Notice on Further Improving Democratic Decision-Making System of Hangzhou Municipal Government (H.Z. [1999] No.16), Notice on Implementation Advice of Suggestions Collection and Rewarding of Hangzhou People (trial) (H.Z. [2000] No.11), and Notice on Unifying E-government Affairs Internet Platforms in Hangzhou (H.Z.B.H. [2004] No.26) stipulate the following: promote open government affairs; receive supervision of people; establish Internet channels to collect public opinions; collect public advice and suggestions on decision-making of governments and analyze them in a quantitative way on time; enhance the democracy and scientificity of decision-making of governments. Therefore, participation of citizens in Internet public forums is guaranteed by policies.

Second, analysis of participants. Participants mainly include net friends, the construction bureau and bus company. The first group is net friends. Identities of net friends participating in the discussion are unknown; in terms of quantity, by June 30, there were 28 replying posts with page views of 703. Among over 6 million people in Hangzhou, only a few people participated in this topic. But it is sure that net friends who participate in the discussion are interested in the topic. The operation of BRT has influence on participants, so they reply on the Internet with a hope of their voice being heard by the government, not just their complaints. The second group is the construction bureau and the bus company. They fail to have an interaction with net friends on forums, that is to say, they do not reply to the advice and suggestions of net friends.

Third, process analysis. Since the construction bureau and bus company fail to join the discussion, net friends develop the discussion on right of way and potential safety hazard, listing disadvantages and advantages of BRT. During the interaction, two kinds of opinions arise: one opinion is that BRT has too many problems, causing complaint; the other opinion is that BRT is an exploration on solving problems in the city. Hence, such communication is a two-way communication between citizens. They interact by questioning and answering in the forum. The model of their interaction is based on several questions and various opinions and has several centers. However, communication between citizens and the government is indirect.

Fourth, content analysis. First, many net friends criticize the BRT because it is a vanity project causing the public to complain. Also, it causes former buses to be canceled, bringing inconvenience to the public. For example, a net friend signed as "moon in the water" said, "who is more important? Of course, citizens are. It is necessary to have BRT. However, if BRT project becomes a vanity project of Hangzhou government or even some leaders, it has lost its former meaning!" Second, many net friends point out the disadvantages of the BRT. Such disadvantages mainly include potential safety hazards, problems with the BRT itself, setting of isolation strips and resource wasting. For

Chapter 6 Citizen Participation Platform on Internet

example, a net friend signed as "little yellow croaker" said, "the soft isolation strips of BRT are not easy to be recognized at night, which easily causes traffic accidents!" Third, net friends of keen insight analyze interested parties and conclude that the BRT does not benefit anyone. For example, decision-makers—such imported goods would not come from our own thoughts. I do not know the process of decision-making. I can just say that they are very brave. Money users—who empowered you with the right to spend money? Who empowered you with the right to take money from our pocket and spend them? Who empowered you with the right to take so such money from our pocket and spend them without the permission of the people's congress? Bus drivers—just listen to the voice of the drivers. They are so laborious. They go to work so early and drive all day with very few rest days. However, they only get a salary of 2,000 yuan per month. Once I heard drivers discuss on the bus that they might go to work at 5 a.m. to earn extra 100 yuan per month. Private car drivers—the most furious group, because of the traffic jams. Ordinary bus drivers—the poorest martyrs. Traffic police—fellow sufferers. An unknown future: economic benefit always appears when it is necessary. They have spent so much money, so they price the ticket at 4 yuan for they need the money. However, can such money being spent be recollected? If such money cannot be recollected, who will pay for it? Lastly, net friends think it is necessary to hold a hearing, allowing decision-makers to express opinions of the public. Huge input does not relieve the traffic jam in Hangzhou, for only a few people take the BRT. This makes the public think that the BRT is a project wasting man power and money. Of course, the intention of the government is good. However, big decisions like this should be made after hearings.

Fifth, result analysis. By the end of 2008, the right of way of BRT was solved to some extent. Special ways of BRT are also allowed to be used by three other buses. When building other BRT routes, the Hangzhou Construction Bureau and bus company promise to collect public opinions through hearings and other ways.

(2) *Internet discussion on government affairs*

In the early 21st century, Internet discussion on government affairs is preferred by governments at various levels in China. Through the Internet, governments and citizens can communicate and citizens can participate in public affairs. In Zhejiang, CNNB—Dialogue is the representative. Founded in 2001, CNNB—Dialogue has been one of the most influential news interaction and communication platforms in Zhejiang. It aims at building a channel for communication, allowing main government officials and persons-in-charge to have a face-to-face communication with ordinary citizens. By June 8, 2016, CNNB—Dialogue was held 767 times. Its content includes employment, housing, medical health, education, migrant workers, urban development and construction, college entrance examination, environment, party construction, innovation, Internet civilization, a well-off society in an all-round way, Two Sessions (the NPC and the CPPCC), prevention and cure of SARS and bird flu, which are all social focuses and topics attracting attention of the public.

To collect public opinions in a comprehensive way, CNNB—Dialogue has set up several systems, including the system of holding various communication and interaction ways regularly, Internet news speaker system, and information feedback system. First, the system of holding events regularly. CNNB—Dialogue is held 1–2 times per week. Each time the dialogue lasts for 1–2 hours. Dialogue—Government Affairs Discussion presents a comprehensive communication and interaction over problems of concern to net friends. Seen from the page views after each program, netizens have a stronger response. The lowest page view for 1 day is 650,000 and the highest is 1.1 million. Second, release bulletin in advance. The program picks what netizens are concerned about the most as the topic. Three days before the program, the online communication time and subject will be foreshowed at a marked place on the website's homepage. Third, innovative technologies including various interaction ways. Ningbo Internet interaction multi-media paper *Ningbo Broadcast Paper*,

Chapter 6 Citizen Participation Platform on Internet

forums, QQ, MSN, blogs and, WeChat allow net friends to communicate and interact with guests closely. Three-dimensional display, two-way communication and interaction can meet demands of different audiences, effectively enhancing their enthusiasm. Fourth, community reporter system. CNNB sets "CNNB reporters". Around 137 persons from hundreds of communities in Ningbo and other counties become reporters. They participate in the CNNB—Dialogue and provide their advice and suggestions on decisions made by governments, social and economic development, and residents' life improvement from their points of view as community residents. Fifth, news speaker system. In October 2008, Ningbo initiated Internet speaker system in Zhejiang and built the Internet platform along with 22 Ningbo municipal departments. "Internet news speaker" would communicate with netizens regularly and release news on the Internet in the forms of videos, words and pictures after integrating information of traditional news presses. Sixth, information feedback system. Interviewed departments will, within 10 days after online communication between their officials and the public, solve problems posed by netizens and implement general advice provided by them during communication. Then such departments shall give feedback to the coordination team in writing. The coordination team will present such feedback in Dialogue—Government Affairs Discussion. In regard to advice provided by netizens during online communication, relative official departments shall be responsible for collecting such advice and implementing them.

Example 2: Internet dialogues on solving problems and creating excellence

Here we take "Solving Problems and Creating Excellence" held eight times by the CNNB—Dialogue from February 5 to 12, 2006 as an example to present the process.

First, organization process. (1) Picking topics of dialogue. To coordinate with the "Solving Problems and Creating Excellence" work of Ningbo Municipal Party Committee and Municipal Government,

Political Participation and Institutional Innovation:
A Case Study of Zhejiang

CNNB, along with *Ningbo Daily*, decides to hold an activity of "Solving Problems and Creating Excellence Series Dialogues" live video. (2) Inviting guests: invite responsible persons of eight relative official departments. (3) Issuing the announcement. Since February 5, *Ningbo Daily* and CNNB work together for the special program of "Solving Problems and Creating Excellence Series Dialogues". The program invites guests to communicate with net friends on eight aspects including solving problems of employment, housing, medical treatment and traffic, as well as improving schooling, habitation, service, humanity and environment. *Ningbo Daily* also invites responsible persons from the Labor and Social Security Bureau, Construction Committee, Education Bureau, Sanitary Bureau, Urban Management Bureau, Environmental Protection Bureau and Culture Bureau to its editorial office to communicate with citizens through the hotline "87000000". (4) Propagating and reporting: on each dialogue day, *Ningbo Daily* will have a special page to comment on the "dialogue" and announce in advance guests and the time of the next dialogue. The TV stations in Ningbo also report the "dialogue" many times.

Second, participants. There are two types of participants: one is netizens, including Ningbo citizens, migrant workers and other persons who care about the development of Ningbo. Netizens put forward 684 questions with the page view of over 500,000. The other type is responsible persons from eight municipal party committee-related departments and other related departments.

Third, dialogue process. In terms of the way of communication, the dialogue mainly adopts vertical communication, which is easy for citizens to have a direct impact on the government and its decision-making. Each program has a theme at its center and has several questions to be negotiated, reaching a consensus on some questions to some extent. Additionally, besides questioning and answering on forums, there are also online interactions and synchronous live video and audio; in terms of interaction model, it is a multi-centric interaction model.

Chapter 6　Citizen Participation Platform on Internet

Fourth, content analysis. Such dialogues are to express interests and inquire information, while some also appeal for rights of citizens. The following takes relieving employment problem as an example. (1) University students' innovative undertaking. For example, net friend A asks: "There are no preferential policies for innovative undertaking of university students?" Labor and Social Security Bureau answers: "Among the new re-employment policies issued by the State Council last December, university students are encouraged to start up a business. Junior college and technical secondary school students can enjoy interest subsidy for petty loan after being registered as unemployed. Ningbo will make specific measures to implement policies." (2) Minimum salary. For example, net friend B asks: "Will the minimum salary have to deduct 'five social insurances and one housing fund'?" Labor and Social Security Bureau answers: "The present minimum salary in Ningbo are 610 yuan and 670 yuan and the minimum payment per hour are 5.2 yuan and 5.7 yuan. All employers shall not pay a salary less than minimum salary to employees. However, the minimum salary shall include social insurance charges that shall be borne by employees." (3) Employment injury insurance. For example, net friend C asks: "If there is no labor contract, can employees get compensated if they get hurt?" Labor and Social Security Bureau answers: "Employers shall sign contracts with employees after recruitment within time specified by laws. Even if employers fail to sign contracts with employees, employers shall compensate for any occupational injury of employees."

Fifth, performance analysis. Internet discussion on government affairs provides citizens with an opportunity to express their concerns, especially for migrant workers. This has improved the image of the government, enhanced government credibility, and provided a reference and basis for its decision-making. After the dialogue, the implementation of Ningbo Comprehensive Traffic Rules, Ningbo Urban Road Traffic Management and Development Planning, and Urban Public Transport Special Planning of Ningbo Center is approved, Research on Recently Easing Ningbo Urban Traffic Problems is pushed to be organized, and "system of analyzing impact of major construction projects on traffic" is established. Suggestions on Improving Urban Housing Supply System are implemented, and relative policies are improved to match with them.

(3) *Collecting livelihood things on Internet*

Collecting public opinions on the Internet is an important way to allow citizens to join in decision-making of governments and to absorb public advice. In recent years, collecting public opinions on the Internet in Zhejiang has not been a single activity, but is a part of governments' agenda and people's congress's decision-making. Governments at various levels have always paid high attention to the collection of social conditions and public opinions. As early as in 2007, Hangzhou government set up a public opinions collection system. After that, all other governments in Zhejiang started to use the Internet to collect public opinions, which is more convenient. Internet public opinions collection is mainly used in the public service sector relevant to the daily life of citizens, namely the practical things for citizens. Within Zhejiang, governments of Hangzhou, Ningbo and Jinhua are doing best in terms of Internet public opinions collection in China. Here we take Zhejiang livelihood things collection in 2016 as an example to describe the microcosmic process of Internet public opinions collection.

Since 2015, every year People's Government of Zhejiang Province would arrange 10 livelihood projects to do practical things for citizens, solving their general difficulties in terms of daily life and medical treatment. Livelihood things are chosen from public opinions collection. Every year public opinions would be collected before Two Sessions. For example, in 2015, Li Qiang, Provincial Governor of Zhejiang then, released an open letter on Zhejiang Government Affairs Information Network and invited netizens to provide advice and suggestions. With standard decision-making procedures, including online voting of net friends, 10 livelihood things were written into the government work report and were being implemented after being approved by provincial people's congress.

Chapter 6　Citizen Participation Platform on Internet

Example 3: Collecting 10 livelihood things of Zhejiang Provincial Government in 2016

Internet livelihood things collecting mainly includes opinions collection, advice classification, Internet poll, offline advice collection and provincial people's congress's approval.

First, Internet advice collection. On October 20, 2015, Zhejiang Provincial Government decided to draft a government work report, so the Provincial Governor Li Qiang then released an open letter to all the people of Zhejiang to collect livelihood projects that Zhejiang people wanted the government to do for them. The open letter received support and response of net friends. Some net friends asked: "Can the government promise us safe food?", "Can the government help solve difficulties of going to school for children of migrant workers?" and so on. By December 22, 2015, when Internet advice collection finished, Zhejiang Government Affairs Information Network totally received over 8,000 suggestions from net friends.

Second, offline advice collection. During the process of netizens' advice to 10 livelihood things of Zhejiang Provincial Government, there were many advice-listening steps. Advice collection is not just limited to net friends. Many provincial people's congress deputies, municipal people's congress director and chairman of CPPCC also replied to the open letter. After sorting out 20 livelihood things, Zhejiang Provincial Government specially held a work arrangement meeting of "project of serving people with practical work", in which relevant provincial departments were required to put forward advice for the content and goal of such 20 livelihood things. In fact, this step was to supplement the public opinions. For example, Zhejiang Disabled Persons' Federation put forward a system of providing living allowances to the disabled with financial difficulties and nursing subsidy to severely disabled people. The direct beneficiary of this advice is a group which may not use the Internet.

Political Participation and Institutional Innovation:
A Case Study of Zhejiang

Third, classification of Internet advice. Provincial government research room that is responsible for advice collection will print all the advice. Then they review each advice of net friends and sort out 20 livelihood things based on principles of integrating the same, livelihood-related opinions, operable and practical advice. After collecting feedback of relevant provincial departments, they submit such collection to provincial deputy secretaries for review and then to provincial executive meeting for discussion and approval. Finally, 16 projects are listed as alternative projects, which dealt with most concerned livelihood problems including transportation, environment protection, education, social security, food security, pension service, housing security, culture and handy service for the public. Finally, these projects are listed as alternative livelihood projects in the 2016 government work report.

Fourth, Internet voting. On December 28, 2015, the Provincial Governor Li Qiang then released the announcement of "Ten Livelihood Things of Zhejiang Provincial Government in 2016" on Zhejiang Government Affairs Information Network, asking netizens to vote 10 out of 16 alternative livelihood projects. He pointed out that livelihood things shall be put forward by the public and decided together, and the provincial government would include those with highest votes into the provincial government work report of the following year. With reposting in WeChat Moments of netizens, over 10,000 persons voted per day. By January 20, 2017, 180,769 persons voted.

Fifth, decision-making. Result of netizens' voting is not similar to the final result of 10 livelihood things chosen. Actually, voting results have overlaps with finally included livelihood things. On January 24, 2016, 10 livelihood things approved by provincial people's congress were not similar to the voting results of netizens. First, there is no doubt that things with 10 highest votes are included into 10 livelihood things. Second, besides the 10 things with highest votes, the 11th, 12th, 14th and 16th things are also included into 10 livelihood things, with only 13th and 15th

Chapter 6　Citizen Participation Platform on Internet

being left out. This shows that the decision-making of Zhejiang Provincial Government has fully respected the public opinions. For things included without obtaining the highest number of votes, they are chosen because their votes are very close to 10 things with highest votes.

Of course, on provincial Two Sessions, people's congress deputies, CPPCC members, democratic parties, responsible persons of association of industry and commerce, figures without party affiliation, officials, experts and scholars have a discussion on livelihood things put forward on the Government Work Report. Before being released to the society, 10 livelihood projects have dozens of modifications before being approved on Two Sessions. Then such 10 livelihood projects are duly authorized.

6.3.2 People's congress deputies, CPPCC members Internet participation platform

In the era of the Internet, people's congresses at all levels actively adapt to the Internet, establishing people's congress deputies' duty performance platform to extend and expand the links between members and the people, which lets them really play their parts. People's congresses at various levels and their members use portals of local people's congress and governments to establish online interaction platforms for people's congress deputies and citizens. For example, they establish people's congress deputies' duty performance platform and online liaison stations; some local people's congress standing committees also use the Internet to organize people's congress deputies to have online interviews to answer questions from netizens.

(1) *People's congress deputies' Internet duty performance platforms*

In the age of the Internet, the people's congress as legislature uses the Internet to innovate their duty performance ways, expanding their channels to connect with citizens. In 2013, Zhejiang Provincial People's Congress established and started to use the people's congress deputies' performance service platform (http://dblz.zjrd.gov.cn/?zid=4haskuvuzjll4yujqy05g6cufk8kdixi111). This platform includes two sub-systems: the representative performance service system and the representative–people contact system. Although the two sub-systems have independent access rights, their data are shared in the background.

The representative performance service system is mainly for the people's congress deputies to perform their duties and allows the people's congress standing committee and the government, people's court and people's procuratorate to have interactions. Through this system, representatives can understand the work dynamics of the people's congress and the government, people's court, people's procuratorate, submit and follow up proposals, suggestions and their implementation, and participate in the work of people's congress. The standing committee of the people's congress and the government, people's court and people's procuratorate can use this system to carry out work contacts, handle work and share information resources. The representative–people contact system is mainly for representatives to provide services to the public through this system, while the public can contact the representatives to learn the performance of their duties and present their interests to the representatives. Representatives can, through the service platform, interact with the public, listen to public opinions, understand public opinions, access the public's wisdom, report to the voters and receive supervision.

This platform includes people's congress deputies from provinces, cities, counties and towns. Around 89,000 people's congress deputies can use this platform to provide important political information, set up new Internet channels between representatives and the people's congress, and establish electronic performance files for representatives.

This platform not only allows people's congress deputies at all levels to perform their duties through the Internet, but also erects a bridge for the people's congress standing committee to contact representatives. People's congresses members at all levels in Zhejiang can upload social information and public opinions at any time by taking photos, videos

Chapter 6　Citizen Participation Platform on Internet

and other forms. The platform will, through circulation, distribute such information and opinions to relevant departments. In order to enhance the effectiveness of representatives' duty performance and liaison with the public, when representatives report problems to government departments through the duty performance platform, emails and reminding SMS messages will be sent to such departments at the same time by the platform, so that such departments can promptly check and handle the issues. The standing committees of people's congress at all levels will take major issues reported from representative as an important basis for people's congress to carry out legislation and supervision.

For example, in May 2014, Xu Bo, the provincial people's congress deputy, put forward through the platform the Proposal to Solve the Problem of College Students' Mandarin Testing Work in Zhejiang Province, pointing out that due to rising prices and increased examination costs, Zhejiang Province's Mandarin Proficiency Test would not be able to make ends meet, which affected the normal operation. More than 10 minutes after the opinion was expressed, officials from Zhejiang Education Department called and said that they would solve the problem as soon as possible. Later, the relevant department stipulated that the paid application fee would be reduced from the original 30% to 20%, reducing the economic pressure on mandarin test centers and college test stations in various cities. The number of visits on the performance service platform has been increasing continuously. The platform had a total of over 6.7 million visits by the end of May 2014, and representatives had over 1,000 spontaneous discussions on it. During the closing of Two Sessions, the platform ensures the effective connection between the duty performance of people's congress deputies and the government departments.

(2) People's congress deputies' Internet liaison station

People's Congress Deputies' Internet Liaison Station and App of Zhejiang People's Congress Deputies' Duty Performance Service Platform are Internet windows for voters to contact representatives

Political Participation and Institutional Innovation:
A Case Study of Zhejiang

launched by the provincial people's congress standing committee based on Zhejiang People's Congress Deputies' Duty Performance Service Platform. The online liaison station provides convenient and quick online channels for representatives to contact the public to strengthen the analysis, follow-up and supervision of the public opinion. Through interaction by offline liaison station and online liaison station, "online" supervision and "offline" daily work is organically combined. On the one hand, representatives inspect, research and contact people through "offline" means to collect public information. On the other hand, the public reflect stereoscopically, visually and vividly "online" social conditions and public opinions by way of pictures, videos, texts and so on. Then they will receive rapid response and handling from the government, people's court and people's procuratorate. This forms a positive interaction with the government work and promotes a number of hot spots and difficult problems to be solved, realizing the virtuous circle and interactive communication between representatives and voters.

Since 2013, the practice of interacting with people on the Internet through People's Congress Deputies' Liaison Station has been promoted throughout Zhejiang. In 2015, the standing committee of Zhejiang Provincial People's Congress took promoting pilots of representatives Internet liaison stations as key work. Later, the people's congress of Shangcheng District in Hangzhou fully implemented representatives online reception work through website forums, WeChat groups and APPs. People's congress's Internet liaison station of Keqiao District in Shaoxing opens the "voter message" section to collect public opinions; Jiangshan People's Congress builds three major network communication carriers, including representative duty performance service platform, proposal handling system and Jiangshan People's Congress network, which makes it easy for the standing committee to contact representatives and the public; a total of 10 online communication stations have been built in nine counties (cities, districts) of Lishui. In recent years, Zhejiang Province's people's congress deputies' performance platform played its role by building

Chapter 6 Citizen Participation Platform on Internet

offline representative liaison stations and online representative liaison stations, which permits a close link between representatives and the people. By October 2016, over 2,600 representative liaison stations and over 430 Internet representative liaison stations based on townships and sub-districts have been established in Zhejiang Province. They almost include 85,000 representatives at level five in Zhejiang into the network system to contact the public.

The Internet allows the grassroots people's congress deputies to break through time and space limitations. People's congress deputies' liaison stations move from "offline" to "online". Formerly, only on fixed "conference reception days" would representatives interact with voters. It is suitable for the elderly, but most young people are outside, which makes them unable to participate in "conference reception days" at a fixed time and place. With online liaison stations, voters who find it inconvenient to report problems at home can report them through the Internet, which allows real-time zero-distance contact between people's congress deputies and the public. This provides another channel for people to contact representatives, and problems can be reported and solved in a quicker and more convenient way. Although the people's congress deputies' Internet liaison stations are required to be promoted throughout the province by the provincial people's congress, such stations are being widely applied due to the fact that they satisfy the needs of the people in real life and are an endogenous innovation.

In addition to people's congress deputies' Internet reception stations, some grassroots people's congresses have successively launched new practices such as "online reception room", "online express train" and "representatives QQ Group" to adapt to the age of the Internet. They truly move representative stations and receptions in real life to the Internet world. For example, the "People's Congress Deputies' Liaison Station" section of Hangzhou Binjiang District People's Congress Standing Committee's official website has 18 representative liaison station locations. You can randomly click on any one of the online liaison stations of any representative, then you can find information about the representative including the phone number and position. There is also an interactive part called "I want to ask questions". The public can put forward any questions and suggestions, and representatives will reply. For any issues that cannot be handled by representatives, the people's congresses of higher levels will study or urge relevant departments to handle them. Some grassroot people's congress deputies may connect their online liaison stations with the community client-side and the WeChat public account. Residents can also log on to representative's online liaison stations through these two methods to communicate with representatives. In order to shorten the distance with the voters, some representatives also open microblogs and establish WeChat groups, which not only expands the space for them to perform their duties, but also prompts government departments to take public opinions and suggestions seriously and respond in a timely way. This platform not only makes it easy for people to report problems to representatives, but also promotes and supervises the performance of members, where some representatives only appear during meetings and become "invisible" during other times.

(3) *Internet communication between people's congress deputies and the public*

Besides the people's congress deputies' duty performance platforms and representatives' Internet liaison stations, the Internet also allows other online communication between netizens and representatives. Especially during the Two Sessions each year, people's congress deputies at all levels will communicate online with netizens. Each year, Zhejiang Province carries out online communication activities between "people's congress deputies at all levels and netizens face to face". In 2010, 23 people's congress members of Zhejiang, invited by Zhejiang Online, had face-to-face communication with net friends.

Local people's congress also launches live webcasts. For example, the Standing Committee of the Hangzhou Municipal People's Congress established a webcasting system for the standing committee meeting on

Chapter 6 Citizen Participation Platform on Internet

August 2010. Before the meeting, Hangzhou Municipal People's Congress asks for topics of the Standing Committee meetings by making special subject webpages and releasing announcements of live webcasts and so on. In order to ensure an active and effective participation of netizens in discussions on live broadcasts, it has done a lot of basic work. During the conference, the scene will be webcasted as a video and in a graphic way, and netizens can freely "enter the venue" through the Internet to participate in the discussion and express their opinions with messages. By October 2012, the total webcasting of the Standing Committee had reached over 70 hours with more than 1.72 million netizens browsing special subject webpages, 290,000 netizens watching the webcasting, and over 10,000 netizens posting messages. The enthusiasm and width of netizens' participation are obvious. In another example, on January 19, 2016, during the Two Sessions of Yuhang District of Hangzhou, the Direct Contact to Two Session Series Interviews of Yuhang Conference Hall of Yuhang News Network invited Lv Qi, the People's Congress Deputy of the District, Director of the Linping Environmental Protection Institute, to communicate with netizens. She talked about issues including market fairness issues caused by small restaurants without licenses, food safety issues, firefighting, environmental protection and neighborhood disputes. Netizens actively participated in the interview, thinking that such topics of representatives were close to people's livelihood and leaving their opinions and suggestions on the webcasting interview page. Netizens interacted with interviewed guests over issues of fast food order by mobile phones, community delivery lockers and restaurant hygiene. People's congress deputies answered the questions of netizens one by one. They also taught some garbage classification knowledge to enhance the awareness of garbage classification of the public.

At the same time, in order to overcome the limitation that netizens cannot participate in real time during webcasting, some local people's congresses allow netizens to leave a message to communicate with representatives. For example, when Two Sessions of Hangzhou was held in February 2015, Hangzhou Network opened a column and invited eight representatives to listen to the voices of netizens on social hot topics. Netizens can open pages of representatives and leave a message in the forum, letting representatives bring their opinions to the venue of Two Sessions. In addition, Hangzhou Network also opened a WeChat voice and text message window. After following WeChat of Hangzhou Network, marked with "I have words for Two Sessions", you can leave voice or text as suggestions for Two Sessions.

(4) *People's congress deputies have real-time supervision on governments*

The Internet not only contributes to the political participation of the ordinary citizens, but also helps the legislature to supervise the administrative organs, especially their budget execution. In September 2016, the Standing Committee of the People's Congress of Binjiang District of Hangzhou established a financial real-time supervision station, supervising all government financial usage situations and the use of funds in a real-time way. By clicking on the homepage of Hangzhou Binjiang District People's Congress, one can find six sections. The most concerned part is the financial supervision section. The section is divided into three sub-sections: departmental budget and final accounts, government investment project supervision, and payment management supervision.

Through this program, people from all walks of life can check the budget and final accounts of 45 departments and sub-districts in Binjiang District at any time. The members of the Standing Committee of the Binjiang People's Congress can also check the real-time use of financial funds at any time. In the past, the supervision of people's congress and its standing committee on the government's financial situation was mainly carried out by reviewing in June the government's final account report for the previous year and the implementation of the budget for the first half of the year; at the end of the year or the beginning of the second year, they review the implementation of the government's budget throughout the year, and selectively review the budget execution and other situations of several departments. After establishing the "real-time supervision station", members of people's congress standing committee can view and supervise the real-time use of funds in various departments, the progress of major project investments, and the progress of practical projects for the public through the government investment project supervision column and payment management supervision column. The supervision of people's congress has changed from a procedural review to a substantive supervision.

(5) *CPPCC members' Internet liaison office*

The Internet not only affects the way people's congresses and people's congress deputies work, but also improves the work methods of the CPPCC and CPPCC members. In recent years, the local CPPCCs have actively established new carriers and platforms for grassroot consultations. For example, CPPCC of Shangcheng District in Hangzhou established the "CPPCC members workroom" to listen to public opinions of grassroot entities, collect social situations and public opinions, and organize special thematic consultations. With research on social conditions and public opinions, Shangcheng CPPCC reports its results to the party committees and the government with proposals. The Shangcheng District CPPCC small group spontaneously establishes a "CPPCC members into the community to negotiate 365" working mechanism, sending 35 CPPCC members to 12 communities. Such CPPCC members take root and have their professional fields matched with appeals of the community residents, promoting their interaction with residents. Establishing consultative platforms and building new Internet duty performance platforms for "South Star Commissioner E Home" have expanded the CPPCC's duty performance from offline to the online platforms. The online platforms focus on the people's livelihood and environmental protection, and two offline "E homes Stations" for duty performance of CPPCC members are built. CPPCC members have face-to-face dialogues with residents every quarter to collect social situations and public opinions. More and more CPPCC members perform their duties with "Internet +" by establishing CPPCC members Internet workrooms, connecting online workrooms, video dialogues with offline workrooms, and face-to-face dialogues, extending and expanding the space for intervention, through which social situations and public opinions are precisely collected and reflected.

6.3.3 Party and government information collection platform and mobilized participation

Maintaining social stability is an important function of local governments. Security is one of the important public products provided by local governments. During the construction of local security, the Internet plays an important role. The work of building a secure Zhejiang will change from the form provided by government service to participation of all citizens. Every citizen is a participant and builder of security construction.

(1) Evolution of security information platform

In 2014, Zhejiang Politics and Law Committee established the Secure Zhejiang Information Network. In 2015, it launched the mobile version of the Secure Zhejiang Information Network, which is Ping An Tong. In 2016, Secure Zhejiang App went online and formed Secure Zhejiang Information Network, Ping An Tong and Secure Zhejiang APP. Secure Zhejiang Information Network has its information mainly processed by the PC. With the popularization of smart mobile phones, the security information system began to extend to mobile terminals, which allows security information to be handled anytime anywhere with the emergence of Ping An Tong. However, as Ping An Tong is confidential, it is not popular. With the advancement of technology, Secure Zhejiang APP went online. It is an APP open to the public, which means anyone can download and install it. However, Secure Zhejiang Information Network, Ping An Tong and Secure Zhejiang APP can share data in the background, ensuring both data security and citizen participation.

Smartphones, mobile terminals and APPs have become important means for collecting information. Zhejiang Province promoted the

Chapter 6 Citizen Participation Platform on Internet

application of 92,000 mobile terminals of Ping An Tong for follow-up recording, instant recording and reporting, instant video recording and messaging, real-time collecting and dynamic recording by grassroots network grid managers, so as to collect first-hand information as much as possible. In addition to the Secure Zhejiang APP, totally 139 WeChat official accounts and APPs have been opened at county and township levels in Zhejiang. In some places, network grid managers are encouraged to establish WeChat groups with the network grid as units. Network grid members collect public appeals, and then report to the security information system. Mobile terminals and APPs allow security volunteers, civil affairs liaison officers and ordinary residents who are active at the grassroots level to become peripheral nerves of the Secure Zhejiang APP.

(2) *Main functions of platforms*

With the diversification of the form of Security Information Platform, the platform also has to increase its functions. At first, the platform is just required to collect information, but finally it is required to handle events.

First, information collection. The Security Zhejiang Information Network was established as a security information collection system. Of course, information collection is not implemented by ordinary citizens, but by Municipal Politics and Law Committee, County (District) Politics and Law Committee, and Township Comprehensive Management Office. Initially, information which was needed during reporting was simple, such as demographic information, including names, ID numbers, addresses, telephone numbers, etc., and later corporate information was included. With the continuous improvement of Secure Zhejiang Information Network and the application of Ping An Tong, the daily information of villages and communities and their network grids also need to be collected, such as contradictions and disputes mediation, and supervision of corporate safety production. However, such information is still submitted by staff of the comprehensive management office of the township (sub-district) or village officials. This is because the information system is confidential with the account number kept confidential. However, with the promotion of the Secure Zhejiang APP, information collection is no longer confined to grassroots officials or village officials. Any resident can download and install the Secure Zhejiang APP, and he/she can participate in the security construction by providing information at any time through the APP.

Second, event handling and event circulation. With the advancement of technology and the state's higher requirements for security construction, Zhejiang Politics and Law Committee requests that the Municipal Politics and Law Committee, the County (District) Politics and Law Committee and the Township (Sub-district) Comprehensive Management Office not only need to collect information through the Security Information Platform, but shall also use this platform to coordinate multiple departments to jointly handle a specific event. The process and results of the disposal will leave electronic traces on the system platform.

(3) *Mobilized participation*

Secure Zhejiang information is mainly collected in three ways: first, mobilized participation. The order is sent to the lower politics and law committee from the higher level politics and law committee, and finally is sent to the township (sub-district) comprehensive management office. The township (sub-district) comprehensive management office gives the order to the villages and communities under its administration. For example, in 2016, when Ping An Tong App was promoted, based on the requirement that 5% of the permanent population shall install the APP, a town in Zhejiang Province had to install 1,887 APPs. To implement this task, its comprehensive management office mobilized parents of students from middle schools and primary schools in the town to install the APP. Only by this way did the town complete the task given by its superiors.

Chapter 6　Citizen Participation Platform on Internet

Second, induced participation. In order to guide residents to effectively participate in security construction, a county in Zhejiang introduced a reward policy. The reward is applicable for network grid managers and full-time (part-time) staff, grid information men, volunteers, village (resident) representatives, etc. from each village (community) with the "grid management, group service" work. For any effective information submitted by a person for the first time, after being confirmed by the township (sub-district) comprehensive management committee (office), the person will be rewarded according to the classification of the information: for information with various unstable factors, having low risks but needing to be handled in a timely and proper manner, the person will be rewarded with 5–20 yuan per item of information; for information with various unstable factors, having moderate risks and that if not stopped and disposed timely, may cause greater impact, resulting in greater loss, the person will be rewarded with 100–200 yuan per item of information.

In short, the political participation of the citizens in the Internet age is the result of interaction between technological empowerment and active institutional reform. However, technological empowerment is not a one-way but a two-way empowerment. The state will use technology, on the one hand, to enhance institutional absorption capability, and on the other hand, to restrain and supervise the participation of citizens.

6.4 Information technology, government supervision and restrictive participation

Technology empowers the government and the government uses technology to regulate citizen participation. The government regards the Internet as a tool and a means to govern the society. Fine management and scientific management are common features in the production and social fields in the age of major industrialization. However, unlike the industrial era, in an era of new economy, the zero marginal cost driven by the Internet of Things is theoretically possible. This will greatly strike and destroy the production concept, organizational structure, management model, social structure, social psychology and government functions of enterprises in the age of major industrialization. It may also mean that a technology platform composed of the Internet of Things will replace enterprises and social governance models designed according to the concept of industrialization. At least, in the field of social governance, the trend of

Chapter 6 Citizen Participation Platform on Internet

technology-managerialism has become extremely obvious. Based on the grassroots network grid and according to segmentation, the technology platform can achieve precise and dynamic management by coordinating the actions of multiple governance entities.

Citizen participation in the Internet age is subject to dual constraints and supervision from the technology and government systems. Citizens are guided to participate in public services and social governance, rather than the politics. The constraints, supervision and guidance restrain the group polarization effect and political polarization effect of Internet political participation, ensuring the citizens' orderly political participation on the Internet and in real life. This prevents overburden of the government system caused by excessive participation of citizens that may bring destructive strike to the present system.

6.4.1 Technical constraints of Internet political participation

Citizen participation in the Internet era must be continuously supported by technology. Since 2000, technologies involved in citizen Internet participation include emails, BBS, ICT, 1G technology, 2G technology, 3G technology, 4G technology, sensors, smartphones, big data, cloud computing, Internet of Things, APPs and so on. In fact, the maturity of 4G technology, big data, cloud computing and the Internet of Things as well as the popularity of smartphones has supported the efficient operation of social governance system in the Internet era in terms of technology and equipment. This has really raised the curtain of citizens' participation and government Internet governance in the Internet era.

(1) *Application of big data and cloud computing in government service section*

Zhejiang not only supports big data and cloud computing industries, but also applies them to social governance. The government, taking advantage of big data industry agglomeration, cooperates with industry leaders in Zhejiang such as Alibaba Group, NetEase, Hikvision and

H3C to integrate system platform resources of various departments and promote the construction of "Seven Centers and One Demonstration Zone" that includes National Cloud Computing Industry Center and National Big Data Industry Center, and builds the initial "Cloud Zhejiang" system platform. In June 2014, relying on Alibaba Cloud, Zhejiang realized 67 information-sharing programs among 13 provincial departments and Zhejiang Government Affairs Service Network officially went online. In September 2015, Zhejiang Government Affairs Service Network launched the "Data Openness" service, which opened to the public more than 1,500 data categories provided by 68 provincial units, including 403 downloadable data resources and 135 data interfaces.

(2) *Application of Internet of Things in social governance*

The Internet of Things connects people and things, things and things with ICT and then achieves remote control. Zhejiang has fully applied the Internet of Things technology to social governance, connecting 1.84 million monitoring probes in Zhejiang to establish an articulated naturality web for comprehensive management, and then integrating the security construction information system, articulated naturality web for comprehensive management, and public security video surveillance network to form a three-dimensional and information-based public security prevention and control system. This system can synchronously monitor more than 70% of key public areas in Zhejiang such as stations, plazas, airports and intersections. It can sensitively capture information of abnormal gathering of people in public places and give warnings. In the police information system, the Internet of Things allows locations of all police forces, patrol cars and walking routes to be visualized and orders can be sent directly to policemen, realizing precise deployment and precise command of the police force.

(3) *Application of sensor and its identification technology*

To achieve dependence on sensors and intelligent identification technology of Internet social governance, Zhejiang has its main

Chapter 6 Citizen Participation Platform on Internet

intersections, all villages and communities and their network grids fully equipped with monitoring probes. Especially, in the suburban areas that have concentration of migrant population, each household has installed monitoring probes to conduct real-time dynamic monitoring all day. At the same time, places such as subway stations, train stations, hospitals, plazas, courier delivery/pick-up points not only have high-definition video surveillance, but also have facial recognition systems and vehicle capture systems, which can realize real-time collection of personnel and vehicle information. The vehicle capture system, connected to Hawkeye vehicle analysis system, can automatically capture and analyze each passing vehicle and then automatically share such information with related departments.

It should be pointed out that the development and application of technologies and equipment such as big data, cloud computing, the Internet of Things and sensors are not free. Citizen participation in the Internet era relies on these technologies but is also constrained by these technologies. The constraint of technology mainly comes from two aspects: one is the technology developer and the other is government as the technology buyer. Technology developers develop technology and equipment for the purpose of profit, and government purchases such technology and equipment for providing services, consolidating systems. Citizen participation and goal of such participation shall be subordinate to goals of the enterprise and government. Therefore, in the era of Internet technologies led by the enterprise and government, citizen participation can only be approved if it helps to achieve corporate profits and government governance goals rather than restraining and challenging them.

6.4.2 Construction of Internet participation mechanism and strengthening of government supervision

Samuel Huntington points out that in order to promote development and avoid political turmoil, countries in transition must expand their

Political Participation and Institutional Innovation:
A Case Study of Zhejiang

political systems to enhance their institutional capacity for absorption.[2] For China, a country in transition, the practice of its provinces is strikingly consistent with Huntington's suggestion, which was put forward half a century ago. Zhejiang has gradually refined the system design of Internet governance, established the Zhejiang Government Affairs Service Network with all government departments incorporated into this network. Through this, interdepartmental and cross-level cooperation and governance are promoted; the comprehensive command and coordination platform is established; the power for social governance is sublimated to grassroot entities; an open and joint governance is implemented; and social forces are integrated to build a mass prevention and mass treatment system. Besides passively absorbing Internet participation, the government also actively uses technologies and systems to supervise the society.

(1) *Refine the system design and establish "One Network"*

Internet governance is an important measure to refine the national governance system and improve the state's governance capacity. In 2016, Zhejiang Province promoted the reform focused on "Four Lists and One Network". The reform integrates the provincial security construction information system with the "network grid management, group service" network, uses Internet technology to integrate horizontal departments and vertical levels, and establishes a social governance network covering horizontal departments and vertical levels. "One Network" brings together functions such as information collection, contradictions resolution, security protection, professional supervision, democratic supervision, public services, volunteer services, etc. With the "One Network", the grid-based management and service work system of unified leadership of the party committee and government, coordination led by comprehensive management departments, cooperation by relevant departments, and participation of all parties in society is formed

---

[2]Huntington, S. P. *Political Order in Changing Societies*. New Haven, CT.: Yale University Press, 1968.

Chapter 6　Citizen Participation Platform on Internet

to achieve a seamless connection between the local governance system and the grassroots governance system.

The comprehensive technology service platform is the core infrastructure of "One Network". It can achieve data sharing, solve the problem of buck-passing among departments and promote cooperation of departments. Based on the existing resources of Zhejiang Government Affairs Service Network, Zhejiang Province, taking Zhejiang's security construction information system as the backbone, integrating information resources of departments including public security, civil affairs, human resources and social security, education, judicial administration, sanitation, safety supervision, environmental protection, industry and commerce, food and medicine, and fire protection, establishes the Zhejiang Social Governance Information Sharing and Exchange Platform, prepares shared directory standards, and builds a comprehensive service platform of provincial social governance that allows linkage between lower and higher level departments, overall coordination and efficient service. Local governments at all levels, based on meeting the needs of residents, enterprises and social organizations, have constantly upgraded their service platforms, such as five sub-centers for public security, urban management, civil affairs, social and public services, and intelligence information in Qingyuan County to form a comprehensive management system. Jinhua City has created a "four-in-one" service platform for cities, counties and townships, and a "four-in-one" service platform for telephone, Internet, SMS and WeChat. These platforms effectively achieved the sharing of information, improved the comprehensive utilization of social governance information resources, and effectively alleviated the problems of "information isolated islands" and "data gaps".

(2) *Cross-department and cross-tier cooperative governance*

The Internet governance in Zhejiang emphasizes sector cooperation, insists on territorial management and principle of who takes charge and takes responsibility. Therefore, responsibility for Internet governance directly goes to persons-in-charge of party committees and governments at various levels, and departments and units, and a responsibility investigation system is strictly implemented. Using technology as a means and multi-tiered service platform as a node, a six-level comprehensive information service platform of network grid–village and community–township (sub-district)–county (city, district)–city–province is established. The platform allows event handling, distributary disposal, command and dispatch, analysis and judgment, supervision and feedback. Information entry, service, process supervision and responsibility target assessment can be simultaneously realized on one network. Through efficient and accurate collaboration among the sectors, collaborative management and services across multiple levels, regions, systems, departments and businesses are realized.

Dynamic collaboration is one of the mechanisms that drive efficient operation of a comprehensive technology platform. The comprehensive technology platform integrates information, functions and services in various fields including public security, urban management, and civil affairs, and effectively solves practical problems through a set of efficient event circulation and disposal mechanisms. First, establish a dynamic departmental coordination mechanism. In the background of the platform, departments of public security, urban management, market supervision, human resources and social security all have dedicated personnel to handle the information and do a good job of scientific and reasonable diversion of these hotlines. Second, establish the hierarchical responsibility and multi-link mechanism. Establish a comprehensive command platform for county-level social governance and a sub-platform for townships, and then develop an innovative event circulation and disposal system in the platform. Through the two-tier platform and event circulation and disposal system, the county-level platform can be linked with townships (sub-districts), villages (communities) and network grids vertically, as well as connect with other horizontal departments to realize the linkage treatment of all events.

Chapter 6 Citizen Participation Platform on Internet

(3) *Improve governance ability of county and township government*

In the design of Internet participation system, Zhejiang Province promotes county-level law enforcement to the construction of integrated command platforms of grassroots level and county and township levels. With townships (sub-districts) as the hub, the platform can, horizontally, integrate departmental information and service resources, and vertically, open up social governance from counties (cities, districts) to villages (communities). Through township (sub-district)-integrated command platforms, online event circulation and force linkage will be brought into use to maximize the integration and use of management service resources of grassroots governments such as administrative resources, public service resources, social resources and market resources, to strengthen abilities of coordinative handling of events and services for the people of townships (sub-districts), and to improve the overall capacity of social governance of grassroots governments.

(4) *Integrate social forces to build a mass prevention and mass treatment system*

The Internet participation platform has created a platform and opportunity for social forces to participate in grassroots governance. Platforms at various levels link the comprehensive management network, government affairs extranet and Internet for communication. With websites, WeChat groups, APPs, Government Affairs Microblog, and emails such as Ping An Zhejiang Information Network Group, Zhejiang Government Affairs Service Network Group, network grid managers, security personnel of enterprises and public institutions, sanitation workers, taxi drivers and other social forces are integrated to participate in social governance, achieving mutual interaction between the police and the public, forming a mass prevention and mass treatment atmosphere, realizing overall response to social group of mass prevention and mass treatment, and improving grassroots governance ability. Party committees and governments at all levels establish an incentive mechanism for information collection and reporting, and provide incentives such as "WeChat red packet" and prepaid recharges to network grid staff and the public for their effective information. This will increase the enthusiasm and activeness of the grassroots governments in finding problems and submitting information.

6.4.3 Diversion mechanism: Public service and social supervision

Citizen participation by Internet in China, which is in transition, is not spontaneous and disorderly but is under a government-induced diversion mechanism that allows citizen participation in public services and social governance rather than in politics. In recent years, Internet governance in Zhejiang Province has been not only used for political participation, information collection and public opinions communication, but also widely applied to new areas such as public services, volunteer services, public safety and public crisis warning.

Information is the core element of social governance in the Internet age. In essence, the "Internet +" social governance system is a system for information collection and information processing. Zhejiang Province collects basic information such as population, housing, vehicles and places, as well as event information including contradictions, disputes and hidden dangers through 1.84 million monitoring probes, 235,000 network grid personnel from 109,000 network grids, and increased persons who are using mobile terminals and APPs.

The Internet governance system has built a platform for communication between party and government offices and the public, becoming a carrier for people to participate in politics and express their opinions. In recent years, Zhejiang Province has created a number of influential interactive platforms such as "Our Round Table Meeting" in Hangzhou, "CNNB—Dialogue" in Ningbo and "Intermediate Station for Political Situations and Public Opinions" in Wenzhou. These platforms center around democratic consultation and democratic

Chapter 6   Citizen Participation Platform on Internet

government affairs discussion on social conditions, public opinions and public policies, helping to ease the public's sentiments and collect the public wisdom. Such platforms have played an important role in the democratic decision-making and resolution of social conflicts.

Comprehensive service platforms, mobile terminals and APPs are tools for governments to perform the duty of public services, integrate cross-sector and cross-departmental resources, and provide volunteer services. The "Internet +" social governance system is widely applied to urban public services such as urban management, sanitation, greening and transportation. In the meanwhile, the comprehensive service platform allows party and government organizations to integrate social forces, lead the public to become "eyes" and "touching points" for finding sources and feeding back problems as they act as public situation information officers and network grid supervisors, and guide and integrate social forces to carry out various forms of volunteer service.

"Internet +" social governance system is not only applied to public services, but also widely used in social supervision. In recent years, Zhejiang Province, through "Internet +", has strengthened its supervision over food safety, rental housing management, express delivery, traffic accidents, illegal construction, and environmental problems such as sewage and air quality, as well as strengthened warning for public safety crisis in scenic spots, train stations and plazas, so as to prevent social risks to the maximum extent. "Internet +" is also widely used in law enforcement and judicial areas including information sharing of parties involved, document delivery, financial crime prediction and prevention. By this way, people and institutions entering the blacklist of dishonesty cannot do anything, which effectively solves the problem of difficult execution of judgment.

In short, when China is in transition, local governments have taken the initiative to use Internet technology to expand the capacity

Political Participation and Institutional Innovation: A Case Study of Zhejiang

of the system to enhance the institutional absorption, to guide citizens' Internet participation to public services and social supervision. Local governments, through the construction of Internet participation mechanism, strengthen their supervision on society and ensure orderly and controllable Internet participation of citizens, so as to reduce the negative impact of Internet participation on the system.

6.5 Discussion and conclusion

The forms of citizen participation in the Internet era are diverse. The aforesaid practice of Internet participation throughout Zhejiang, namely the orderly participation under the guidance of technological empowerment and government constraints, is just one form of citizen participation in China. The feature of such participation helps us to think about universal issues such as Internet governance, technology and politics, public services, government and citizens.

6.5.1 Asymmetry of technological empowerment and constraint

In the era of the Internet, technology plays an important role in the political participation of the citizens. It empowers citizens to provide more convenient means to participate in the governance of public affairs and to supervise the government. However, technology is not neutral. Although it will empower

Political Participation and Institutional Innovation: A Case Study of Zhejiang

its developers and users, the content and extent of empowerment are not exactly the same. As Professor Zheng Yongnian points out: "Some interactions on the Internet can create more power for both parties. The state and social forces are in a mutual empowerment relationship. However, other interactions damage the interests of both parties. The struggle does not empower each other but aims to exclude each other".[3]

Then, in what areas is technological empowerment symmetrical? In what areas is technological empowerment asymmetric? In politics, people's congress deputies' duty performance platforms make it convenient for citizens to contact members anytime and anywhere to present their own demands. In terms of community services, Internet participation platforms facilitate residents' lives and improve government efficiency, and technology empowers the government and the public. Secure Zhejiang APP' and "Ping An 365" strengthen the government's control over residents, and technology empowers the country and society in an asymmetrical manner. More importantly, technology gives developers the power to make rules, while giving users the power to follow rules. In essence, the power to make rules and the power to follow rules are asymmetrical. Technology information system is a microcosm of relationships between man and machine, state and society, government and community. In terms of regulation, it plays a key role in reproduction and supervision of social relations by using non-obtrusive back-links that attract no attention from the public.

As a means of governance, technology is seen as a catalyst for the urban economic recovery in the post-recession era. Who is advocating and designing technical governance? Who benefits most from technical governance? Is technology governance truly the cure-all of urban prosperity and sustainable development? Technology is an activity

---

[3] Zheng Yongnian. *Technological Empowerment: The Internet, State and Society in China*. Palo Alto: Stanford University Press, 2008: 181.

carried out by multi-national companies and countries as powerful private and public actors under a policy framework that aligns their interests. Multi-national companies in the ICT fields such as IBM, Cisco and Siemens participate in the smart city initiative and receive active support from the national and local governments. Against such a background, these multi-national companies prefer to develop and use advanced information technologies in relatively profitable fields of urban governance, especially in environmental protection, energy, water and sustainable urban development. But sometimes they will also, based on demands of urban residents, work for ordinary goals such as improving the living conditions of urban residents. However, benefits sharing and costs sharing of governance are not equal. The development of technology projects is mainly implemented by multi-national technology companies with the criteria of profit maximization. In the construction and operation of technology projects, technology companies have gained most benefits, while public sectors bear most of the risks for they are responsible for the investment of projects, and the public, with no more choice, have to adapt to a new urban life model coordinated by a new technology. In fact, the real driving force of technological governance and the relationship between government and citizens is only calculated and controlled on the basis of ultra-high speed. They do not want to change the real society.

6.5.2 Insertion and absorption

In the political participation of the Internet age, the role of the local government is to supervise, constrain and ensure the orderly participation of the public. It will not push the Internet participation to the opposite of consolidating the legitimacy of the system. It, by inserting Internet participation of citizens into functional departments of people's congress, CPPCC, party committee and the government, incorporates demands of citizens expressed in the Internet into the policy process and the political process, which allows the decision-making to be scientific and democratic, thereby improving the flexibility of the system.

For the government, citizen Internet participation is only one of the functions of the technology platform. The important function of the technology platform is that the country transforms society in the name of science. In the operation of technology platforms including people's congress deputies' duty performance platform, Min Qing E Dian Tong and the "Ping An 365", the government transforms the society like engineers and architects. The engineering-technical orientation of social transformation is the encyclopedia sent by the Enlightenment period to modern society, being in central position of modern government governance. However, can technical experts transform society to a better one? This is still a difficult question to answer. Rousseau believes that morality is the nature of human moral character and social relations. Engineering-technical orientation cannot solve all socio-economic problems and does not improve the meaningful moral life of citizens and the community. On the contrary, it leads to deterioration of moral quality. Because the community is first of all social and moral, and only then is it technical. If technology is prioritized over social morality as a measure of social governance, then technology may intentionally or unintentionally destroy the community's quality of political negotiation and the nature of social interaction.

6.5.3 Internet citizen participation not equal to democracy

Participation is an essential element of democracy, but it is not equal to democracy. The relationship between the participation and democracy in the Internet age has not yet been solved. The practice of China in transition provides an opportunity to reflect on this issue. The advancement of communication and information technology has indeed provided citizens with opportunities and means to participate in political processes and social governance, and the ruling party and the government have indeed made efforts to promote citizen participation. However, from all this, we cannot conclude that citizen participation in the Internet era will surely lead to a smooth transition to democracy. The process of democratization in developing countries is complex and we cannot lay hope on technology for democracy. The practice of

Chapter 6　Citizen Participation Platform on Internet

citizen participation in Zhejiang Province of China is a participation induced, restrained and supervised by the government. To a certain extent, this kind of participation avoids the devastating impact of excessive participation on the political system. If participation in the Internet age does not lead to democratic governance, then where will it lead to? There are at least three possibilities.

The first possibility is to expand polarization. The technology that supports citizen participation has the tendency of capital expansion and values of the consumer society. Behind the scale expansion of public participation is the temptation of technology and capital. Although many scientific and technological innovations are completed with government funding, such as the federal government-funded information highway program, the development of big data technology has fallen into the hands of large multi-national companies such as Google, Cisco, IBM and Alibaba, which will further widen the digital divide and the income gap between technology companies and users and between the government and citizens, creating a new Matthew effect. In addition, large-scale enterprises which engaged in technology development have induced people to behave as they expected by embedding intentions and ideas into technology, injecting the value of capital into ordinary people's behavioral concepts and social order.

The second possibility is the surge of social risks. Technology has features of production and empowerment, but also has invasive, opaque and restrictive features. The intrusive, opaque and restrictive nature of technology will make the social consequences of technology unpredictable, leading to a surge in the risks of citizen participation and technological governance, and negative effects on economy, environment, culture, law, morality and community. Political elite or economic elite can control the initial choice of technology; however, if they do not fully consider the consequences of their decisions, then society may be fundamentally shaped in a way beyond what humans can expect. At that time, society will face a "new governance dilemma".

The third possibility is that humans take initiative to give up their judgment. We are worried that political participation in the Internet era is mired in mob politics, as well as that such participation goes to another extreme of technological rule. Since the Enlightenment Movement, instrumental rationality has become the essence of technical science. It also guides science and technology to dehumanization, inducing humans to use parameters, standards and scripts to replace their intuition, emotion, imagination and empirical judgment. In the future, we have reasons to worry that humans will have their judgment based on biological and historical experience give way to judgment based on parameters, standards and scripts. In the era of big data, we are concerned about human beings falling into risks and pitfalls of computer simulations.

In short, in this era of the Internet, advancement of information and Internet technology has brought new opportunities for promoting citizens' political participation, as well as provided new tools and means for participants. However, Internet and information technology have also brought citizens and society face to face with underlying risks and governance crises. Therefore, it is far from enough only to know opportunities brought on by the Internet, one should also carefully take potential risks of the Internet into consideration.

6.5.4 Government and citizens in the era of the Internet

In today's Internet age, the relationship between citizens and the government is more complex. On the one hand, technology empowers both the state and citizens to enhance the status of both parties. On the other hand, the country controls technology to constrain and supervise citizens. At the same time, citizens use technology to break through such supervision of the country. In the Internet era, the relationship between the state and citizens is not only influenced by technical variables, but also by the governance system and government capabilities. The endogenous relationship between the governance system and technology further enhances or undermines government capabilities.

Chapter 6　Citizen Participation Platform on Internet

The practice of Internet participation across Zhejiang shows that technology is used to improve the quality of national governance and national capabilities. Technology is often used as governmentality. Foucault points out that governmentality is the sum of systems, procedures, analysis, reflections and calculations. Political economy is its main form of knowledge. Security sector is its fundamental technological tool. It also develops a set of governance knowledge and order of power.[4] In this sense, as Hummel points out, "computer bureaucracy"[5] can accurately understand the essence of the wisdom of governance in reality: new technologies, knowledge and order of power. Internet technology is used by the country to strengthen the knowledge and power of bureaucracy, and to transform citizen participation into a means consistent with rationality and legitimacy. Multinational corporations and national and local governments distinguish between "good" and "bad", draw out what is "acceptable" and what is "unacceptable", and form recognition and knowledge through the government's control or mandatory process and introduce specific technical parameters, which set a new moral order for the society. The establishment of this moral order, including control of norms of conduct, discipline mechanism of compulsory system and the cultural mechanism of assigning specific identities to the governors and the governed, permits the reproduction of new orders and powers. In other words, the Internet does not break the path dependence problem of citizen participation and democratic development. The reason is not that relevant technology is not good enough, but that its bureaucratization has made it a part of the bureaucratic knowledge–power order.

---

[4] Foucault, M. Governmentality. In G. Burchell, C. Gordon and P. Miller, (eds.), *The Foucault Effect: Studies in Governmentality*. London: Harvester Wheatsheaf, 1991: 87–104.

[5] Hummel, R. P. *The Bureaucratic Experience: The Post-Modern Challenge*. Armonk, NY: M. E. Sharpe, 2007: 9.

Chapter 7

Zhejiang Experience in Promoting Orderly Public Political Participation and Its Value

Political Participation and Institutional Innovation: A Case Study of Zhejiang

The basic value of modern democracy is to confirm for the first time in the history of mankind that the sovereignty belongs to the people. The organization of the government must be authorized by the people. The purpose of the government is to protect the freedom and rights of citizens. Therefore, the exercise of government power and the government's public policy must be based on public opinion, obey the public opinion, comply with the constitution and the law, and rigorously follow the constitution and the laws to govern and exercise power. In the era of globalization, informatization and urbanization, the society is bound to be one with diversified interest subjects and value pursuits. Since different social groups have different values and value orientations, different personal positions and perspectives, their interest appeals also vary a lot. In the pattern of social pluralism, it is almost impossible to achieve total consensus. Under this circumstance, since the public policy is concerned with the distribution of social interests and values, it must be the result of all levels of society, especially stakeholders, participating in the negotiation and game. All citizens, regardless of their origin, gender, age and belief, have the opportunity to participate in the policy process and formulate policies on the basis of full deliberation and consultation. If the policy process lacks the justified procedure, and if the public policy formulation has no public participation, with sufficient interest expression and negotiation, the governmental decision-making is bound to lack legitimacy and justification, and wouldn't be supported by the people. Therefore, emancipating the mind, deepening political reforms, opening up public space and promoting citizens' orderly political participation are the necessary requirements for the development of the times and society.

Zhejiang Province is one of the most developed areas in China's market economy. Since the reform and opening-up, during the gradual formation of the market economy system and the diversified social interests pattern, the party committees and governments at all levels in Zhejiang Province keep exploring and trying to expand the ways

Chapter 7 Zhejiang Experience in Promoting Orderly Public Political Participation and Its Value

of orderly public political participation due to the needs of citizen's from all social walks' to participate and express interests in the rapid development of the private economy during the transition period and an increasingly stratified social structure and social class. Thus, while improving and optimizing existing democratic participation systems, they have also created a series of new public consultation platforms providing the channel of participating in the local public affairs for the interest expression of all social walks. As a response to the real needs of the society and the people in the transition period, these new participation mechanisms and methods have, to some extent, met the growing desires and demands of the people to be in charge of their own affairs. At the same time, the Zhejiang Provincial Party Committee and the Provincial Government also carried out standardized guidance on non-institutional participation such as mass protests against rights' violations in some localities, initiated public consultations, developed democratic politics, and promoted social stability, harmony and development.

7.1 Characteristics of Zhejiang's experience in institutional innovation

We believe that Zhejiang's institutional innovation to expand orderly public politics is a supplement and improvement to existing institutional arrangements such as the people's congress system, the people's political consultation system, and the grassroots democratic self-government system formed since the founding of the People's Republic of China. It is the timely response to reality of the diversified social interest demands, the desire for citizen participation, and the surge of enthusiasm formed by the transition from traditional agricultural society to modern industrial society. From the perspective of the performance of these participation platforms and participation methods, Zhejiang's response is undoubtedly prompt and effective, and it is a major innovation in China's grassroots democratic political construction. Specifically, Zhejiang's experience

Political Participation and Institutional Innovation:
A Case Study of Zhejiang

and institutional innovations in promoting orderly public political participation have the following characteristics.

7.1.1 Providing concrete and practical approaches for public participation in local governance

In today's China, the subjects of social interests are increasingly divided; the pluralistic game in the public sphere is becoming increasingly fierce; the awareness of citizen rights and democracy is constantly awakening; the enthusiasm for democratic participation is rising. Promoting public political participation has become a real issue that needs to be resolved.

The system of soliciting opinions for the improvement of the projects for people's well-being after years of practice at the two levels of government in Zhejiang and Hangzhou is exactly such a concrete and practical participation way. According to the relevant regulations, all government projects that concern the people's well-being, including local economic and social development and urban construction management, must openly solicit suggestions and opinions from the public (including migrant workers). Before the local Two Sessions are held each year, the people's congresses, the political consultative conferences and the government must solicit opinions and suggestions from all social walks of life on the planning and determination of the projects for people's well-being of that year. What does the government need to do to improve people's well-being? Which projects should be prioritized? The citizens usually only need to write a letter or e-mail to the people's congress, CPPCC and the government to offer their suggestions, with the name, content and requirements of the proposed project and the expected goals. Then the people's congress and the government confirm the list of the projects for people's well-being according to public opinions and submit to the people's congress committee for approval. Another example is the public participation mechanism of major projects in Hangzhou. Before launching the renovation of the West Lake Scenic Area and the construction of major

Chapter 7   Zhejiang Experience in Promoting Orderly Public Political Participation and Its Value

urban projects, the Municipal Party Committee and the Municipal Government invited experts to design several plans and then widely solicited the public opinions. For the projects of West Lake Scenic Area's Beishan Road Line, Nanshan Road Line, Yanggong Dike and West Lake Westward, before the construction of the projects, the relevant government departments must publicly display the relevant construction plans to hear the criticism and questioning of the public about the plan. Some projects, such as the architectural styles of various venues and halls, also allow citizens to visit, comment and vote on the spot. The above-mentioned participation channels and methods involving the people's well-being are specific and practical, and they bring great convenience to the public participation, which has lasted for more than a decade.

In Wenling, Zeguo Town and Xinhe Town have introduced the democratic discussion system into the decision-making process of the township government and formed a set of standardized procedures in the formulation of local public policies. For example, in 2005, Zeguo introduced democratic talks into the decision-making process for the use of funds for urban construction: Should the limited government finance be used for image-building projects or municipal construction closely related to people's well-being? Build a road first or a landfill first? Which road should be built first? For all these questions, we must listen to the opinions of people from all areas of the town. In Xinhe, the democratic talk has been introduced into the review process of the 2006 financial budget plan to form a participatory budget. Whether the budget of the government finance is reasonable and whether the expenditure is necessary must be discussed and negotiated by attending representatives. There must be debates and questions of representatives and citizens to clearly express different interest claims so that delegates and citizens could deeply discuss the pros and cons of government-related decisions. The practice of democratic talks in Zeguo and Xinhe provides a practical platform for the public to participate in local governance. Through democratic discussion on the institutional platform for public consultation, the government allows the public to participate in and witness decision-making. This decision-making process not only enhances the scientific and democratic decision-making of the government, but also greatly strengthens the legitimacy of decision-making, which greatly contributes to the implementation and execution of the decisions.

7.1.2 Innovative public participation system has clear objectives and roles

The institutional innovations of Zhejiang Province in promoting citizens' orderly political participation, be it the village democratic talks, the city's hearings, the people's suggestion solicitation system, television inquiries, the government's website administration forums or the democratic participation system of major well-being projects, are all forms of participation which are highly and functionally differentiated. From the standpoint of institutional arrangements itself, the objective and roles of these participation mechanisms are to promote citizens' orderly political participation and provide channels for expressing their interests, instead of political functions of publicizing the will of party committees or implementing government policies.

The innovative citizen participation mechanism has clear participation functions and goals, which makes it strictly separated from the political functions of other functional agencies in the national institutional arrangement, reflecting the distinctive value implications of modern democratic participation. First, the main participants are citizens, not officials. Second, the autonomy of the participation system is significant, and as far as possible distinguished from the people's congress, CPPCC and other systems to perform the role of public participation, which is unconducive to be carried out by other traditional systems. Third, the participation mechanism weakens the nature of the ruling party as a social control tool, the participation forms such as democratic talks, hearings, television

Chapter 7　Zhejiang Experience in Promoting Orderly Public Political Participation and Its Value

inquiries and public forums on the Internet, all clearly demonstrating the function of citizens participating in local affairs, expressing interest claims and influencing government decision-making. It rarely takes on the functions of the ruling party's will expression, social mobilization and policy advocacy, showing a high degree of functional differentiation.

Take Wenling's democratic talk system as an example. Since its beginning in 1999, it has been running for 18 years and the democratic talks have become a decision-making process that must be performed during the formulation of policies by some functional departments of the municipal government. It has become a public negotiation platform with powerful operational and explicit citizen participation functions and goals. According to the Regulations of the CPC Wenling Municipal Committee on "Democratic Talk" published and launched on September 29, 2004, "Democratic Talk" is the original form of grassroots democracy of the city. It is an important carrier for democratic expansion, democratic decision-making promotion, democratic management and democratic supervision. Several Provisions of Songmen Democratic Talk System forwarded by the Wenling Municipal Committee to all towns more clearly regulate that the democratic talk is a new grassroots democratic pattern for the government to hold equal dialogue, democratic negotiation and full demonstration with the citizens regarding the public affairs. Songmen also clearly stipulates that the democratic talk can be conducted regularly or irregularly, no less than four times a year, generally held once every quarter, and it can be held at any time in special circumstances. Scholars at home and abroad highly acknowledge this and believe that Wenling's democratic talk has already become institutionalized. The democratic talk has developed exhaustive procedural regulations about "how to negotiate" and it does not rely solely on ideology, but considers individual interests and preferences to respond to the demands of the people with the characteristics of democratic elements such as consultation and voting.

Political Participation and Institutional Innovation: A Case Study of Zhejiang

The development of Wenling democratic talk has gradually weakened the ideological propaganda function it had when it was first created, and gradually positioned itself in the function of expressing, negotiating and integrating interest in democratic consultations, to realize citizens' influence on the local public policy.

Hearings and television inquiries have become specialized institutional platforms for citizen interests expression, public consultation and interests integration in cities like Hangzhou, Wenzhou and Ningbo. All social walks of life have begun to review its value and significance according to its influence on government public decision-making. Some local governments tried to use hearings as a political publicity tool for decorating public opinion and strengthening policy legitimacy, which has been seriously disapproved of and questioned by the social communities. To some extent, the new participation channels have already been separated from traditional participation systems and become a procedural participation system for modern citizens to safeguard their own legal rights and interests, showing highly differentiated political participation orientation. As for the public opinion solicitation system, it has become a channel for the government to absorb folk wisdom and understand public demands and interests. The government decision-making is improved based on the collected opinions so that the public goods and services could better comply with the majority's needs. It is a specific and operational approach to realizing traditional public participation and social monitoring system, separated from the previous multi-function integration state to become a centralized public opinion expression and decision-making influencing mechanism. Government website forums are almost unable to exercise the traditional policy publicity and education function since they were established; instead, they serve as a platform for ordinary people to express opinions, show their attempts and realize interests expression and communication as well as a channel for party committees and governments at all levels to understand public information and adjust the public policy.

Chapter 7 Zhejiang Experience in Promoting Orderly Public Political Participation and Its Value

7.1.3 Innovative public participation system reflects the values of democracy and the advanced participation technology

Institutional innovation in political participation should meet the needs of citizens to play a practical role in promoting citizens' participation, making them enjoy the participation. The participation system must not only reflect the value of contemporary democracy, but also be facilitated by the latest participation technologies in today's information society. The reason that the institutional innovation of promoting citizens' orderly political participation in Zhejiang can be accepted and acknowledged by citizens is that these innovations apply the latest public political participation theories and technologies in the field, such as the theories of deliberative democracy and responsive democracy. Especially with the rise of the Internet and network technology as well as the gradual improvement of the hearing process and technology, the application of these latest participation theories and technologies serves citizens' interest expression, integration and maintenance. For example, Wenling's democratic talk not only embodies the value implications of the deliberative democracy theory, one of the latest democratic theories in the world today. Under the guidance of Professor James Fishkin from Stanford University and Professor He Baogang from Deakin University, the democratic talk in Zeguo and other places also absorbs the ideas like consultation polls and testing techniques, including a series of technical processing methods, which involves the random sampling, grouping (including control groups and non-control groups) and questionnaires during the consultation process as well as abundant statistics and calculations. In a sense, Wenling democratic talk has already conformed with the deliberative democracy theory and technology in the frontier areas of international social science. The hearings held in several places and the statutory procedures for the relevant hearings are not only the application of the deliberative democracy theory, but also the application of legal procedures and technological democracy, and the government process theory of the government's public decision-making. The public opinion solicitation

Political Participation and Institutional Innovation: A Case Study of Zhejiang

is essentially the application of responsive democratic theory, involving the legal orientation, institutional design, collection methods, operability design, statistics and opinion information processing techniques. Of course, the well-implemented public opinion solicitation may become the most advanced quantitative democracy at present; on the contrary, it may degrade into formalism and the public opinion solicitation system will inevitably become a superficial form of qualitative democracy, which is why the public opinion solicitation could be successfully run in Zhejiang but not in other provinces.

In the Internet era, ICT empowers both citizens and governments, and creates a basic structure for the adjustment of state–society relations. As far as Zhejiang is concerned, the local people's congress, CPPCC and the government have established their own platforms for citizen participation, including the Zhejiang People's Congress Performance Platform, Zhejiang Provincial Government Service Network, the China Hangzhou Network—Government Affairs Forum, and China Ningbo Network—Dialogue. The Internet expands the capacity of the political system and improves its resilience so that a platform for citizen participation can be set up on the Internet. Internet technology has been used as a new way for citizens to be the masters of the country, expressing interest claims and starting achievable attempts in realizing the goal of people taking charge through information technology. Of course, the political participation of the citizens on the Internet doesn't come without any constraints. The local people's congress, CPPCC and the government use the Internet to monitor the participation of citizens, reduce the impact of citizen participation on the political system and divert citizen participation to public services through "Internet +" social governance. And in the area of social governance, they could improve the quality of government public services. Under the combined effect of Internet empowerment and the expansion of the state system, and government supervision and diversion mechanisms, the participation of Zhejiang citizens on the Internet has exhibited an orderly expansion. In other words, the Zhejiang Government's Internet Public Forum is a combination of typical respondent democracy and network technology.

Chapter 7 Zhejiang Experience in Promoting Orderly Public Political Participation and Its Value

It relies on Zhejiang's advanced economy, strong government funding and leading edge construction of government websites at all levels to better apply network technology to local governance and public affairs. The process of formulating policies, through the use of network technology, collects citizens' feedback on the government's public decision-making, thus expanding the space for public political participation. The experience of Zhejiang's Internet citizen participation shows that it is necessary to synchronize the Internet technology with the capacity expansion system, so as to avoid the fatal impact of citizen participation in the Internet era.

7.1.4 Institutional innovation is the supplement and improvement for the national political system

In recent years, the institutional innovation of citizen participation in Zhejiang has risen from time to time. It is the result of systematic exploration at the institutional level by the party committees and governments at all levels in Zhejiang based on the social reality and increasing political participation need of people in the transition period. Regarding the innovative participation system itself, whether it is rural democratic talks, the city's administrative hearings, legislative hearings, public opinion solicitation, major social well-being project, democratic participation system, television inquiries or the online citizen participation platform, they are all participation forms with highly differentiated functions. Since they were created, these systems do not appear as social control tools. They no longer shoulder the political functions of propagating and implementing the policies of the ruling party and the government. They are based solely on the functional goals of promoting citizens' orderly political participation. It has become a public negotiation platform for different social communities to express interest appeals, display citizens' wishes and realize interest expression and interest integration.

What needs to be pointed out is that while these innovative public participation mechanisms and forms show the side of institutional autonomy, we must also see that the institutional innovation of the participation mechanism is not built beyond the people's congress system and the political consultation system. In other words, in recent years, a series of institutional innovations for promoting citizens' orderly political participation in Zhejiang have been carried out on the basis of the fundamental political system of the country. Essentially, it is the improvement of the socialist system with Chinese characteristics.

Promoting the construction of the provincial and municipal people's congresses and the CPPCC system and promoting citizens' orderly political participation are important parts of the modernization of the state governance system since the reform and opening-up. For example, the Standing Committee of the Zhejiang Provincial People's Congress allows citizens' representatives to attend the meetings so that the general public could have an opportunity to understand the legislative process of the standing committee of local people's congress. The open legislation and legislative negotiation procedures of the Zhejiang Provincial People's Congress and the Hangzhou Municipal People's Congress have promoted the democratization and openness of the local people's congressional legislative process, so as to advance the legitimacy of the local regulations formulated and promulgated by local people's congresses. Another example is that the standing committee of the Zhejiang Provincial Committee of the Chinese People's Political Consultative Conference also allows citizen representatives to attend the meetings. The monthly social well-being forum of the provincial CPPCC invites representatives from relevant social walks to participate in the speech and speak with the members of the CPPCC and government functional departments upon the hot topics in medical, health, education and food safety, land acquisition and arbitrary administrative charges issues concerning the public. Citizens are allowed to participate directly in the political consultation process of the local CPPCC. This not only promotes citizens' orderly political participation, but also enhances the representation of political consultation, and the pertinence and effectiveness of consultation opinions.

The practice of promoting citizens' orderly political participation in several places in Zhejiang also shows that only when the innovative

Chapter 7 Zhejiang Experience in Promoting Orderly Public Political Participation and Its Value

participation system and participation model are integrated into the country's fundamental political system can the system innovation be lasting and effective and maintain the vitality. The practice of citizen participation in Zhejiang shows once again that the system that encourages prosperity forms a positive feedback loop. A series of hearings on specific issues in Hangzhou, Ningbo and Wenzhou have widely accepted the participation of representatives from all walks of life. Different interests, positions, opinions and appeals have all been placed together to be discussed in an open, truthful and extensive way, even fiercely debated, questioned and argued. These hearings on the one hand, of course, offer the opportunity to the community, especially stakeholders to express, so that different interest groups can voice their opinions, but the absorption of these public opinions into the government decision-making still depends on the interest coordination and integration by the host units such as the CPPCC and the people's congress in the process of hearings and negotiations. The public participation performance of the government website and governmental affairs forum also depends on the attention and the integration mechanism of the government's functional departments. In the first few years of Wenling democratic talk, due to the lack of support from national laws and macro-level institution, consultations and discussions were unlikely to go deeper, and it was not only difficult to promote it to areas beyond Wenling, even its local development was seriously challenged. Later, some villages and towns in Wenling tried to combine democratic talk with the people's congress system. For example, through the consultative democratic talk on the municipal public projects in Zeguo, based on the consensus reached by the democratic talk and the results of public opinion polls, the decision-making mechanisms of town party committees and governments preliminarily settled down the annual municipal construction pre-selected projects, which then were submitted to the town people's congress meeting and finally became the confirmed projects after deliberation and approval by the deputies to the people's congress. The same holds true for the success of Wenling's participatory budgeting. Once the operation of the

Political Participation and Institutional Innovation:
A Case Study of Zhejiang

democratic talk is linked to the town party committee, the government's decision-making system, and the people's congress system, it becomes a basic procedure for the decision-making process of the town people's congresses and the government. The democratic talk system has been injected with new vitality and the legitimacy of the new system has also been strengthened.

7.2 Why did institutional innovation occur in Zhejiang?

In the discussion of the latest progress in the construction of basic democratic politics in Zhejiang, we pointed out that the rapid development of the private economy and the deepening reform of the country's political system are important motives for the institutional changes that promote the development of grassroots democracy in rural areas. The actual dilemma of local governance brought on by the rapid development of private economy, marketization and urbanization is the opportunity for the changes in the grassroots democratic system in Zhejiang, people's rising awareness of democracy and rights, and the institutional innovations of the local government to promote local governance are the direct motives for local governments to promote citizens' orderly political participation and innovate public participation channels to encourage citizens to participate in local governance. What needs to be emphasized is that the reasons for the series of institutional innovations, which increase citizens' orderly political participation and promote the participation of citizens in local governance, that have occurred in Zhejiang lie in the following factors.

7.2.1 Local party committees and governments respond positively to the growing demand for participation in the transitional society

Zhejiang is the province where the private economy was first developed, and its private economy is the most developed across the country. With the rapid advancement of industrialization, marketization and urbanization, the society has undergone a major transformation, with social interest subjects undergoing fierce differentiation and social stratification undergoing rapid changes. As a result, various social issues have emerged in an endless stream. Citizen interest expression and interest integration have therefore been put on the agenda. While the ruling party and the government are striving to maintain stability, it is impossible to ignore these issues. Faced with the new social pattern of the multi-interest game during the transition period and the growing demand for political participation by citizens, the ruling party and the government took the initiative to respond and promote institutional innovation and institution building.

Current modernization in China featuring industrialization, marketization and urbanization is late-stage, exogenous modernization, while modern China's democracy is also the passive democracy driven by the elite. Therefore, first the ruling party and the government need to respond to the increasing participation need of citizens, which is the basic feature of contemporary Chinese citizens' political participation and the key to the development of democratic politics. Second, it is the responsibility of the modern government to respond to the increasing participation needs of citizens. The purpose of the modern government should only be to ensure the realization of the basic rights of citizens. Citizens' basic rights include the right to life, liberty, property and

Chapter 7 Zhejiang Experience in Promoting Orderly Public Political Participation and Its Value

political participation of the citizens. Citizens' political participation is an important means for citizens to realize their rights. Each government has the responsibility to actively respond to citizens' participation needs. Third, China's national conditions and realistic system determine that the current stage of democratic politics can only take deliberative democracy as its main content. Consultative democracy emphasizes communication and negotiation between citizens and the government, and does not emphasize the confrontation and opposition of citizens to the government. The premise of consultation and communication between citizens and the government must be the prompt response of the government to the needs of citizens for political participation. China's traditional political culture is a culture of subjects. The majority of the general population lacks the independent spirit of liberal democracy. They are highly dependent on the government. The relationship between the people and the government is characterized by the obedience of the people to the government. The government policy process tends to focus on output but lacks input. In the relation to the government, they often tend to negotiate with the government. The success or failure of the negotiation usually depends on the government's response to citizens' negotiation request. If the government is sincere and responds quickly, a deliberative democracy may develop; if the government responds slowly or lacks sincerity, the deliberative democracy will shrink. If it refuses to respond and ignores the participation needs of citizens, it will force citizens in to non-institutional participation and eventually lead to social conflict and turmoil.

According to the practice of grassroots democracy development in Zhejiang, the promotion of the orderly participation of citizens in institutional innovation largely depends on the fact that party committees and governments at all levels have seized the opportunity for development, responded quickly to the participation needs of citizens and promoted government–public cooperation to advance the formation of the institutional innovation.

Political Participation and Institutional Innovation:
A Case Study of Zhejiang

Take Wenling's democratic talks as an example. Before this system was created, Zhejiang's agricultural and rural modernization education had been carried out for 12 years. This kind of mobilization by the government bringing the farmers together to listen to lectures by experts or officials appeared to be somehow unsuitable for the current stage of development and social interest differentiation. It did not regard the peasants as an equal object of dialogue, nor did it have a clear relationship with peasant interests. Farmers were very disgusted with such activities. What they needed was an equal dialogue platform to discuss issues that were of vital interest to them, such as village and town construction projects, investment environment projects, village and town security and order, and disputes between villages and towns. Farmers wanted to participate in the policymaking process and influence government decision-making so that they could realize the benefits they could see. The Publicity Department of Wenling Municipal Party Committee and the township party committees and governments have resolutely put an end to the original ideological education model and introduced a deliberative democracy mechanism that transformed agricultural and rural modernization education into "democratic talk", in which the government and citizens directly and indirectly negotiate on an equal basis. The democratic talk system provides farmers with a platform for equal dialogue and open discussion. The officials and the people come together to discuss and respond to public affairs that are of interest to the public, such as village planning and construction projects, and finally make decisions. With the development of the democratic talks, the government has also constantly updated the topics and procedures of the democratic talks according to changes in the participation of farmers, so as to integrate them with the village elections and the people's congress system. At the same time, the Wenling local party committee and government also resolved the implementation and supervision of the results of the democratic talk through a number of basic institutional norms, so that the democratic talk could become a system that guarantees and realizes the rights and interests of citizens.

Chapter 7　Zhejiang Experience in Promoting Orderly Public Political Participation and Its Value

The improvement of the hearing system is also a positive response of local governments to the growing demand for citizen participation and interest expression. For example, the Hangzhou taxi fare adjustment hearing was held because of the public's doubts about the unilateral pricing of the government; Zhejiang's legislative hearings were held because of ordinary people's dissatisfaction with the private legislation session of the people's congress. The establishment of the government website public forums is the government's affirmation and guidance of the behavior of citizens participating in politics in the Internet age. The public opinion solicitation system is a product of the government's desire to collect public opinions, understand public sentiments and respond to citizen participation in government decision-making. In order to meet the needs of the people for political participation and to improve the scientific and democratic decision-making of the government, the Hangzhou Municipal Government established the Public Opinion Solicitation System in 2000. The Hangzhou Municipal Government has set up a public opinion solicitation office, which is specifically responsible for collecting and sorting public opinions. In recent years, a series of major decisions made by the Hangzhou Municipal Government were based on the suggestions of ordinary citizens in Hangzhou, such as building a new image of Hangzhou's Sudi and Baidi, the establishment of the exhibition hall of the Western Fair in the Hangzhou History Museum, and adding and extending some bus lines. In the first half of 2005, the Public Opinion Solicitation Office of the Hangzhou Municipal Government received 8,749 suggestions from various communities. About one in every 100 proposals was adopted and implemented by the municipal government. In the proposed form of solicitation, Hangzhou has introduced three forms, namely daily collection, special collection and media solicitation, to solicit opinions and suggestions of the public from multiple levels and in all aspects. Hangzhou has also established a reward system recommended by the people, which commends and encourages citizens who have provided good suggestions for government decision-making, and effectively promoted the implementation and improvement of the public opinion solicitation system.

Political Participation and Institutional Innovation:
A Case Study of Zhejiang

In China, citizens' attitudes to and actions of political participation, development of their participation skills and interests are largely based on the trust of the government in the development of political participation, and the government's timely response to the needs of the people for participation will encourage citizens to maintain perseverance and interest in political participation, and will continue to improve their participation skills and capabilities in their participation. In short, the government's positive response to the growing demand for citizens' political participation can stimulate and accumulate the trust of citizens for the government, promote the harmony between citizens and the state, and lay a solid foundation for the development of democratic politics.

7.2.2 A large number of local officials made active moves, bold exploration and practical innovation

In the transitional society, interest division and conflict have become increasingly fierce, and people's awareness of rights and democratic participation has been continuously enhanced. This is not a phenomenon exclusive to Zhejiang Province. During the rapid transformation of the Chinese society from a traditional agricultural society to a modern industrial society, the reason for a series of institutional innovations of promoting the orderly public political participation that first occurred in Zhejiang lies in the fact that Zhejiang is a development highland of Chinese civilization in history. After the Song dynasty, China's economic center was transferred to the Jiangnan region. Zhejiang became the land with the most prosperous economy and the most developed culture during that period. It was known as the "land of fish and rice" and "province of cultural relics". In modern times, Zhejiang was the first to accept the baptism of Western industrial civilization due to its proximity to Shanghai. Therefore, the genes of Zhejiang people carry the spirit of being civilized, pragmatic, open and daring to be the best in the world. The officials in Zhejiang are practical and pragmatic, open-minded, and more aware of democracy and the rule of law. Faced with the reality of social interest

Chapter 7 Zhejiang Experience in Promoting Orderly Public Political Participation and Its Value

differentiation and social stratification during the transitional period, local officials at all levels in Zhejiang are also paying attention to safeguarding the harmony and stability of the society while respecting the people's pioneering spirit and while developing the local economy. They are good at improving the system through innovation and the quality of local governance.

Zhejiang is one of the provinces with the most developed private economy and the highest degree of marketization. The private economy often accounts for the largest proportion of the national economy and enjoys the fastest development. Naturally, it also stimulates citizens' participation needs and strong desire to be the masters. However, institutionalized public participation channels are currently under-supplied in contrast with the huge demand for interest expression. This supply–demand asymmetry has once also led to the occurrence of public crises in certain areas of Zhejiang due to mass rights-defending incidents. For example, the Huaxi Incident of Dongyang a decade ago, the Xinchang Jingxin Pharmaceutical Incident and the Pollution Incident in Changxing Battery Factory were all social crises triggered by non-institutional political participation.

Some active and promising officials from party committees and governments at all levels in Zhejiang have sensitively felt the influence of social interest differentiation and social stratification, and thus initiated the impulse of institutional innovation. The courage of the Zhejiang people to dare to enter the world is also reflected by government officials at all levels. While promoting the development of the private economy, they are actively exploring institutional innovations to promote citizens' orderly political participation, opening up more public space to the public, and putting the public's ever-increasing demand for political participation and energy-oriented systems on track. Through a series of platforms such as democratic conferences, hearings, and television and government affairs forums, citizens are encouraged

Political Participation and Institutional Innovation:
A Case Study of Zhejiang

to participate in local governance, so that the people can express their views on local public affairs, and put forward views different from that of the government, through the institutional platform of public participation and public consultation, to resolve social conflicts and disputes and promote social harmony, stability, and social and economic development.

7.2.3 The cooperation between the government and citizens promotes institutional innovation in an orderly manner

Citizens are the main participants. Since the reform and opening-up, in the process of social transformation driven by marketization, the awareness of the rights, democracy, and the rule of law of the people in Zhejiang has been continuously enhanced. The people's growing enthusiasm for democratic participation has interacted with the innovation impulse of the local government, and has promoted systematic innovation of citizens' orderly political participation in various regions of Zhejiang. With the advancement of industrialization and urbanization, the rapid development of the private economy, modernization has also led to many new conflicts while stimulating social progress. At the same time, citizens' rights awareness and democratic awareness are also constantly increasing with social mobility and social interaction, which constitutes an external pressure on local governments at various levels to promote institutional innovation. It can be said that the interaction and game between the government and the people have promoted the innovation system and system construction to enhance citizen participation.

From the perspective of the government, the contemporary Chinese government is undoubtedly the dominant force in promoting political development and the only provider of the system. For example, the Wenling Democratic Conference is the government's promotion. The government no longer engages in the "false, big, and empty" preaching, and shifts the retreat of political propaganda and education

Chapter 7 Zhejiang Experience in Promoting Orderly Public Political Participation and Its Value

to pragmatic citizen participation in order to respond to the growing interest of citizens. The democracy talks started in the "Forum on Rural Modernization Education" in Songmen Township, Wenling City in 1999. Its original intention was to try to use a form of face-to-face communication between the cadres and the public to promote the policies of the ruling party to the villagers. At that time, modern education in agriculture and rural areas had been carried out in Zhejiang Province for 12 consecutive years. The education methods basically consisted of mobilizing the general assembly first, and then invited some experts or officials to teach the people. In fact, the broad masses of the people have been deeply annoyed by this kind of brainwashing propaganda and education. In response to this problem, the Publicity Department of Taizhou Municipal Party Committee and the Publicity Department of Wenling Municipal Party Committee held pilots in the town of Songmen in an attempt to "get out of the old form of education to educate" and hoped to bring the government and the people closer to each other through democratic communication, candid dialogue and doing things for the people. On June 15, 1999, more than 150 people spontaneously came and participants enthusiastically expressed their opinions and demands on the town's investment environment, village and township construction plans, daily liquefied gas prices, and neighborhood disputes. Town leaders answered more than half of the questions on the spot. If they couldn't solve the problems on the spot, they would make detailed explanations or would promise concrete solutions in time. This new type of communication caused a positive response from the villagers. In the four "Education Forum" activities held in 1999, the total number of spontaneously participating people reached more than 600. More than 100 questions were raised by the participants, more than 80 questions were explained and answered by relevant leaders on the spot, and more than 20 promised to be delivered. This activity was intimately described by the masses in Songmen Town as "a great way to do big things and solve difficult problems without spending money". It was a "focus interview" in Songmen Town.

Political Participation and Institutional Innovation:
A Case Study of Zhejiang

The success of the "Forum on Rural Modernization of Education" in Songmen Town greatly encouraged the democratic innovation practice in other townships in Wenling and increased the enthusiasm of ordinary people to participate in politics. People find that in government management and local public affairs, they can no longer simply act as passive players. The active participation of villagers can also influence the government's decision-making. Citizens can use their political rights to exercise their rights and protect themselves. The awakening of civic awareness, combined with the promotion and guidance of the government, has brought vitality to the practice of grassroots democracy. The experience of Songmen was summed up and promoted in a timely manner by the Publicity Department of Wenling Municipal Party Committee. Various forms of democratic communication and democratic dialogue activities took place across the city, including "public opinion talks", "village affairs referendum" and "personal affairs night talks", etc. Although the names are numerous, they are basically the same in form and essence as the "Forum on Rural Modernization Education" in Songmen Town. They use local officials to communicate with the people in a face-to-face manner and make decisions or promises on the issues of interest to the people and solve the problems. In order to further standardize and deepen these forms of deliberative democracy, Wenling Municipal Party Committee decided in 2001 to collectively refer to them as "democratic talks".

7.3 What does Zhejiang's experience tell us?

Citizens' political participation is an important indicator to measure the development level of a country's democratic politics. At the same time, it is an important marker of a country's political modernization and the degree of political civilization development. Therefore, promoting citizens' orderly political participation, and allowing citizens to participate extensively in local governance and exercising their constitutional rights as the masters of their own affairs are not only inherent requirements for the development of democratic politics, but also important parts of building a socialist democracy and political civilization. The promotion of institutional innovation in Zhejiang, the expansion of citizens' orderly political participation and the wide participation of citizens in the practice of local governance are important experiments in the construction of local democratic politics in China. From the experience of grassroots democratic politics and system innovation in Zhejiang, we can at least draw the following inspirations.

7.3.1 Citizens totally have the capability of taking care of their own affairs

Democracy is a universally pursued value, a system of state governance and a way of life for modern citizens. As a governance system, each specific form of democracy is developed by members of the community based on their social, economic, political, cultural and geographic environment, and their interaction and adaptation with their civic cultural environment. The character and basic qualities of citizens directly determine the quality of democracy. In modern times, political theorists such as Tocqueville and Almond have explored the characteristics and causes of democracy, paid more attention to the cultural characteristics of citizens, attached importance to the basic conditions of democracy, and studied the main factors of society to explore the birth, development and decline of democracy and the reasons. For the Chinese, democracy is an exotic product imported from abroad in modern times. Therefore, the first problem encountered in the promotion of democracy in China is the following: Do the Chinese have the consciousness of democracy and the ability to practice democracy?

China has thousands of years' history of absolutist political tradition. The traditional political culture is a typical subject culture. The official culture is characterized by a royal and authoritarian rule, emphasizing personal surrender to monarchs and rulers, and to groups and nations as well as the absolute obedience to the superior; the political tradition emphasizes individual responsibilities and obligations, not individual rights. The entire society was characterized by the absolute dependence and obedience to the monarch, the supreme, power, authority and honor. Almost everyone in the society was in a relationship of attachment to rank and external human relations. Fei Xiaotong called such an autocratic and hierarchical

Chapter 7　Zhejiang Experience in Promoting Orderly Public Political Participation and Its Value

vertical structure of traditional Chinese society a "differential pattern". In this "differential pattern", the relations between two persons, between individuals and groups (family and clan), between superiors and subordinates, was a relationship of attachment, and a subordinate affiliation based on hierarchy. The traditional principle used to stipulate such relations was the "three cardinal principles and five constant virtues" advocated by Confucianism, that is, the so-called "King is the ruler of the official, the father is the ruler of the son, and the husband is the ruler of the wife". In the family, the children were required to obey and adhere to their parents. In the country and society, people were required to subordinate themselves and absolutely obey the superiors, attach themselves to and obey the officials at all levels, and finally bow to the emperor. The obligation of children and subjects was to obey and show ethical requirements. In such a culture of subjects, the relationship between human beings was the relationship between obedience and dependence, and individuals completely lost autonomy and independence of personality. Politics was a career of bureaucrats and doctors. The state affairs had nothing to do with the ordinary people. The emperors, ruling groups, and bureaucrats at all levels monopolized the power of the state. The emperor relied on the bureaucracy to become the master of all people. The subjects and the lower ones had to accept their position and became the minions or servants of emperors and rulers.

After the baptism of the modern revolution and culture, the Chinese gradually came into contact with the concepts of democracy, republicanism, freedom and equality, and gradually came to understand the concept of rights, but the implementation of the planned economy and the continuous development of the class struggle led to the reversion of the culture of dependent subjects in the past. Once the Chinese people lost their autonomy, their awareness of civil rights and democratic consciousness disappeared, and their awareness of participation in democracy and ownership were almost lost. Even today, especially in the economically underdeveloped

Political Participation and Institutional Innovation: A Case Study of Zhejiang

rural areas of the central and western regions, the phenomenon of weak citizen participation and low democratic capacity seems to be relatively common. Even in the economically developed coastal areas such as Zhejiang, there is still a prevailing phenomenon of political indifference whereby villagers give up voting during village elections. However, this does not mean that the general public hold negative attitude toward political participation, nor does it mean that they lack the ability to participate in politics.

After 40 years of reform and opening-up, the market-oriented economic and political reforms have reconstructed a space for the free flow of social resources for the contemporary Chinese. The social pattern featuring multiple interest groups with independent interests and subjective awareness has been gradually formed in the marketization process, while the awareness of citizens' rights has been continuously enhanced and the awareness of democracy has increased. At the same time, the development of the private economy has also promoted the construction of a contractual relationship based on equality and self-government from the social level, nurturing the people's awareness of their rights and of democracy, which has also promoted the passion, confidence and impulse of citizens to participate in politics. Therefore, in today's China, people do have a considerable sense of rights and participation. In the increasingly fierce game of interest among various stakeholders, the general public has made important decisions concerning public affairs. In particular, major decisions that are related to the interests of the people and belong to the scope of the people's well-being, driven by vital interests, have witnessed strong enthusiasm and aspiration for participation. They only lack the proper participation ways and methods, therefore they are either skeptical about the authenticity or do not believe in their influence on politics. They are no longer as obscure as they were during the "Cultural Revolution". Only when they are convinced that participation can achieve their interests will they take the initiative to participate. Faced with multiple values and diversified choices, the temporary wait-and-see and indifference

Chapter 7 Zhejiang Experience in Promoting Orderly Public Political Participation and Its Value

expressed by the people at some time do not mean that they do not have the willingness and ability to participate. In a sense, this just shows their maturity. In the practice of grassroots democratic politics in Zhejiang, especially rural democratic talks, city hearings, major project democratic participation system, television inquiries, public opinion solicitation system, Internet public forums, official–civilian dialogues, etc., and the active participation of citizens in public consultation show that the concept of democratic awareness and rights of Chinese citizens have already changed. They are actively participating in politics to express their interest demands and strive for and safeguard their own rights and interests. The practice of grassroots democracy and citizen participation in Zhejiang also clearly demonstrates to the world that contemporary Chinese people have the ability to participate democratically.

Zhejiang's public orderly participation in politics also shows that the nature, content, scope and objects of public participation in China today have all undergone great changes during the social transformation. The people's political participation ability and level have greatly improved. They not only dare to participate, but also are good at participating. Professor James Fishkin from Stanford University has summed up a large number of democratic talks around the world, including the Wenling democratic talk. He believes that people from different backgrounds, rich or poor, regardless of their level of knowledge, could concentrate on issues of common concern and exchange discussions. As an observer from a foreign country, Professor James Fishkin clearly affirms the ability of citizens of all countries, including China, to participate. The Wenling democratic talk is a testament to the high political participation of Zhejiang citizens. Mu Yifei, the Vice Minister of Wenling Municipal Party Committee Publicity Department then, spoke about the personal experience of the 2005 democratic talk of Zeguo: "When I first talked about it, I didn't agree with it. After the morning and afternoon, I was totally overwhelmed, and the effect of the miracle was the participation of the people. We were simply not expecting. The ability of the people to participate changed greatly from morning to afternoon".

A series of hearings in Hangzhou, Ningbo and Wenzhou in recent years also show that citizens not only have the ability to participate, but also are good at participating. In fact, the general public is increasingly disgusted with the practice of official hearings as "shows". Hearings should only have genuine content, and openness to get the public's support, otherwise the people will not buy in. The increased awareness of citizen participation has prompted some government officials to change their thinking and practice of using the hearing only as a tool to gain the legitimacy of governance, and has prompted the organizers of the hearing to continuously improve and perfect the hearing system so as to enrich the content of the hearing. The scope of the hearing is broader; the participants are more representative; the debates of all parties are more intense; the hearings show more equality; the hearing is more open and transparent; the hearing results are more effective; the implementation of the consensus reached by the hearing receives more supervision. All these show that citizens' political participation has improved.

The popularity of mobile Internet and mobile phones, and the rapid development of Internet citizens' political participation are the latest features of contemporary Chinese citizen participation. Although China's Internet has risen relatively late, the scale of Internet users has grown rapidly. According to statistics, at the end of 2005, there were a total of 970 million Internet users in the world. In July 2006, the number of Chinese Internet users was 123,000. In recent years, with the popularization of the mobile Internet, by December 2016, the number of Chinese netizens reached 731 million. The size of Chinese netizens has been equivalent to the total population of Europe. The Internet penetration rate was 53.2%, 3.1% points higher than the global average and 7.6% higher than the Asian average. (On January 22, 2017, CNNIC released the Statistical Report on the Development of China's Internet

Chapter 7 Zhejiang Experience in Promoting Orderly Public Political Participation and Its Value

Network.) Netizens have used the website citizen forum to post stickers and use blogs, microblogs, and WeChat tools to express their sentiments on the Internet and influence public opinion.

The rise of we-media such as microblogs and WeChat has brought unprecedented development to Internet political participation. Therefore, today's Chinese society has gone out of the age of subjects, and has made great strides toward the era of citizenship. People's awareness of rights is awakened and democratic participation is rising. The era of the reform and opening-up is, in a sense, the "era of rights", and it is an era in which the concept of civil rights, democracy, and the rule of law are increasingly strengthened. It can be said that in modern times, democracy has always been the dream of the Chinese people. The contemporary Chinese people yearn for democracy, pursue democracy, study democracy, and are open to participation. Judging from the situation in Zhejiang at least, the Chinese people have the ability to implement democracy. Any attempt to delay the democratic process or hinder citizens' political participation, and even to deprive them of their rights to participate in local governance, will be futile.

7.3.2 Democracy relies on the tangible participation system and channel

Expanding citizens' orderly political participation and realizing the people's right to be the masters of the country is the national goal that the ruling party and the government have clearly declared to the world. However, democracy cannot stop in the theoretical or constitutional text alone, let alone stay in slogans or ideals. Citizens are the masters of the nation. They are not nominal in nature. Citizens exercise the rights to be the masters of their own affairs and directly or indirectly participate in public affairs. They need to have specific institutional arrangements and have practical and effective channels for participation. Without channels or enough channels for participation, citizens will have no

Political Participation and Institutional Innovation: A Case Study of Zhejiang

way to participate in politics, influence government decisions, and safeguard and realize their own interests. Over time, citizens will lose their enthusiasm and confidence in democratic politics. The so-called democratic system will eventually become a tool of elite rule.

Democracy must first address the construction and improvement of the participation system. This involves a series of institutional issues such as the channels of citizens' political participation, participation tools and means of participation. Citizens should have perfect and effective channels and methods, and a series of formal or procedural democracy. These are the most basic requirements of modern democracy. Modern representative democracy marks the transition from substantive democracy to formal democracy. In such an era with formal democracy as the mainstream, it is more important than real democracy. The level of formal democracy in a country is also a measure of the country's level of democratic political development. After the Second World War, the democratic theorists represented by Schumpeter praised formal democracy, paid more attention to and emphasized the opening and improvement of channels and methods of civic participation, and no longer rigidly adhered to whether the people really could be the masters of their own affairs. In the opinion of these democratic theorists, if the participation system is not perfect, citizens lack the actual channels of participation, and any empty talks and debates about democracy have no meaning. Democracy is concrete and real. Essentially, it is about whether or not the people have a perfect channel and method for political participation, so that the right to participate can be implemented and citizens can directly or indirectly participate in public affairs.

Due to political cultural traditions and various practical conditions, the People's Republic of China has not totally resolved the problem of letting the people be the masters of their own affairs. For many years, the people's mastery of the country has remained more of an ideal. The platforms and channels for citizen participation

Chapter 7   Zhejiang Experience in Promoting Orderly Public Political Participation and Its Value

in the national institutional arrangements are mostly lacking effective mechanisms. This is like putting a democratic machine in front of people, but it cannot be powered on and cannot be operated, leading to the inability of the machine to function effectively. Since the reform and opening-up, China's democratic political construction, especially the villagers' self-government as the content of the rural grassroots democratic political construction process, is remarkable. However, with the rapid advancement of industrialization and marketization and the major transformation of economic and social structures, the social stratum is increasingly differentiated and the main body of interest is diversified. The general public's awareness of democracy and rights has been continuously enhanced, and the enthusiasm and desire for political participation have also increased. In recent years, there have been continuous outbreaks of mass protests across the country. From economically developed Zhejiang and Guangdong to the rural areas of the central and western China, more and more citizens express their interest demands through non-institutional channels. Safeguarding their legitimate rights and interests in such extreme ways demonstrates, on the other hand, the failure of the participation platform within the system, and the obstruction of participation channels highlights the importance and necessity of advancing political reform and institutional innovation. The ruling party and the government have an urgent need to speed up the opening of public space, expand the channels for citizen participation, and promote citizens' orderly political participation to meet their growing desire for the same.

Zhejiang is one of the provinces with the most developed private economy and the highest degree of marketization. The advantages of social and economic development have created Zhejiang people's awareness of democracy, rights awareness and the need for greater participation. The party committees and governments at all levels in Zhejiang have thus felt the pressure from non-governmental democracy earlier than the officials in the central and western regions, felt the enthusiasm of the majority of the people as the masters of their own family, and felt the desire to open up local politics and expand the channels or methods of citizen participation. It has prompted the government and the private sector to have the impulse to expand the system of citizen participation. In recent years, party committees and governments at all levels in Zhejiang have continuously explored and promoted system construction and system innovation from five aspects, encouraging the public to actively participate in local public affairs. The first of these institutional innovations is rural democracy talks and local governance, including democratic talks, citizen councils, residents' or villagers' representative meetings, democratic wealth management meetings, and residents' forums; the second is the city's hearings, including legislative hearings, administrative hearings and judicial hearings; the third is the people's proposal solicitation system, which includes daily suggestions and solicitations for thematic proposals; the fourth is the democratic participation in major political projects and people's livelihood, institutions, etc.; the fifth is government affairs forums on government websites, including government affairs public relations forums, government effectiveness nets, "Citizens Council", social networks and government online service halls. These systems have innovated and improved the existing political participation system, provided a feasible way for citizens to participate in local governance, and ensured the political rights of citizens to participate in public affairs.

7.3.3 Safeguarding the public rights needs multi-level, functionally complementary participation system supply

Safeguarding citizens' rights and freedom and providing citizens with equal opportunities for participation are the basic responsibilities of the ruling party and the government given by the constitution. Whether citizens' rights to participate in politics can be guaranteed is an important indicator of the government's legitimacy.

The practice of grassroots democracy in Zhejiang shows that in this province with a highly developed private economy and a high degree

Chapter 7 Zhejiang Experience in Promoting Orderly Public Political Participation and Its Value

of marketization, citizens' rights awareness, democratic awareness, and the concept of the rule of law have increased, and citizens' aspirations and enthusiasm for participation have been very strong. A series of typical cases such as hearings, democratic conferences, and television and government affairs in which citizens participated demonstrates the enormous energy of participation embedded in ordinary citizens. They participate with a clear goal and are good at using all opportunities. Through their participation, they influence the public decision-making of the government to realize their own interests and safeguard their legitimate rights and interests. The facts show that with years of experience in the market economy, after years of education in democracy and the rule of law, the citizens of the economically developed coastal areas in China today have already bid farewell to what they were, as the social observers depicted in the early 20th century—the people with a weak sense of rights, lacking awareness and ability to participate—they have grown into a generation of modern citizens who have rights awareness, the rule of law concept and political participation ability.

For the new generation of citizens, the question now is no longer whether they have the need or ability to participate, but whether the institutionalized participation channels are adequate and whether they can produce real profit. From the practice of grassroots democracy in Zhejiang, we have also discovered that in a multi-interest society, citizens' rights and interest appeals are multi-faceted and multi-level and each type of citizens' participation in the channels and forms can play a limited role in democratic participation. In other words, a single institutional innovation can no longer guarantee the realization of citizens' basic rights and freedoms, and it cannot meet the demands of the diverse social interests. Therefore, what the government needs to do is to advance with the times, promote institutional innovation, and solve the problem of lack of adequate channels for participation in the system to implement the slogan of the development of democracy. The government needs to establish a participating network of multi-channel, multi-level and complementary functions, gradually promote citizens' orderly political participation, and meet citizens' increasing demand for participation.

From the perspective of the civic participation system, the series of institutional innovations that have been introduced by Zhejiang in recent years to promote civic participation and the various innovative forms of participation that emerged have complementary functions. These innovations include rural democracy talks, city public hearings, democratic participation in major projects for people's well-being, public opinion soliciting system, citizens attending provincial and municipal people's congresses, citizens attending the provincial CPPCC people's livelihood forums, participating in consultations, and television system, etc. In terms of the functions of these systems, they seem to be limited, but none of the channels can be replaced by other channels. The scope of their respective applicable citizen groups is very different. Each type of participation adapts to the characteristics of participation of different participants and social groups. It satisfies the needs of citizens participating at different levels and in environments. At the same time, this organic combination of individual systems and different forms of participation can realize the complementary functions of the participation mechanism, promote citizens' orderly political participation, and improve citizens' participation character and ability.

7.3.4 Enhancing public's orderly political participation is the basic way to promote social stability and construct a harmonious society

In today's China, with the dramatic transformation of society, the social stratum after years of differentiation and reorganization tends to be structurally solidified, and the social pattern of diversification of interest subjects and diversification of interest demands has basically taken shape. On the one hand, the awareness of citizens'

Chapter 7 Zhejiang Experience in Promoting Orderly Public Political Participation and Its Value

rights has become increasingly strong, and the sense of democracy and enthusiasm for participation has been rising. On the other hand, the inflexibility and obstruction of existing channels for participation within the system create a sharp contradiction. Under the condition that the channels for participation within the system are not smooth, many people tend to seek non-institutional participation. In recent years, citizens' rights-defense incidents in various parts of the country due to land acquisition, house demolition and environmental pollution were basically caused by obstructed access to citizens' political participation.

The practice in Zhejiang shows that advancing institutional innovations, establishing a variety of uninterrupted channels of participation for the people within the system and enhancing citizens' orderly political participation can effectively promote social harmony and stability. On the contrary, under the circumstances that the channels of participation in the system are not smooth, the people will be forced to consider out-of-system participation. If the government handles it improperly, it may even cause local social unrest, leading to social instability. The democratic talks, the hearings, the public opinion solicitation system, and the major project democratic participation system related to the people's livelihood have provided a relatively effective channel for citizens to participate in the local governance, and safeguarding their own legitimate rights and interests. As a result, social stability will be promoted and harmonious development will be achieved.

The establishment of a deliberative democracy negotiation system provides a new platform for citizens to participate in grassroots social affairs and express their interests. It satisfies the needs of citizens to participate. Citizens participating in local public affairs through various channels and communicating directly with officials are not only helping to reduce conflicts between citizens and governments, but also making government decisions easier to implement. At the same time,

Political Participation and Institutional Innovation:
A Case Study of Zhejiang

as public participation in the formulation of decisions reflects more public opinions, the government is recognized by the citizens, and the political legitimacy of the government has also been consolidated and promoted. Citizens have also been democratically trained in this democratic practice, with their citizen awareness raised. As a result, social conflicts have been eliminated in the practice of democratic dialogue, effectively reducing social shocks. Jiang Zhaohua, Secretary of the Party Committee of Zeguo, said in an interview with Xinhua News Agency's *China Comment*: "In the past, the government had big powers and risks. Now it has a small power, but things are done smoothly, and there are fewer aftereffects. Things are determined by the democratic talks, and the pressure on the government is light". Many social conflicts and disputes have been effectively resolved through various forms of citizen participation in politics. There are many villages where the original villagers and cadres have a great deal of conflicts. Now that public decision-making has been implemented, and transparent decision-making has been implemented, citizens will participate in decision-making and the contradictions will be easily solved. Through several years of democratic practice, there are now almost no petitioners in the towns and townships that had relatively high petitioning rates. Similarly, the implementation of the hearing will also help reduce the conflicts between the government and citizens, and ease the conflicts among social interest groups. The legislative hearings have reduced citizens' dissatisfaction with the people's congress's closing-door legislation. Price hearings have reduced citizens' dissatisfaction with the government's arbitrary pricing and judicial hearings have protected the legitimate interests of the parties concerned. The hearing system promotes the stability of the social order by solving the specific interest demands of citizens and preventing the expansion and spread of contradictions and conflicts. In short, the development of grassroots democratic politics and the promotion of citizens' orderly political participation can improve the information exchange and understanding between the government and citizens, reduce social conflicts and

Chapter 7 Zhejiang Experience in Promoting Orderly Public Political Participation and Its Value

tensions caused by inadequate information communication, and contribute to social harmony and stability.

On the contrary, the legitimate rights and interests of citizens might be violated and there might be no channel for participation within the system, in particular when local governments contend for profit with the people, neglecting the rights of citizens, and even resorting to high pressure or even violent methods to resolve various social conflicts and interests disputes. These possibilities can easily lead to sharp conflicts and conflicts between citizens and the government, and bring about serious social shocks. In previous years, non-institutional participation events in Dongyang, Xinchang and Changxing in Zhejiang Province all occurred when the participation channels were not smooth and the interests of the masses were not taken seriously and resolved by the local government. Therefore, improving the system and broadening the channels for citizens' participation, innovating forms of citizens' participation, and promoting citizens' orderly political participation are the basic conditions for achieving social stability and building a harmonious socialist society.

The systematic innovation of promoting citizens' orderly political participation in Zhejiang Province is generally in the start-up phase, and there are still many imperfections in related institutional construction. Although Zhejiang's institutional innovation still has problems and deficiencies, these innovative forms of citizens' participation have enriched and improved the political participation system since the founding of the People's Republic of China, opening up more public space for citizens and allowing more citizens to have the possibility of participating in politics, expressing interest claims, and influencing the decisions of local governments so as to realize and safeguard their own legitimate rights and interests. Since Zhejiang has the advantage of being one step ahead in the process of industrialization, marketization and urbanization in China, in recent years, it has faced the dilemma of citizens' political participation in the social transformation period

Political Participation and Institutional Innovation:
A Case Study of Zhejiang

and the difficulties in the participation of channels for participation in the system. It is a common problem across the country. Therefore, the institutional innovation experience of Zhejiang in grassroots democracy and promoting the orderly participation of citizens is not only of important reference value for other provinces in China, but also can be replicated.

Chapter 8

Summary and Discussion

Political Participation and Institutional Innovation: A Case Study of Zhejiang

In the previous chapters, we studied a series of institutional innovations, including rural democratic talks, urban hearings, politics discussions on TV, systems of public opinion collection and public forums on government websites, etc., from perspectives of industrialization, marketization, social transformation and local democratic development in China. In addition, we discussed the performance of Zhejiang in respect to enhancing citizens' orderly political participation and promotion of democracy and we also discussed related problems and summed up Zhejiang's experience. Before ending this book, we will discuss some theoretical issues on institutional innovation of democracy and enhancing citizens' orderly political participation.

It should be pointed out that during the development of grassroots democracy and promotion of institutional innovation, party committees and governments at all levels of Zhejiang, based on national conditions and social facts during transition, strive to establish and develop systems of political participation of the citizens with Chinese characteristics, such as rural democratic talks and systems of public opinion collection. So to speak, these systems are definitely "made in China". Though some forms of participation are imported goods, they can be accepted and applied by Chinese people. This is mainly because they are combined with national conditions of China. If innovation on enhancing citizens' orderly political participation is not based on national conditions, it can neither be accepted by the ruling party and the government nor necessarily evoke democratic consciousness among common people. However, theoretical tools used by current political scientists in China, including the author of this book, to study China's political participation of the citizens are almost copied from Western scholars. After investigating Zhejiang's experience of enhancing citizens' orderly political participation and institutional innovation, it is necessary to study and review foreign political theories or explanation patterns, such as democratic theory, political participation and political development, from perspectives of construction of a theoretical system of Chinese political science and the logic of this study.

8.1 Characters of citizens and cultivation of participation-type citizens

Increasing research has shown that democracy does not simply mean a constitution or system, but a lifestyle and political life. Implementation of democracy and efficient operation of a democratic machine first require democratic people who approve, look forward to and pursue democracy and freedom, and are eager to master the destiny of the country. In other words, democracy is rooted in people's characters, behaviors and lifestyles. Since Tocqueville, speaking of conditions of democratic politics, democracy theorists always emphasize the importance of characters of citizens. In the eyes of democratic theoreticians, if there's no participant of democracy, there will be no successful democracy, which almost becomes a consensus in practice of democracy. Therefore, all democratic theoreticians attach great importance to and stress on the cultivation of the democratic character of citizens.

Political Participation and Institutional Innovation:
A Case Study of Zhejiang

For a long time, people have always thought that Chinese citizens were short of awareness and character of democratic participation, so it was not suitable for the Chinese to participate in democracy and it was even not necessary to vest citizens with rights and qualification of political participation. As early as in the debate on Chinese and Western culture in the 20th century, Goodnow, an American political scientist, held that it was not suitable for Chinese to participate in democracy yet, for Chinese didn't have the quality of citizens; and enlightened despotism was more proper for the Chinese before democracy. At that time, many people agreed with Goodnow as political culture based on Confucianism in traditional China stressed on social class and praised strict hierarchy and relationships of dependence among people. This is a dependent political culture, where common people are used to being obedient to the authority in their daily political life and usually passively accept and submit to the country, the government and output of the political system, with little input into the system. Since modern times, the political character of the Chinese has been characterized by lack of autonomy, indifference toward political and public affairs and low will and ability to participate.

In the early 20th century, Liang Qichao, Sun Yat-sen and Lu Xun among others realized that the primary cause for the decline of modern China was that nationals were benighted and lacked the senses of freedom, autonomy, capacity of self-government, civism, patriotism and public spirit. In *New People* published by Liang Qichao in 1902, he pointed out that the primary cause for no political progress and the decline of the nation was that common people did not know there was civism. Therefore, the top priority to save the nation from subjugation and ensure its survival was to remold the national character. He advocated to change old Chinese concepts and thoughts by learning new thoughts and culture from the West and training new citizens in freedom, individuality, independent personality, rights and obligations. Only in this way could

Chapter 8 Summary and Discussion

the society be autonomous and the country be democratic. Liang held that to arouse the wisdom of common people, promoting civil rights was the basis. And to improve moral quality of common people was its core and essence. So to speak, over more than one century, Chinese intellectual and political elite have puzzled over how to develop people's civic awareness and transform them from subjects into citizens.

Since the reform and opening-up, the ruling party and the government have promoted construction of democracy and nomocracy. They promote village self-governance in rural areas and community autonomy in cities, attach great importance to citizens' education and train participants through constant education on citizenship, democracy and nomocracy. Since the reform and opening-up, for 40 years, democracy at the grassroots level has been developed and political rights and political participation of urban and rural residents have been greatly enhanced. In fact, 40 years of the reform and opening-up is the right era of citizens. With increasing freedom and rights of citizens during change of political systems, their rights' consciousness starts to be awakened and enhanced obviously.

First, citizens' consciousness of individual subjects and rights is gradually enhanced. Before the reform and opening-up, personal interests would be subordinated to national and collective interests unconditionally. Sacrificing one's personal interests was stressed and any personal interest was regarded as something relating to bourgeoisie, leading to criticism from public power and through public opinions. Since the reform and opening-up, especially with the rapid development of market economy in recent years, personal interests have gradually become obvious and clear and been separated from national and collective interests. Different interests have become distinct. With the market-oriented reform and the development of private economy, people's values have undergone fundamental change and subject consciousness of individuals has become clear. Individuals no longer ignore their personal interests. When there's a conflict between

Political Participation and Institutional Innovation: A Case Study of Zhejiang

personal interests and national and collective interests, people no longer sacrifice their interests, but start to ask the collective or state for proof of appropriateness of their action and play interest games with the collective or state.

Second, people's contract concept is strengthened because of the strengthening of subject consciousness as citizens. Traditional administrative and clan ties are greatly weakened and boundaries of citizen groups are clear. Contractual relationships of both sides in commercial intercourse are valued and ideas of Western social contract theory are gradually accepted by the public. Hence, opinions of social contract theory, for example, the legitimacy of government's power is given by citizens and public power must be oriented by public interests, gradually become self-evident norms of political life. The existence of private rights of citizens allows citizens to avoid great irrational intervention in private and social spheres. In a sense, China is undergoing a transformation from identity to contract and the separation between a civil society and a political state.

Third, right and democracy consciousness and the will of direct political participation are strengthened. Individualization of interests, frequent movement of population and selectivity of social roles of individuals force people to enter strangers' society from circles of acquaintances. Diversification of social-interest subjects leads to contradictions and conflicts among different interest subjects. With the change of social structure and values, people's attitude to and solutions for these contradictions and conflicts also change. Right and democracy consciousness of citizens and their will for direct political participation are increasingly strengthened.

However, it's worth noting that citizen training has not been very successful since modern times. There's a big gap between Chinese nationals and mature citizens in developed democratic society in respect to their democracy quality. Citizens' sense and skills of participation

Chapter 8 Summary and Discussion

still need breakthrough promotion, which is a key factor restricting the development of China's democratic politics. Sound development of democratic politics greatly depends on corresponding views of citizenship and democracy consciousness of citizens. (1) Public spirit: citizens should love public life, be warmhearted in public utilities and take active part in public affairs. (2) Spirit of participation: citizens should take active part in various related affairs. (3) Spirit of tolerance: citizens should express their opinions, respect the participation of others and get used to teamwork. (4) Spirit of compromise and win–win: differences and disputes among various interest groups should be solved by law only. Therefore, democracy should follow the principle of majority decision, which doesn't mean that winners take all, but respect and protect rights and freedom of the minority. Thus, compromise is necessary to achieve a win–win situation. (5) Spirit of nomocracy: citizens should develop a law-abiding habit and observe and revere the law; all actions should accord with the law and all disputes should be settled within the scope of the law.

Speaking of training participants, we should know that training and formation of a participation character and enhancement of democracy consciousness and skills of citizens cannot be accomplished in one day, but require long-term democracy education and political participation. Through practice, citizens can improve their ability for political participation and deepen their democracy consciousness.

In addition, we should not complicate or even deify issues. In today's China, democracy has been regarded as a universally pursued value. People look forward to democracy unprecedentedly and naturally hope to get rid of bondage and constraint from external power. They hope to master their fate and the future of the country, so they are passionate about participation in public affairs. In real political life, democracy and political participation, in essence, are related to interests. Great decisions about public affairs, especially relating to interests of common people, belong to the field of the people's livelihood, so

Political Participation and Institutional Innovation: A Case Study of Zhejiang

people have every incentive to participate in them. Even people with poorest awareness and education care about their interests. Sometimes, citizens are indifferent to political participation and have no impetus to participate. The reason is not that they have no awareness or spirit of participation, but that they can see no interest or benefit from participation or they don't believe that they can get any interest or benefit from participation. Thus, their indifference reflects their awareness of participation and is a rational behavior. In some regions of developed economy and society, people are indifferent to public affairs and not willing to participate, primarily because their passion and desires cannot be expressed via fixed approaches and proper forms, instead of having no quality of citizenship or enthusiasm for participation. Otherwise, they are distrustful of the government and not confident in expression, protection and realization of interests by political participation.

We should understand that the democratic character of citizens cannot be formed without foundation and gradual improvement of awareness and capacity of democratic participation requires practice. It may make sense that it was not suitable for the Chinese to adopt democracy in the 20th century, for democracy was just introduced into China from abroad, and the Chinese hadn't adapted to democracy without citizenship quality and ability for participation. However, after practice of democracy for more than one century, some people insist on hackneyed and stereotyped expressions of Goodnow *et al.* and refuse to offer necessary approaches of political participation for citizens by using lack of quality and ability as an excuse. In fact, they deprive basic political rights of citizens and their words are worth pondering on. According to the process of Western democratic development, the participation character, for example, can be attributed to lots of club activity and, more importantly, elections. Obviously, to develop the democratic character of citizens requires frequent and repeated democratic practice.

Hence, in our eyes, what's important is neither that the Chinese citizens don't want to be in power nor that the Chinese citizens

Chapter 8 Summary and Discussion

don't know how to be in power, but that various conditions should be created for citizens to offer them chances of being in power. Thus, they can learn democracy in democracy and participation in participation. It's not the right thing to claim to promote democracy but refuse to offer citizens chances of participation on the excuse of scarce participation capacity of citizens. Thus, the experience gathered by party committees and governments at all levels of Zhejiang during institutional innovation and enhancing citizens' orderly political participation and allowing citizens to be transformed from subjects into participants is quite valuable.

Party committees and governments at all levels of Zhejiang realize the extreme importance of democratic exercise for cultivation of a democratic character and the great significance of the practice of democratic participation for being the masters of the country. During construction of grassroots democracy, party committees and governments at all levels of Zhejiang don't blindly criticize citizens without democratic quality and ability. Instead, they face up to social structural differentiation, rise of new classes and interest diversification and actively promote institutional innovation. They allow citizens to take part in various forms of democratic participation, such as rural democratic talks, urban hearings, political discussions on TV, systems of public opinion collection and public forums of government websites, so that citizens in Zhejiang can learn and improve their ability and skills of democracy through participation in local governance, democratic elections, democratic management, democratic decision-making and democratic supervision.

Rural democratic talks of Wenling reflect the importance of training people with a democratic character. Mu Yifei, Vice Minister of Publicity Department of the Municipal Committee of Wenling, points out that, "It can improve quality of both officials and citizens. We call it a democratic talk, namely a democratic school. It can help cadres strengthen their democratic consciousness and common people learn

Political Participation and Institutional Innovation:
A Case Study of Zhejiang

everything about procedures".[1] Democratic practice in Zhejiang shows that the cultivation of democratic character of citizens requires real democratic activities and the democratic character of citizens cannot appear without foundation. Orderly participation and institutional innovation of citizens in Zhejiang indicate that citizens are fully capable of learning how to be in power from democratic practice. The only thing that the government and the ruling party needs to do is to provide citizens with numerous channels for participation. To sum up, institutional innovation relating to expansion of orderly participation must follow an active, safe and progressive principle. There's a mutually dependent and synergistic dialectical relationship between institutional innovation relating to expansion of orderly participation and formation of the participation character of citizens. Institutional innovation allows citizens to take part in local governance, promotes citizens' orderly political participation and enhances citizens' ability for political participation. Moreover, improvement of citizens' ability can promote innovation, development and perfection of participation systems, which further improves the democratic quality and citizens' ability for participation.

---

[1] Chen Shengyong and He Baogang. *Development of Deliberative Democracy*. Beijing: China Social Sciences Press, 2006: 464.

8.2 Unbalance between political power and governing power in democracy and its solution

Democracy is a universally pursued value in modern society. Theoretically, democracy is a form of government of popular sovereignty. In this form of government, people are the masters of the country with supreme power and all power of governing a country. However, in modern democracy, the representative system is the only choice of a system of government. As subjects of state sovereignty, people can only entrust government officials with state power reluctantly and government officials are responsible for governing the country and dealing with public affairs. However, once representatives and government officials get power from people, it's easy for them to be self-righteous and do what they wish without restraint against people's will, leading to infringement of civil rights. This is a paradox in modern democracy.

Political Participation and Institutional Innovation:
A Case Study of Zhejiang

In a realistic society, on the one hand, the constitution stipulates that people are the masters of the country and all power belongs to the people, so the power of the government, including power of all officials, comes from the people and officials exercise power and administer state affairs in accordance with the people's commission. On the other hand, due to lack of constraints and limitations of state power caused by system arrangement, officials often turn from a guest into a host and refuse the restriction and supervision of power by the people. As a result, public servants turn into the host, while the people become their subjects. In the eyes of powerful officials, democracy, or "the people are the masters of the country", is equal to "making decisions for the people by them at will". Ironically, if concrete links of receiving and authorizing the people's power are not defined well and the people actually have no channel of political participation, totalitarian dictators also can claim that their sovereignty belongs to the people and is on behalf of the people. They can carry out tyrannies in the name of the people, which is not rare in history. As a result, democracy turns into an excuse for despotism and a popular slogan advertising despotism or a fig leaf concealing violation of popular will and abuse of power.

So far, it is still a difficult problem for theorists of modern democracy to remove antagonism or unbalance between political power and governing power in a democratic system, ensure that administration of the government follows the will of the people and guarantee freedom and rights of citizens. The development of democracy since modern times shows that the only solution for this problem is to regulate and restrict governing power by using political rights of citizens to decide national affairs, choose government officials and supervise and restrict state power of government officials conferred by the constitution.

Hence, the system where a country is ruled by the people covers three aspects. (1) Granting and receiving of rights: it is primary in

Chapter 8 Summary and Discussion

institutional arrangement, involving institutional design of fundamental granting and receiving of rights, namely workable universal suffrage; (2) citizens' rights of participating in the administration and discussing state affairs, namely direct or indirect participation of citizens in public affairs and influence of citizens on government's public decision-making, involving universal and effective channels of citizens' participation in a national political system; (3) people's supervision over state power. The development of democracy since modern times shows that though universal suffrage cannot be realized in a country within a short time because of the fact that the process of democratization is hindered by various subjective and objective factors, democracy can be promoted to remove unbalance between political power and governing power by opening up public space, creating various approaches for citizens' participation and interest expression, promoting citizens' orderly political participation and allowing citizens to directly participate in public affairs, express interest demands, influence government's decision-making and supervise power operation of the government. In other words, the more perfect the institutionalized channel of participating in public affairs and conducting interest expression, interest integration and interest maintenance is, the smaller the gap between political power and governing power will be.

In China, since the Revolution of 1911, through the ages, statesmen including Sun Yat-sen, Mao Zedong and Deng Xiaoping explored and designed various solutions. However, due to arduousness of institutional improvement, complexity of institutional arrangement and other reasons, it is still difficult to carry out national institutional improvement.

Precious opportunities for enhancing citizens' orderly political participation and institutional innovation are created because of the development of market economy, especially the rapid development of private economy, social structure transformation and stratification. With the spirit of bold exploration and innovation, party committees and governments at all levels of Zhejiang have created some new forms of participation of citizens, such as rural democratic talks, urban hearings, political discussions on TV, systems of public opinion collection and public forums of government websites, in the process of construction of grassroots democracy. These citizens take part in institutional innovation and build an institutional platform of interest expression, interest integration and interest maintenance, reflecting the spirit of responsive democracy and consultative democracy. Through repeated consultations and discussions among different interest groups, interest expression, interest integration and interest maintenance of citizens are realized, meeting participation needs of citizens to some extent. As a result, citizens can conduct orderly participation in local public affairs and affect government's decision-making. As these new forms of participation play an unprecedented role, they alleviate social contradictions and conflicts of interest to some extent and narrow the gap between political power and governing power as far as possible, promoting development of local democracy in depth and breadth within the current institutional framework.

Institutional innovation in Zhejiang reveals that, at the present stage of democratic development in China, one of the basic approaches of removing unbalance between political power and governing power, avoiding alienation of democratic development and realizing the great deal of ruling the country by the people, is to establish smooth channels for participation, promote citizens' orderly political participation, encourage the people to participate in local governance and realize interest expression, interest integration and interest maintenance of citizens.

8.3 Political participation, institutional innovation and political stability

In developing countries, one major challenge in the process of modernization is to promote democracy, promote citizens' orderly political participation and maintain stability of social order at the same time. Huntington points out that, "Spreading of political turmoil in Asia, Africa and Latin America in the 20th century is mainly attributed to their over quick modernization, which is far quicker than that in early modernized countries. Modernization in Europe and North America has lasted for several centuries. In general, they only settled one problem or crisis every time. However, in other regions in the world except the West, in the process of modernization, centralization of authority, national amalgamation, social mobilization, economic development, political participation and social welfare, etc. occur at the same time".[2] As these problems come one after another, political instability is common in developing countries. On this basis, Huntington puts forward a famous statement: "Modernity leads to stability, but the process of mobilization results in instability".[3] In other words, the main reason for common political instability, disordered politics in developing countries lies in their efforts of realizing modernity, instead of lack of modernity.

In combination with the political development course in developing countries, Huntington elaborates on relations between political participation and political stability. Economic development leads to widening of the gap between the rich and the poor and enlargement of social inequality, but social mobilization in the process of modernization reduces legality of inequality, leading to political instability. "Urbanization, improvement of educational levels and public application of media raise people's pursuit and expectation. If the expectation cannot be met, individuals and groups are more likely to participate in politics. If there's no powerful political system with strong adaptability, expansion of participation means instability and riots".[4] Huntington states relations among economic development, political participation and political stability and proposes three famous formulas as follows:

(1) Social mobilization/economic development = Social frustration;
(2) Social depression/mobility opportunities = Political participation;
(3) Political participation/institutionalization = Political turmoil.[5]

---

[2] Chen Shengyong and He Baogang. *Development of Deliberative Democracy*. Beijing: China Social Sciences Press, 2006: 43.

[3] Huntington. *Political Order in Changing Societies*. Translated by Li Shengping, et al. Beijing: Huaxia Publishing House, 1988: 41.

[4] Huntington. *Political Order in Changing Societies*. Translated by Li Shengping, et al. Beijing: Huaxia Publishing House, 1988: 47.

[5] Huntington. *Political Order in Changing Societies*. Translated by Li Shengping, et al. Beijing: Huaxia Publishing House, 1988: 51.

Chapter 8 Summary and Discussion

Specifically, economic development results in the improvement of the social living standard and raises people's desires and needs. However, in a society in the middle of modernization transformation, strengthening the ability of meeting these desires is far slower than generating these desires, leading to social frustration. The social frustration then results in political unrest. Huntington holds that political unrest depends on the nature of economic and social structure of a traditional society, longitudinal flow (change of income and occupation) and transverse flow (urbanization and secularization, etc.). Due to low economic flow in most countries during modernization, in order to get rid of social frustration, citizens ask for expansion of political participation to influence government's decision-making and meet desires brought on by economic development. With the improvement of citizens' awareness of political participation, strength and extent of political participation have been enlarged continuously. If a political system is so advanced that it can satisfy participation needs of citizens and include behavior of political participation into institutionalized channels, the political order will be stable. Otherwise, it will be unstable and lead to unrest and violence. Huntington also holds that a stable political system should be regarded as the primary value of political development and political stability is measurable. The political order partially depends on relations between the development level of a political system and the degree of political participation of mobilized new social forces. That is to say, political stability depends on a political system and political participation. Huntington thinks that the way of avoiding political turmoil and realizing stability of a political system is to enhance the institutional level of a political system and ensure orderly political participation of the citizens. In order to enhance the institutional level of a political system, a powerful and effective government system should be built first to guarantee smooth modernization. In addition, a political system should have the ability to mobilize and absorb openly new social forces and groups of political participation. Therefore, a system undergoing modernization must have the ability of absorbing social forces created by modernization into the system.

Political Participation and Institutional Innovation: A Case Study of Zhejiang

In China, since the reform and opening-up, with the process of industrialization, marketization and urbanization, people have gradually formed their consciousness of rights, participation and equality and have higher awareness and demands for politics. Due to profound changes of economic systems and production modes and promotion of democracy and nomocracy, the broad masses of the people start to pursue political rights and are eager for participation in decision-making, management of public affairs and protection of their economic interests and other interests. As a result, the urgent demand of the broad masses of the people to participate in the administration and discussion of state affairs is of objective necessity. Therefore, a task of top priority for the ruling party and the government is to meet people's pursuit of political rights, set up participation channels, promote citizens' orderly political participation and make citizens masters of the country.

Meanwhile, political development, especially democratization and enhancing of citizens' orderly political participation require a stable political order. Otherwise, they will lead to chaos and a disordered society, which cannot ensure political participation interests of anyone. Huntington holds that in a developing country, order is more important than democracy, namely citizens' participation. "For many modernizing countries... the primary problem is not freedom but establishment of a legal public order. Obviously, people can be unfree with order, but cannot be free without order. Authority should be created first to restrict it".[6] In order to ensure the political order of a developing country, Huntington even holds that a country with a powerful autocratic party is better than a country without a party, for strong ability of maintaining order of a government is necessary to completely guarantee no total loss of interests of citizens in disputes and conflicts. Thus, it can be seen that

---

[6] Chen Shengyong and He Baogang. *Development of Deliberative Democracy*. Beijing: China Social Sciences Press, 2006: 278.

Chapter 8　Summary and Discussion

order and stability are quite important during political participation of the citizens.

A stable political order is the basis of social, economic and political development. Therefore, the supreme stability is beyond all doubt. However, one precondition of supreme stability is that the government or the ruling party must ensure rights and an equal opportunity of participation of each citizen. Otherwise, no one would like to accept a stable order as such. If a government suppresses or deprives citizens' rights to maintain its order and protect interests of the ruling class or a part of people, the ruling legitimacy of an autocratic government or an autocratic party surely will be completely lost. In the 20th century, lots of military autocracies in Asia, Africa and Latin America appeared in the name of order control, but they also completely lost their ruling legitimacy and gave way to a government that could ensure rights and opportunities of each citizen in the end because of order control.

The fundamental purpose of a modern government is to guarantee rights of political participation of each citizen and an equal opportunity of interest expression, interest integration and interest maintenance of each citizen, reflecting the legitimacy of a modern government. Rural democratic talks, urban hearings, political discussions on TV, systems of public opinion collection and public forums of government websites, etc. in Zhejiang have strengthened the capacity of the political system, absorbed citizens to participate and ensured equal rights and opportunities of political participation of each citizen. The reason for successful democratic talks in Wenling is that they reflect more equality during negotiation. Professor He Baogang thinks that democratic talks in Wenling created a new political culture and changed the political structure, leading to an increasingly equal political structure. In addition, he says, "In fact, democratic talks allow common people, instead of officials, to decide, where the power center changes. Each link behind the whole method guarantees equality. Through abstract selection, everyone is equal in terms of probability. During discussion,

Political Participation and Institutional Innovation:
A Case Study of Zhejiang

everyone has an equal opportunity to speak".[7] The key to success of hearings in Hangzhou, Ningbo and Wenzhou, etc. in recent years is that they offer citizens equal opportunities of participation and allow them to express their interests.

On the contrary, if a government doesn't deal with institutional supply, or provide citizens with institutional channels for basic participation and expression of interests or equal rights and opportunities of political participation in time, citizens will adopt non-institutional forms to express and protect their interests. Based on this, Locke seldom condemned rebellion of citizens. In *Two Treatises of Civil Government*, he states that the establishment of a government is to ensure natural equal rights and freedom of citizens. If a government fails to ensure them, citizens have a right to create a new government. Obviously, if a government fails to ensure equal rights and chances for citizens and even turns opposite to the public to aggressively maintain interests of some people and damage interest of some others, with non-effective approaches of participation in the system, citizens surely will express and protect their interests through non-institutional participation.

Democracy represents the general trend, but promotion and development of democracy require a stable order. On the one hand, the government should open up public space, expand the scope of political participation and absorb and deal with participation demands of citizens via institutionalized channels. On the other hand, a stable order should be ensured at the same time to promote stability of the political and social order, which is a problem for various countries during modernization. In order to solve this problem, the only way of promoting political participation and ensuring rights of citizens and a stable political order at the same time is to realize legalization of political participation. Through institutional innovation and construction,

---
[7]Chen Shengyong and He Baogang. *Development of Deliberative Democracy*. Beijing: China Social Sciences Press, 2006: 278.

Chapter 8 Summary and Discussion

the government builds institutionalized, standardized and programmed channels of participation, so that each citizen can conduct political participation, express their interests and demands equally and realize and protect their legitimate rights and interests. Huntington believes that the political order partially depends on relations between the development level of a political system and the degree of political participation of mobilized new social forces. That is to say, political stability depends on a political system and political participation. An institutionalized channel means that the channel is open, diverse, transparent and equal, in which any citizen can participate. If only a few people can participate, the more institutionalized the system is, the less likely will citizens become the masters of the country. Institutionalization for participation of the minority or the privileged class cannot gain moral support and is not institutionalization of democracy.

Institutionalization allows every citizen to participate freely and equally and express and integrate their interests, so it asks both the government and citizens to follow the unified constitution and law of the country. As the non-institutional interest expression is massive, sudden and collective, it threatens social stability and political order, which is what Huntington was worried about. According to Huntington's research, modernization of a developing country can lead to instability and strong mobilizing participation of citizens can cause problems relating to social order. Hence, Huntington stresses that political participation should be promoted with a stable order.

In contrast to Huntington, Almond never worries about the stability of developing countries. In his eyes, as long as a developing country builds the same democratic system as that in developed countries with a highly open political process and ensures effective interest expression and interest integration of citizens and participation of citizens in policy development and implementation, there will be no political instability. Otherwise, if the public political process of a government is closed and citizens cannot conduct basic interest expression and interest

Political Participation and Institutional Innovation:
A Case Study of Zhejiang

integration and have no right to affect government's decision-making and implementation, it indicates that there are problems with the political development, political democracy and freedom of the country. Therefore, it's no surprise that its politics is not stable, for citizens will adopt various approaches to maintain and realize their rights conferred by the constitution. In fact, there's no substantive divergence between Almond and Huntington and they just focus on different parts. Almond holds that only when structural differentiation of the political system of a developing country is as mature as that of a developed country, can citizens participate in politics and achieve their interests freely. Thus, there's no instability in this condition. On the contrary, if citizens do not have equal status of participation in terms of institutional structure, it will lead to instability. Though Huntington worries about instability in developing countries, he doesn't equate political participation of the citizens in developing countries with instability. What he worries about is not instability caused by citizens' participation by institutionalized approaches, but that citizens don't have institutionalized channels for political participation, leading to unstable political order caused by non-institutional participation of citizens. In Almond's words, this is because the political process is immature and unprepared. Thus, it can be seen that the thoughts of two masters of politics is the same in essence. In other words, political participation is a basic right of citizens and every government should guarantee it; institutional participation is beneficial to stability, while non-institutional participation can lead to instability.

Development of local democracy and institutional innovation in Zhejiang shows the potential of development of grassroots democracy in China. According to the investigation on enhancing citizens' political participation and institutional innovation in Zhejiang and empirical research and theoretical analysis on various social stratums and cases of political participation of the citizens, we think that with the formation of the social structure with marketization of Chinese economy and diversification of interests, political participation featured

Chapter 8 Summary and Discussion

by interest demands and rights' protection constantly increases, which not only reflects increasingly complex social interest patterns during current adjustment of interest relations in China, but also provides live power for socialist political civilization and democratic construction. Hence, during social transformation with prominent social stratum differentiation, increasingly complex interest relationships and endless emergence of new problems and phenomena, it is an important task for socialist democratic construction to expand and promote citizens' orderly political participation through institutional improvement. The key to promoting political stability and realizing China's democratization and legalization is to promote institutional innovation and build various channels of political participation of the citizens, so that the pursuit of democracy and appeal for lawful rights and interests of citizens can be included into the present system, bringing increasingly high enthusiasm of citizens about political participation in the course of modernization.

In addition to exploring institutional innovation, governments at all levels in Zhejiang have also developed and perfected potentials of the present political institutions in respect to coordination of interests and integration of public opinions. They guide citizens in rational orderly political participation through institutionalized approaches and legitimate procedures, which not only promotes construction of these governments, but also protects political rights and interests of citizens. Successful experience in direct and orderly participation of citizens in local governance in Zhejiang has laid a good foundation for construction of grassroots democracy in China, achieved good social and political benefits and offered valuable experience for participation of citizens in other areas. Of course, it can be seen that there are still many problems and defects in the course of enhancing political participation of the citizens and institutional innovation in Zhejiang.

In political participation of the citizens and institutional innovation in Zhejiang, there are at least a few disadvantages, as follows: first,

Political Participation and Institutional Innovation: A Case Study of Zhejiang

innovation channels are still limited. At present, only democratic talks, hearings, systems of public opinion collection and public forums of government websites in Wenling perform noticeably well. In principle, they are just mechanisms supplementing information of public opinions for original decision-making systems of party committees, governments and the people's congress and merely preliminary concretization of originally abstract surveillance by the masses, and the principle that the people are the masters of the country. Second, equality of participation is still insufficient and not all people can enjoy these channels. Perhaps the democratic talk in Wenling is the participation form involving most people, but they only account for a small proportion of over 50 million people in Zhejiang. In terms of hearings, many citizens do not have knowledge of legal procedures of hearings or enough money or information, etc. People who take part in hearings are unit staff and social elite who have spare time and money or are interested parties, but few ordinary citizens are able to participate. Third, institutional innovation is not creative enough. Rural democratic talks, urban hearings, politics discussion on TV, systems of public opinion collection and public forums of government websites, etc. depend on enthusiasm, determination and even conscience and ambition of local officials to a large extent. Hence, even if democratic talks have grown vigorously in Wenling and been praised highly by leaders of the provincial party committee, they do not work in other cities, reflecting rule of man during institutional innovation. Fourth, effects of institutional innovation are limited and local. Democratic talks are not popular outside Wenling. Even in Wenling, negotiation results of democratic talks may come to nothing. Though policymaking of the people's congress and the government in Xinhe and Zeguo is based on democratic talks, policymaking in other areas is still in line with original decision-making procedures. Sustainability of democratic talks is still questioned by people. Many people don't think that democratic talks are promising, let alone popularize and copy democratic talks in other counties and cities. Similarly, though hearings have been used by many local governments as a consultation mechanism

Chapter 8 Summary and Discussion

for local public policy, most of them become a mere formality. In addition, functions of systems of public opinion collection and public forums of government websites have not been completely fulfilled and many citizens are suspicious of feasibility of online communication between officials and common people.

In the Internet era of democratization, globalization and marketization, to promote citizens' political participation is a world trend and a symbol of political civilization and social progress of a country. Institutional innovation in Zhejiang has shown that political participation is necessary and possible in China and the key to citizen participation is not the ability and quality of citizens, but channels and means of participation and institutionalization and legalization of these channels and means. As long as political rights of citizens conferred by the constitution are put into practice, systems of political participation are perfected and opportunities of participation are increased, Chinese citizens have sufficient wisdom and ability to take part in national and local governance and strengthen their capacity of democracy and develop their quality as citizens during participation. Therefore, enhancing of political participation of the citizens and institutional innovation should be generalized across the country. Institutional innovation in Zhejiang needs to be further deepened, improved and perfected and also generalized across the country. The scope of political participation of the citizens and institutional innovation should be extended and more effective legal participation channels should be created for citizens to form a multi-channel, multi-form and multi-level participation system.

Democracy is a process. Enhancing of political participation of the citizens and institutional innovation is a link in the development of democracy in China. It is normal that some problems arise in this process. In order to develop democracy and enhance the level of democracy and quality of local governance, citizens should learn democracy, gradually develop the spirit of modern citizens, enhance

Political Participation and Institutional Innovation: A Case Study of Zhejiang

their consciousness of political participation and enthusiasm for participation, and study and master methods and techniques of participation during participation. In addition, the ruling party and the government should actively promote democracy and the rule of law in China, explore Chinese characteristics of democracy and the Chinese path of democratic development, carry out political restructuring and construction of a modern national system, establish and perfect the political participation system, widen channels of citizens' orderly political participation and promote institutionalization and legalization of political participation of various stratums. Meanwhile, they should conduct a civic education movement, develop the civic spirit and democratic character of the people and enhance the ability and skills of participation of citizens, making democracy the form of political life of modern Chinese. Based on this, the autonomous level of citizens gradually rises, where village and community autonomy is extended to township and county autonomy, so that concepts of liberty, democracy and the rule of law are rooted in people's mind, and democracy and the rule of law can be operated effectively at all social and political levels and develop and mature in China.

Bibliography

Chinese books

Almond, G. A. and Powell, G. B. *Comparative Politics: System, Process, and Policies*. Translated by Cao Peilin. Shanghai: Shanghai Translation Publishing House, 1987.

Almond, G. A. and Verba, S. *Civic Culture: Political Attitudes and Democracy of Five Countries*. Translated by Ma Dianjun. Hangzhou: Zhejiang People's Publishing House, 1989.

Aristoteles. *Politics*. Beijing: The Commercial Press, 1997.

Barber, B. R. *Strong Democracy*. Translated by Peng Bin and Wu Runzhou. Changchun: Jilin People's Publishing House, 2006.

Bohman, J. and Rehg, W. *Deliberative Democracy: Essays on Reason and Politics*. Translated by Chen Jiagang. Beijing: Central Compilation and Translation Press, 2006.

Bohman, J. *Public Consultation: Complexity of Pluralism and Democracy*. Beijing: Central Compilation and Translation Press, 2006.

Cass, R. S. *The Commonwealth of the Internet*. Translated by Huang Weiming. Shanghai: Shanghai People's Publishing House, 2003.

Chen Jiagang. *Consultative Democracy*. Beijing: SDX Joint Publishing Company, 2004.

Chen Shengyong and He Baogang. *Development of Deliberative Democracy*. Beijing: China Social Sciences Press, 2006.

Chen Shengyong, Wang Jinjun and Ma Bin. *Organization, Self-governance and Democracy: Research on Wenzhou Chamber of Commerce of Zhejiang*. Beijing: China Social Sciences Press, 2004.

CNNIC. *A Statistical Report on the Development of China's Internet (2006/1)*. Beijing: China Network Information Center, 2006a.

CNNIC. *A Statistical Report on the Development of China's Internet (2006/7)*. Beijing: China Network Information Center, 2006b.

Dahl, R. *Preface to Democratic Theory*. Beijing: SDX Joint Publishing Company, 1999.

Davis, L. E. and Knous, D. C. *Theory of Institutional Change and Innovation: Description, Analogy and Explanation*. Shanghai: SDX Joint Publishing Company and Shanghai People's Publishing House, 1996.

Dentrives, M. P. *Democracy as a Public Consultation: A New Perspective*. Translated by Wang Yingze. Beijing: Central Compilation and Translation Press, 2006.

Easton, D. *Systematic Analysis of Political Life*. Beijing: Huaxia Publishing House, 1989.

Fang Jiangshan. *Non-Institutional Political Participation: Analysis on Chinese Farmers During Transition*. Beijing: People's Publishing House, 2000.

Fantine, J. *Constructing Virtual Government: Information Technology and System Innovation*. Translated by Shao Guosong. Beijing: China Renmin University Press, 2004.

Gao Xinjun. *Local Government's Governance in the USA: A Case Study*. Xi'an: Northwest University Press, 2005.

Gao Xinmin and Wu Guihan. *Selection and Evaluation of the Cases of Leading Cadres Dealing with Mass Incidents*. Beijing: Press of Party School of the Central Committee of CPC, 2011.

Garson, G. D. *Public Sector Information Technology: Policy and Management*. Translated by Liu Wuyi. Beijing: Tsinghua University Press, 2005.

Guo Qiushui. *Three Contemporary Great Democracy Theories*. Beijing: New Star Press, 2006.

Habermas. *Three Normative Models of Democracy: The Concept of Deliberative Politics*. Translated by Lee Andong and Duan Huaiqing. Shanghai: Shanghai People's Publishing House, 1997.

Habermas. *Public Sphere*. Beijing: SDX Joint Publishing Company, 1998.

Habermas. *Legitimation Crisis*. Translated by Liu Beicheng and Cao Weidong. Shanghai: Shanghai People's Publishing House, 2000a.

Habermas. *Rebuilding Historical Materialism*. Translated by Guo Guanyi. Beijing: Social Sciences Academic Press, 2000b.

Bibliography

Habermas. *The Structural Transformation of the Public Sphere*. Translated by Cao Weidong. Shanghai: Xueling Press, 2002.

Habermas. *Between Facts and Norms: Contributions to a Discourse Theory of Law and Democracy*. Beijing: SDX Joint Publishing Company, 2003.

Hangzhou Committee of the CPPCC. *Theory and Practice of CPPCC: Volume Eight*. Beijing: China Shuji Press, 2016.

He Baogang and Lang Youxing. *Seek a Balance Between Democracy and Authority*. Wuhan: Huazhong Normal University Press, 2003.

He Qinglian. *The Trap of Modernization*. Beijing: Today China Press, 1998.

Held, D. *The Model of Democracy*. Translated by Yan Jirong, *et al*. Beijing: Central Compilation and Translation Press, 2000.

Holmes, D. *E-Government Affairs*. Translated by Zhan Junfeng. Beijing: China Machine Press, 2003.

Hughes. *Introduction to Public Management*. Beijing: China Renmin University Press, 2001.

Huntington and Dominguez. *Political Development*. Translated by Chu Fuyun. Beijing: The Commercial Press, 1996.

Huntington and Nelson. *No Easy Choice*. Translated by Wang Xiaoshou *et al*. Beijing: Huaxia Publishing House, 1989.

Huntington. *Political Order in Changing Societies*. Translated by Li Shengping, *et al*. Beijing: Huaxia Publishing House, 1988.

Ke Wugang and Shi Manfei. *Institutional Economics*. Beijing: The Commercial Press, 2000.

Li Chunyan. *Research on Public Hearing in China*. Beijing: Law Press China, 2009.

Li Peilin. *Off-Farm Workers: Economic and Social Analysis of Off-farm Workers in Cities of China*. Beijing: Social Sciences Academic Press, 2003.

Li Qiang. *The Social Structure of China in the 21st Century*. Beijing: The Eastern Publishing Co., Ltd., 2001.

Lin Shangli. *Community Democracy and Governance: A Case Study*. Beijing: Social Sciences Academic Press, 2003.

Lin Shangli. *Party Politics and Modernization*. Shanghai: Shanghai People's Publishing House, 1998.

Liu Junning. *Direct Democracy and Indirect Democracy*. Beijing: SDX Joint Publishing Company, 1998.

Liu Wenfu. *Network Politics*. Beijing: The Commercial Press, 2002.

Political Participation and Institutional Innovation: A Case Study of Zhejiang

Lu Xueyi. *Research Report on Contemporary Chinese Social Stratums*. Beijing: Social Sciences Academic Press, 2002.

Lu Xueyi. *Contemporary Chinese Social Mobility*. Beijing: Social Sciences Academic Press, 2004.

Luo Chuanxian. *Basic Theory of Administrative Procedure Law*. Taipei: Wu-Nan Book Inc, 1993.

MacAdam, Tarrow and Tily. *Dynamics of Contention*. Translated by Li Yizhong and Qu Ping. Nanjing: Yilin Press, 2006.

Marx and Engels. *Collected Works of K. Marx and F. Engels: Volume IV*. Beijing: People's Publishing House, 1972.

Meng Qingguo and Fan Bo. *Theory and Practice of E-government*. Beijing: Tsinghua University Press, 2006.

Miller, D. *The Blackwell Encyclopedia of Political Science*. Translated by Deng Zhenglai. Beijing: Press of China University of Political Science and Law, 2002.

Min Qi. *Chinese Political Culture: Social and Psychological Factors of Dystocia in Democratic Politics*. Kunming: Yunnan People's Publishing House, 1989.

Nee, N. H. and Verba, S. *Political Participation*. Translated by Chu Fuyun. Beijing: The Commercial Press, 1996.

Norris, N. *New Political Communication: Political Communication in Post-Industrial Society*. Shanghai: Shanghai Jiao Tong University Press, 2005.

North, D. C. North. *System, Institutional Change and Economic Performance*. Translated by Liu Shouying. Shanghai: SDX Joint Publishing Company, 1994.

North, D. C. *Structure and Change in Economic History*. Translated by Li Yiping. Beijing: The Commercial Press, 2005.

Office of Beijing Municipal Information Work. *An Introduction to E-government*. Beijing: Tsinghua University Press, 2003.

Olson. *Logic of Collective Action*. Translated by Chen Yu. Shanghai: SDX Joint Publishing Company and Shanghai People's Publishing House, 2004.

Olson. *Power and Prosperity*. Translated by Su Changhe. Shanghai: Shanghai People's Publishing House, 2005.

Orum. *Introduction to Political Sociology: Social Analysis of Political Entity*. Translated by Dong Yunhu and Li Yunlong. Hangzhou: Zhejiang People's Publishing House, 1989a.

Bibliography

Orum. *Political Sociology*. Translated by Zhang Huaqing. Shanghai: Shanghai People's Publishing House, 1989b.

Osborne, D. and Gaebler, T. *Reform of Governments: How Entrepreneurship Reforms the Public Sector*. Translated by Zhou Dunren. Shanghai: Shanghai Translation Publishing House, 2006.

Pan Yihe. *Concept and System: A Comparative Study of Political Culture*. Shanghai: Xueling Press, 2002.

Peng Zongchao, Xue Lan and Kan Ke. *Hearing System: Transparent Decision-making and Public Governance*. Beijing: Tsinghua University Press, 2004.

Portman, C. *Participation and Democratic Theory*. Shanghai: Shanghai People's Publishing House, 2006.

Putnam, R. D. *Making Democracy Work: Civic Traditions in Modern Italy*. Translated by Wang Lie, *et al*. Nanchang: Jiangxi People's Publishing House, 2001.

Research Group of Research Office of the State Council. *Research Report on Off-farm Workers in China*. Beijing: China Yanshi Press, 2006.

Ries, A. and Ries, L. *11 Immutable Laws of Internet Branding*. Translated by Mei Haihao. Shanghai: Shanghai People's Publishing House, 2006.

Rozman, G. *The Modernization of China*. Translated by a subject group of the National Social Science Fund of China. Nanjing: Jiangsu People's Publishing House, 2003.

Satori. *New Theory of Democracy*. Translated by Feng Keli. Shanghai: The Eastern Publishing Co., Ltd., 1998.

Sun Baiying. *Contemporary Local Governance: Challenges in the 21st Century*. Beijing: China Renmin University Press, 2004.

Tao Dongming and Chen Mingming. *Contemporary Chinese Political Participation*. Hangzhou: Zhejiang People's Publishing House, 1998.

Tao Wenzhao. *Research on Electronic Governments*. Beijing: The Commercial Press, 2005.

Thomas, J. C. *Citizen Participation in Public Decision-Making: New Skills and Strategies of Public Administrators*. Translated by Sun Baiying. Beijing: China Renmin University Press, 2005.

Toffler, A. and Toffler, H. *Create a New Civilization: The Third Wave of Politics*. Beijing: SDX Joint Publishing Company, 1996.

Tullock, G., Seldon, A. and Brady, G. L. *Government Failure: A Probe into Public Choice*. Translated by Xu Renhui. Taipei: Zhisheng Culture, 2005.

**Political Participation and Institutional Innovation:
A Case Study of Zhejiang**

Wang Bangzuo. *New Politics*. Shanghai: Fudan University Press, 2006.
Wang Luli. *Introduction to Political Culture*. Beijing: China Renmin University Press, 2002.
Wang Puqu. *Politics Basis*. Beijing: Peking University Press, 2001.
Wang Yong. *Transparent Governments*. Beijing: Press of Chinese Academy of Governance, 2005.
Xiao Gongquan. *Constitutionalism and Democracy*. Beijing: Tsinghua University Press, 2006.
Xu Yong. *Rural Governance and Chinese Politics*. Beijing: China Social Sciences Press, 2003.
Xu Zengyang. *Rural Governance in Flow*. Beijing: China Social Sciences Press, 2003.
Yao Guozhang and Lin Ping. *Cases of International E-government*. Beijing: Peking University Press, 2005.
Yu Jianrong. *Yuecun Politics*. Beijing: The Commercial Press, 2002.
Zhang Jiansheng. *Research on Administrative Hearing System*. Hangzhou: Zhejiang University Press, 2010.
Zhang Jingping. *What Happened in Zhejiang: Democratic Life in the Transitional Period*. Shanghai: Orient Publishing Center, 2006.
Zhu Enen. *A Documentary Report on the Investigation of a Criminal Gang with the Nature of a Large Criminal Syndicate in Zhangwang, Zhejiang*. Beijing: Mass Publishing House, 2006.
Zhu Guanglei. *The Process of Contemporary Chinese Government*. Tianjin: Tianjin People's Publishing House, 2002.
Zhu Guanglei. *Modern Government Theory*. Beijing: Higher Education Press, 2006.

Chinese periodicals and newspapers

Bai Shuying and He Ming. Structure and process of BBS interaction. *Sociological Study*, 2003 (5).

Chao Longqi. Black forces and the grassroots regime in contemporary China. *Journal of Chinese People's Public Security University*, 2001 (5).

Chen Huaping and Dong Juan. Construction of public policy hearing platform based on new media. *Chinese Administration*, 2015 (11).

Chen Jiagang. Consultative democracy: System design and practice exploration. *Journal of China National School of Administration*, 2017 (1).

Chen Shengyong. Theory of deliberative democracy and China. *Zhejiang Social Sciences*, 2005 (1).

Chen Shengyong and Du Jie. Internet public forum and deliberative democracy. *Academics*, 2005 (5).

Chen Shengyong and Du Jie. Internet public forum and deliberative democracy. *Journal of Zhejiang University (Humanities and Social Sciences)*, 2005 (5).

Dong Hua. Exposure of 3.23 Wenling Exemplary Case. *Lawyer World*, 2001 (6).

Fang Qinxian. Conflicts and identity dilemma behind anti-tax: Take Zhili mass incident as an example. *Journal of Yichun University*, 2014 (11).

Feng Ying. From a show to a hearing. *China Society*, 2005 (16).

He Baogang and Wu Jinjin. Political legitimacy function of public consultation: A survey of citizens' public service satisfaction. *Zhejiang Social Sciences*, 2016 (9).

He Wei and Wang Huanchen. Restraining rent-seeking corruption by institutional innovation. *Political Science and Law*, 2000 (1).

Huang Fenglan. The evolution and path from traditional community meeting to modern community hearing in China. *Chinese Administration*, 2016 (12).

Hua Zhengxue. Analysis of current patterns, characteristics and performance of private enterprise owners' political participation in China. *Journal of Guangzhou Institute of Socialism*, 2005 (2).

Hu Tongxin. Analysis of the democratic value of network political participation. *Politics*, 2005 (12).

Hu Zuguang. Gini coefficient and statistics: Take Zhejiang as an example. *Zhejiang Social Sciences*, 2005 (4).

Political Participation and Institutional Innovation:
A Case Study of Zhejiang

Liang Ying and Huang Jianrong. Public governance in consultative democracy. *Chinese Administration*, 2005 (9).

Li Baoliang. From super-economic compulsion to relational consensus: Analysis of the process of political participation of private enterprise owners. *Sociological Study*, 2001 (1).

Li Shuchang, *et al*. How to make our community a better environment. *Yuhang Morning News*, 2016-01-20 (1).

Li Xiaoming. Citizens annoyed officials through sharp questions in a hearing of Hangzhou Planning Bureau. *Morning News*, 2011-01-07 (1).

Li Yubi. Perfection of China's legislative hearing system from the perspective of constitutionalism. *People's Congress Studying*, 2004 (7).

Ma Baobin and Ma Zhenqing. Group political participation in the Chinese society in the new era. *Cass Journal of Political Science*, 2005 (2).

Peng Zongchao, Xue Lan and Shen Xuhui. Comparative analysis of foreign legislative hearing systems. *Cass Journal of Political Science*, 2003 (1).

Qi Yanxing and Fang Fang. The status and countermeasures of mass incidents in Zhejiang. *Journal of Zhejiang Police College*, 2000 (5).

Research Group of Chinese Public Administration Society. A study on the main characteristics, causes and government countermeasures of group unexpected events in the transition period of China. *Chinese Administration*, 2002 (5).

Shi Jinchuan. Institutional change and economic development: A study on "Zhejiang Model". *Zhejiang Social Sciences*, 2005 (5).

Xing Leqin and Yang Fengyin. Analysis of the current situation of private enterprise owners' political participation in Zhejiang. *Chinese Administration*, 2004 (11).

Xu Ying. Internet, public domain and life politics: Digital democracy. *The Journal of Humanities*, 2002 (3).

Xu Yunpeng and Zhang Xukun. The American price hearing system and its enlightenment. *Social Science Front*, 2008 (12).

Xu Zengyang. Political and sociological analysis of the tide of off-farm workers. *Cass Journal of Political Science*, 2004 (1).

Yan Jirong. Democracy: Election or negotiation: Value and enlightenment of consultative democracy. *Scientific Socialism*, 2006 (6).

Yu Chunjiang. The function of social consultation and its realization path of discussing policies on: Take "Round Table" of Hangzhou TV Station as an example. *Journal of Party School of CPC Hangzhou*, 2017 (1).

Yu Gechun. A perspective on the political participation of off-farm workers in "chasing wages". *Journal of Provincial Party School of Fujian*, 2005 (1).

Yu Hao. Internet + representative. *The People's Congress of China*, 2016 (12).

Yu Jianrong. Black forces in rural areas and degradation of grassroots power. *Strategy and Management*, 2003 (5).

Zhang Bingxuan and Zhou Tao. Can wisdom bring governance: Calm thought on the hot construction of intelligent cities under the new normal conditions. *Journal of Wuhan University (Philosophy and Social Sciences)*, 2016 (1).

Zhang Chunsheng. College campus BBS: From bulletin board system to campus portals. *Youth Studies*, 2005 (10).

Zhang Wenlin, *et al*. Constructing collaborative public services: Research on the top-level design method of government informatization. *Management World*, 2013 (8).

Zhang Yongyi. Status and prospect of citizen network participating in the work of National People's Congress: Research on live webcast of Standing Committee of Hangzhou People's Congress. *People's Congress Studying*, 2013 (4).

Zhao Shukai. Rural governance. *Organization and Conflicts*, 2003 (6).

Zheng Chuangui. The marginality of off-farm workers' political participation should not be ignored. *Theory and Reform*, 2004 (5).

Zhu Guanglei and Yang Liwu. Forms, significance and limits of political participation of private entrepreneurs in China. *Nankai Journal*, 2004 (5).

Zhu Jialiang. The path and characteristics of Zhejiang economic system reform. *Research on Reform and Development*, 1998 (12).

English literature

Acemoglu, D. and Robinson, J. A. *Why Nations Fail: The Origins of Power, Prosperity, and Poverty*. New York: Crown Business, 2013.

Barber, B. *Strong Democracy: Participatory Politics for A New Age*. Berkeley: University of California Press, 1984.

Chambers, S. *Reasonable Democracy: Jürgen Habermas and the Politics of Discourse*. Ithaca: Cornell University Press, 1996.

Political Participation and Institutional Innovation:
A Case Study of Zhejiang

Dryzek, J. *Deliberative Democracy and Beyond: Liberals, Critics, Contestations.* Oxford: Oxford University Press, 2000.

Elster, J. *Deliberative Democracy.* Cambridge: Cambridge University Press, 1998.

Gould, C. *Rethinking Democracy: Freedom and Social Cooperation in Politics, Economy and Society.* Cambridge: Cambridge University Press, 1988.

Habermas, J. *Communication and the Evolution of Society.* Boston: Beacon Press, 1979.

Horan, T. A. Planning digital places: A new approach to community telecommunications planning and development. In: G. Garsaon, (ed.), *Handbook of Public Information Systems.* New York: Marcel Dekker, 2000.

Latour, B. Where are the missing masses? Sociology of a door. In: W. E. Bijker and J. Law (eds.), *Shaping Technology/Building Society: Studies in Sociotechnical Change.* Cambridge: MIT Press, 1992.

McGinnis, J. O. *Accelerating Democracy: Transforming Governance Through Technology.* Princeton: Princeton University Press, 2012.

Morozov, E. *To Save Everything, Click Here: Technology, Solutionism, and the Urge to Fix Problems that Don't Exist.* London: Allen Lane, 2013.

Pateman, C. *Participation and Democratic Theory.* Cambridge: Cambridge University Press, 1970.

Rifkin, J. *The Zero Marginal Cost Society: The Internet of Things, the Collaborative Commons, and the Eclipse of Capitalism.* New York: Palgrave Macmillan, 2014.

Scavo, C. and Shi Y. World Wide Web site design and sue in public management. In: G. Garson and C. Scavo, (eds.), *Information Technology and Computer Application in Public Administration: Issues and Trends.* Hershey, PA: Idea Group Publishing, 1999.

Storper, M. *Keys to the City: How Economics, Institutions, Social Interaction, and Politics Shape Development.* Princeton: Princeton University Press, 2013.

Turner, J. H. *The Structure of Sociological Theory.* Homewood, IL: Dorsey Press, 1978.

Verba, S. and Norman H. N. *Participation in America: Social Equality and Democracy.* New York: Harper & Row, 1972.

Warren, M. Deliberative democracy. In: A. Carter and G. Stokes (eds.), *Democratic Theory Today.* Cambridge: Polity Press, 2000.

Bibliography

Williams, M. The uneasy alliance of group representation and deliberative democracy. In: Will Kymliika and Wayne Norman (eds.), *Citizenship in Diverse Societies*. Oxford: Oxford University Press, 2000.

Zheng Yongnian. Technological empowerment: The Internet, state and society in China. Palo Alto: Stanford University Press, 2008.

Postscript

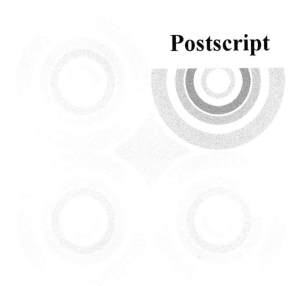

Since I began working in Zhejiang University in 2000, I have been engaged in teaching and research of politics at college for quite a few years. It is not a short period in my life. However, it seems that time passes away so swiftly. I started my teaching career at the beginning of the 21st century when a popular saying was that, in the field of China's social sciences, economics and economists had taken the lead in the past two decades and it would be the turn of politics and political scientists to appear on the scene in the new century. Another opinion then was more exaggerated: The 21st century would be an era of politics.

Actually, the saying is quite pertinent to the social development of current China.

Since the reform and opening-up, starting with the rectification of the name of market economy and its enlightenment, Chinese economists studied economic development and market construction and put forward relevant countermeasures and advice at each stage of the reform of the economic system. Lots of economists, represented by Wu Jinglian (known as "Market Wu" because of advocating the market system), Li Yining (known as "Stock Li" because of supporting the joint-stock system reform), Justin Yifu Lin and Lang Xianping *et al*. have achieved great accomplishments in respect of research on market-oriented economic restructuring and socio-economic development. However, with the rapid development of industrialization, marketization

Political Participation and Institutional Innovation:
A Case Study of Zhejiang

and urbanization, lots of institutional malpractice and social problems appear. Unfair social distribution and polarization between the rich and the poor lead to a social gap during transformation, and social inequality results in increasingly acute social conflicts. Unbalanced development between east and west, urban and rural areas, corruption and low efficiency of governments and further perfection of the initially established market system, etc. involve far more than economics. In my opinion, the greatest challenge for China is how to deepen its structural reform and institutional innovation and complete the great construction of the national system. In this respect, economics alone is not enough. However, it makes sense that politics touches upon construction of the national system.

The reform and opening-up in China requires politics and the era calls for political scientists. However, are China's politics and political scientists ready?

In China, disciplines such as politics, law and sociology didn't return to the system of philosophy and social sciences and were yet to be developed until Deng Xiaoping brought order out of chaos after the reform and opening-up. Due to various reasons, politics is hysteretic in China, more than a decade behind the development of economics, law and sociology, etc. According to reality, we have to admit that applying both politics and economics to national institutional improvement in the 21st century for the construction of the market system still has a long way to go.

First, economics is the most mature science in social sciences. After development and perfection for more than two centuries, Western economics not only has normative theoretical systems and research paradigms, but has also built a set of scientific research methods. However, the research on politics started 150 years later than that on economics. Though it underwent a behavioral revolution, its theoretical systems and research methods still need further exploration. In circles of international politics, the debate on politics as a subject has never stoped since the behavioral revolution in the USA. In October 2004, a set of articles on subject nature, status and future of politics were published in *Political Science and Politics*. In "Where Is Political Science Going?", Giovanni Sartori, a famous professor at Columbia University and the author of *The Theory of Democracy Revisited*, harshly criticized the status of politics since the behavioral revolution, especially the excessively quantitative tendency in current research of political science in the USA. Two other articles, namely "Whither Political Science?" and "Political Science Is Going Ahead", were written by David D. Latin from Stanford University and Josep M. Colomer from the Mexican Economic Research and Teaching Center, respectively. Is politics a subject, can it become a subject and should it be a subject? Whether the study on politics should imitate that on economics to stress quantification or statistics or carry out more logical thinking? There's great divergence between both sides of the debate, highlighting immature property of politics and uncertainty of future development of politics.

Second, objects of study of politics are more complicated than those of economics. Economic behavior of both Chinese and Westerners pursues benefit maximization. The market system is the same in the East and the West and so in socialist or capitalist countries. Economists can copy mature market systems in Western developed countries and apply them in China. However, this method cannot be used for political behavior, because political behavior is guided by a series of different motives and is not as simple and common as economic behavior. Though institutional arrangement in all modern countries seeks fairness and justice, there are great differences in respect of national characters, historical tradition and political culture, etc. because of different national conditions. In addition, due to different economic development, characteristics of social structure, levels of education, value preference and behavior forms of different countries, Western democratic systems are divided into many types in different countries. A political system

Political Participation and Institutional Innovation:
A Case Study of Zhejiang

cannot be copied or simply applied, which has been confirmed by many cases of unsuccessful national systems since the Revolution of 1911.

As the immature discipline of political science and hysteretic Chinese political science have to confront China's institutional reform and national institutional construction in the 21st century, Chinese political science and political scientists indeed shoulder heavy responsibilities. As a political professional, I should start with the academic tradition, promote the development of the discipline, gradually construct a political theory system, bring forth new ideas about research methods and build a Chinese type of politics to make every effort for the reform and opening-up and institutional improvement in China. However, I also understand that institutional improvement of the country is a great task and to build a Chinese type of politics cannot be accomplished in an action, but requires arduous exploration, practice and repeated experiments, generation after generation. Hence, current political professionals should train related talents for future research, for the development of Chinese politics depends on a galaxy of talents and efforts of future generation.

I was born in the 1950s and was one of the first students who took the college entrance examination after the "Cultural Revolution". I feel lucky that I became a scholar, but it is occasional. Scholars in our generation stole a march on others when there was a shortage of talents. After years of hard work, we became a little famous. However, we were destined to become scholars serving as a link between the past and future. It takes 10 years to grow trees, but a 100 to educate people. Therefore, to train talents is more important for us than to study. As a result, as an idealist, I was transferred from an R&D institution to Zhejiang University with a high-strung working pace. In the 8 years, I worked selflessly and happily and tried my best to create a small teaching world. Starting with controlling the study style of freshmen of the department, I always enjoyed teaching the course of principles of political science for freshmen. I set up the master's program in

Postscript

politics, the doctoral program in politics and a key research base for social sciences in Zhejiang, namely the Research Center for Local Governments and Social Governance. Finally, I built a system platform for training professionals of political science. Over the years, I have accepted and guided many master's students and doctoral students as well as many college graduates.

Though the subject attribute of politics is still controversial among political scientists, in terms of professional training, both normative theory and interpretation theory are stressed and students should pay attention to both theoretical basis and methods of scientific research. The biggest difference between social sciences and humanities is that scholars or amateurs of humanities can enclose themselves in their ivory towers. However, as social sciences are tools of understanding and transforming the society, professionals have to face social reality and understand civil society to grasp the times. Therefore, beginners of politics should strengthen their ability of logical thinking by reading classics and attempt to conduct some studies on realistic problems. In other words, they should apply the theory while observing the reality, deepen their understanding of realistic problems and then correct and even revise the current theory. In addition, they should master methods of social surveys and empirical research by conducting social surveys and empirical research. One basic approach for professors to teach students methods of empirical research is to do projects. If students can follow laws of learning and research properly while doing a project instead of regarding it as a tool for dealing with inspections, conferring academic titles or earning money, doing projects may become the most effective means for the major.

This book is the final result of a national project "Citizens' Orderly Political Participation and Institutional Innovation" (Project No.: 04BZZ012). It is also the second book written by me in collaboration with graduate students of Zhejiang University after *Organization, Self-Governance and Democracy: Research on Wenzhou Chamber of*

Political Participation and Institutional Innovation:
A Case Study of Zhejiang

Commerce of Zhejiang. In addition, co-authors of the first book are some of my graduate students, while those of the second book are some of my doctoral students. However, the research methods adopted in these two books are similar. To be specific, I determined the thoughts and methods of research, provided some preliminary research data and chose a student to take charge of research and to compose a subtopic in accordance with the research contents.

For this book, I mainly composed the Chapters 1, 7 and 8, with the help of Zhang Bingxuan and Zhong Dongsheng in basic work. The co-authors of other chapters are Wu Xingzhi (Chapters 2 and 3), Zhong Dongsheng (Chapter 4), Gao Yiqing (Chapter 5), Zhang Bingxuan (Chapter 6) and Meng Jun (whose chapter had to be deleted regretfully due to the limit of book). I'd like to thank leaders, including Chen Yonghao and Zeng Hua *et al*. of Zhejiang Allied Social Science Association for their great support in publishing this book; and all the people who ensured the publishing of this book on behalf of my students and me.

Chen Shengyong

CPSIA information can be obtained
at www.ICGtesting.com
Printed in the USA
LVHW082013070420
652563LV00003B/4